The Ultimate Scene and Monologue Sourcebook

An Actor's Guide to Over 1,000 Monologues and Scenes from More Than 300 Contemporary Plays

Ed Hooks

BACK STAGE BOOKS
An imprint of Watson-Guptill Publications/New York

Ed Hooks has been acting in theater, film, and television for more than 20 years, and has taught acting and auditioning technique for more than a decade. He is also the author of *The Audition Book* (Back Stage Books, 1989).

Senior Editor: Paul Lukas
Editor: Liz Harvey
Book and Cover Design: Areta Buk
Production Manager: Ellen Greene

First published in 1994 by Back Stage Books,
an imprint of Watson-Guptill Publications,
a division of VNU Business Media, Inc.,
770 Broadway, New York, NY 10003
www.wgpub.com

Library of Congress Cataloging-in-Publication Data

Hooks, Ed.
    The ultimate scene and monologue sourcebook: an actor's guide to over 1000 monologues and dialogues from more than 300 contemporary plays / by Ed Hooks.
        p. cm.
    ISBN 0-8230-7771-3
    1. Acting—Bibliography. 2. Monologues—Bibliography.
3. Dialogues—Bibliography. 4. American drama—20th century.
I. Title.
Z5784.A27H66 1994
[PN2080]
016.80882—dc20   93-43030
                                                 CIP

Manufactured in the United States of America

First printing, 1994

11 12 13 14 15 / 07 06 05

"I had a friend once said, 'Norman, I don't care if there are only three people out front, or if the audience laugh when they shouldn't, or don't when they should, one person, just one person is certain to know and understand. And I act for him.' That's what my friend said."

The Dresser by Ronald Harwood

ACKNOWLEDGMENTS

First thanks must go to Roy Johnson of Limelight Film & Theatre Bookstore on Market Street in San Francisco, who allowed me to take and read, 10 at a time, as many plays from his shelves as I could endure. He, along with his knowledgeable associates Ken Bullock, Stephen Sack, and Derek Gavin Mutch, have been simply invaluable to the process.

My acting students not only suggested favorite scenes, monologues, and plays, but also were dragged into service as something of a test kitchen when I was in doubt about whether a selected scene would play or should be included. Their contributions give this book a practical and concrete-solid foundation, and I am grateful to them.

Talented friends who have been particularly helpful include playwright/author Jeffrey Sweet, who challenged and stimulated me with his concepts about what constitutes a good scene, and Amy Potozkin, casting director for Berkeley Repertory Theatre, with whom I enjoyed a spirited discussion about what makes a good audition monologue. Tom Hardy, Janet Rotblatt, Dorothy Horstman, Cynthia Hart, Paul Collins, Sharon Omi, Alice Elliott, and Jane Carmichael all offered significant input, and Jeanne Beacom provided special inspiration. Tone Forrest and Joyce Mehess helped a lot one cold and rainy Tuesday in the Studio City branch of the Samuel French Theater Bookshop. Tone and Joyce possess encyclopedic knowledge of plays-in-print and were extremely generous with their time. Paul Lukas, Senior Editor at Back Stage Books, made the initial decision to publish *The Ultimate Scene and Monologue Sourcebook*. His standard of excellence and wise counsel have been a continual inspiration to me. My editor, Liz Harvey, brought an artist's eye and an engineer's precision to an extraordinarily difficult task involving thousands of small details, and she deserves special thanks.

Writing a book is tantamount to bringing a stranger to live in your house, a guest who becomes more demanding as editorial deadlines approach. My wife, Cally, has made this guest welcome, suggesting and discussing potential plays, reviewing drafts of the manuscript, and giving me the benefit of her objective and critical opinions. Her influence is on every page, and my gratitude to her is endless.

Finally, I want to thank my 10-year-old daughter, Dagny, who has contributed mightily to this book by "not interrupting dad when he is working."

Contents

Introduction

The scenes and monologues referenced in this book are intended for workshop and audition use by the serious actor. They range from the innocence of *Ah, Wilderness!*, which deals with the maturing of a young boy at the turn of the century, to the lurid canvas of *Toyer*, with its focus on the crimes of a contemporary serial rapist. They also represent a variety of acting styles, from Oscar Wilde and Noël Coward's high comedy and sharp repartee, to Michael Gazzo's quintessential Actors Studio drama, *A Hatful of Rain*.

I read more than 1,000 plays while preparing *The Ultimate Scene and Monologue Sourcebook*, finally settling on selections from just over 300 of them. To be included here, scenes had to be emotionally compelling, to a minor degree at least, and monologues had to do more than merely tell a story. I excluded a great deal of potential material because it struck me as immature or emotionally shallow and unworthy of consideration by intelligent actors. This isn't to suggest that every single scene and monologue in this book should be the subject of a doctoral dissertation. There is always room in an acting class for a well-written selection from a comedic piece of fluff or a clock-stopping potboiler, and I included more than a few simply because they are fun to work on. In the final analysis, however, an actor is, as Artaud observed, "an athlete of the heart," and source material for an acting workshop should serve that definition.

HOW TO USE THIS BOOK

The Ultimate Scene and Monologue Sourcebook contains seven sections, which you can cross-reference. For example, if you're searching for material of a particular genre, such as a drama or comedy, you can peruse "Part One: Play Synopses and Analyses" until you find a play that you like. Next, you can cross-reference to the scenes and/or monologues cited from that particular play. You might want to go to Part Two for a male monologue or to Part Six for a male/female scene.

If, on the other hand, you already have specific scene requirements in mind, turn to the corresponding reference section first. For example, if you're searching for a mother/daughter scene, you'll want to consider the plays in the female/female section. You can go about this two ways. Your first option is to turn to the indexes at the back of the book, which are broken down into such categories as gender, nationality, and age, and scan the titles listed in the "Female/Female Scenes" index. Your other option is to go directly to "Part Five: Female/Female Scenes" and scan the selections until you find one that meets your needs. In either case, your next step is simply to cross-reference back to Part One, the synopsis/analysis section, for more information on the play. Then get a copy of the play and, if the material seems appropriate, get to work.

As you read this book, you'll find my opinions about the difficulty level of the material, as well as occasional historical reference points, in the analysis portion of Part One. For instance, this is where you'll discover that Elia Kazan won the first Tony Award in 1947 for directing Arthur Miller's *All My Sons;* that Tennessee Williams based the role of Laura in *The Glass Menagerie* on his sister, Rose; and that August Strindberg deeply influenced Eugene O'Neill.

While writing this book, I also made every effort to provide easy reference to the scenes and monologues, which I indexed extensively. In addition to the indexes, I included specific page numbers for scenes and monologues from the Samuel French (SF) and Dramatists Play Service (DPS) acting editions, as well as provided first- and last-line designations throughout.

Finally, as you use this book, keep the following provisos in mind. Just because I listed only one or two scenes from a play doesn't mean that there isn't other suitable material. This book is a reference guide, and scene selection is a matter of taste. I chose the scenes and monologues that I consider to be the strongest.

Wherever possible, I used acting editions as source material. This can lead to confusion if you get your copies of the plays from the library, particularly classics by Tennessee Williams. He originally wrote many of his plays in a three-act format, but the works also appear in two-act versions. To complicate matters further, Williams continually tinkered with his plays, leading to variations even within the three-act versions. To a lesser degree, I encountered this problem with plays by Lillian Hellman and William Inge. As a result, if you select a scene or monologue that is referenced here but then can't find the material in the compilation from your local library, don't despair. It is probably in the text somewhere; you just need to do a little more investigating. If, however, you are unable to locate the scene or monologue in question, you might wind up having to order an acting edition of the play. For this reason, and because many of the referenced plays can't be found in libraries, I included addresses for a few major theatrical retailers that sell plays via mail order.

Ed Hooks
Palo Alto, California
January 1994

Part One
Play Synopses and Analyses

ABDICATION, THE
by Ruth Wolff [The New Women's Theatre (Random House)]
Synopsis: Set in the Vatican, 1655. Christina, the Virgin Queen of Sweden, has abdicated the Protestant throne to convert to Catholicism and has made the long journey to seek the Pope's blessings. His emissary, Cardinal Azzolino, is assigned to hear Christina's confession and to recommend or disapprove of her acceptance into the Church. The heart of the play involves the confrontation between these two strong-willed people, who are in conflict about their sexuality. An air of sexual tension permeates their debates about the Church and philosophy.
Analysis: Although *The Abdication* is widely available in libraries, you might have some trouble finding it, but it is worth the search. A movie starring Liv Ullman and Peter Finch was based on the play. All levels.
Scenes/Monologues: Female Monologues (2)

ABSENT FRIENDS
by Alan Ayckbourn (Samuel French)
Synopsis: Colin's fiancée recently drowned, and a group of former friends have invited him to a tea party to lift his spirits. The problem is that his friends have marital and other personal problems of their own, and Colin is quite happy with his sentimental memories. The more they try to take his mind off his deceased lover, the more he insists on talking about her, which depresses everyone. Then he good-naturedly tries to solve their problems, which makes the get-together even more disastrous.
Analysis: This play is one of Alan Ayckbourn's less-performed comedies, significant for its lack of physical action. For the most part, the characters sit around a table talking, so the humor comes from what the audience members discover about their lives. All levels.
Scenes/Monologues: Male Monologues (1), Female Monologues (1), Female/Female Scenes (1)

ABSURD PERSON SINGULAR
by Alan Ayckbourn (Samuel French)
Synopsis: Three couples gather on three consecutive Christmas Eves, and the action takes place in their respective kitchens. During the three years, the characters go through reversals of fortune. The struggling couple in Act I become real-estate moguls in Act III, while the bank manager who lends them money in Act I watches his marriage and business fall apart at the same time. The third couple, an architect and his wife, go from blue skies to attempted suicide.
Analysis: This 1972 comedy starts out funny, almost becomes a farce in Act II, and by the end, turns dark. With Alan Ayckbourn, the structure is frequently the thing. All levels.
Scenes/Monologues: Male Monologues (2), Three-Person Scenes (1)

ABUNDANCE
by Beth Henley (Dramatists Play Service)
Synopsis: Bess and Macon are mail-order brides who meet at a stage-coach depot in the Wyoming Territory during the 1870s. *Abundance* tracks the two women and their relationships for the next 25 years. During this time frame, Bess changes from a wallflower into a cynical novelist/lecturer, and Macon's confident, outgoing nature is transformed into one of syphilitic despair.
Analysis: Overall, this play isn't Beth Henley's best, but it contains a couple of scenes that are interesting, and the milieu is unusual. All levels.
Scenes/Monologues: Three-Person Scenes (1)

AFTER THE FALL
by Arthur Miller (Dramatists Play Service)
Synopsis: The action takes place in Quentin's mind and memory as he desperately tries to find meaningful connections in his life. There is no plot per se; the scenes jump around like the workings of his mind, involving confrontations with former wives, as well as his parents, brother, and business associates.
Analysis: Difficult, intellectually challenging material appropriate for advanced actors.
Scenes/Monologues: Male Monologues (1), Male/Female Scenes (3)

AGNES OF GOD
by John Pielmeier (Samuel French)
Synopsis: A troubled young nun with practically no exposure to the outside world surprises everyone by having a baby at the convent. At birth, the infant is killed and stuffed into a wastebasket. Who is the father? Who killed the baby? Was Agnes alone in the room when the baby was born? She claims not to remember anything about the event and refuses to name the father, even under hypnosis. The core of the drama centers on the efforts of a court-appointed psychiatrist to determine whether Agnes is sane and the psychiatrist's conflict with Agnes's Mother Superior.
Analysis: This marvelously theatrical drama, which is played on a bare stage, is chock-full of tense scenes that address universal issues. Each of the characters is strongly defined. Amanda Plummer won a Tony for playing Agnes in the 1982 production. All levels.
Scenes/Monologues: Female Monologues (2), Female/Female Scenes (3)

AH, WILDERNESS!
by Eugene O'Neill (Samuel French)
Synopsis: An innocent coming-of-age story set on the Connecticut shore, July 4, 1906. Exploding fireworks provide the background for exploding passions, both romantic and political, for 16-year-old Richard Miller, fresh out of high school and already a confirmed individualist. When he presents his lady love with verses of purple poetry from the pages of Algernon Charles Swinburne, all hell breaks loose. Everyone gets upset for a while but in the end, the young lovers are together once again—and probably forever.
Analysis: Completed in 1942, this is Eugene O'Neill's only full-length comedy. It draws from his memories of a boyhood love for one Maibelle Scott. The famous George M. Cohan played Nat Miller in the first production. All levels.
Scenes/Monologues: Male Monologues (2), Male/Female Scenes (2)

ALBUM
by David Rimmer (Dramatists Play Service)
Synopsis: A coming-of-age story set in the 1960s. A small group of teenagers address various issues, including whether or not to "do it," who to "do it" with, what the consequences of "doing it" are, and whether or not Bob Dylan is musically superior to the Beatles.

Analysis: David Rimmer doesn't condescend to his characters, a likeable, serious, and impassioned group. Nice dialogue. All levels.
Scenes/Monologues: Female/Female Scenes (1)

ALL MY SONS
by Arthur Miller (Dramatists Play Service)
Synopsis: The background: Joe Keller and Steve Deever were neighbors and business partners until their company sold defective airplane-engine parts, a crime for which Steve went to prison. Joe maintained his innocence, served a very short prison sentence, and continued to build a prosperous business alone. But he was more at fault than Steve. The defective parts resulted in 21 plane crashes, and when Steve's Army-officer son, Larry, learned the truth about his father's complicity, he was so deeply shamed that he committed suicide in combat.

During the play, Joe's youngest son, Chris, becomes engaged to Steve's daughter—and Larry's former fiancée—Ann, and everyone in the family finally has to confront the facts of Joe's crime. Unable to live with the guilt of his actions once they are out in the open, Joe commits suicide.
Analysis: A classic from 1947 about the decisions people make in life and their consequences. Elia Kazan won the very first Tony Award for directing the play. All levels.
Scenes/Monologues: Male Monologues (1), Female/Female Scenes (1), Male/Female Scenes (1)

AMADEUS
by Peter Shaffer (Samuel French)
Synopsis: The story of Mozart's life and early death as told by Antonio Salieri, a less-talented, fatally jealous composer and court favorite. The premise of the play is that Salieri himself orchestrated Mozart's tragic demise.
Analysis: While brilliant in concept and presentation, *Amadeus* unfortunately provides little opportunity for scene work. It won Tony Awards for Best Play and Best Director in 1980. All levels.
Scenes/Monologues: Male Monologues (1), Male/Female Scenes (1)

AMEN CORNER, THE
by James Baldwin (Samuel French)
Synopsis: Sister Margaret Alexander is the pastor of a small Harlem church located above the apartment where she lives with her son, David, and her older sister. To all appearances, Margaret is a passionate, committed spokesperson for the Lord. But her entire life starts to crumble when her former husband, Luke, shows up, clearly nearing the end of his life. His presence in the home rivets the couple's 18-year-old son, who has been trying to decide whether or not to follow in the footsteps of his musician father, a life that his mother claims is sinful. Luke also affects Margaret, reminding her of the pleasures of marriage she left behind 10 years ago when she walked out with David.

Meanwhile, the church elders are watching this family drama play out and have come to question Margaret's sanctity. They conspire to have her removed as pastor. In the final moments of the play, David leaves home for good, determined to be a professional musician, and Margaret acknowledges her love for Luke as he dies in her arms. Although she'll no longer lead the small church, she has found a more profound peace in human love and acceptance.
Analysis: A lovely 1961 drama by a major American writer, full of insight and poetry. The entire cast is African American. All levels.
Scenes/Monologues: Male Monologues (3), Female Monologues (1), Male/Male Scenes (1), Male/Female Scenes (2)

AMERI/CAIN GOTHIC
by Paul Carter Harrison [*Totem Voices, Plays from the Black World Repertory,* edited by Paul Carter Harrison (Grove Press)]

Synopsis: Harper, a private investigator responsible for reconnoitering a Memphis motel before Martin Luther King's arrival, is distracted by Cass, a recluse living in the rooming house that the fatal bullet is ultimately fired from. Cass is suffering from a grave sense of imminent violence and solicits Harper's help.

Analysis: Difficult two-character play requiring strong, intelligent, trusting actors. There is a continual air of danger and sexual attraction.

Scenes/Monologues: Male Monologues (1), Female Monologues (1), Male/Female Scenes (1)

AMERICAN BUFFALO
by David Mamet (Samuel French)

Synopsis: Three small-time crooks plot to steal a coin collection. Don Dubrow, the owner of the junk shop where they hang out, is calling the shots. Teach maneuvers to cut Bob, his rather slow-witted gofer, out of the job and the money. In the end, violence erupts, and the robbery doesn't take place.

Analysis: This play, David Mamet's first on Broadway, won the Drama Critics Circle Award for Best American Play in 1977. All levels.

Scenes/Monologues: Male/Male Scenes (3)

AMERICAN PLAN, THE
by Richard Greenberg (Dramatists Play Service)

Synopsis: Eva Adler, her daughter, Lili, and their maid, Olivia, are spending another summer in the Catskills. Lili meets, falls in love with, and becomes engaged to a nice young man staying in the hotel across the lake. Then everything unravels as the audience learns that the young man is gay, Lili is emotionally frail, and Eva is haunted by memories of Nazi Germany. The play covers a 20-year span from the 1950s through the 1970s.

Analysis: Very complex characters populate this finely imagined 1991 play. It feels almost like a romantic comedy at first but then turns quite dark. Most individual scenes are fairly straightforward, but the subtext takes them to a different level; this makes for some interesting acting challenges. For sophisticated actors.

Scenes/Monologues: Male Monologues (1), Male/Male Scenes (1), Male/Female Scenes (3)

ANASTASIA
by Marcelle Maurette [adapted by Guy Bolton (Samuel French)]

Synopsis: Bounine, former aide-de-camp to the late Russian tsar Nicholas II and more recently a cab driver in Berlin, discovers a young woman who has confided in a hospital nurse that she is the tsar's only-surviving daughter, Anastasia. When Bounine confronts her with this rumor, she denies it, claiming that she just made up the story for something to do. However, he is aware that if the real Anastasia were ever to surface, she would inherit the huge fortune left behind when all of the other members of her family were assassinated in 1918. So Bounine and some unscrupulous cohorts conspire to pass the woman off as the real Anastasia, thereby gaining access to the money.

The trouble with the men's scheme is that the woman is inconsistent: sometimes she cooperates, and sometimes she doesn't. She may, in fact, be brain-damaged from a big factory explosion. Nonetheless, the men persist until they finally persuade the woman to go along with their plan. Then, at the very moment she is to be presented to the public and the press, she walks out the back door and disappears in the streets. The play ends with a strong implication that the woman may indeed be the real Anastasia, but life has become too complicated for her to handle.

Analysis: Big subject, minor 1954 play, a couple of good scenes. All levels.

Scenes/Monologues: Female/Female Scenes (1), Male/Female Scenes (3)

ANDERSONVILLE TRIAL, THE

by Saul Levitt (Dramatists Play Service)

Synopsis: Based on the actual 1865 trial of Confederate officer Henry Wirz, who was in charge of the infamous Andersonville Prison in Georgia during the Civil War. Approximately 14,000 Union soldiers died there, most of whom fell prey to bad food and water, insufficient clothing, and disease. Wirz was found guilty of conspiracy to kill the soldiers and was executed.

Analysis: Courtroom dramas can be fun because they frequently address moral issues head-on. On the other hand, the plays provide few if any two-person scenes. Young George C. Scott played Colonel Chipman in the 1959 premiere. All levels.

Scenes/Monologues: Male Monologues (1), Male/Male Scenes (1)

AND MISS REARDON DRINKS A LITTLE

by Paul Zindel (Dramatists Play Service)

Synopsis: The ultimate dysfunctional family, full of religious guilt and plenty of dirty little secrets. Probably set in Queens, New York, although the location isn't specified. Three sisters work in the educational system: Anna is a high-school-chemistry teacher, Catherine is an assistant principal, and Ceil is a member of the school board. After their mother's death, Anna had a nervous breakdown and was sexually involved with a high-school student. His parents are now threatening to sue the school unless Anna is sent to a hospital for psychological treatment. The action of the play centers on Ceil and Catherine's struggle to decide what to do with Anna. Ultimately, they put her in the hospital.

Analysis: Well-written, caustic. Played Broadway in 1971. Estelle Parsons was nominated for a Tony, and Rae Allen won one. All levels.

Scenes/Monologues: Female/Female Scenes (1), Three-Person Scenes (1)

ANGELS IN AMERICA: A GAY FANTASIA ON NATIONAL THEMES, PART I: MILLENNIUM APPROACHES

by Tony Kushner (Theatre Communications Group)

Synopsis: A simple description of the characters and plot is not only impossible but also can't begin to do justice to this remarkable play, which blends reality with fantasy, humans with angels, and the past with the present—and then asks the audience to look at the meaning of it all through the rosy prism of Ronald Reagan's America. The vast canvas of this challenging work is anchored by two couples, one gay and one heterosexual, whose respective relationships dissolve and recombine in unexpected ways.

Analysis: *Angels in America: A Gay Fantasia on National Themes* is presented in two parts, the first of which is *Millennium Approaches*. (The second part, *Perestroika*, isn't included here because as of this writing it was still being revised in anticipation of the Broadway production.) Graphic and frequently disturbing as the play wrestles with sexual and political themes, scene work from *Angels in America* is appropriate for experienced actors. The play won the 1993 Pulitzer Prize, as well as four Tony Awards, including Best Play.

Scenes/Monologues: Male/Male Scenes (2), Male/Female Scenes (3)

ANNA CHRISTIE

by Eugene O'Neill (Vintage Books)

Synopsis: Anna has traveled from middle America to New York City for a reunion with her father, whom she hasn't seen for 15 years. She moves in with him on the coal barge he captains and is happy in the fresh sea air and crisp fog. A few days later, a group of shipwrecked sailors are brought on board, and Anna immediately falls in love with one of them, an Irishman named Mat Burke. He proposes marriage but, strangely, Anna won't accept. Then, in a tumultuous confession, she tells Mat and her father that she isn't the innocent farm girl they presume her to be, and that she was abused by her foster family and turned to prostitution.

The men react not with compassion and understanding, but with horror and anger. Both feel betrayed by Anna's sordid past. When they stumble off on a drunken binge, Anna concludes that all men are despicable and that reform is futile.

But as Anna prepares to return to the street, the men come back, full of remorse. Mat still wants to marry her after all, and her father has made arrangements for her financial security while he is away at sea. Ironically, the two men are going to ship out on the same boat to Cape Town. Anna accepts Mat's proposal and, as the men depart, she promises to have a nice home for them to return to.

Analysis: Eugene O'Neill took a great deal of heat for—and was defensive about—putting a too-pat happy ending on *Anna Christie*. Still, this 1921 drama popularized O'Neill's name once and for all and won him a second Pulitzer Prize. Greta Garbo's first "talking" film was the 1930 version of *Anna Christie*. All levels.

Scenes/Monologues: Female Monologues (1), Male/Female Scenes (3)

ANOTHER ANTIGONE
by A. R. Gurney, Jr. (Dramatists Play Service)

Synopsis: Henry Harper is an intellectually aloof teacher of Greek drama at a Boston college. One of his senior students, Judy Miller, hands in a new version of the Greek classic *Antigone,* adapting it as an antinuclear-arms statement. Unimpressed by Judy's efforts, Henry considers the rewrite to be "another *Antigone,*" lacking in discipline and ignorant of the meaning of tragedy, just like similar efforts made by previous students; he refuses to give her a passing grade. When Judy decides to follow through with her play, to see it produced at the college, teacher and student divide into warring camps. In the spirit of Greek tragedy, these opposing forces cause each other grief.

Analysis: This is a relatively unknown gem from A. R. Gurney, Jr.: intellectually challenging, full of excellent scenes and monologues, beautifully written and conceived. All levels.

Scenes/Monologues: Male Monologues (1), Female Monologues (1), Male/Female Scenes (4)

APPROACHING ZANZIBAR
by Tina Howe (Samuel French)

Synopsis: The Blossom family drives 2,000 miles from Hastings, New York, to Taos, New Mexico, in order to visit Aunt Olivia, a famous artist, before she dies. On the way they frolic, argue, meet strangers, have nightmares, play jokes, sleep in tents, and learn about life.

Analysis: Terrific comic monologue for an older actress. No two-person scenes. All levels.

Scenes/Monologues: Female Monologues (1)

ARTICHOKE
by Joanna M. Glass (Dramatists Play Service)

Synopsis: Walter fathered a daughter by another woman 14 years ago, and he and his legal wife, Margaret, raised the child. At the same time his wife took in the child, however, she banished Walter to the smokehouse on their 500-acre farm. This odd living arrangement has continued up to the present, with Walter taking monthly excursions into town to visit a prostitute "for relief." The action of the play begins as Gibson McFarland, Ph.D., an expert on Alexander Pope, arrives from Vancouver for a summer visit. He is really "family," having been adopted at the age of eight by Margaret's father and raised in the same house. In short order, Gibson and Margaret begin a romance, and Walter moves off the farm. Then Margaret realizes that she and Gibson will never be the natural fit that she and Walter are, so at summer's end, Gibson returns to Vancouver and Walter moves back in to Margaret's bedroom.

Analysis: This 1975 play is a favorite with community theaters. Although it is a bit saccharine and moralistic, the scenes work. Just don't expect major fireworks. All levels.

Scenes/Monologues: Male/Female Scenes (2)

AUTUMN GARDEN, THE
by Lillian Hellman (Dramatists Play Service)
Synopsis: Constance Tuckerman hosts the same visitors each year at her summer boardinghouse near the Gulf of Mexico, about 100 miles from New Orleans. Most of the people are middle-aged or older, facing the autumn of their lives, and the play, which takes place during September 1949, provides a platform for them to take stock of their personal values and prospects.
Analysis: Lillian Hellman must have been influenced by Anton Chekhov's style of probing the human character when she wrote *The Autumn Garden*. She and producer Kermit Bloomgarden even hired Harold Clurman of Group Theater fame to direct this character-driven 1951 work on Broadway. It received mixed notices and closed after 102 performances. All levels.
Scenes/Monologues: Male Monologues (1), Female/Female Scenes (1), Male/Female Scenes (3)

BABY DANCE, THE
by Jane Anderson (Samuel French)
Synopsis: Rachel and Richard are a childless, upwardly mobile, educated Hollywood showbiz couple who advertise for, and then decide to purchase, the as-yet-unborn child of Wanda and Al, a dirt-poor Louisiana couple. Act I takes place in Wanda and Al's trailer home, and Act II is set in the hospital on the day the baby is born. As the play evolves, the baby suffers oxygen deprivation, and the Hollywood couple back out of the deal on the possibility that they might be purchasing damaged goods.
Analysis: Clearly inspired by a few highly publicized cases in the late 1980s, this play forces the audience to consider some volatile issues. *The Baby Dance* is billed as a drama, a good point to keep in mind since there is considerable opportunity for comedy. All levels.
Scenes/Monologues: Male/Male Scenes (1), Female/Female Scenes (1), Three-Person Scenes (3)

BABY WITH THE BATHWATER
by Christopher Durang (Dramatists Play Service)
Synopsis: The story follows the mostly irrational events in the life of a male child named Daisy. That's right, this boy has a girl's name, and most people think he is a girl.
Analysis: An outlandish 1984 comedy that is full of unexplained leaps and transitions. Actors who work on the piece should carefully read Christopher Durang's notes (in the back of the DPS acting edition, pp. 55–62).
Scenes/Monologues: Female/Female Scenes (1), Three-Person Scenes (1)

BAD HABITS
by Terrence McNally [1990 revised edition (Dramatists Play Service)]
Synopsis: On either side of a tranquil lake somewhere near New York City are two sanitariums where people come to be cured of their bad habits. At Dunelawn the patients are encouraged to revel in self-indulgence. They can, for example, smoke, drink, and eat high-cholesterol diets on the premise that it is best to be happy and, if you are, the habits aren't bad. The regimen at Ravenswood, on the other hand, calls for extreme self-denial and injections of serum that transform the patients into identical automatons. There are no plots per se in these back-to-back, one-act plays, just a crazy-quilt assembly line of neurotic characters trying to work out their problems.
Analysis: Actors love to work on this material. It is broad, wacky, in-your-face comedy. All levels.
Scenes/Monologues: Female Monologues (1), Female/Female Scenes (1), Male/Female Scenes (3)

BALTIMORE WALTZ, THE
by Paula Vogel (Dramatists Play Service)
Synopsis: After Paula Vogel's brother died of AIDS in 1988, she wrote this short and whimsical play about the European vacation they never took together. The cast consists of a brother and

sister, and one other actor who plays everyone else. Stylistically fun, the whole work takes place in the sister's imagination.
Analysis: Winner of the 1991–92 Obie Award for Best Play. All levels.
Scenes/Monologues: Male Monologues (2)

BEAR, THE
by Anton Chekhov [*The Sneeze, Plays and Stories* by Anton Chekhov, translated and adapted by Michael Frayn (Samuel French)]
Synopsis: Widow Popova's late husband owes Smirnov 1,200 rubles. When she can't pay the debt, Smirnov flies into a rage, refusing to leave her home until she comes up with the money. They argue and bicker until they finally agree to a pistol duel. But as Smirnov teaches the widow how to use the weapon, he realizes that he has fallen in love with her. So he proposes to her. After some brief resistance, she accepts.
Analysis: Delightful short comedy, truly funny. Michael Frayn does with Anton Chekhov what Richard Wilbur does with Molière. All levels.
Scenes/Monologues: Male Monologues (1), Male/Female Scenes (1)

BEAU JEST
by James Sherman (Samuel French)
Synopsis: Sarah Goldman is a nice Jewish woman whose parents won't leave her alone about being single. The truth is that she is happy being single. Furthermore, her boyfriend, Chris, isn't Jewish. To get her parents off her back, Sarah invents a "proper" boyfriend, a Jewish doctor. They then insist on meeting him, so Sarah calls an escort service, requests a Jewish fellow for the evening, and arranges a small dinner party. When the escort, Bob Shroeder, arrives minutes before her parents, Sarah is horrified to discover he isn't Jewish. Fortunately, however, he is an actor and plays his part perfectly during the dinner, completely winning over Sarah's parents. Later, Sarah and Bob fall for each other for real. Amid much comedic confusion, romance prevails as the whole charade is put on the table. In the end, Chris steps aside, and Sarah and Bob look toward the future together.
Analysis: Cute, warm, and innocent 1989 comedy. All levels.
Scenes/Monologues: Male/Female Scenes (1)

BEDROOMS: FIVE COMEDIES
by Renée Taylor and Joseph Bologna (Samuel French)
Synopsis: Five unrelated, contemporary mini-comedies comprise this collection. In "David and Nancy," David is the nervous father of the bride-to-be. He wakes his daughter, Nancy, in the middle of the night to tell her that he has changed his mind about allowing her to get married. The scene ends with a tender embrace and, naturally, the wedding is on. In "Bill and Laura," a recently separated couple meets unexpectedly at a party, and their claws come out again. Laura and Bill's argument builds to a fever pitch, culminating in a reunion.

"Alan, Betty and Riva" centers on an adulterous relationship. Alan, a chiropodist, tries to revive the four-year affair he has been having with Betty, his nurse, by arranging a menage-à-trois. After Betty reluctantly participates, she is overcome with remorse and threatens to jump from the hotel ledge unless Alan agrees to leave his wife. In a panic, Alan commits to Betty.

In "Nick and Wendy," which consists of five brief scenes, a married couple tries unsuccessfully to iron out their problems during a self-encounter weekend. Nick and Wendy ultimately end up exactly where they started. And in "Mrs. Wexel and Mr. Lewis," love, or at least lust, comes to two residents of a retirement community. As it turns out, their imaginations are much more active than their bodies.
Analysis: Consistently amusing. All levels.
Scenes/Monologues: Male Monologues (1), Male/Female Scenes (2)

BELL, BOOK AND CANDLE

by John Van Druten (Dramatists Play Service)

Synopsis: Gillian Holroyd is an honest-to-goodness witch who lives in the Murray Hill section of New York City among her relatives. She becomes smitten with Sheperd Henderson, the handsome publisher who lives in her building, so she casts a "spell" to guarantee his affections. When Sheperd finds out what Gillian did, he storms out. By then, however, she is truly in love and has lost her magic powers. (Witches can't fall in love, you see.) But in the end, they get back together and proceed down the proverbial yellow brick road into a rosy sunrise.

Analysis: Silly stuff, but this 1951 comedy holds up surprisingly well. All levels.

Scenes/Monologues: Female/Female Scenes (1), Male/Female Scenes (3)

BENT

by Martin Sherman (Samuel French)

Synopsis: One of the few groups of people lower than Jews in Nazi Germany were homosexuals. Jews were required to wear yellow stars, and homosexuals were forced to wear pink ones. Here, Max and Rudy are forced to flee Berlin after a high-ranking homosexual Nazi officer is murdered. They are caught and while being transported to Dachau, the guards kill Rudy. In the camp, Max begins a relationship with another gay prisoner, Horst, an act of love that sustains them even though they can't touch one another. In the end, both men die in the camp.

Analysis: Dismal, powerful, sexually graphic, beautifully written. Absolutely inappropriate for novice actors.

Scenes/Monologues: Male/Male Scenes (4)

BETRAYAL

by Harold Pinter (Dramatists Play Service)

Synopsis: This one-act play begins two years after the end of Jerry and Emma's seven-year affair and moves progressively backward in time, ending with the day they decided to begin their relationship. Along the way, the consequences of their choices are sifted and exposed.

Analysis: Adult, literate, complex relationships starkly evolve. This 1978 play was turned into an excellent 1983 movie starring Jeremy Irons, Ben Kingsley, and Patricia Hodge. All levels.

Scenes/Monologues: Male/Male Scenes (1), Male/Female Scenes (4)

BETWEEN DAYLIGHT AND BOONVILLE

by Matt Williams (Samuel French)

Synopsis: Set against a background of the strip-mining industry in southern Indiana, the story focuses on three miners' wives, Carla, Marlene, and Lorette. Carla wants to take her child and escape her dreary trailer-park existence and a husband who has let himself go to pot. Marlene, pregnant and the mother of two, thinks she should stand by her man. Lorette has seen it all in her 60 years and thinks that the other two women are silly. When Marlene's husband is killed in a mining accident in Act II, the issues facing the women take on new meaning.

Analysis: There is a nice flow of middle-American dialogue in this 1979 comedy-drama. The play is a little corny at times and, perhaps, too talky, but it is worthwhile. The issues addressed are valid, and the women are searching for dignity. All levels.

Scenes/Monologues: Female Monologues (2), Female/Female Scenes (1), Male/Female Scenes (1)

BEYOND THERAPY

by Christopher Durang (Samuel French)

Synopsis: Bruce and Prudence meet through a personal ad, but they don't click at all. It turns out that Bruce is living with his male lover, Bob, and Prudence is sleeping with her psychiatrist. Soon, both of their therapists and Bob are mixed up in a bizarre quest for romance and happiness. There doesn't seem to be a sane character in the play. But then, what is sanity?

Analysis: Wild, wonderfully improbable, and frequently hilarious, this 1981 comedy is a send-up of therapy, existentialism, and the "me" generation. All levels.

Scenes/Monologues: Male/Female Scenes (5), Three-Person Scenes (1)

BIRDBATH

by Leonard Melfi [*Encounters, Six One-Act Plays* by Leonard Melfi (Samuel French)]

Synopsis: Velma and Frankie work at a New York City cafeteria, she as a waitress, he as a cashier. Tonight, for the first time, they speak to one another, and Velma winds up going to Frankie's apartment for some tea. There, he drinks premixed martinis until he is stoned and, after a while, she joins him. As the alcohol takes effect and as Frankie pushes Velma gently but insistently toward the bed, the audience learns how deeply troubled and strange Velma is. She becomes increasingly agitated until, finally, in an outburst, she pulls a blood-encrusted knife from her purse, threatening to stab Frankie. Then she confesses that she killed her mother that very morning. Exhausted by hysteria and fear, Velma falls asleep on the bed as Frankie writes a poem about her.

Analysis: If you want to work on vintage 1960s Off-Off-Broadway material, this intensely emotional drama, which premiered at Theatre Genesis, is a classic.

Scenes/Monologues: Male/Female Scenes (2)

BLOOD MOON

by Nicholas Kazan (Samuel French)

Synopsis: Manya's uncle introduces her to his womanizing friend, Alan, who lives in a New York City bachelor pad. Later that evening, Alan rapes Manya in a violent and ugly scene. A year later, she invites both men to dinner at her small Upper West Side apartment, tricking them into believing that she wants to let bygones be bygones. During the evening, she tells them that she was impregnated during the rape, aborted the late-term fetus, and then had an emotional breakdown. But, Manya says, she is okay now, happy with life. The men heartily enjoy the gourmet meal she prepared and just as they're wiping their mouths, she announces that this evening is, in fact, her revenge—that she froze both the placenta and fetus and served them for dinner. The men, shocked and sickened, quickly exit. In a curtain speech, Manya explains her actions to the audience, saying that she chose this course for its symmetry.

Analysis: Definitely adult material, but appropriate for all levels. Dana Delaney of "China Beach" fame created the role of Manya in New York.

Scenes/Monologues: Male/Female Scenes (2)

BLUE WINDOW

by Craig Lucas (Samuel French)

Synopsis: Libby is hosting a dinner party, her first attempt to socialize since her husband was killed and she was seriously injured in a freak fall from an apartment-building balcony. The action of the play follows the goings on in three different apartments as the party guests prepare for and then attend Libby's party. The blue window of the title refers to a wished-for window into people's emotions.

Analysis: It is sometimes hard to read this play because of the unusual overlapping scene structure and the way the dialogue is laid out on the printed page. It works well on the stage, however. All levels.

Scenes/Monologues: Female Monologues (1), Male/Female Scenes (1)

BORN IN THE RSA

by Barney Simon and the cast [*Woza Afrika! An Anthology of South African Plays,* edited by Duma Ndlovu (George Braziller, Inc.)]

Synopsis: Through a series of monologues directed to the theater audience, a South-African interracial ensemble cast depicts the horrors of apartheid.

Analysis: Journalistic and expository in style, this 1986 drama is frequently compelling and presents an excellent history lesson. All levels.
Scenes/Monologues: Female Monologues (3)

BORN YESTERDAY
by Garson Kanin (Dramatists Play Service)
Synopsis: Harry Brock, a self-made millionaire and brash con man, is worried that his beautiful-but-dumb girlfriend, Billie Dawn, is going to be an embarrassment to him as he wines and dines the movers and shakers in Washington, DC, trying to "purchase" self-serving legislation. So, as he continues on his path of corruption, he arranges for a serious-minded journalist to tutor Billie Dawn, to "show her the ropes" in Washington. Naturally, the tutor and his charge fall in love and as she becomes better educated, Billie develops a social conscience. In the end, the new lovers exit together, managing to thwart Harry's dastardly scheme.
Analysis: A delightful comedy that opened on Broadway in 1946 and ran for 1,642 performances. Judy Holliday became a star playing the ex-chorine, Billie Dawn. All levels.
Scenes/Monologues: Male/Male Scenes (1), Male/Female Scenes (3)

BOYS' LIFE
by Howard Korder (Dramatists Play Service)
Synopsis: Jack, Don, and Phil navigate the dating/marriage scene during the disjointed, upwardly mobile, spiritually empty, sexually threatening 1980s.
Analysis: This one-act play, which was nominated for a Pulitzer Prize in 1988, captures the undercurrent anxiety of dating in the 1980s and hints at major confusion in male/female relationships. All levels.
Scenes/Monologues: Male Monologues (2), Male/Female Scenes (1), Three-Person Scenes (1)

BREAKING THE CODE
by Hugh Whitemore (Samuel French)
Synopsis: Based on the true story of Alan Turing, a gay British mathematician who broke an important secret German code during World War II. Homosexuality was a crime in England during the 1940s, and Turning's government trial caused him acute public embarrassment and humiliation. Ultimately, he committed suicide.
Analysis: Derek Jacobi and Michael Gough received Tony nominations in 1988 for their work in this play. While essentially a biography of Turing, the playwright makes important points about homosexuality, hypocrisy in society, and the limits of science versus humanity. Written in the British vernacular. All levels.
Scenes/Monologues: Male Monologues (1), Male/Male Scenes (2), Male/Female Scenes (2)

BUCK
by Ronald Ribman (Theatre Communications Group) [*New Plays USA, 1983* (Theatre Communications Group); *The Rug Merchants of Chaos and Other Plays* by Ronald Ribman (Theatre Communications Group)]
Synopsis: This play depicts life in a low-budget cable-television station where the hit show of the moment involves staged reenactments of violent crimes. Buck, the producer, is in the midst of an acrimonious fight with his ex-wife and her current husband for custody of his 10-year-old son. No plot per se.
Analysis: Bleak, violent, sexual, a comment on the deteriorating standards of American society as represented by television. Well written, but contains rough adult material. Definitely not appropriate for inexperienced actors. *Buck* was originally co-produced in 1983 by The American Place Theatre and Playwrights Horizons in New York City. Ronald Ribman has been a serious contributor to the American theatre since the early 1960s. One of his plays,

Journey of the Fifth Horse (1966), also produced at The American Place Theatre, was an important early showcase for Dustin Hoffman.
Scenes/Monologues: Male Monologues (1), Female Monologues (1), Male/Female Scenes (1)

BURN THIS
by Lanford Wilson (Hill & Wang/Noonday; HarperCollins Canada Ltd.)
Synopsis: This play deals with the people who come together after a freak boating accident during which Robbie, Anna's gay roommate, is killed. Pale, Robbie's erratic and volatile brother, comes to collect Robbie's belongings and immediately begins a tempestuous romance with Anna, who has become bored by the sterile relationship she has with Burton, a Hollywood screenwriter. Anna, however, is frightened by Pale's powerful personality, his unpredictability, and her own needs. When Larry, Anna's other gay roommate, realizes that she should be with Pale and not Burton, he choreographs a situation that brings them together by the final curtain.
Analysis: Hip and well written. The character of Pale, played first by John Malkovich, is colorful and challenging. Appropriate for bright actors of all levels.
Scenes/Monologues: Male Monologues (1), Female Monologues (1), Male/Female Scenes (1)

BUTLEY
by Simon Gray (Samuel French)
Synopsis: Ben Butley is a bisexual English professor at the College of London University, a man burnt out on teaching and love. The play follows him through a single day during which he learns that his estranged wife plans to remarry, and that his male lover—and former student—is going to move in with another man. All of the action takes place in Butley's cluttered office.
Analysis: Alan Bates successfully nailed the title role in the London production, which was directed by Harold Pinter, and again later on Broadway. Be warned: this character is a true challenge. To play Butley well, an actor needs to get in touch with his very cynical, black humor. For literate actors of all levels. Written in the British vernacular.
Scenes/Monologues: Male/Male Scenes (3)

CAMERAS
by Jon Jory [*Twenty-Five Ten-Minute Plays from Actors Theatre of Louisville* (Samuel French)]
Synopsis: Several professional photographers dispassionately discuss what comprises the perfect shot and the relationship between a photograph and the person who looks at it. Then a young woman walks on stage and describes a horrible car accident in which a motorist ran into a working road crew. Bodies were strewn all over, and a person was screaming silently inside the car. Passersby tried desperately to rescue him while a photographer stopped and took pictures of the scene. What if the photographer had put down the camera and helped with the rescue? Would the person have lived?
Analysis: A small kick in the gut. All levels.
Scenes/Monologues: Female Monologues (1)

CANDIDA
by George Bernard Shaw (Signet)
Synopsis: In 1894 London, Candida Morell and her minister husband, James, befriend a sensitive and rather helpless young poet, Eugene Marchbanks. Subsequently, she has to choose between the men, who have radically different notions about love and marriage. In the surprising final moments of the play, she chooses "the weaker of the two," namely, her strong, manly, vigorous husband. By doing this, she benevolently rejects the romantic premises of each man, establishing her own turf as an independent woman.

Analysis: George Bernard Shaw's fifth play, frequently revived. Actors who enjoy the lush use of language will enjoy working on this most. All levels.
Scenes/Monologues: Female Monologues (1), Male/Male Scenes (1), Male/Female Scenes (1)

CAT ON A HOT TIN ROOF
by Tennessee Williams (Dramatists Play Service)
Synopsis: Big Daddy, a wealthy southern landowner with an estate of some 28,000 acres as well as cash and stock valued at $10 million, is dying and doesn't have a will. The central event of this play revolves around a family celebration for Big Daddy's sixty-fifth birthday, and while he doesn't realize yet that his illness is terminal, everyone else does. So there is a great deal of jostling for favor in the will they all hope he'll write.

Big Daddy's greedy older son, Gooper, is in a nasty contest of one-upmanship with Brick's sexually frustrated wife, Margaret. If anyone is a sentimental favorite to be named in the will, however, it is Brick, the alcoholic son who is indifferent to Big Daddy's wealth and bored by the spectacle of everybody kissing up to him. Brick is also deeply depressed by the death of his longtime friend, Skipper. A constant background question in *Cat on a Hot Tin Roof* is whether or not Brick and Skipper were, in fact, lovers. What is certain is that Brick no longer has sex with Margaret, and everyone knows it.
Analysis: Although Tennessee Williams was criticized in some quarters for not resolving the question of Brick's sexuality, this great American classic won the 1955 Pulitzer Prize. All levels.
Scenes/Monologues: Male/Male Scenes (1), Male/Female Scenes (1)

CAT'S-PAW
by William Mastrosimone (Samuel French)
Synopsis: A low-level employee of the Environmental Protection Agency (EPA) is abducted by a group of urban guerrillas. The organization demands that local newspapers publish a statement concerning the urgent dangers of water pollution and, when the papers don't comply, a car bomb is set off near the White House, killing 27 innocent people. Subsequently, a local-television reporter is brought to the guerrilla hideout to interview the hostage and the group leader. During the session, it becomes apparent that the EPA is, at the very least, negligent in containing the water-pollution problem.
Analysis: A 1986 "message" play that is unrelentingly tense. All levels.
Scenes/Monologues: Male/Male Scenes (1), Male/Female Scenes (1)

CHAPTER TWO
by Neil Simon (Samuel French)
Synopsis: Novelist George Schneider is recovering from the death of his wife. Actress Jennie Malone is rebounding from a divorce. So George's brother arranges a blind-date introduction. After an ecstatic two-week courtship, George and Jennie marry and leave on their honeymoon. But memories of George's deceased wife haunts him, and he is unable to commit to this new union. When Jennie realizes that she can't successfully compete with a memory, the newlyweds split up. Within weeks, however, George undergoes a catharsis and reunites with Jennie, presumably to live happily ever after.
Analysis: This semiautobiographical 1977 play is dedicated to actress Marsha Mason, whom Neil Simon married shortly after the death of his first wife. Witty and moving. All levels.
Scenes/Monologues: Female Monologues (1), Male/Male Scenes (1), Male/Female Scenes (3)

CHASE, THE
by Horton Foote (Dramatists Play Service)
Synopsis: Law-abiding citizens in the tranquil Texas town of Richmond are terrorized by Bubber Reeves, a home-grown escaped murderer who is bent on revenge against the local sheriff.

One by one, frightened business leaders turn against Sheriff Hawes when he is frustrated in his search for the killer and won't provide each of them with individual guard service. They remind him who pays his salary, threaten to see him defeated in the next election, and promise to deny him the farm loan he wants badly. By the time Hawes finally shoots down Bubber in a shack outside of town, the citizens have shown their true colors. They prove themselves to be the moral and ethical equals of the man they've been hunting

Analysis: Written almost like a movie and feeling close to *High Noon* in a contemporary setting, *The Chase*, first presented in 1952, provides fun challenges for actors who want to try some high drama. Horton Foote, author of the award-winning film and play *The Trip to Bountiful*, is one of America's finest naturalistic writers. All levels.

Scenes/Monologues: Male/Male Scenes (2), Male/Female Scenes (1)

CHEATERS
by Michael Jacobs (Samuel French)

Synopsis: Michelle walks out on Allen because he won't seriously commit to their relationship. She thinks that it is time for them to stop living together and get married. The breakup leads to the involvement of their respective parents who, it turns out, are having affairs with one another! In the end, Michelle and Allen set a wedding date.

Analysis: A thoroughly convoluted 1978 comedy that, fortunately, has one excellent funny scene for class work. All levels.

Scenes/Monologues: Female Monologues (1), Male/Female Scenes (1)

CHERRY ORCHARD, THE
by Anton Chekhov [*Chekhov, The Major Plays,* translated by Ann Dunnigan (Signet Books)]

Synopsis: Unable to pay taxes on the family estate, Lyuboff Ranevskaya and her brother wind up losing the property in a public auction rather than allowing their beloved cherry orchard to be sold for subdevelopment.

Analysis: Anton Chekhov's last play, arguably his best. There isn't much in the way of scene work, however, because the stage is almost always full of characters. The few possibilities that exist are, in my judgement, too short. All levels.

Scenes/Monologues: Male Monologues (1)

CHILDREN OF A LESSER GOD
by Mark Medoff (Dramatists Play Service)

Synopsis: James Leeds is a teacher at a state school for the deaf, and his new student, Sarah Norman, is a deaf woman who adamantly refuses to speak; she prefers to sign. The teacher/student relationship evolves into a love affair that by Act II results in their marriage. Their union isn't a perfect one, however, because Sarah suffers with very deep shame. Before long her attempts to turn away from her deaf friends and to merge completely with the hearing world force Sarah and James to reassess the basis of their relationship and, indeed, the basis of all communication.

Analysis: Written in 1980 as a vehicle for deaf actress Phyllis Frelich, *Children of a Lesser God* won a Tony for Best Play. Frelich won for Best Actress, and John Rubinstein won for Best Actor. The role of Sarah requires expert use of signed English.

Scenes/Monologues: Male Monologues (1), Male/Female Scenes (5)

CHILDREN'S HOUR, THE
by Lillian Hellman (Dramatists Play Service)

Synopsis: Karen and Martha saved their money for eight long years to purchase a farm and start a girls' school, and the place is just starting to pay for itself when their world falls apart. A 14-year-old student accuses the women of being lesbians, and the resulting public furor destroys their reputation and business. When Dr. Joseph Cardin, their only ally and Karen's fiancé, admits that he, too, suspects that the allegations are true, the women are thrown into utter desperation. Martha, in a moment of deep introspection, wonders aloud if perhaps she does love Karen in an "unnatural" way. When Karen responds to this insight with hostility, Martha walks into the next room and kills herself. Then, in an anticlimax, it comes to light that the charges were false, the construction of a maladjusted child.

Analysis: On one level, *The Children's Hour* is the story of a devilish child running amok; on a more serious level, it is an examination of the relationship between two women. Ultimately, playwright Lillian Hellman doesn't resolve this bigger issue, and the ending is something of a letdown. Still, this was Hellman's first produced play and her biggest hit, running 691 performances on Broadway. In 1934, lesbianism was a controversial subject, and the play was widely banned, most notably in London and Boston.

Scenes/Monologues: Female/Female Scenes (2), Male/Female Scenes (1)

COASTAL DISTURBANCES
by Tina Howe (Samuel French)

Synopsis: The play is set in an upscale beach community on Massachusetts' North Shore during the last two weeks of August. Leo and Holly are both rebounding from troubled relationships and find each other.

Analysis: A light 1986 treatment of contemporary relationships. Cute at times, cloying at others. A bit self-aware. The individual scenes are fine, if not long on conflict. All levels.

Scenes/Monologues: Male Monologues (1), Female Monologues (1), Male/Female Scenes (2)

COLD STORAGE
by Ronald Ribman (Samuel French)

Synopsis: Two cancer patients get to know each other on the roof garden of Hope Memorial Hospital. Parmigian is an existentialist to the core. Landau is more hopeful.

Analysis: A philosophical debate, actually, written by a talented and serious playwright. Ran on Broadway in 1977.

Scenes/Monologues: Male Monologues (1), Male/Male Scenes (1)

COLORED MUSEUM, THE
by George C. Wolfe (Broadway Play Publishing)

Synopsis: Theatrical device is a museum tour of 11 exhibits that force black stereotypes into the light.

Analysis: The play's inventive milieu presents an excellent opportunity for flashy monologues. The entire cast is African American. All levels.

Scenes/Monologues: Male Monologues (1), Female Monologues (2)

COME BACK, LITTLE SHEBA
by William Inge (Samuel French)

Synopsis: Lola and Doc have endured a marriage of convenience for 20 years, and both are fixated on their lost youth. Doc's alcoholism has nearly ruined the union and has brought them close to poverty. Sober now and attending Alcoholics Anonymous meetings for almost a year, Doc thinks that things are looking up until he discovers that the couple's boarder, a seemingly innocent young woman, is sleeping with her casual boyfriend. This kind of promiscuity throws Doc into a philosophical tailspin, and he goes on a bender. Lola, for reasons of her own, is also disillusioned to learn that the woman is sleeping around. When Doc dries out, he and Lola move into the future with mutual diminished expectations about the prospects for goodness and purity in this world. Little Sheba, by the way, is a puppy Lola used to own, one that disappeared one day, never to grow old. She wishes it would come back, just as she longs for her youth to be restored.

Analysis: William Inge's first play, *Come Back, Little Sheba* was stylistically influenced by his mentor, Tennessee Williams, and is full of symbols. First performed in 1950, the drama feels dated now, but still packs a punch for scene work. Shirley Booth won a Tony for her stage performance as Lola and an Oscar in 1952 for the same film role. All levels.
Scenes/Monologues: Female Monologues (1), Male/Female Scenes (3)

COME BACK TO THE 5 & DIME, JIMMY DEAN, JIMMY DEAN

by Ed Graczyk (Samuel French)
Synopsis: The "Disciples of James Dean" reunite in a tiny, drought-afflicted west Texas town on the twentieth anniversary of the actor's death. They drink, party, and reminisce about how it was to be teenagers in 1955 when *Giant* was filming in nearby Marfa, and many of the locals were extras. Then Joanne arrives, a mysterious woman whom the women soon discover is former Disciples-member Joe; she underwent a sex-change operation. Joe/Joanne's brutally honest perspective leads to some serious truth-telling among the old gang members. Sissy discloses that she lost her man after she had a mastectomy, Mona admits that her son wasn't fathered by James Dean after all, and Juanita faces the probability that her late husband was a lecherous alcoholic.
Analysis: A wonderfully theatrical play, jumping back and forth in time between 1955 and 1975 as well as in and out of reality. The work is full of poetry, humor, and magic. For sophisticated actors of all levels.
Scenes/Monologues: Female Monologues (2), Female/Female Scenes (1)

COMMANCHE CAFE

by William Hauptman (Samuel French)
Synopsis: Set in a cafe in southern Oklahoma during the late 1930s, where Mattie has been a waitress for 14 years. Ronnie is a newcomer. They sit and peel potatoes, talking about life, love, and leaving Oklahoma.
Analysis: This 8-page work is more a theatrical exercise than a play, but the southwestern flavor is strong, and the language is poetic. All levels.
Scenes/Monologues: Female Monologues (2), Female/Female Scenes (1)

COUPLA WHITE CHICKS SITTING AROUND TALKING, A

by John Ford Noonan (Samuel French)
Synopsis: The women are unlikely friends: Maude is a reserved lady from Westchester County, New York, and Hannah Mae is a newly arrived gregarious Texan. Their relationship is oddly strengthened when Maude impulsively makes love with Hannah Mae's husband, Carl Joe. Overcome with guilt, Maude confesses the act to Hannah Mae, who, instead of reacting with anger, contends that they are closer now—and anyway, who could resist a hunk like Carl Joe? Subsequently, Maude confides in her new friend, telling about her troubled marriage to Tyler, who is at that very moment out of town on a romantic fling. The women unite to set their respective husbands straight.
Analysis: Very funny two-character comedy, even if a truck can fit through the big holes in the plot. All levels.
Scenes/Monologues: Female/Female Scenes (1)

COVER

by Jeffrey Sweet with Stephen Johnson and Sandra Hastie [*Twenty-Five Ten-Minute Plays from Actors Theatre of Louisville* (Samuel French)]
Synopsis: Marty wants Frank to lie and tell his lady friend, Diane, that the two of them were together last night, but the truth is that Marty had a date. Frank doesn't want to lie but when Diane brings up the issue, he finds the false words coming out of his mouth. Diane sees right through the lie but doesn't challenge the men's story.

Analysis: Although the whole play is only 7 1/2 pages long, the undercurrent of negotiations going on makes it interesting.
Scenes/Monologues: Three-Person Scenes (1)

CRIMES OF THE HEART
by Beth Henley (Dramatists Play Service)
Synopsis: A glimpse into the lives of the very eccentric Magrath sisters, Babe, Meg, and Lenny, of Hazlehurst, Mississippi. They rediscover the value of family ties when Babe, the youngest, shoots Zachary, her abusive husband and a prominent local attorney, and faces the prospect of a jail sentence.
Analysis: This pitch-black Southern-Gothic comedy, a 1979 Pulitzer Prize winner, was first produced at the Actors Theatre of Louisville and later on Broadway. It was made into a successful 1986 movie starring Tess Harper, Diane Keaton, Jessica Lange, and Sissy Spacek. All levels.
Scenes/Monologues: Female/Female Scenes (1), Male/Female Scenes (3)

CROSSING DELANCEY
by Susan Sandler (Samuel French)
Synopsis: Isabelle is an independent, young Jewish woman who, when she isn't working in a bookstore, spends time with her elderly, spunky grandmother on the New York's Lower East Side. Bubbie, as the grandmother is known, is a lady with one foot still in the old country. She is concerned about Isabelle still being single and arranges for a matchmaker to cook up a romance. The matchmaker then introduces Isabelle to Sam, a sensitive fellow who works as a pickle-maker. Isabelle, however, has her sights set on a romantic, handsome novelist who frequents the bookstore. As the plot unfolds, she discovers that the novelist is a shallow cad and that Sam has some wonderful virtues, so their match turns out to be a good one after all, and everyone lives happily after.
Analysis: Delightful comedy that capitalizes on generational and cultural differences. The play was successfully adapted for the movies in 1988, starring Amy Irving. All levels.
Scenes/Monologues: Male Monologues (1), Female Monologues (1), Male/Female Scenes (3)

CRUCIBLE, THE
by Arthur Miller (Dramatists Play Service)
Synopsis: Set amid the Salem witch trials the late seventeenth century, the story involves John Proctor, a man suffering from guilt because he committed adultery with young Abigail Williams some months earlier. When Abigail and a group of her friends claim to be affected by the devil and accuse various citizens of being witches, Proctor knows she is lying but is afraid to speak up for fear his sin will be disclosed. He tries to ignore the ongoing trials; however, this becomes impossible when his own wife, Elizabeth, is accused of being a witch. Finally, Proctor steps forward and, when he does, he himself is accused of being a witch. To save his own life, he shamefully signs a false confession, but when he is pressed to reveal the names of others who might be witches, he refuses and is led to his death in the gallows.
Analysis: This 1953 drama strongly parallels the struggles of McCarthyism in the United States, but it stands on its own as a powerful and well-drawn work of art. It ran for 197 performances on Broadway in 1953 and for more than 500 performances in a later Off-Broadway revival. All levels.
Scenes/Monologues: Male/Female Scenes (3)

DANCE AND THE RAILROAD, THE
by David Henry Hwang (Dramatists Play Service)
Synopsis: In 1867, Chinese laborers working on the American transcontinental railroad launched an unsuccessful strike against their employers. During the strike, two of the men get

to know each other in a nearby mountaintop clearing when Ma discovers Lone practicing his dance steps. It turns out that Lone is a trained opera dancer whose parents abruptly took him out of opera school two years ago, sending him to America to get rich. Ma asks to be trained, too, so that he can play the grand role of Gwan Gung, the God of Fighters and the God of Adventurers, in an opera. Lone tests Ma's dedication, leaving him to crouch and imitate a locust overnight. When the strike ends the next morning, Ma has successfully proved that he has the fortitude to learn but he no longer wants to dance. He wants to get rich in America.

Analysis: David Henry Hwang, the author of *M. Butterfly,* runs elements of Chinese myth up against American culture. In this 1981 one-act play, he attacks the image of the passive and subservient "coolie" laborer. All characters are Asian American. All levels.

Scenes/Monologues: Male Monologues (1), Male/Male Scenes (1)

DANNY AND THE DEEP BLUE SEA

by John Patrick Shanley (Dramatists Play Service) [*13 by Shanley* (Applause Books)]

Synopsis: Danny and Roberta are violent, battered people. They meet in a Bronx bar and, despite their tough and defensive façades, are drawn to each other. They spend the night together and before dawn, Danny proposes marriage, an act of kindness and hope that neither seems to be able to accept or tolerate. Finally, their emotional barriers fall, and they face the future together.

Analysis: John Patrick Shanley's insightful, poetic, sensitive characterizations shine a bright light on the heavy toll that childhood abuse and neglect can take. Challenging material for actors of all levels, at times funny, ultimately very moving. Shanley is best known for writing the delightful 1987 film comedy *Moonstruck.*

Scenes/Monologues: Female Monologues (1), Male/Female Scenes (3)

DARK AT THE TOP OF THE STAIRS, THE

by William Inge (Dramatists Play Service)

Synopsis: The year is 1920, and Cora's friends are getting rich in this oil-soaked Oklahoma town. She longs to climb the social ladder with them, but her husband, Rubin, a simple man and harness-salesman by trade, doesn't share the gambling inclinations of the oil drillers. They continually fight about money, and everything comes to a head over the issue of a new party dress for their shy daughter, Reenie, who has been invited to a fancy country-club party. Rubin storms out of the house in frustration, perhaps never to return.

The party turns out to be a disaster, ending in the suicide of Reenie's blind date, a Jewish boy from Hollywood. Cora then asks her sister, Lottie, if she and the children can come live with her and her husband in Oklahoma City. Lottie refuses, saying that her home isn't a happy one either, so the arrangement won't work out. Rubin returns, makes amends with the family and, in a touching speech, explains his frustrations as a man. The family moves forward with greater love and resolve, seemingly more in touch with the values that truly matter.

Analysis: This 1957 drama is dedicated to Tennessee Williams, and his influence is evident through the play. Reenie, for example, is very reminiscent of Laura in *The Glass Menagerie.* Beautifully written, if perhaps a little too neat at the end. All levels.

Scenes/Monologues: Male Monologues (2), Female/Female Scenes (1), Male/Female Scenes (1)

DAY IN THE DEATH OF JOE EGG, A

by Peter Nichols (Samuel French)

Synopsis: Ten-year-old Josephine is spastic, given to frequent seizures, completely dependent on her parents for every imaginable human need, and unable to speak or walk. Her presence in the family has skewed Sheila and Bri's marriage to the point of breaking. Sheila believes that hope rings eternal, that there is always a chance that Joe will develop normally. Bri, however, has no hope at all. He considers his daughter to be essentially without life and has resorted to black humor to deal with the situation. The playwright employs a theatrical device where Bri and Sheila relive the events of the child's birth and early years, play-acting various characters in their lives, such as a doctor and priest.

Analysis: A very disturbing, sometimes funny, two-act drama. Albert Finney starred as Bri during its 1968 Broadway run. Scene work is possible but difficult because of the fast-moving, almost cabaret-style presentation. Written in the British vernacular. All levels.

Scenes/Monologues: Male Monologues (1), Female Monologues (1)

DAYS OF WINE AND ROSES
by J. P. Miller (Dramatists Play Service)

Synopsis: Joe and Kristen are alcoholics in denial. They marry quickly, have a daughter, and then continue a slow and boozy decline into poverty. Finally, Joe admits his sickness and joins Alcoholics Anonymous. Kristen, however, stays in denial and at final curtain, the audience realizes that she'll be doomed unless she comes to terms with the truth.

Analysis: Originally a 1958 "Playhouse 90" production, this drama went to Broadway and, ultimately, to film, where Jack Lemmon stopped the clocks with his portrayal of Joe. The dialogue rings true. All levels.

Scenes/Monologues: Male/Female Scenes (1)

DEATH AND THE MAIDEN
by Ariel Dorfman (Penguin)

Synopsis: Paulina was held in captivity, blindfolded, and brutally tortured by a "doctor" during the reign of a now-collapsed South American military dictatorship. This horror is reborn when her husband, Roberto, innocently brings home a man who gave him a lift on the road. Recognizing the man's voice as that of her torturer, Paulina takes him prisoner, demanding his confession and repentance. Roberto, convinced that she is serious about killing the man if he doesn't confess, goes along with her. Although her prisoner passionately denies that he is the torturer, Paulina tricks him into disclosing the truth. The title, by the way, refers to a Schubert quartet that was played during the torture sessions.

Analysis: Intelligent, topical. The Broadway cast included Glenn Close, Richard Dreyfus, and Gene Hackman. Even though these characters have Hispanic names, all roles can be played by non-Hispanics. All levels.

Scenes/Monologues: Female Monologues (1), Male/Male Scenes (1), Male/Female Scenes (2)

DEATH OF A SALESMAN
by Arthur Miller (Dramatists Play Service)

Synopsis: Willy Loman, an aging traveling salesman, realizes that he is getting too old to be on the road so much. He curtails an unfinished trip through New England and abruptly returns to his Brooklyn home. There he locks horns with his visiting eldest son, Biff, who disagrees with him about which life choices lead to "success." Willy has bought heavily into the American Dream, but Biff doesn't believe that working your way up the financial ladder is particularly worthwhile. This conflict, which profoundly changes the relationship between them, is the central issue in the play. Willy is forced to take stock of himself and realizes that he has, indeed, lived his life on false premises. Depressed, he commits suicide in a car crash in order to collect insurance money for the final payment on his home, a home that is a necessary component of the American Dream.

Analysis: Arthur Miller's great modern tragedy won the Pulitzer Prize in 1949. As he does in *All My Sons,* he explores a man's basic values. Is it better to reach for society's suggestion of an ideal or to look within? Lee J. Cobb was 37 in 1949 when he created the role of Willy on Broadway, and Dustin Hoffman was in his forties when he played Willy. All levels.

Scenes/Monologues: Male Monologues (1), Female Monologues (1), Male/Male Scenes (1)

DEATH OF BESSIE SMITH, THE
by Edward Albee (Plume)
Synopsis: Two whites-only hospitals near Memphis refuse to treat Bessie Smith, the great blues singer, when she is brought in after a car wreck in 1937. In eight fast-moving scenes, Albee exposes the circumstances and underlying racism of this tragic event.
Analysis: One of Edward Albee's more enduring plays, this 1959 drama is rough in its depiction of racism and sexuality. For sophisticated actors.
Scenes/Monologues: Male/Female Scenes (3)

DELICATE BALANCE, A
by Edward Albee (Samuel French)
Synopsis: Agnes and Tobias live a highly ordered existence in the spacious suburban home they share with Agnes's sister, Claire. But this isn't a happy domestic scene by any means, for this is a family in strong denial. These are the kind of people who have a civilized drink before breakfast and bury their true emotions in intellectual repartee. One night, longtime friends Harry and Edna arrive, bags in hand. They want to sleep over because they are afraid of some nameless thing, perhaps the darkness of their own home and lives. Harry and Edna retreat into an upstairs bedroom and, days later, announce that they intend to move permanently out of their own place and to live here full time.

Julia, Agnes and Tobias's daughter, arrives home a short time later, licking her wounds from the demise of her fourth marriage. She is pushed to the edge of hysteria and violence by the presence of the strangers who are now residing in her old bedroom. Harry and Edna eventually recognize they aren't welcome and, with deflated spirits, depart.
Analysis: Psychologically dense, mysterious, adult drama that ran on Broadway in 1967. Marian Seldes won a Tony for portraying Julia. Best for experienced actors.
Scenes/Monologues: Female Monologues (1), Female/Female Scenes (1), Male/Female Scenes (3)

DIVISION STREET
by Steve Tesich (Samuel French)
Synopsis: Chris Adrian, a Tom Hayden-like former leader of the radical movement during the 1960s, resurfaces as an insurance salesperson in Chicago in the early 1980s. After his picture unexpectedly appears in the newspapers, fellow radicals converge on his apartment, imploring him to lead a new revolution. But Chris has gone straight and is no longer interested in boat people or other causes, so he turns them away. Finally, everyone agrees to get back in touch with the honorable principles that led to the revolution.
Analysis: Madcap 1980 comedy that ran on Broadway for 21 performances. Full of mistaken identities, pratfalls, disguises, sex changes, and characters with strange international accents. A great deal of fun for actors who can ride the wave. All levels.
Scenes/Monologues: Male Monologues (3), Female Monologues (1), Male/Male Scenes (1), Male/Female Scenes (2)

DOES A TIGER WEAR A NECKTIE?
by Don Petersen (Dramatists Play Service)
Synopsis: The play is set "in a rehabilitation center for juvenile narcotic addicts located on an island in a river bordering a large industrial city." There is no major plot line. The works consists of character exploration as incarcerated young people from life's underbelly try to find their way.
Analysis: Definitely not for novice actors. Gritty dialogue and situations, very primal at times. Al Pacino won a Tony Award in 1969 for creating the role of Bickham.
Scenes/Monologues: Male Monologues (1), Male/Male Scenes (2), Male/Female Scenes (1)

DOLL'S HOUSE, A

by Henrik Ibsen [a new version by Christopher Hampton (Samuel French)]

Synopsis: Nora forged her father's name to a loan document to get money to pay for Helmer's recuperation from a serious illness. She has secretly been repaying the debt out of her meager household allowance. And now that her husband is healthy again and has been promoted to the prestigious position of bank manager, it appears that life is taking a positive turn.

Suddenly, however, Nora finds herself being blackmailed with the old forgery by a unscrupulous and desperate bank employee who is afraid of losing his job when Helmer becomes manager. Helmer discovers the forgery anyway and rather than protecting his wife, reacts by turning against her, damning her for jeopardizing his job. She concludes that she has been nothing more than a possession to her husband all along, never an equal partner. So at the final curtain, Nora walks out on him and her children, determined to become an independent, self-reliant woman.

Analysis: Henrik Ibsen's powerful 1879 indictment of Victorian society's treatment of women is still relevant today and is, along with *Hedda Gabler,* his most enduring legacy. All levels.

Scenes/Monologues: Female/Female Scenes (1), Male/Female Scenes (4)

DRAMA

by Anton Chekhov [*The Sneeze, Plays and Stories* by Anton Chekhov, translated and adapted by Michael Frayn (Samuel French)]

Synopsis: Pavel Vasilevich, a well-known writer, is working at home when an admirer with literary ambitions shows up to get feedback on the drama she has written. Although he agrees to take a look at it if she'll leave it, she begins to read it to him right away. Pavel tries diplomatically to stop the reading, but the woman seems oblivious to his growing discomfort. She goes on and on and, to be truthful, her writing is awful. Finally, when all else fails, he takes out a knife and kills her.

Analysis: Thin—the whole play is only 8 pages long—but very funny. All levels.

Scenes/Monologues: Male/Female Scenes (1)

DREAM GIRL

by Elmer Rice (Dramatists Play Service)

Synopsis: Aspiring novelist Georgina Allerton is a daydreamer living a mundane life, finding spice only in her very active fantasies. She confronts this fact about herself when her secret love, her very married brother-in-law, decides to get a divorce and suggests that they get together. Finally given the opportunity to act on her fantasy, however, Georgina retreats. Clark Redfield, a hardboiled realist and newspaperman, then enters her life. Although there is a chemistry between them, she feels threatened when he accuses her of preferring fantasy to reality. Eventually, however, Georgina falls in love with Clark and at the play's end, they marry.

Analysis: This 1945 play is the very definition of innocence. Stylistically dated, but still good scene-study material. All levels.

Scenes/Monologues: Female Monologues (1), Male/Female Scenes (1)

DRESSER, THE

by Ronald Harwood (Samuel French)

Synopsis: Sir is an aging actor-manager whose showcase role is King Lear. He travels the English provinces with his entourage, portraying that character and others. *The Dresser* focuses on his final performance, set in war-torn England in 1942, and explores the relationships Sir has formed over the years with his dresser, Norman, the woman he lives with, and others in the ragtag company.

Analysis: A lovely ode to the theater, a Valentine to a lifestyle now regretfully long gone, and Sir is a role to be cherished. To do it justice, however, an actor needs to have seasoning,

insight, and technical power. Albert Finney played Sir to Tom Courtenay's Norman in the 1983 movie version. Written in the British vernacular.
Scenes/Monologues: Male Monologues (4), Male/Female Scenes (1)

DUET FOR ONE
by Tom Kempinski (Samuel French)
Synopsis: World-famous violinist Stephanie Abrahams finds her career abruptly halted at the young age of 33 when she is afflicted with multiple sclerosis. Losing the skill that literally defines her life and marriage, she becomes suicidal. Seven months after the diagnosis, Stephanie begins psychotherapy. *Duet for One* is a session-by-session diary of her progress. The early denial of her pain turns into hostility, then fury and, finally, acceptance.
Analysis: Very intense material, a tear-jerker showcase for Stephanie, who is in a wheelchair almost the entire play. Scene work will be enhanced if you have one. Anne Bancroft and Max Von Sydow starred in this sometimes verbose two-character 1981 drama on Broadway. All levels.
Scenes/Monologues: Female Monologues (1), Male/Female Scenes (1)

DYLAN
by Sidney Michaels (Samuel French)
Synopsis: Based on *Dylan Thomas in America* by John Malcolm Brinnin and *Leftover Life to Kill* by Caitlin Thomas, *Dylan* tracks the famous Welsh poet's final American lecture tours, ending with his death at 38 in the White Horse Tavern in New York City's Greenwich Village. Journalistic in style, hopping back and forth across the Atlantic and all around the United States on a bare stage, this is very effective theater. Dylan speaks with an English accent, while Caitlin has an Irish accent.
Analysis: This is the kind of material that, if done well, can create that powerful a memory. All levels.
Scenes/Monologues: Male Monologues (1), Male/Female Scenes (2)

EASTERN STANDARD
by Richard Greenberg (Dramatists Play Service)
Synopsis: Five upwardly mobile young people meet a bag lady in a Manhattan restaurant in 1987. They all wind up at Stephen's beach house where various romances bloom, and the bag lady steals from everyone.
Analysis: Hard to categorize. Bizarre and funny at times, occasionally poignant. The play is finally a bit too shallow. It is the kind of piece where one of the characters admits to having attempted suicide on "a whim; don't you ever have whims?"
Scenes/Monologues: Male/Female Scenes (1)

ECCENTRICITIES OF A NIGHTINGALE, THE
by Tennessee Williams (Dramatists Play Service)
Synopsis: This later version of *Summer and Smoke* features a much more aggressive and high-strung Alma, and John isn't so obviously a hell-raiser. It also has fewer characters and more focused scenes. Furthermore, Alma actually goes to bed with John on New Year's Eve in a hotel room that is rented by the hour. In the end, however, she still winds up alone, although this version doesn't mention John and Nellie's marriage. The final moments are exactly the same: Alma picks up a traveling salesman at the fountain.
Analysis: Although *Summer and Smoke* is the better-known work, Tennessee Williams preferred this later version. The scenes are more pointed, the conflict is more overt, and Alma is a little closer to the edge. All levels.
Scenes/Monologues: Female Monologues (4), Male/Female Scenes (6)

ECHOES
by N. Richard Nash (Samuel French)
Synopsis: Sam, a high-school history teacher, and Tilda, occupation unknown, share a room in a mental institution. They spend most of their time in a safe, pretend world, excluding the doctors and all the threatening reality they bring with them. Sam, however, is getting better and, as he begins shifting toward lucidity—and away from Tilda—she panics, trying desperately to hold him in their world. At the final curtain, he moves into the next room so he can see his wife and 3-year-old son, and Tilda is left alone with her fantasies.
Analysis: Winner of the 1972 Best Play Award from The American Playwrights Theatre, an association of university and community theaters. Difficult material. N. Richard Nash questions where reality begins and ends, and the meaning of sanity. Excellent for actors who want to work on imagination and concentration. All levels.
Scenes/Monologues: Female Monologues (2), Male/Female Scenes (6)

EDUCATING RITA
by Willy Russell (Samuel French)
Synopsis: Like *Pygmalion,* this comedy features an educated but burnt-out literature professor who takes an uneducated but young, spunky, lower-class woman under his wing. Rita excels, perhaps outdistancing Frank in understanding the deeper implications of the assigned material. During the year the play covers, her shallow husband kicks her out because she is trying to better herself, and Frank drifts into and out of a merely comfortable relationship. At the final curtain, it looks like Frank and Rita might get together, now that she is educated.
Analysis: A lovely 1981 two-character, two-act romantic comedy that was the basis for a 1986 movie starring Michael Caine and Julie Walters. Written in the British vernacular. The difference between Frank and Rita's upper- and lower-class accents, respectively, is important. All levels.
Scenes/Monologues: Female Monologues (1), Male/Female Scenes (2)

EFFECT OF GAMMA RAYS ON MAN-IN-THE-MOON MARIGOLDS
by Paul Zindel (Bantam)
Synopsis: Tillie is an emotionally isolated teenager who is consumed with love for science. She finds a kind of symmetry and beauty in the study of atoms that is missing from her home life. When she becomes a finalist in her school's science fair, the play turns into a family drama in which her alcoholic mother and seizure-prone older sister ruin any possible honors.
Analysis: Winner of the 1971 Pulitzer Prize, this haunting drama is chock full of metaphors. The colorful role of the mother was created on stage by Sada Thompson and later played by Joanne Woodward in the movie version. All levels.
Scenes/Monologues: Female Monologues (3), Female/Female Scenes (1)

EMPRESS OF CHINA
by Ruth Wolff (Broadway Play Publishing)
Synopsis: The story of the Dowager Empress Tzu-Hsi and her rise to power in China. Starting as the emperor's concubine, she ultimately ruled the country for 50 years, keeping the tentacles of Western civilization at bay.
Analysis: Ruth Wolff specializes in dramas with strong, central female characters. All characters are Asian American. All levels.
Scenes/Monologues: Female Monologues (2), Male/Female Scenes (2)

END OF THE WORLD WITH SYMPOSIUM TO FOLLOW, THE
by Arthur Kopit (Samuel French)
Synopsis: A mysterious, wealthy industrialist commissions an out-of-work playwright to write a play based on the premise that the world is going to end. As the playwright researches the

topic, interviewing generals and war experts, he is shocked to learn that nuclear proliferation makes no sense at all—that, in the final analysis, it resembles an M. C. Escher drawing.
Analysis: A 1984 comedy-drama by the very talented Arthur Kopit, written before anybody dreamed that Russia would self-destruct and that the nuclear threat would, at least temporarily, seem to subside. All levels.
Scenes/Monologues: Male Monologues (2), Male/Male Scenes (1)

ENEMY OF THE PEOPLE, AN
by Henrik Ibsen [adapted by Arthur Miller (Dramatists Play Service)]
Synopsis: A small Norwegian city seeks financial salvation through the development and promotion of a health spa. Everything moves forward happily until Dr. Thomas Stockmann discovers that the local water is polluted. It is filled with disease-causing bacteria that are washing downstream from a tannery, which, ironically, his father-in-law owns. When it becomes clear that Stockmann intends to publicize the danger, the local power elite, including his brother the mayor, conspires to ostracize him, officially labeling him an "enemy of the people." Stockmann stands on principal, even though this translates into personal financial ruin and hard times for his family. Despite local hostility, he remains true to his sense of what is right.
Analysis: Henrik Ibsen's most militant play, reportedly based on an actual 1830 incident. All levels.
Scenes/Monologues: Male/Male Scenes (2)

ENTER LAUGHING
by Joseph Stein (Samuel French)
Synopsis: This play is set in New York City during the 1930s. David Kolowitz is a "nice Jewish boy" with a predictable future as a pharmacist, and he has a sweet, simple local girl-friend named Wanda. When David sees an ad for the Marlowe Theater and School for Dramatic Arts, he thinks that he is better suited for the glamorous life of an actor. The Marlowe school turns out to be a seedy nickel-and-dime operation, the kind of place where aspiring actors' wallets are more important than their talent, and the owner's jaded daughter is the company ingenue. David, who has almost no talent, is cast opposite the ingenue and has an important (to him) kissing scene. Opening night is almost a disaster but wonderful or not, David is happy to have made his theatrical debut. Although his parents think he is making a big mistake if he doesn't go to pharmacy school, Wanda believes he is doing the right thing.
Analysis: Based on a novel by Carl Reiner, this comedy is delightful, innocent, and great fun to perform. All levels.
Scenes/Monologues: Male/Female Scenes (1)

EQUUS
by Peter Schaffer (Samuel French)
Synopsis: Martin Dysart, a doctor at the Rokesby Psychiatric Hospital in southern England, accepts Alan Strang as a patient. The 17-year-old has blinded six horses with a metal spike, and the court has ordered him to be treated at the hospital rather than sent to prison. Dysart and Strang come to understand and respect each other as the young man's complex motives are understood. In the process of working with Alan, Dysart questions his own values.
Analysis: Extraordinarily intelligent script dealing with religion, sexuality, and guilt. Much of the play's power, however, comes from the original, highly theatrical staging by John Dexter. All new actors should read the play, but the scenes aren't the best for workshop application. There is one wonderful monologue for Dora, Alan's mother. Dysart has several introspective monologues, the best of which is in Act 2, Scene 22. Keep in mind that auditors will probably be mystified by the self-searching material unless they are familiar with the play's context.
Scenes/Monologues: Female Monologues (1)

EVERYTHING IN THE GARDEN
by Edward Albee [adapted from the play by Giles Cooper (Dramatists Play Service)]
Synopsis: Richard is outraged to learn that his wife has started earning money by working as a high-priced prostitute downtown, and he threatens to throw her out. On the other hand, they're living beyond their means in an upscale neighborhood, and they could use the money for a new greenhouse. To complicate matters, several other wives from the country-club set are also prostitutes, but their husbands like the money and condone the practice. Then the wealthy man next door is accidentally killed after he discovers the neighborhood secret, so the husbands bury him in the backyard. At the final curtain, the women decide to continue hooking, and their very charismatic madam, Mrs. Toothe, sets up shop in the neighborhood.
Analysis: This 1968 drama has some excellent scenes for workshops but as an evening of theater, fails by a mile. For sophisticated actors of all levels.
Scenes/Monologues: Female/Female Scenes (1), Male/Female Scenes (2)

EVILS OF TOBACCO, THE
by Anton Chekhov [*The Sneeze, Plays and Stories* by Anton Chekhov, translated and adapted by Michael Frayn (Samuel French)]
Synopsis: Nyukhin is the father of seven unmarried daughters and the henpecked husband of a domineering woman who owns and operates a school for girls. In this 15-minute monologue, he addresses an assembly of female students on the evils of tobacco. Nyukhin doesn't, however, really make his points because he gets lost in relating incidental details of his personal life. Toward the end of the speech, he returns to the subject at hand when he hears his wife approaching.
Analysis: A one-act comedy with a poignant edge. The more Nyukhin talks, the more the audience realizes how he has wasted his life. Anton Chekhov initially considered this monologue to be inconsequential, but over the years he revised it many times, which explains its richness. For experienced actors.
Scenes/Monologues: Male Monologues (1)

EXTREMITIES
by William Mastrosimone (Samuel French)
Synopsis: Marjorie is alone in her house when Raul appears, supposedly looking for "Joe." Quickly, he becomes menacing and tries to rape her. She sprays insecticide in his face, blinding him, and then ties him up with extension cords and shoves him into the fireplace. By the time Marjorie's roommates return, Raul appears to be the victim, not the criminal. Marjorie is wild-eyed and bent on revenge. After an extended psychological game of cat and mouse in which Raul cleverly turns the women against each another, he agrees to confess his crime to the police. Satisfied that he won't walk away free, Marjorie turns him over to the legal system.
Analysis: William Mastrosimone was motivated to write *Extremities* after developing a friendship with a rape victim who lived in constant terror that her rapist would return. He decided to create a scenario that gives the victim the opportunity for revenge. But is Marjorie's desire to hurt the man evil in itself? As the playwright asks in the afterword to the acting-edition of the play, "How does one deal with evil without becoming evil oneself?" Physically violent and sexual material, appropriate for mature actors of all levels.
Scenes/Monologues: Male/Female Scenes (2)

FALLEN ANGELS
by Noël Coward (Samuel French)
Synopsis: Jane and Julia, friends since childhood, were involved romantically with the same handsome Frenchman before their respective marriages. Now, five years later, their marriages have become merely comfortable; they love their husbands, but aren't in love. Suddenly, the Frenchman arrives in town, throwing both women into a frenzy of romantic anticipation and guilt. In the

end, the two couples stay married, but the former lover moves into a flat upstairs, so the audience suspects that the juiciest moments are yet to come.

Analysis: Another vintage piece of fluff from playwright Noël Coward. The plot is ridiculously improbable, but he milks it for all it is worth. Appropriate for all levels, but novice American actors, schooled in theatrical realism, may have trouble with Coward's brand of high comedy and sharp repartee.

Scenes/Monologues: Female/Female Scenes (1), Male/Female Scenes (1)

FAR COUNTRY, A

by Henry Denker (Samuel French)

Synopsis: A dramatization of one of Freud's breakthrough cases, detailing the treatment of an attractive young woman, Elizabeth von Ritter, who is plagued by phantom leg pain. With Freud's encouragement, she puts the pieces together in her memory just before succumbing to total paralysis and . . . and . . . voilà! She can walk again!

Analysis: Overly dramatic and undoubtedly an unrealistic depiction of the actual events, this material is still a great deal of fun for scene work. Actors who like to let all the stops out will love it. The great Kim Stanley played von Ritter in the 1961 production. All levels.

Scenes/Monologues: Male/Male Scenes (1), Male/Female Scenes (2)

FATHER'S DAY

by Oliver Hailey (Dramatists Play Service)

Synopsis: It is Father's Day, so the women in a New York City coop apartment are having a get-together while their ex-husbands take the children for the day. Because the play is character-driven rather than plot-driven, in Act I the audience learns all about each of the women. They discuss, for example, how they came to marry the way they did, what they think of motherhood and sex, and why they're divorced. In Act 2, when the ex-husbands join them on the patio, the audience discovers that, in most cases, the women and men have false illusions about one another. Richard, for example, is actually bisexual, but Marion doesn't have a clue. She thinks he is promiscuous with other women. The major event in the play, however, is the custody battle between Louise and Tom. Their 7-year-old son has chosen to live with his father, and Louise is trying to cope.

Analysis: Biting, intelligent, sophisticated comedy/drama. Good scenes. All levels.

Scenes/Monologues: Female Monologues (2), Female/Female Scenes (1), Male/Female Scenes (1)

FENCES

by August Wilson (Samuel French)

Synopsis: Troy Maxson, the son of a sharecropper, is a powerful, sometimes violent, man who understands the virtues of hard work and the value of an education. Here, in Pennsylvania in 1957, he has a home, a good woman, a grown son from a former marriage, and a teenage son from this union. *Fences* covers the years 1957 through 1965, ending with Troy's death. During this time, the audience sees him involved in a standoff with his young son, father a child by another woman, get promoted from garbage collector to garbage-truck driver, and have his simple-minded brother jailed. Troy also finishes putting up a fence around the house, more to keep people in than to keep people out.

Analysis: Winner of the 1987 Pulitzer Prize, *Fences* is a major achievement. The role of Troy Maxson, tailor-made for James Earl Jones, is on a par with that of Willy Loman from *Death of a Salesman*. Unfortunately, most of the scenes in the play involve Troy, which limits scene study. The entire cast is African American. All levels.

Scenes/Monologues: Male Monologues (2), Female Monologues (2), Male/Male Scenes (1), Male/Female Scenes (1)

FIRST BREEZE OF SUMMER, THE

by Leslie Lee (Samuel French) [*Black Thunder, An Anthology of Contemporary African American Drama* (Mentor/Penguin)]

Synopsis: Gremmar is in her mid-seventies when the audience first meet her, and already her cough and dizzy spells signal that she won't live too much longer. As her children and grandchildren sort out their lives in the present day, Gremmar's story is told in flashback sequences. The audience meets the three men, two black and one white, with whom she had children and finds out why she never married any of them. When Louis, the grandson who dotes on Gremmar the most, learns that the father of his Aunt Edna was a white man, he flies into a rage, embarrassed by what he perceives to be Gremmar's wild sexual past and lack of racial pride. Before she actually gets an opportunity to respond to Louis's rage, however, she is gone.

Analysis: Winner of the Obie for Best Play in 1975 and later a Tony Award nominee, this is a wise and outstanding drama, well written, excellent for scene work. All levels.

Scenes/Monologues: Male Monologues (1), Male/Female Scenes (6)

FOB

by David Henry Hwang (Dramatists Play Service)

Synopsis: *FOB* (an abbreviation for "Fresh Off the Boat," a derogatory term for a newly arrived Chinese person) is set in the back room of a Chinese restaurant in Torrance, California. Grace is a first-generation Chinese American, a college journalism student. Her cousin, Dale, is an American of Chinese descent, second generation. Steve is a Chinese newcomer, a man who mysteriously appears and claims to be Gwan Gung, the Chinese god of warriors, writers, and prostitutes. To Dale, this new fellow is a grinning, pidgin-speaking stereotype of everything Asian Americans have tried to outgrow; to Grace, who is initially skeptical, Steve becomes part of a Promethean struggle against the loss of divinity.

Analysis: David Henry Hwang, author of *M. Butterfly*, wrote *FOB* while an undergraduate student at Stanford University during the late 1970s. The play is stylistically innovative, blending mythic and contemporary characters, as well as elements of Chinese opera and kitchen-sink drama. *FOB* won the 1981 Obie for Best Play after running at New York's Public Theater. The entire cast is Asian American. All levels.

Scenes/Monologues: Male Monologues (1), Female Monologues (1), Male/Female Scenes (1)

FOOL FOR LOVE

by Sam Shepard (Dramatists Play Service)

Synopsis: May is Eddie's half sister, but they've been romantically involved for 15 years, living in a trailer in some unnamed place out west. She may have been pregnant at one time, but this isn't clear. Eddie disappears now and then, and the last time he went, May hit the road herself, landing in a motel on the edge of the Mojave desert. Eddie finds her and wants to take her back but, when he arrives, she is dressing to go out on a date with Martin, a local fellow she met. After a while, Martin arrives, and he and Eddie have something of a standoff.

Then a mysterious woman in a black Mercedes, perhaps a countess Eddie has been dating, firebombs Eddie's truck and horse trailer in the parking lot outside the motel. When Eddie goes out to confront her, May starts packing her suitcase to move on, telling Martin that Eddie isn't coming back.

Analysis: The meaning of this 1983 one-act play is subject to interpretation, but the events of the plot, taken at face value, coupled with some colorful characters, make for interesting scene work. All levels.

Scenes/Monologues: Male/Male Scenes (1), Male/Female Scenes (1)

FOX, THE

by Alan Miller [based on D. H. Lawrence's short novel of the same name (Samuel French)]

Synopsis: The year is 1918. Jill and Nellie purchased the old Bailey Farm and moved here three years ago intending "to live our own lives, without having to strut about to other people's ideas and demands." It has been hard going, however, and the women's experiment is about to end when a young soldier appears unexpectedly at the door. Jill and Nellie invite him to stay for a few days, and he immediately begins to charm and dominate them. Nellie is smitten when he proposes marriage to her the next day. Alarmed by this sudden threat to her relationship with Nellie, Jill tries to force him out and to talk Nellie out of marriage. She finally convinces Nellie that he wants only the farm and a couple of women to take care of him. Henry, recognizing that Jill has become his enemy, kills her. At the final curtain, the audience knows that he'll have his way with Nellie—and that Jill was right about him.

Analysis: A big question left unanswered in the script is whether or not the women are lovers. It is much better for scene work if you come down on the "yes" side. Written in the British vernacular, but can be transposed to American English. All levels.

Scenes/Monologues: Male Monologues (1), Female Monologues (1), Female/Female Scenes (1)

FRANKIE AND JOHNNY IN THE CLAIR DE LUNE

by Terrence McNally (Dramatists Play Service)

Synopsis: All of the action takes place in Frankie's Tenth Avenue apartment in New York City between 3 A.M. and dawn. She and Johnny, her co-worker at a greasy-spoon restaurant, have made love for the first time, and she doesn't want him to stay the whole night. Their emotionally defensive dating dance becomes more intimate, and by sunrise the audience realizes that Frankie and Johnny are good for each other.

Analysis: A lovely, honest 1987 drama about two good people on society's lower rungs. All levels.

Scenes/Monologues: Male Monologues (1), Female Monologues (1), Male/Female Scenes (3)

GENIUSES

by Jonathan Reynolds (Samuel French)

Synopsis: A Hollywood movie company is shooting a major motion picture entitled *Parabola of Death* (read *Apocalypse Now*) in the Philippines. The hotshot young director is woefully behind schedule because of monsoons, the necessity of coordinating a cast of thousands, an incomplete script, and a Playmate of the Year with the runs.

Analysis: Fun parody of big-time movie making. All levels.

Scenes/Monologues: Male/Male Scenes (2), Male/Female Scenes (1)

GETTING OUT

by Marsha Norman (Dramatists Play Service)

Synopsis: After spending most of her young life in jail, Arlene is getting out. But this isn't going to be easy. Her former pimp appears and tells her how much she can make on the streets of New York; a former guard at the prison is hanging around, trying to make time with her; and her mother has no use for her. All Arlene wants is to stay out of jail and somehow get it together so that she can bring her child to live with her. The child was taken away at birth by prison officials and given up for adoption.

Analysis: The play utilizes a theatrical device in which two actresses play Arlene at different ages. The younger, more confrontational one moves in and out of the action. For scene-study purposes, simply eliminate her. Tough, uneducated, streetwise characters populate this difficult play. Experienced actors.

Scenes/Monologues: Female Monologues (1), Female/Female Scenes (1)

GINGERBREAD LADY, THE
by Neil Simon (Samuel French)

Synopsis: Evy arrives home after 10 weeks of drying out in a Long Island sanitarium. Her daughter, Polly, moves in with her, and best friends Jimmy and Toby are protective, hovering. Sobriety doesn't last long, however, as Evy quickly falls off the wagon directly into a reprise of an abusive relationship with Lou Tanner. At the final curtain, she resolves to try again—and harder—to get sober.

Analysis: Neil Simon's 1970 comedy rips at the heart when applied to a tough subject like alcoholism. All levels.

Scenes/Monologues: Female Monologues (2), Female/Female Scenes (2), Male/Female Scenes (2)

GIRL ON THE VIA FLAMINIA, THE
by Alfred Hayes (Samuel French)

Synopsis: Rome in late 1944 is a war-ravaged city with few economic opportunities for anyone. Many Italian women, therefore, allow themselves to be kept by American "liberation" soldiers who are longing for romance a long way from home, even though such arrangements are a source of Italian shame. Lisa agrees to be "married" to Robert, and the truth is that they might be a perfect match under different circumstances. Before long, however, their charade is exposed. Lisa is officially designated a prostitute and given a yellow government ID card so that she can work the streets.

Analysis: This 1954 drama holds up very well, and the scenes are excellent, full of deep emotion and conflict. All levels.

Scenes/Monologues: Female/Female Scenes (1), Male/Female Scenes (4)

GLASS MENAGERIE, THE
by Tennessee Williams (Dramatists Play Service)

Synopsis: The play is set in the Depression era during the 1930s in the Wingfields' modest apartment in St. Louis. The central event in this classic American drama concerns Amanda's attempts to find a gentleman caller for her crippled and shy daughter, Laura. At Amanda's urging, her son, Tom, brings Jim O'Connor, a co-worker at the shoe factory, home to dinner, not realizing what elaborate and embarrassing attempts his mother would make to impress the visitor. It turns out that Laura once had a crush on Jim in high school and that he is currently engaged. The evening is a major disappointment to Amanda and leaves Laura even more emotionally withdrawn. Tom leaves home shortly after the events of the play in order to pursue the life of a poet.

Analysis: Tennessee Williams's great autobiographical "memory" play, the one that brought him fame in 1945. Williams modeled Tom on himself. Laura, based on his sister, Rose, and Amanda, based on his mother, Edwina, are major female roles. All levels.

Scenes/Monologues: Male Monologues (2), Female Monologues (1), Male/Female Scenes (2)

GLENGARRY GLEN ROSS
by David Mamet (Samuel French)

Synopsis: The play is set amid the dog-eat-dog world of unscrupulous Florida real-estate salespersons, the kind of people who sell swampland to unsuspecting buyers. The central event involves Moss and Levene's theft of leads and contracts from the company office.

Analysis: A stunning character study of salespeople and, ultimately, a comment on free enterprise in America. Rough language. Made into a movie in 1992 starring Alan Arkin, Ed Harris, Jack Lemmon, and Al Pacino. All levels.

Scenes/Monologues: Male Monologues (2), Male/Male Scenes (2)

GOLDEN BOY

by Clifford Odets (Dramatists Play Service)

Synopsis: Joe Bonaparte plays the violin brilliantly, and his Italian-American, simple-living widower-father is hoping to see him pursue a dignified career as a musician. But Joe lusts for the fast lane, money, and adventure—and he also happens to have talent as a boxer. He enters the fight game, getting mixed up with promoters, hustlers, and their women. At first, Joe pulls his punches in the ring to protect his musician hands, but as he emotionally tilts away from his family and toward the lure of the bright lights and big money, he starts giving his all. He works his way up to an important match during which he kills his opponent.

Overcome with grief at the hardened man he has become, a killer of other men, Joe agrees to give it all up and run off with Lorna Moon, the promoter's streetwise girlfriend who has slowly but surely fallen in love with him. Joe and Lorna take a ride in his new car to celebrate their decision, get into an accident, and are killed.

Analysis: Less political than Clifford Odets's other plays, *Golden Boy* rests on an outrageous premise and sometimes corny dialogue. Still, this 1937 drama was the biggest commercial success the Group Theater ever had. The cast was stellar, including Lee J. Cobb, Elia Kazan, Frances Farmer as Lorna, Luther Adler as Joe, and Karl Malden in a tiny role. Harold Clurman directed.

Scenes/Monologues: Male/Female Scenes (2)

GOOSE AND TOMTOM

by David Rabe (Samuel French)

Synopsis: A slice of ugly life with a couple of bleak, miserable, lowlife, women-hating, violent, small-time jewel thieves, presented in the spirit of *Clockwork Orange* and *Blade Runner*. Buddies Goose and Tomtom are continually trying to prove to one another and the world how tough they are. The action in this long two-act play takes place in an underworld apartment the men share with Lorraine, a pretty woman who likes jewels and is impressed with their toughness. After the men's stash of diamonds is stolen, they resort to kidnapping and murder in their attempts to get the gems back.

Analysis: Very surreal at times. The 1986 Broadway workshop production was directed by playwright David Rabe and featured Sean Penn, Madonna, and Harvey Keitel. Only experienced actors who have a true taste for experimental drama should attempt this material.

Scenes/Monologues: Male/Male Scenes (2)

HAPPINESS CAGE, THE

by Dennis J. Reardon (Samuel French)

Synopsis: Set in the cancer ward of a Veterans' Administration hospital. Dr. Freytag, world-famous neurophysiologist, is doing research involving terminally ill cancer patients. By inserting an electrically charged metal probe into a pleasure-inducing region of the brain, he believes he can relieve a patient of pain. Somewhere along the way, however, the doctor gets the idea that perhaps he can deliver pleasure to everyone, even if they aren't terminally ill. The crux of the play involves Freytag's attempts to experiment on a couple of healthy men, and the work becomes an examination of the value of free will.

Analysis: An intensely grim 1969 drama that contains shades of Nazism and Big Brother. The single scene excerpted here confronts life-and-death issues head-on. Experienced actors.

Scenes/Monologues: Male/Male Scenes (1)

HATFUL OF RAIN, A

by Michael Vincente Gazzo (Samuel French)

Synopsis: Johnny Pope is fighting drug addiction, a habit begun when he was recuperating in a military hospital after the Korean War. Borrowing money from his brother, Polo, to support a $40-a-day habit and keeping his addiction secret from his family, Johnny is sinking deeper and deeper into despair. As he becomes more withdrawn and restless, Celia, his pregnant wife, believes that he must be having an affair. Longing for affection, she is drawn to Polo, now living with her and Johnny in their small New York City apartment. Finally, Johnny confesses to his family that he is a junkie. By the end of the play, Celia calls the police to come get Johnny so he can begin a supervised withdrawal.

Analysis: The quintessential Actors Studio drama, developed by Michael Vincent Gazzo in the mid-1950s at the Studio lab in New York. Many scenes grew directly out of improvisations. This gritty social drama was an important early showcase for Shelley Winters, who played Celia, and Ben Gazzara, who played Johnny. All levels.

Scenes/Monologues: Male/Female Scenes (3)

HEDDA GABLER

by Henrik Ibsen [translated by Christopher Hampton (Samuel French)]

Synopsis: The daughter of a prominent Norwegian general, Hedda chooses security when she marries a meek professor with good career prospects rather than pursuing the free-spirited existence she truly wants. Already secretly—and unhappily—pregnant when she and George return from their honeymoon, Hedda tries to adjust to a conventional home life. Then her onetime flame Eilert Lovborg arrives, recovered from alcoholism and again writing prolifically. He proudly shows Hedda and George the manuscript for his next book, which promises to be a groundbreaking success. This news threatens George's imminent appointment to a professorship because it is clear that he'll face competition from Lovborg. Hedda's former schoolmate Thea Elvsted then shows up. Lovborg has been living with her and her much-older husband in the country for the last three years and, in fact, it is she who inspired him to write again. During a complex scene with Hedda and Thea, Lovborg begins drinking again, and then he leaves to join a bachelor party with George's friend, Judge Brack.

The next morning, George returns carrying Lovborg's precious manuscript, explaining to Hedda that Lovborg dropped it while drunkenly heading home. A short time later, Lovborg arrives and confides in Hedda that he has lost his manuscript and has nothing more to live for. Instead of giving him the manuscript, which is in the other room, she gives him one of her father's dueling pistols so that he can commit suicide "beautifully" and "artistically." After Lovborg leaves, Hedda burns his manuscript. George, initially outraged that she destroyed the manuscript, is flattered that she cares enough about him to commit such a heinous act.

Judge Brack, meanwhile, has been floating into and out of the action and has romantic designs on Hedda. He delivers the news that Lovborg has died, but it was far from "beautiful." The pistol accidentally went off, destroying Lovborg's penis ("lower stomach" is the way Brack puts it, but he is actually referring to Lovborg's sexual organ). Brack tells Hedda he knows she gave the pistol to Lovborg and then says he wants to continue his relationship with her. Realizing that Brack has control over her life now, Hedda can't face the future. She goes into the next room and kills herself with her father's other pistol.

Analysis: Henrik Ibsen wrote *Hedda Gabler* while in his sixties, and some scholars believe that there are strong autobiographical characteristics in the female protagonist. As it happens, he was living in a loveless marriage and, late in life, began a series of nonsexual romantic entanglements with younger women. Like Hedda, he didn't have the courage to abandon his marriage or risk scandal to do what his heart said he should. All levels.

Scenes/Monologues: Female/Female Scenes (1), Male/Female Scenes (2), Three-Person Scenes (1)

HEIDI CHRONICLES, THE

by Wendy Wasserstein (Dramatists Play Service)

Synopsis: Beginning in 1965 when Heidi Holland is 16 and progressing to 1989, this play follows the evolution of a New Yorker as she chooses a career, searches for the right man, falls in love, falls out of love, sees friends come and go, tries to make sense of the world, and adopts a baby. All of the characters are urban, nice, witty, and capable.

Analysis: Wendy Wasserstein pushes beyond her earlier, much-narrower focus on women's issues to those that define a generation. This frequently touching comedy, winner of the 1989 Tony Award for Best Play and the 1989 Pulitzer Prize for Drama, also won the New York Drama Critics Circle Prize, the Drama Desk Award, the Outer Critics Circle Award, and the Susan Smith Blackburn Prize. All levels.

Scenes/Monologues: Female Monologues (1), Male/Female Scenes (4)

HELLO AND GOODBYE

by Athol Fugard (Samuel French)

Synopsis: After a bitter 15-year absence and having heard that her Afrikaner father is near death, Hester unexpectedly shows up at his lower-class home in Port Elizabeth to claim her share of his meager estate. She discovers that her gloomy younger brother is tending full time to the old man, having given up dreams of a life on his own. Hester digs through family belongings, trying to find the insurance money she contends her father collected when he lost his leg years earlier. When there are no more boxes for her to open, Johnny admits that their father has, in fact, been dead for several days and that he knew all along there was no money. He has been comforting himself with the delusion that the old man was still alive in the next room. Not wanting further involvement with her emotionally ruined brother, Hester returns to her life in the big city.

Analysis: Powerful two-character drama. Both characters are Afrikaners, so accents would be appropriate. Colleen Dewhurst and Martin Sheen created the roles in 1971. For experienced actors.

Scenes/Monologues: Male Monologues (1), Female Monologues (1), Male/Female Scenes (4)

HELLO OUT THERE

by William Saroyan (Samuel French)

Synopsis: A drifter/gambler coming off a two-year run of bad luck picks up a woman in a small Texas town. After they have sex, the woman demands money; when he refuses, she cries "rape." All of the action takes place in a jail cell in Matador, Texas, and revolves around the relationship the young man strikes up with the young cook/cleaning girl at the jail. Eventually, a lynch mob arrives and kills him, but not before he has given all his money to the cook and urges her to head for San Francisco.

Analysis: Like all of William Saroyan's other plays, this 14-page, one-act drama, written in 1941, is musical and poetic, and evokes a sense of loneliness. All levels.

Scenes/Monologues: Male/Female Scenes (1)

HERE WE ARE

by Dorothy Parker [*24 Favorite One-Act Plays,* edited by Bennett Cerf and Van H. Cartmell (Doubleday/Dolphin)]

Synopsis: A young couple, married precisely 2 hours and 26 minutes, are en route via a Pullman car to New York City for their honeymoon. The groom is eager to consummate the union, but the bride has a bit of anxiety about the prospect. So they talk about everything except the subject at hand.

Analysis: Innocent 1931 fun from Dorothy Parker. The play is just 10 pages long. All levels.

Scenes/Monologues: Male/Female Scenes (1)

HOOTERS

by Ted Tally (Dramatists Play Service)

Synopsis: Cheryl, a 25-year-old working woman, is entertaining a serious proposal of marriage but isn't sure she is ready for adulthood. She has brought her girlfriend Ronda to Cape Cod for a weekend of sun and serious girl-talk. As it happens, they meet Clint and Ricky, a couple of wild and crazy 19-year-olds with sex on their minds and beer in their hands. To Ronda's dismay, Cheryl hops into bed with Clint, evidently trying to hide from responsibility by immersing herself in a party scene. When Clint tells Cheryl that he loves her, however, the party ends abruptly. In the end, Cheryl begins to take a serious look at herself. Clint and Ricky, meanwhile, have come to a Waterloo of their own, facing the same questions about adulthood, responsibility, and friendship.

Analysis: On the surface, *Hooters* is about horny post-adolescents on the make. The language is frequently sexist, of the locker-room variety. There is a purpose to this madness, however, if you look for it. Ted Tally, a talented playwright, has highlighted and isolated the pursuit of hedonistic pleasures in order to make a deeper point about values. All levels.

Scenes/Monologues: Female Monologues (1), Male/Male Scenes (2), Female/Female Scenes (2), Male/Female Scenes (1)

HOPSCOTCH

by Israel Horovitz (Dramatists Play Service)

Synopsis: Elsa is playing hopscotch alone in the park when Will walks up. She seems to be both threatened by and attracted to him. As the play unfolds, the audience learns that they were married in high school for just a week. When he disappeared 12 years ago, she was pregnant. For reasons known only to playwright Israel Horovitz, both characters aren't who they say they are.

Analysis: A cryptic 1977 one-act drama, part of "The Quannapowitt Quartet" series. For experienced actors.

Scenes/Monologues: Male/Female Scenes (1)

HOTHOUSE

by Megan Terry (Samuel French)

Synopsis: The story is set in 1955. Life is in continual turmoil for this lower-class, poverty-stricken, uneducated family of a Washington fisherman. Abuse, both physical and verbal, alcoholism, and despair are the norm. Jody, the daughter, falls in love with a local college student and comes close to leaving the rat's nest to be with him. In the end, however, because abuse breeds abuse, she stays with her mother and pours another drink.

Analysis: This 1974 three-act drama is rough, but it contains a couple of good scenes and is arguably Megan Terry's most accessible work. She is most closely associated with alternative-theater and unrealistic styles and was a major player in the Off-Off-Broadway scene of the 1960s. All levels.

Scenes/Monologues: Female/Female Scenes (1), Male/Female Scenes (1)

HOUSE OF BLUE LEAVES, THE

by John Guare (Samuel French)

Synopsis: Artie's apartment in Sunnyside, Queens, is full of comic madness because of the imminent visit of the Pope to New York City on October 4, 1965. Artie, an untalented but hopeful musician, wants the Pope to bless his music; Bunny Flingus from downstairs wants him to bless her hoped-for marriage to Artie—even though Artie has a mentally deficient wife named Bananas in the next room. Artie's maladjusted son, Ronnie, who is AWOL from the Army, hopes to blow up the Pope with a homemade bomb. Add to this stew three crazed nuns, a Hollywood producer, and a deaf starlet, and stir well.

Analysis: Stylistically influenced by the insanity of the 1960s, this comedy is incredibly funny. All levels.

Scenes/Monologues: Male Monologues (1), Female Monologues (2), Male/Female Scenes (1)

HOUSE OF RAMON IGLESIA, THE
by José Rivera (Samuel French)

Synopsis: Dolores and Ramon Iglesia are trying to sell their dilapidated Long Island home so that they can return with their sons to Puerto Rico after years of unsuccessful struggling to make it in the United States. But the title to the house is a mess. Untangling it involves expensive trips back and forth to Puerto Rico, and Dolores and Ramon are broke. The selling of the house is the central event of the play and against that, the family tries to determine if they are essentially Puerto Rican or American. A great deal of generational conflict.

Analysis: Wonderful material. The drama was broadcast as part of the "American Playhouse" television series on PBS in 1986. The entire cast is Hispanic. All levels.

Scenes/Monologues: Male Monologues (1), Male/Female Scenes (1), Three-Person Scenes (1)

HURLYBURLY
by David Rabe (Samuel French)

Synopsis: Two men coming out of failed marriages share a house in the Hollywood Hills. *Hurlyburly* explores their relationships with each other and with various friends and lovers. The story focuses on a complex, sprawling quest for meaning and connection in the 1980s, filled with drugs, liquor, sex, occasional violence, and, finally, suicide.

Analysis: Bleak, funny, and brilliantly written. The three-act structure is unusual today, and you almost feel that each act could stand alone. The 1984 Off-Broadway production had a dream cast: William Hurt, Harvey Keitel, Christopher Walken, Jerry Stiller, Cynthia Nixon, Sigourney Weaver, and Judith Ivey. Mike Nichols directed. A challenging work for intelligent actors of all levels.

Scenes/Monologues: Male Monologues (3), Female Monologues (1), Male/Male Scenes (3), Male/Female Scenes (2)

HUSBANDRY
by Patrick Tovat (Samuel French)

Synopsis: Harry's aging parents are struggling to make ends meet on their Kentucky farm, and they want him to take over the place. But he has a life of his own in New York, as well as a career-oriented wife who has no interest in farming. Harry is ambivalent about moving, and his wife is actively opposed to it.

Analysis: A "message" play about the plight of the American farmer. All levels.

Scenes/Monologues: Male Monologues (1), Female Monologues (1), Male/Female Scenes (2)

I AM A CAMERA
by John Van Druten (Dramatists Play Service)

Synopsis: Adapted from *The Berlin Stories of Christopher Isherwood,* this play was turned into *Cabaret.* It tells the story of Sally Bowles, would-be actress/singer, and her circle of friends and lovers in 1930 Berlin. As John Van Druten explains in his preface to the acting edition, the play lacks a definable plot; his intent was to create the feel of Berlin at the dawn of Nazism and to inhabit it with richly drawn characters. Van Druten succeeded, particularly with the demonstrative and dramatic Sally Bowles, one of the loveliest roles an actress could hope for.

Analysis: Most scenes are brief, short on conflict, and long on mood and texture. All levels.

Scenes/Monologues: Male/Female Scenes (3)

I HATE HAMLET
by Paul Rudnick (Dramatists Play Service)

Synopsis: Andrew Rally, star of the television hit "L. A. Medical," returns to New York City to "take a few classes, maybe do a play," wanting to edge his way back into the theater.

Instead, Andrew is cast in the title role of *Hamlet* in Shakespeare in the Park. He is terrified, believing the part is beyond his abilities. Both Andrew's girlfriend and agent are encouraging, but his Los Angeles producer/friend thinks he is a fool not to jump into another television show. When Andrew leases John Barrymore's old New York apartment, the actor's ghost appears to "coach" him for the role of his life. Andrew ultimately plays Hamlet, not very well, but at least he has gone the distance.

Analysis: Nicol Williamson played John Barrymore on Broadway and evidently didn't get along with the actor playing Andrew. During one highly publicized performance, the actor stormed off the stage and quit on the spot because Williamson swatted him on the butt with a sword during a mock duel. All levels.

Scenes/Monologues: Male Monologues (1), Male/Male Scenes (1), Male/Female Scenes (1)

IMMIGRANT, THE
by Mark Harelik (Broadway Play Publishing)
Synopsis: The story begins in Hamilton, Texas, in 1909 and continues to the present day. A young Russian Jewish immigrant, Haskell Harelik, arrives in America through the port of Galveston, Texas, instead of the usual New York route. He is befriended by local residents Ima and Milton Perry, who give him a place to live. Subsequently, Milton arranges financing for Haskell's dry-goods business. After Haskell brings his wife over from Russia, the families continue to share a close friendship. The Hareliks have three sons, the youngest of whom they name after Milton.

Both families prosper and enjoy one another until 1939 when a Shabbos mealtime discussion about Hitler turns into a full-fledged argument between the men. After that, they stubbornly refuse to talk to one another for years, meeting only once for a brief time shortly before Milton's death. In a curtain speech, Milton Harelik, American through-and-through, speaks warmly of his parents and of Ida Perry, bringing their story up to the present day.

Analysis: This drama makes you feel optimistic about the United States. Americans may be cut from many different kinds of trees, but they're all planted in the same yard. Lovely 1985 play about Mark Harelik's own family history. All levels.

Scenes/Monologues: Male/Male Scenes (1), Female/Female Scenes (1), Male/Female Scenes (1)

IMPASSIONED EMBRACES
by John Pielmeier (Dramatists Play Service)
Synopsis: This work consists of 14 sketch-like scenes and monologues by the author of *Agnes of God*. No particular theme, just a compilation of odds and ends.

Analysis: Some of these pieces came from a program at the Repertory Theatre of St. Louis, and others from the Actors Theatre of Louisville. All levels.

Scenes/Monologues: Male/Female Scenes (2)

IMPORTANCE OF BEING EARNEST, THE
by Oscar Wilde (Samuel French)
Synopsis: John (Jack), who lives in the country, pretends to have a naughty brother named Earnest who lives in the city. Algernon, who lives in the city, pretends to have an invalid friend named Bunbury who lives in the country. Both men use these fictions as excuses to travel back and forth between city and country, to live two separate existences. This complicated and unnecessary fabrication blows up in the men's faces when they fall in love with Cecily and Gwendolen, who become entangled in the deceit. In the end, the confusion is all straightened out, and everyone gets married, presumably to live happily ever after.

Analysis: Oscar Wilde's famous comedy classic pokes malicious fun at social manners and pretensions in nineteenth-century England. First performed in 1895. Appropriate for all levels, but novice American actors may have trouble with the high comedy and sharp repartee.

Scenes/Monologues: Female/Female Scenes (1)

INDEPENDENCE

by Lee Blessing (Dramatists Play Service)

Synopsis: Kess visits her childhood home in Independence, Iowa, for the first time since moving to Minneapolis four years ago, right after she had her mother committed to the mental hospital. Kess discovers that her sister Jo is pregnant by a man who is about to marry another woman and that their mother, who is back on the street, is planning to raise Jo's baby at home. Kess's sister Sherry, meanwhile, is into meaningless sex, and no member of the family, it seems, is altogether comfortable with the fact that Kess is a lesbian. This all-female household, in short, is very maladjusted. Kess manages to convince Jo that she should return with her to the big city before it is too late for her to salvage a respectable life.

Analysis: An improbable premise with a couple of good scenes and surprisingly well-written dialogue. *Independence* is a "serious comedy." All levels.

Scenes/Monologues: Female/Female Scenes (2)

I NEVER SANG FOR MY FATHER

by Robert Anderson (Dramatists Play Service)

Synopsis: Gene's elderly father, Tom, is a stern, demanding, financially successful man who has never been very available on an emotional level. After Tom's wife dies unexpectedly, he is forced to confront his own physical frailty, as well as the disjointed relationship he has with Gene. The men struggle to find some equilibrium, some common points of communication. Tom believes it is proper that Gene be the dutiful son and live close by in case he is needed, but Gene contends that he has a life of his own and wants to return to California and remarry. In the end, Gene leaves, and his father eventually follows him to Los Angeles, where he dies while still harboring deep feelings of bitterness. Gene has a touching curtain speech.

Analysis: A thoughtful, intelligent, sad exploration of the father/son relationship. Hal Holbrook played Gene on the stage in 1968, and Gene Hackman played him in the 1970 film. All levels.

Scenes/Monologues: Male Monologues (1), Male/Male Scenes (1), Male/Female Scenes (1)

IN PERPETUITY THROUGHOUT THE UNIVERSE

by Eric Overmyer (Broadway Play Publishing)

Synopsis: Ghostwriters for powerful, right-wing American bigots try to spread the Yellow Peril message.

Analysis: An intelligent script that is too cryptic and literary for most scene-study application. A biting comment on racial paranoia in contemporary America. The monologues, however, are terrific. All levels.

Scenes/Monologues: Male Monologues (2)

IN THE BOOM BOOM ROOM

by David Rabe (Samuel French)

Synopsis: This play tracks the struggle and ultimate descent of Chrissy, an unsophisticated young woman who comes from squalid, abusive origins. She works as a go-go dancer in a small club, and she is looking for a way out. Prostitution, childhood incest, and homosexuality are woven into the fabric of this tense story, set in a pre-AIDS, 1970s environment. In the end, Chrissy moves lower from the relative safety of a go-go cage to the stage of a strip joint.

Analysis: The milieu is dated now, but this drama still packs quite a punch. Good workshop material for sophisticated actors. For the latest SF acting edition, David Rabe has revised his play, reverting to the original two-act version that he prefers and that is referenced here.

Scenes/Monologues: Male Monologues (1), Female Monologues (2), Female/Female Scenes (2), Male/Female Scenes (2)

I OUGHT TO BE IN PICTURES
by Neil Simon (Samuel French)
Synopsis: Blocked Hollywood screenwriter Herb Tucker wakes one morning to discover his 19-year-old daughter, Libby, whom he hasn't seen for 16 years, sitting in his living room. She says she wants to be an actress and hopes he'll introduce her to his important movie-business friends. During the next two weeks, Herb and Libby get to know one another, slowly dropping their defenses. Finally, Libby decides to return to New York and her mother, happy now that she at last has a relationship with her father. As for her acting career, she didn't really want to pursue one in the first place.
Analysis: Appealing, warm, good Neil Simon. All levels.
Scenes/Monologues: Male Monologues (1), Male/Female Scenes (2)

ISN'T IT ROMANTIC?
by Wendy Wasserstein (Dramatists Play Service)
Synopsis: Janie and Harriet are prototypes of the urban, educated, upwardly mobile young women of the 1980s trying to solve the career/family puzzle.
Analysis: Wendy Wasserstein addresses this subject probably better than anyone else. Every scene is brief and breezy. All levels.
Scenes/Monologues: Female/Female Scenes (3)

I STAND BEFORE YOU NAKED
by Joyce Carol Oates [*12 Plays by Joyce Carol Oates* (Plume Drama)]
Synopsis: This is a "collage-play," presented as a series of monologues by women. There is the cafeteria worker who is married to a serial killer, the prostitute who is upset by the blood blister on her lip, the anorexic young woman with the orange, the mental patient who talks about Jesus, and more.
Analysis: Joyce Carol Oates is a world-class novelist whose playwriting ventures are a mixed bag, veering toward the experimental. Her work in this arena, much of which has been developed at the Actors Theatre of Louisville, is arguably still too literary. For sophisticated actors.
Scenes/Monologues: Female Monologues (2)

IT HAD TO BE YOU
by Renée Taylor and Joseph Bologna (Samuel French)
Synopsis: Vito Pignoli, a New York City advertising-agency producer feels sorry for actress Theda Blau, who rushes into a commercial audition at the last minute and nervously rambles through the rather hysterical story of her life. Afterward, he assures her in private that she did a good job in the audition but says that her type is a bit too unconventional for his conservative client. Vito and Theda share a cab, wind up at her place, one thing leads to another, one night turns into two, and before you know it, these people with wildly different personalities wind up marrying each other. At the final curtain, Vito plans to quit his coat-and-tie ad-agency job and devote himself to writing plays with Theda.
Analysis: This 1982 physical comedy is standard source material for acting workshops and auditions. All levels.
Scenes/Monologues: Female Monologues (1), Male/Female Scenes (2)

JAR THE FLOOR
by Cheryl West [*Women Playwrights—Best Plays of 1992* (Smith & Kraus)]
Synopsis: Four generations of women from a single African-American family gather for the great-grandmother's ninetieth birthday in Park Forest, Illinois. This is the main event of the play, but the real story is in the way each of the women is trying to escape the expectations of her mother and find her own way in the world. Vennie, the youngest woman, arrives with her

white girlfriend, Raisa, a single mother who has had a mastectomy. Vennie's mother, Maydee, is a college professor with high hopes for her daughter. Maydee's mother, Lola, is a good-time, flashy dresser who, as it turns out, allowed one of her many men friends to molest Maydee when she was 13. Lola's mother, Madear, is senile, delightful, frequently wise, and blunt to a fault. By the final curtain, Lola learns that Vennie isn't going to get her college diploma after all, that she intends to pursue a singing career instead. Lola and Maydee overtly acknowledge the sexual abuse. And Madear escapes into her reveries.

Analysis: Cheryl West has a keen ear for the music of language, ranging from the very uneducated vernacular of Madear, to Maydee's sophistication, to Lola's funky talk. In addition, the playwright puts her finger firmly on the pulse of the mother/daughter dance. All levels.

Scenes/Monologues: Female/Female Scenes (2)

JIMMY SHINE

by Murray Schisgal (Dramatists Play Service)

Synopsis: Jimmy Shine is a loser à la cartoon character Charlie Brown. Jimmy never gets the woman and can't sell his paintings. His friend Michael, in contrast, reaps all the glory with half the effort and marries beautiful Elizabeth. Jimmy decides to give up trying to be an artist and accepts his lot in life as a bachelor. Then, out of the blue, Elizabeth shows up at his apartment, announces that her marriage to Michael is over, and invites Jimmy to run away to Denver with her. Jimmy figures out that the invitation is a sham and that she is just trying to make Michael jealous, so he tells her to flake off. Happy to be his own man at last, he once again picks up his paintbrushes and takes out a canvas. Curtain.

Analysis: Basically, this 1969 comedy was a Broadway vehicle for Dustin Hoffman, who got to play a wide variety of ages in the piece, as well as to do some impersonations of W. C. Fields and others. *Jimmy Shine* isn't Murray Schisgal's best, but it is cute. All levels.

Scenes/Monologues: Male/Female Scenes (1)

JOE TURNER'S COME AND GONE

by August Wilson (Samuel French)

Synopsis: The place is Seth Holly's rooming house in Pittsburgh, Pennsylvania; the time is 1911. The black men and women who stay here are in transit, physically and spiritually. They're moving between memories of farmhand slavery and the promises inherent in an urban future. Sometimes they still practice voodoo while they pray to a Christian god. Herald Loomis arrives with his 11-year-old daughter, seeking a room and information on the whereabouts of his wife, Martha; the two were separated when he was incarcerated in Tennessee on Joe Turner's chain gang. It turns out that Martha has come north and is now a devout member of an Evangelical church.

When Martha and Herald meet face-to-face, thanks to the assistance of Rutherford Selig, a white "people finder," it is clear they can no longer be husband and wife. In fact, they've grown apart spiritually. She has found God at the same time that he has come to distrust a white Jesus. Finally, he turns their daughter over to Martha to raise and walks down the road in search of himself.

Analysis: This is a fascinating play because of the spiritual never-neverland it occupies. The 1988 Broadway production garnered several Tony nominations. All levels.

Scenes/Monologues: Male Monologues (3), Female Monologues (2)

JOINED AT THE HEAD

by Catherine Butterfield (Dramatists Play Service) [*Women Playwrights—Best Plays of 1992* (Smith & Kraus)]

Synopsis: Maggie arrives in Boston on a book-promotion tour and is contacted by her old high-school boyfriend, Jim. She agrees to have dinner with him and his wife, Maggy, who,

Maggie soon discovers, has cancer. The story tracks the relationships among these three individuals and ends with Maggy's death.

Analysis: Stylistically dazzling, this 1992 comedy/drama is moving and funny. The characters take turns addressing the audience, which actually functions as a fourth character. Audience members actively debate which elements of the story should be included. All levels.

Scenes/Monologues: Male Monologues (1), Female Monologues (1), Female/Female Scenes (2), Male/Female Scenes (1)

K-2

by Patrick Meyers (Dramatists Play Service)

Synopsis: Harold and Taylor are stuck on an ice ledge 27,000 feet up the side of K-2, the world's second-tallest mountain. There are only two hours of daylight remaining, and one more night without the protection of a tent or sleeping bags means certain death for both men. To make matters worse, Harold's leg is badly broken, and they have only one rope to use for their descent. Harold and Taylor struggle to save themselves and, while looking death in the face, address the existential questions of life. After a sudden avalanche destroys their remaining equipment, the men decide that Taylor must descend alone, leaving Harold to die.

Analysis: Life-and-death situations make for excellent human drama. Scene work in this 1983 one-act play requires heavy clothing and perhaps some mountain-climbing equipment for authenticity. All levels.

Scenes/Monologues: Male Monologues (1), Male/Male Scenes (1)

KATHY AND MO SHOW, THE: PARALLEL LIVES

by Mo Gaffney and Kathy Najimy (Dramatists Play Service)

Synopsis: The show consists of 14 brief sketch-comedy scenes that were written to be performed by the authors, Mo Gaffney and Kathy Najimy. Ranging from God's reps overseeing the creation of humans, to a straight couple in a gay bar, to a couple of 5-year-olds trying to figure out the Church, to a couple of menstruating men (!), the style is fast-moving and irreverent. There is no central plot line per se, just a theme built on the idea that people of all colors, shapes, sexes, and sizes are equal and should appreciate each other.

Analysis: Can be fun in workshops for actors who just want to cut up and experiment with sketch comedy and the challenges of pace. Nothing heavyweight here. All levels.

Scenes/Monologues: Female Monologues (1), Female/Female Scenes (5)

KEELY AND DU

by Jane Martin (Samuel French)

Synopsis: Keely was raped and impregnated by her ex-husband. On her way to have an abortion, she was kidnapped by Operation Retrieval, a Christian anti-abortion organization. Keely soon discovers that she is a prisoner and that the members intend to keep her in chains in a basement room until her pregnancy is too advanced to terminate. Her constant companion is a grandmotherly woman named Du, who takes her orders from a pastor named Walter.

As the months unfold, Keely and Du gradually form a bond, separated only by the fundamental disagreement about the propriety of abortion. On Keely's birthday, Du secretly arranges a little celebration, allowing Keely to drink some beer and change clothes for the first time since she was captured. The next day Keely grabs the wire hanger that her new dress had been hanging on and performs a self-abortion, causing a massive hemorrhage. Du calls an ambulance, an act that results in her own eventual arrest. In the final scene, Keely is visiting Du in prison.

Analysis: Arguably Jane Martin's finest work to date, this play premiered at the Actors Theatre of Louisville during the seventeenth annual Humana Festival of New American Plays in March 1993. Arresting theater. For sophisticated actors.

Scenes/Monologues: Female Monologues (2), Female/Female Scenes (1)

KEY EXCHANGE
by Kevin Wade (Dramatists Play Service)
Synopsis: Lisa is looking for a deeper commitment from Philip, who doesn't want to be fenced in or pushed too fast. Michael's new wife, meanwhile, runs off with a choreographer but returns a couple of months later. These two conflicts pretty much comprise the plot—the eternal quest for a good relationship.
Analysis: Cute scenes, fun for class work. Other than the question as to whether or not people should live together, no major moral or ethical issues are addressed. All levels.
Scenes/Monologues: Male Monologues (1), Female Monologues (1), Male/Female Scenes (2)

LADY AND THE CLARINET, THE
by Michael Cristofer (Dramatists Play Service)
Synopsis: Luba, a woman in her late thirties, narrates the history of her love life, from when she was 16 up through her present entanglements with Jack. A musician is continually on stage with her, providing clarinet accompaniment for whatever mood she requests. Sometimes she addresses the audience, sometimes the musician and, sometimes, she is involved in reenactments of her past.
Analysis: Although this 1985 play is full of male/female scenes, they are more like musical riffs and, given the narrator's shifting focus, probably aren't the best source material for workshops. A couple of the monologues are nice, however, and Michael Cristofer is a superb writer. All levels.
Scenes/Monologues: Male Monologues (2)

LANDSCAPE OF THE BODY
by John Guare (Dramatists Play Service)
Synopsis: Betty is on the Nantucket ferry, trying to understand why so many people in her life—her family, her employers—have died mysterious, untimely deaths. She herself is under suspicion for murdering her own son in New York City's Greenwich Village some months earlier. As she talks with the investigating detective who has been trailing her, the play turns to flashbacks, combing through the events that led Betty from Bangor, Maine, to New York City, to South Carolina, back to New York, and then to the ferry. But she didn't kill her son, and she never finds out who did. In fact, she learns never to expect answers in life.
Analysis: This 1977 play, which John Guare wrote in two days, is comic, cryptic, and sometimes graphic. All levels.
Scenes/Monologues: Male Monologues (1), Male/Female Scenes (2)

LARGO DESOLATO
by Vaclav Havel [translated by Tom Stoppard (Grove Weidenfeld)]
Synopsis: Professor Nettles's book, *Ontology of the Human Self,* contains a passage that government officials contend "disturbs the intellectual peace," so they pressure him to disown the work. *Largo Desolato,* seven scenes in one act, captures the agony and insanity of this intellectual's dilemma. On one hand, Nettles speaks for many faceless intellectuals when he defies the government; on the other, his life is in shambles. He is a nervous wreck, quickly becoming addicted to drugs and alcohol. In the end, he refuses to cooperate, and the wait goes on. . . .
Analysis: Profoundly disturbing 1985 comedy-drama, probably more valuable as a dramatic document than as source material for scene work. Still, the play contains a couple of worthwhile possibilities for sophisticated actors.
Scenes/Monologues: Male/Male Scenes (1), Male/Female Scenes (1)

LARK, THE
by Jean Anouilh [adapted by Lillian Hellman (Dramatists Play Service)]
Synopsis: A retelling of the story of Joan of Arc, the fifteenth-century French peasant who responded to the "voice" of God and raised the siege of Orleans. The action moves back and

forth in time on a bare stage, beginning with Joan's childhood and ending with her being burned at the stake after standing trial as a heretic.

Analysis: Julie Harris won a Tony as Best Actress in 1956 for her portrayal of Joan. If you like the Jean Anouilh story, you may also want to take a look at the Christopher Fry adaptation. And, of course, there is George Bernard Shaw's *Saint Joan.* All levels.

Scenes/Monologues: Male/Male Scenes (1), Male/Female Scenes (1)

LAST OF THE RED HOT LOVERS

by Neil Simon (Samuel French)

Synopsis: After 23 years of marriage, Barney faces his mortality and wants to have at least one fling. Over the course of a year, he brings three women to his mother's New York City apartment. All three attempts flop, but they cause Barney to develop a new appreciation for his wife.

Analysis: This 1970 comedy is something of a chestnut, but Neil Simon is still the king. All levels.

Scenes/Monologues: Male Monologues (1), Female Monologues (1), Male/Female Scenes (2)

LAST SUMMER AT BLUEFISH COVE

by Jane Chambers (JH Press)

Synopsis: Bluefish Cove, near New York City, has been a lesbian beach colony for 30 years. The rental agent mistakenly presumes that Eva, who is running from a bad marriage, is a lesbian and rents her a cottage, creating an instant threat to the women at the colony who prefer to remain in the closet. As the action evolves, Eva strikes up a romantic relationship with Lil and is happy to discover that she is a lesbian. Then Eva discovers what everyone else at Bluefish Cove already knows: Lil has cancer and has only a few months to live.

Analysis: Frequently touching, this 1982 comedy-drama celebrates lesbian life. All levels.

Scenes/Monologues: Female/Female Scenes (3)

LAST YANKEE, THE

by Arthur Miller (Dramatists Play Service)

Synopsis: Two men meet for the first time in the waiting room of a state mental hospital where both of their wives are being treated for depression. Frick has money, but Leroy, although a direct descendent of Alexander Hamilton and the son of a lawyer, is a carpenter by trade. He has seven children and is living hand-to-mouth. The men's conversation is full of class sensitivities and prejudices. Frick's attitude finally makes Leroy mad.

Analysis: A 9-page, two-character, one-act work that Arthur Miller wrote for a 1991 play festival in New York. Not a great deal of fireworks, but plenty of subtext and a deceptively subtle build. All levels.

Scenes/Monologues: Male/Male Scenes (1)

LATER

by Corrine Jacker (Dramatists Play Service)

Synopsis: Malachai Dowson died a year ago, and his widow and two daughters have gathered at the family's summer place on Labor Day, trying to come to terms with his memory and with each other.

Analysis: *Later* first surfaced as a 1978 radio drama. Chock full of subtle and telling detail, poetic, gentle. All levels.

Scenes/Monologues: Female Monologues (3), Female/Female Scenes (2)

LAUGHING WILD

by Christopher Durang (Dramatists Play Service)

Synopsis: Two strangers violently confront one another in the tuna-fish aisle of a New York City supermarket. Because the man is blocking the woman's path, she hits him over the head and curses at him. This crazy incident is then combed repeatedly, as the action moves back and forth in time. Both the woman and the man tell their version of what really happened in the store. In the process, the audience learns that she is a frequent resident of mental institutions, and he is a magazine writer seeking meaning in life.

Analysis: *Laughing Wild* is an outlandish theatrical experiment more than a play, breaking the fourth wall and jumping back and forth in time, but it is very funny. All levels.

Scenes/Monologues: Male Monologues (1), Female Monologues (1)

LAUNDRY AND BOURBON

by James McLure (Dramatists Play Service)

Synopsis: A one-act character study of three Texas friends. Hattie happily escapes her nagging children by visiting Elizabeth, who turns out to be quite worried about something. Roy, her husband, suffers from post-traumatic-stress syndrome from the Vietnam War (the syndrome hadn't been named when this play was published in 1979), and has been gone for two days. Furthermore, Roy doesn't know that Elizabeth is pregnant with their first child. After a while, Amy Lee arrives, sells a couple of tickets to the church's pancake supper, and gets into a fight with Hattie. When Amy Lee departs, Hattie and Elizabeth gaze appreciatively at the sunset and feel closer to one another.

Analysis: Corny at times, the writing invites a "Hee-Haw" kind of acting, which is a challenge and requires actors to remain motivated. All levels.

Scenes/Monologues: Female/Female Scenes (1), Three-Person Scenes (1)

LES BELLES SOEURS

by Michel Tremblay [translated by John Van Burek and Bill Glassco (Talonbooks, Canada)]

Synopsis: Germaine has won a million trading stamps in a contest and is having a stamp-pasting party. Her sisters and friends steal the stamps as they paste them in. There is no plot per se in this all-female comedy-drama that is set in a small Catholic parish in Canada. Most of the women are pretty hostile. They put all of their energy into such unimportant activities as playing bingo and entering contests; the women aren't involved in the outside world at all.

Analysis: A stylistically dazzling, frequently bewildering play, grotesquely comic, sometimes poignant and troubling. The playwright seems to be suggesting that the Catholic Church and men are responsible for this sad state of affairs. Scene work isn't practical because of the large ensemble cast that is always on stage. However, the play does contain several outstanding monologues. All levels.

Scenes/Monologues: Female Monologues (3)

LES LIAISONS DANGEREUSES

by Christopher Hampton [based on Choderlos de Laclos's novel of the same name (Samuel French)]

Synopsis: The action in this two-act drama takes place in and around Paris during the 1780s and involves wealthy, decadent, sexually cynical members of the aristocracy. The main plot line centers on a deal struck between the dashing and immoral Valmont and his sometimes lover, widow Madame Merteuil. She is seeking revenge against a former lover who jilted her and who now intends to marry Cécile, a virgin. Merteuil enlists Valmont to seduce (ruin) the younger woman before her wedding night, an assignment he at first refuses because he doesn't see enough sport in the pursuit of a 15-year-old. In addition, he is stalking bigger game, namely the virtuous, married, straightlaced Madame de Tourvel. Eventually, Valmont, using various deceptions, successfully seduces both Cécile and de Tourvel.

The fun, however, goes out of the game for Valmont because he has allowed himself to fall in love with de Tourvel, a mortal error according to the upside-down code of morals he and other aristocrats share. Entanglements become even more complex as Le Chevalier Danceny beds Merteuil even though he is in love with Cécile. In the end, Valmont is killed in a duel with this man.

Analysis: It is hard to keep all the liaisons on stage in focus, but it is worth the effort. During its 1987 Broadway run, *Les Liaisons Dangereuses* received several Tony nominations. Later, it was made into a film starring Glenn Close, John Malkovich, Michelle Pfeiffer, Keanu Reeves, and Uma Thurman. Wonderful material for sophisticated actors who want to play with scenes of seduction and deceit in oh-so-formal but oh-so-decadent French salons.

Scenes/Monologues: Male/Female Scenes (5)

LIE OF THE MIND, A
by Sam Shepard (Dramatists Play Service)

Synopsis: Jake beat up his wife again, and this time he thinks he killed her. He travels south, hiding out with his younger brother, Frankie, in a shabby motel room while he tries to sort out his options. Beth, meanwhile, doesn't die, but suffers brain damage and is being nursed by her parents in Billings, Montana. Jake moves into his childhood room in his mother's house, and Frankie heads to Montana to find out if Beth is dead or alive. He winds up getting shot in the leg by Beth's dad, who mistakes him for a deer. In the end, Jake also shows up in Montana, wrapped in the American flag, only to discover that Beth's mind has snapped, and she is going to marry the relatively gentler Frankie.

Analysis: Sam Shepard paints with bold colors, mainly red, white, and blue. His plays are full of symbolism as he claws at the underpinnings of the Great American Myth. Wide-open spaces, good old boys, women who stand by their men, American flags—and guns, always and forever, guns. All levels.

Scenes/Monologues: Male/Male Scenes (1), Female/Female Scenes (1), Male/Female Scenes (1)

LIFE AND LIMB
by Keith Reddin (Dramatists Play Service)

Synopsis: Franklin joined the army to fight in the Korean War, leaving his new wife, Effie, behind. He lost his right arm during the battle at Pork Chop Hill and now, back in the United States, is unable to find work. Franklin descends into a depressed, alcoholic haze. Just when he is at his most desperate point, he is hired by Tod Cartmell, the sadistic owner of a company that sells prosthetic devices. Finally gainfully employed, Franklin purchases a new television as a surprise gift for Effie, who is having an affair with another man. Before she sees the television, however, she and her girlfriend Doina are killed in a freak accident at a movie theater. Franklin becomes more and more subservient to Cartmell and at the final curtain dies and joins Effie in hell.

Analysis: Keith Reddin has an excellent feel for dialogue and stage craft, and the milieu of this drama, 1952–1956, is unusual. Most scenes are suitable for actors of any level, but the office confrontation between Franklin and Cartmell involves sexual humiliation and is appropriate for advanced actors only.

Scenes/Monologues: Male/Male Scenes (1), Female/Female Scenes (1), Male/Female Scenes (3)

LION IN WINTER, THE
by James Goldman (Samuel French)

Synopsis: Henry II still has a deep affection for his wife, Eleanor of Aquitaine, but keeps her in prison because they can't agree on which of their three sons will inherit the English throne. Complicating their long-term dispute is an agreement Henry made with the French king regarding the marriage of Princess Alais to one of his sons in exchange for the grant of an important plot of land 20 miles outside of Paris. Henry is himself now hopelessly in love with Alais and is unwilling to see her marry anyone but himself. In the end, he disinherits all of his sons and leaves for Rome in order to have his marriage to Eleanor annulled. This will free him to marry Alais. Henry hopes that this marriage will produce worthier sons.

Analysis: An appealing and fanciful 1966 comedy-drama with a peculiar, almost flippant tone in the face of life-and-death stakes. Although the action is set in 1183, the language is contemporary. All levels.
Scenes/Monologues: Male/Female Scenes (4)

LIPS TOGETHER, TEETH APART

by Terrence McNally (Dramatists Play Service)
Synopsis: Sally's brother died of AIDS and willed his Fire Island home to her. She, her husband, Sam, and another couple, John and Chloe, are spending the Fourth of July weekend there. It turns out that Sally and John have been having an affair for a while, that John has been diagnosed with cancer of the esophagus, and that no one really gets along with each other. Everyone laughs a great deal, but there is always underlying tension.
Analysis: This 1991 comedy-drama displays Terrence McNally's usual excellent ear for dialogue. Unfortunately, all four characters are on stage continually, so excerpting scenes for workshop isn't practical. The play's title refers to the fact that Sam grinds his teeth when he sleeps. His dentist has advised him to try falling asleep at night while saying "lips together, teeth apart" to himself. All levels.
Scenes/Monologues: Female Monologues (1)

LISBON TRAVIATA, THE

by Terrence McNally (Dramatists Play Service)
Synopsis: Terrence McNally wrote two separate endings for this play, which deals with the shifting relationships among several gay men. In both versions, Stephen is jealous of his lover Mike's involvement with a new man. In one version, he murders Mike; in the other, he doesn't. The first act is the same in both plays, a funny extended scene between Stephen and his friend Mendy.
Analysis: Terrence McNally can't make up his mind if this is a comedy or a drama, and therein lies the problem. The first act, without question, is quite comic. All levels.
Scenes/Monologues: Male/Male Scenes (1)

LITTLE FOXES, THE

by Lillian Hellman (Dramatists Play Service)
Synopsis: Set in the deep south in 1900, *The Little Foxes* is about a ruthless family that turns on itself and the innocent people who get hurt in the crossfire. Ben and Oscar Hubbard are brothers who will stop at nothing to make a dollar, including overcharging uneducated blacks and even marrying for money instead of love if necessary. They've arranged the deal of their lives, but they need their sister Regina's assistance to raise the investment. When she can't persuade her ailing husband, Horace, to participate, Oscar's spineless son, Leo, simply steals the money from him. Horace discovers the crime but before he can take legal steps to do anything about it, he suffers a massive heart attack and dies.
Analysis: This 1939 Broadway drama would be better titled *The Little Pit Vipers* because of its immoral cast of characters. Tallulah Bankhead played Regina to the hilt. All levels.
Scenes/Monologues: Female Monologues (1), Male/Male Scenes (1), Male/Female Scenes (2)

LONELY IMPULSE OF DELIGHT, A

by John Patrick Shanley (Dramatists Play Service) [*Welcome to the Moon and Other Plays* (Dramatists Play Service); *13 by Shanley* (Applause Books)]
Synopsis: Walter is in love with a mermaid who lives in the lake in New York City's Central Park. He brings his best friend, Jim, to see her late one night. Jim, understandably, doesn't think it is a fun idea to be in the park at night, especially since Walter took him away from a good party where he was about to score with a pretty woman. Sally the Mermaid doesn't

appear, and Jim, who is concerned for his friend's mental stability but is running out of patience with this game, leaves Walter in the park. Then Sally shows up. Or does she?
Analysis: This comedy is a gem for scene-study use because it depends heavily on the actors' use of imagination. All levels.
Scenes/Monologues: Male/Male Scenes (1)

LONG DAY'S JOURNEY INTO NIGHT

by Eugene O'Neill (Yale University Press)
Synopsis: The action takes place during a single day at the Tyrone summer home in 1912, during which aging actor James Tyrone is forced to recognize that his wife Mary has once again descended into morphine addiction; his youngest son, Edmund, has contracted tuberculosis; and his shiftless eldest son, Jamie, will never reform. Mary is still tortured with guilt over the death of their 2-year-old son 25 years ago. In addition, she has never been able to adjust to the nomadic lifestyle of an actor. She would rather live with her drug-induced fantasies of a long-gone youth than suffer more pain in the real world.

James has saved almost every penny he ever earned and is now quite rich. Still, he lives in fear of poverty and is slow to part with a dollar even when it comes to paying for medical care for his own family. Jamie, at 33, can find no profession he likes or is good at and is still financially dependent on his father. This situation further robs Jamie of his self-esteem. Edmund, though ill with tuberculosis, is actually the healthiest member of the family.
Analysis: Eugene O'Neill's wrote this famous autobiographical drama (O'Neill based Edmund on himself) in 1940 but it wasn't published until after his death in 1956. A major achievement for the American theater and a must-read for all acting students. The difficult material is appropriate for thoughtful and serious actors of all levels.
Scenes/Monologues: Male Monologues (2), Female Monologues (1), Male/Male Scenes (2), Male/Female Scenes (1)

LOOK HOMEWARD, ANGEL

by Ketti Frings [based on Thomas Wolfe's novel of the same name (Samuel French)]
Synopsis: World War I is raging in Europe, but time is measured more slowly in Altamont, North Carolina where young Eugene Gant lives in a ramshackle, family-run boarding house. His tight-fisted mother appears to control his destiny just as she has that of Eugene's brother, Ben; sister, Helen; and artistic, alcoholic father, W. O. Gant. Then, one month during the fall of 1916, everything changes. Ben suddenly gets sick and dies, and Eugene falls in love with Laura, a pretty boarder. Their romance, while sweet and pure, is destined to fail because she is older than he is—and she is engaged to someone back home. At the final curtain Eugene is bound for college, which his mother only grudgingly agrees to pay for. With his imminent departure, she begins to realize how hollow she has become.
Analysis: Thomas Wolfe's autobiographical novel is a treasure of American literature, and Ketti Frings's adaptation, which won a Pulitzer Prize in 1958, does it proud. The role of Eugene was an early showcase for Anthony Perkins. All levels.
Scenes/Monologues: Female Monologues (1), Male/Female Scenes (4)

LOSS OF ROSES, A

by William Inge (Dramatists Play Service)
Synopsis: The life of an actress was rough in 1933, especially if her show folded in a remote city. Lila Green, finding herself stranded in just such a situation and with no employment prospects, temporarily moves in with Helen Baird and her son, who she worked for years ago as a housekeeper and baby sitter. Although 32 years old, Lila is, in many ways, an unsophisticated and immature woman; she needs a man to baby and care for her. Ricky Powers, her current beau, is

an insensitive and domineering actor who tries to entice her into performing in blue movies in Kansas City. Lila resists this proposition until an impulsively romantic night with Helen's young son, Kenny, turns into a disappointment the following morning. Forced to confront her advancing age and dismal employment prospects, Lila abandons her dreams of success on the stage, departing with Ricky for Kansas City, where the sordid world of pornography awaits her.

Analysis: William Inge was a protégé of Tennessee Williams, and this drama carries the same air of poetry and symbolism that typifies Williams's work. All levels.

Scenes/Monologues: Female Monologues (1), Male/Female Scenes (2)

LOST IN YONKERS

by Neil Simon (Samuel French)

Synopsis: After Arthur and Jay Kurnitz's mother dies of cancer in 1942, they live for a year with their Grandma Kurnitz in Yonkers while their father works his way out of debt via out-of-town employment. It is through their eyes that the audience meets the family. For the most part, *Lost in Yonkers* is a character-driven work. The primary action centers around the evolution of the relationship between Grandma, an iron-fisted, humorless, old-school German-Jewish immigrant, and Bella, her childlike 35-year-old daughter who lives at home and takes care of her. After the year passes, the boys' father returns to New York City, and they move back in with him.

Analysis: Winner of the 1991 Pulitzer Prize for Drama as well as the Tony for Best Play. Mercedes Ruehl (Bella) and the wonderful Irene Worth (Grandma) also won Tony Awards as Best Actress and Best Supporting Actress, respectively. The role of Bella is among Neil Simon's finest achievements. She is a vulnerable, hopeful, and eccentric woman-child. All levels.

Scenes/Monologues: Female Monologues (1), Female/Female Scenes (1)

LOU GEHRIG DID NOT DIE OF CANCER

by Jason Miller [*Three One-Act Plays by Jason Miller* (Dramatists Play Service)]

Synopsis: Victor Spinilli is the good but demanding coach of the Spinilli Spoilers, a Long Island little-league baseball team sponsored by the Spinilli family business, which Victor's father runs. After Victor gets into an on-field fist fight with an umpire, his father has him fired from the coaching job. This event, coupled with a late-afternoon conversation with the mother of a shy and sensitive boy on the team, leads Victor to serious introspection about his values, his relationship with his overbearing father, and his marriage.

Analysis: A haunting, sometimes cryptic, 1972 one-act drama by the man who wrote *That Championship Season*. The interplay among the characters rings true, and Jason Miller has an excellent ear for dialogue. All levels.

Scenes/Monologues: Male Monologues (1), Male/Female Scenes (2)

LOVER, THE

by Harold Pinter (Dramatists Play Service)

Synopsis: Sarah and Richard, married 10 years, have an unusual arrangement. After he leaves for work, she prepares herself to receive a lover. Richard returns in midafternoon, pretending to be someone else. When he becomes jealous of the relationship his wife is having with his "pretend" self and tries to end the game, she feels threatened because they're both addicted to it. The tempo of their role-playing accelerates and, by the end of the play, it is unclear which are their "real" relationships.

Analysis: Although this very short (one act) play can be fun, it deals directly with sexual attraction and role-playing. As a result, this 1963 drama is a challenge for advanced actors. They need to be secure and professional in their approach.

Scenes/Monologues: Male/Female Scenes (1)

LOVERS AND OTHER STRANGERS
by Renée Taylor and Joseph Bologna (Samuel French)
Synopsis: Each of the five sketchy mini-comedies under the umbrella title of *Lovers and Other Strangers* deals with romantic relationships. The plots are minimal, and the dialogue is frequently hilarious.
Analysis: There is an old New York saying: If you're from New York, and you're not Jewish, you're Jewish; if you're from Texas, and you're Jewish, you're not Jewish. Actors who do scenes from this 1968 comedy should keep that in mind. Very funny material. All levels.
Scenes/Monologues: Male Monologues (1), Female Monologues (1), Male/Female Scenes (3)

LOVE SUICIDE AT SCHOFIELD BARRACKS, THE
by Romulus Linney (Dramatists Play Service) [one-act version; *Seventeen Short Plays by Romulus Linney* (Smith & Kraus)]
Synopsis: The commanding general of Schofield Barracks in Hawaii and his wife commit joint suicide in a very public, highly ritualized Japanese ceremony, and this play involves the subsequent court hearing into the events. The action consists of testimony from various people who knew the general.
Analysis: Set in 1970, the play is a devastating indictment of American military policy in Asia. Romulus Linney has a razor-sharp feel for dialogue. All levels.
Scenes/Monologues: Male Monologues (2), Female Monologues (1)

LUDLOW FAIR
by Lanford Wilson [*Balm in Gilead and Other Plays* by Lanford Wilson (Hill & Wang/Noonday)]
Synopsis: Rachel is distressed because she turned her boyfriend in to the authorities after she caught him stealing money from her and her roommate, Agnes. Now that he is in jail, Rachel thinks that she may have overreacted. Agnes thinks Rachel did the right thing in this case but that she has had entirely too many boyfriends (six) in the last nine months. Still, Agnes admits that Rachel's social life may have been more exciting than her own dull one during the same period. All Agnes has to look forward to is tomorrow's lunch with her boss's skinny son—if she can get over her cold, that is.
Analysis: A 1965 one-act play that is only 16 pages long. The dialogue remains fresh, and the relationship between the roommates is well drawn. All levels.
Scenes/Monologues: Female Monologues (1), Female/Female Scenes (2)

LUV
by Murray Schisgal (Dramatists Play Service)
Synopsis: Ellen is married to Milt, who is doing very well in business. Then she divorces him and marries Harry, Milt's old school chum who is climbing up from the depths of depression. Then Ellen divorces Harry and remarries Milt. Everyone tries to figure out the meaning of life, the mysteries of death, and, of course, love.
Analysis: Wonderful dark comedy. The characters are rich, full, sad, and funny. Stylistically difficult for novice actors.
Scenes/Monologues: Male Monologues (1), Female Monologues (1), Male/Male Scenes (1), Male/Female Scenes (2)

MAN FOR ALL SEASONS, A
by Robert Bolt (Samuel French)
Synopsis: King Henry VIII wants to have his marriage to Catherine of Aragon annulled by the Catholic Church so that he can marry the younger Anne Boleyn, who he hopes will give him a male heir. The problem is that the Church has already "forgiven" one marriage and isn't willing to make any additional exceptions for Henry. He then seeks assistance and public

endorsement from the prominent statesman Sir Thomas More. Although More sympathizes with the king's plight, he won't help Henry. The monarch puts increasing pressure on More, and when the statesman continues to refuse to capitulate, Henry has him executed. The drama is told from More's perspective, who has the king pulling him one way, and the Church and his family pulling him the other.

Analysis: Surely one of the best plays ever written, *A Man for All Seasons* raises questions about the roles government and religion play in people's lives. What price are people willing to pay for their integrity? More paid with his life. For sophisticated actors.

Scenes/Monologues: Male/Male Scenes (2)

MA RAINEY'S BLACK BOTTOM

by August Wilson (New American Library)

Synopsis: A recording session for Ma Rainey, "the mother of the blues," brings her together with her musicians who discuss, debate, and fight about the plight of the black person in America during the 1930s. After some fits and starts, they finally get the record cut, but that isn't the real point of the play. Among the colorful characters, Levee, the cornet player, has the most interesting development. He is a more serious musician than the others and has hopes for a recording contract of his own. When that dream is thwarted by some white record producers, he sinks to the level of a street thug, knifing and killing another musician who accidentally stepped on his new shoes.

Analysis: Nominated for several Tony Awards in 1985, *Ma Rainey's Black Bottom* was August Wilson's first play to reach Broadway. The monologues are terrific. All levels.

Scenes/Monologues: Male Monologues (5)

MARCO POLO SINGS A SOLO

by John Guare (Dramatists Play Service)

Synopsis: This is a futuristic comedy in the Absurdist tradition, set in the year 1999 on an iceberg off the coast of Norway. Stony McBride is making a movie about Marco Polo, starring his father. Stony's pregnant wife, a celebrated pianist, is involved in an affair with a politician who has discovered a cure for cancer. During the play, the audience experiences a cataclysmic earthquake that destroys much of Italy (Hawaii is already long gone), the discovery of a new planet, the astral impregnation of a woman by an astronaut, and a sudden change of power in Washington, DC.

Analysis: John Guare intended *Marco Polo Sings a Solo* to be a philosophical counterpoint to *The House of Blue Leaves*. While the latter play deals with the limitations the characters face, this comedy presents unlimited possibilities. All levels.

Scenes/Monologues: Male Monologues (2), Female Monologues (1)

"MASTER HAROLD" . . . AND THE BOYS

by Athol Fugard (Samuel French)

Synopsis: Set in the South-African town of Port Elizabeth in 1950. Hally, a white schoolboy, spends an hour and a half with Sam and Willy, longtime black employees of his family. The shifting relationships among these people are the centerpiece of the play. Loving and playful on the one hand, Hally can quickly revert to anger, treating Sam and Willy like children even though both are 20 years older than he is. After Hally learns that his alcoholic and abusive father is coming home from the hospital, he turns on Sam with a vengeance, spitting in his face and demanding that he be referred to as "Master Harold" from now on instead of "Hally." Sam responds with dignity and self-restraint.

Analysis: An extraordinary one-act play that, unfortunately, is hard to use for scene work because the three characters are on stage the entire time. Danny Glover created the role of Willy in the 1982 Yale Rep production. Written in the South-African vernacular. All levels.

Scenes/Monologues: Male Monologues (3)

MATCHMAKER, THE
by Thornton Wilder (Samuel French)
Synopsis: This play is set in the early 1880s. Horace Vandergelder is a sweet, blustery, unmarried, self-made bag of hot air. Miss Dolly Levi is going to take care of that just as soon as she gets the cupids in place for his niece, Ermengarde, and her beloved, Ambrose the artist. There is a great deal of running here and there, hiding behind screens and under tables, mistaken identities, and all sorts of charming diversions. In the end, everything comes up roses.
Analysis: Was life ever really this simple? *The Matchmaker* is a classic American comedy, adapted in 1964 as the musical *Hello Dolly!* All levels.
Scenes/Monologues: Male Monologues (2), Female Monologues (1), Male/Female Scenes (1)

M. BUTTERFLY
by David Henry Hwang (Dramatists Play Service)
Synopsis: Inspired by the true 1986 story of a French diplomat who passed state secrets to a Chinese actress who turned out to be not only a spy, but a man. Here, Gallimard truly believes the illusion Song creates. The play unites these basic facts with a fable that highlights Western misconceptions and fantasies about Eastern women and their countries. The glue that holds it all together is the parallel story told in the opera *Madame Butterfly*.
Analysis: A couple of potent scenes involving Song and Gallimard, when Song is dressed as and perceived to be a woman, should be attempted by advanced actors only. All of the other scenes are appropriate for all levels.
Scenes/Monologues: Male/Female Scenes (1)

MEDAL OF HONOR RAG
by Tom Cole (Samuel French)
Synopsis: Dale Jackson, an African-American army sergeant was who was awarded the Congressional Medal of Honor for bravery in Vietnam, is experiencing post-traumatic-stress syndrome. Unable to deal with the idea of being a credit to his race for behavior that took place under enemy fire, Dale thinks that he should have died along with his buddies in Vietnam. As such, he is being treated in the Valley Forge Army Hospital in Pennsylvania. The action takes place on April 23, 1971, and involves Dale's therapy session with a prominent psychiatrist.
Analysis: This material is sometimes blistering in its intensity; it raises the issues of racism in America and hypocrisy. For sophisticated actors.
Scenes/Monologues: Male Monologues (1), Male/Male Scenes (1)

MIDDLE AGES, THE
by A. R. Gurney, Jr. (Dramatists Play Service)
Synopsis: The action takes place in the trophy room of a men's club in a large city from the mid-1940s to the late 1970s. Naturally, the small cast of actors must age during this lengthy time span. The club is a symbol of a kind of highly structured, conservative, moneyed lifestyle that the various characters are continually seeking or avoiding, and the play tracks the way their shifting values alternately pull them together and drive them apart.
Analysis: A. R. Gurney, Jr. is firmly anchored in WASP America, and this 1976 comedy holds the underlying values up for examination. All levels.
Scenes/Monologues: Male Monologues (1), Male/Female Scenes (2)

MIDDLE OF THE NIGHT, THE
by Paddy Chayefsky (Samuel French)
Synopsis: A kindly 53-year-old widower falls in love with a 23-year-old woman who is unhappily married to a musician. No one in their circle of acquaintances approves of this union, but their love is true.

Analysis: Excellent human drama, frequently touching. Actors who play the widower need to have a good feel for New York City/Brooklyn/Jewish speech patterns. This sensitivity isn't as essential for the part of the woman. All levels.
Scenes/Monologues: Female/Female Scenes (1), Male/Female Scenes (2)

MISS JULIE
by August Strindberg [*Six Plays of Strindberg*, translated by Elizabeth Sprigge (Doubleday/Anchor)]
Synopsis: During a midsummer night's revelry that takes place while her father, the Count, is away visiting relatives, Miss Julie makes love with Jean, the family valet. Unable to accept the consequences of her actions, she commits suicide, presumably after the final curtain. The sexual interplay between Miss Julie and Jean violates the taboo of class boundaries, pushing a conflict between her "instincts" as a woman and the propriety of her status in society.
Analysis: Eugene O'Neill, accepting the 1936 Nobel Prize for Drama, said of August Strindberg: "(his) . . . influence runs clearly through more than a few of my plays. . . . For me, he remains, as Nietzsche remains, in his sphere, the master, still to this day more modern than any of us, still our leader." Written in 1888 by a renowned misogynist and controversial in its time, *Miss Julie* is noted for the psychological complexity of its characters, the straightforward approach to sexual realism, and its unusual one-act format. All levels.
Scenes/Monologues: Male Monologues (1), Male/Female Scenes (2)

MISS LONELYHEARTS
by Howard Teichmann [adapted from Nathanael West's novel of the same name (Dramatists Play Service)]
Synopsis: A young, cynical, and ambitious newspaper reporter becomes an advice-to-the-lovelorn columnist during the 1930s. Known now as Miss Lonelyhearts, he finds that his life changes dramatically as the terrible problems of his readers force him to examine the concept of a merciful God. In an almost Christ-like fashion, he tries to heal everyone who asks for his help. He gives himself sexually to a sad and lonely woman who then turns on him when he refuses to have sex with her again. Her husband, a handicapped meter reader for the gas company, finds Lonelyhearts and kills him.
Analysis: Nathanael West's 1933 novel is a classic of American literature. This stage adaptation doesn't come close to the disturbing power of the book, but some of the scenes are good. All levels.
Scenes/Monologues: Male Monologues (1), Male/Female Scenes (3)

MISS MARGARIDA'S WAY
by Roberto Athayde (Samuel French)
Synopsis: A one-woman show in which the audience is treated as a rather stupid eighth-grade class by an arrogant, frequently abusive, foul-mouthed teacher.
Analysis: Written by a young Brazilian playwright in 1977, this controversial play may or may not be a metaphor for an imperialistic United States. Estelle Parsons drew raves and received a Tony nomination for her portrayal of the teacher. Very rough language. Challenging material for experienced actors.
Scenes/Monologues: Female Monologues (2)

MISTER ROBERTS
by Thomas Heggen and Joshua Logan (Dramatists Play Service)
Synopsis: The action takes place aboard a supply ship operating in the back areas of the Pacific in May 1945. Lieutenant AJG Roberts, otherwise known as Mister Roberts, dropped out of medical school to get into the war and is frustrated by his noncombat assignment. An irreverent free spirit, he has conflicts with the self-made captain, an ambitious high-school

dropout who resents educated know-it-alls. In order to secure a much-needed recreational shore leave for the crew, Roberts strikes a secret deal with the captain, agreeing to be a better team player. Then, in frustration, he tosses the captain's beloved potted palm overboard.

During the ensuing shouting match between Roberts and the captain, which is inadvertently broadcast over the ship's loudspeakers, the crew learns about the deal and conspires to forge a transfer request to help Roberts get off the ship. Their scheme works, Roberts goes to combat, and is killed. His spirit and courage are inspirational to the crew, who begin to assert themselves in newer, stronger ways.

Analysis: A well-crafted comedy-drama that ran for three years on Broadway, making Henry Fonda a star. A warning: the dramatized attitude of the men toward women is sometimes offensive. On an all-male ship during a war, some macho posturing takes place. However, the sailors degenerate into uncivilized marauders during their shore leave, brawling, grabbing women, and ripping off their clothes. Boys may have been boys in 1950, but this type of behavior is less acceptable today. All levels.

Scenes/Monologues: Male Monologues (1), Male/Male Scenes (2), Three-Person Scenes (1)

MODIGLIANI
by Dennis McIntyre (Samuel French)

Synopsis: The police are hunting for Modigliani, who broke the front window of a fancy restaurant in Paris. He desperately tries to borrow money from friends so that he and his lover, Beatrice, can flee to Martinique. In the meantime, Modigliani's agent, Zborowski, has made an appointment to show the artist's work to an important gallery owner. A sale would solve all of the couple's financial problems. When the deal doesn't go through, Modigliani's situation gets even worse: his health deteriorates, and Beatrice leaves him. At the end of the play, he and his friend Utrillo begin again with blank canvases.

Analysis: A lusty, vibrant drama filled with colorful characters who care intensely about life. All levels.

Scenes/Monologues: Male/Male Scenes (2), Male/Female Scenes (1)

MONDAY AFTER THE MIRACLE
by William Gibson (Dramatists Play Service)

Synopsis: This is a sequel to *The Miracle Worker,* which deals with Annie Sullivan and her work with Helen Keller. Here, the action begins when Helen is in her early twenties and Annie is 35, and tracks them for the next 15 years or so. Annie marries John, a young academic who comes to help Helen with her writing. In time, however, he feels slighted by the growing fame of the two women and turns to drink. His marriage to Annie then flounders.

Analysis: Any scenes involving Helen are impossible for workshop use because of technical requirements. People communicate with her by tapping on her palm, and the words are interpreted over the theater's public-address system. But a couple of the scenes with Annie and her lover are suitable for scene-study purposes. All levels.

Scenes/Monologues: Male/Female Scenes (3)

MOON FOR THE MISBEGOTTEN, A
by Eugene O'Neill (Samuel French)

Synopsis: After Tyrone's mother died in California, he escorted her body across the country by rail, spending most of the trip in a drunken stupor and sleeping with the trashiest whore he could find on the train. *A Moon for the Misbegotten* begins a year after that trip. Tyrone feels deeply guilty and seeks forgiveness from Josie Hogan, the daughter of a tenant farmer on Connecticut land owned by Tyrone's family. Josie is nearly 6 feet tall and weighs 180 pounds She is a powerful, full-breasted woman, not mannish at all, just big. She claims to have slept with half the men in the nearby village, but the big secret is that she is actually a virgin.

Tyrone sees through her façade, she sees through his, and their confrontation on the porch in Act III is one of the most complex and revealing in dramatic literature. As their defenses fall, Josie realizes that Tyrone is looking for forgiveness, not a lover, and that the romance she hoped for will never happen. At the final curtain, Tyrone heads down the road, bound for New York City, following the lure of bright lights and Broadway.

Analysis: The last script completed by the Nobel Prize playwright, *A Moon for the Misbegotten* is a sequel to *Long Day's Journey Into Night*. The second play tracks the tragic path of James Tyrone, Jr., a character based on Eugene O'Neill's real-life brother, Jamie. World-class material for serious actors.

Scenes/Monologues: Male Monologues (1), Male/Female Scenes (1)

MRS. CALIFORNIA
by Doris Baizley (Dramatists Play Service)

Synopsis: The action takes place backstage at the 1955 Mrs. California contest. Present are Mrs. San Francisco, Mrs. Los Angeles, Mrs. San Bernardino, and Mrs. Modesto, as well as various friends and sponsors. The women compete by sewing an apron, preparing a full meal, ironing two men's white shirts, and giving miscellaneous testimonials. In the end, Mrs. Modesto wins by a spatula.

Analysis: Devastating satire. Chock full of short, funny monologues. All levels.

Scenes/Monologues: Female Monologues (4), Female/Female Scenes (1), Male/Female Scenes (1)

MRS. DALLY HAS A LOVER
by William Hanley (Dramatists Play Service)

Synopsis: Mrs. Dally, 38, is a closet romantic and a reader of John Donne's poetry who longs to experience the more sensitive possibilities in life. She is trapped, however, in a joyless 15-year marriage with a distant, insensitive, blue-collar husband in a small New York City apartment. The play concerns the ongoing sexual relationship she has with Frankie, an 18-year-old who lives in the same building. On the surface of it, the age difference between Mrs. Dally and the young man makes their involvement seem almost perverse but as the audience learns, this is a warm, meaningful union.

Analysis: This lovely and unusual 1963 one-act play, winner of the Vernon Rice Award for distinguished production Off-Broadway, is frequently poetic and always tender. The age difference between the characters causes the audience—and actors—to reevaluate their preconceptions about romantic love. For sophisticated actors.

Scenes/Monologues: Male/Female Scenes (3)

MRS. WARREN'S PROFESSION
by George Bernard Shaw (Signet)

Synopsis: Vivie Warren, a strong, confident, Cambridge-educated young woman, discovers that her mother has amassed considerable wealth from the operation of brothels. Despite Mrs. Warren's explanations about her impoverished origins and the scarce opportunities afforded women in the business world, Vivie is repulsed by her mother's occupation and at the final curtain banishes Mrs. Warren—and her money—from her life.

Analysis: George Bernard Shaw's 1894 drama pits daughter against mother in an effort to highlight the dilemma of the average woman. All levels.

Scenes/Monologues: Female Monologues (1), Female/Female Scenes (1)

MURDER AT THE HOWARD JOHNSON'S
by Ron Clark and Sam Bobrick (Samuel French)

Synopsis: This zany comedy tracks the shifting relationships between Arlene Miller; her husband, Mitchell, a used-car salesperson; and their dentist and her lover, Mitchell Lovell. As the play's title suggests, all of the action takes place in Howard Johnson's. In Act I, Scene 1, Arlene and Mitchell plot to murder Paul. But in Act I, Scene 2, Arlene and Paul reunite and plot to kill Mitchell, who has begun an affair with his dental assistant. By Act II, Arlene has abandoned both men in favor of a relationship with her guru, so Mitchell and Paul get together and plot her murder. At the final curtain, Arlene and Paul reconcile, and Mitchell resolves to be just a dentist. **Analysis:** A wildly improbable premise can lead to wonderful acting fun if everyone goes along with it. All levels. **Scenes/Monologues:** Male/Male Scenes (1), Male/Female Scenes (2), Three-Person Scenes (1)

NATURE AND PURPOSE OF THE UNIVERSE, THE
by Christopher Durang (Dramatists Play Service)
Synopsis: Eleanor is having a terrible time. As the curtain goes up, she is sobbing because her oldest son is a dope pusher and pimp; her middle son is a homosexual; and her youngest son, Andy, lost his penis in a freak reaping-machine accident. Then things really start to deteriorate. Sister Annie de Maupassant shows up at the house and announces that she is the new Pope, the census taker (who looks suspiciously like Sister Annie) advises Eleanor to commit suicide because she is such a failure, and the athletic coach at Andy's school insists that since he has no penis, he must compete in girls' gymnastics. And that's not all . . . the chaos continues. **Analysis:** Another delicious detour into Christopher Durang's dementia. Too crazy overall for scene study, but two funny monologues have potential. All levels. **Scenes/Monologues:** Female Monologues (2)

NERD, THE
by Larry Shue (Dramatists Play Service)
Synopsis: Rick Steadman, who saved Willum's life during the Vietnam War, unexpectedly turns up at his home for a visit. Willum, eternally grateful, rolls out the red carpet, only to discover that Rick is the worst house guest in history, a thoughtless, clumsy, self-involved nerd. After suffering in silence for a week, Willum and his friends plan to get rid of Rick. **Analysis:** Dinner-theater comedy: physical, silly, dumb at times, and fun. All levels. **Scenes/Monologues:** Male Monologues (1), Male/Male Scenes (1)

NEVIS MOUNTAIN DEW
by Steve Carter (Dramatists Play Service)
Synopsis: Set in Queens, New York, in 1954, this drama revolves around a West-Indian family headed by Jared Philibert, who is disabled with infantile paralysis. From his bedroom where he rests in an iron-lung machine, he coordinates the family income, which comes from six rental houses, and referees the continually shifting tensions between his sisters and his wife.

On his fiftieth birthday, Jared's wife buys him a television and an "elevator" to raise it up and down so that he can see the screen from his prone position. Two co-workers from the wife's job have helped carry the gifts, and it becomes readily apparent that one of them has romantic designs on her. But Jared can see that his wife will never leave him as long as he is alive. Neither will his attentive sisters. So in the final moments of the play, Jared arranges an assisted suicide. The audience never knows for sure who helped him turn off the iron lung. **Analysis:** West-Indian heritage and references, the iron lung, and the 1950s color this unusual family portrait. The play was a Burns-Mantle Theater Yearbook "Best Play" of 1978–79. All levels. **Scenes/Monologues:** Female Monologues (1), Male/Female Scenes (1)

'NIGHT, MOTHER
by Marsha Norman (Dramatists Play Service)
Synopsis: Jessie lives with her mother in a small house on a country road. Having decided that her life isn't worth living, she tells her mother that she has decided to commit suicide and

methodically begins the final preparations for that event. Jessie contentedly attends to details as her mother's horror and desperation grow. Exactly 90 minutes from the opening curtain in real time, she walks into the next room and shoots herself.

Analysis: Winner of the 1983 Pulitzer Prize for Drama, the play is nerve-shattering at times, humorous at others, but always insightful. It made Kathy Bates a star. All levels.

Scenes/Monologues: Female Monologues (1), Female/Female Scenes (1)

NIGHT OF THE IGUANA, THE

by Tennessee Williams (Dramatists Play Service)

Synopsis: The events in this play occur in 1940, during one long day in the off-season of the ramshackle Costa Verde Hotel on the Mexican coast, the kind of resort that attracts drifters and travelers off the beaten path. Reverend T. Lawrence Shannon, a defrocked Episcopal priest, seducer of young girls and, for many years, a nickel-and-dime tour conductor, arrives with a bus load of unhappy female tourists. He is suffering another of his nervous breakdowns and has come to see his friend, Fred, the owner of Costa Verde. But Fred died a month ago, and now his lusty widow, Maxine, hanging on by a financial thread, is deciding whether to close the place and move to Texas or to make a go of it alone. She immediately begins trying to convince Shannon to move in with her.

Then two other unwanted guests arrive, a dying, financially destitute 97-year-old minor poet from Nantucket and his unmarried sketch-artist granddaughter. All of these lost souls interact and by the day's end, Shannon agrees to stay with Maxine, the old man composes a fine poem and dies, and Hannah decides to continue the world tour alone. Some native boys capture an iguana and tie it under the verandah to fatten it before eating it. The iguana's continual tugging against the rope becomes a metaphor for the predicament of all the guests in the hotel, each struggling against his or her own unseen restraints and trying to escape.

Analysis: Bleak is too happy a word to describe this 1961 Tennessee Williams drama, but his poetry can't be denied. Difficult material for experienced actors.

Scenes/Monologues: Female Monologues (1), Female/Female Scenes (1), Male/Female Scenes (1)

NO PLACE TO BE SOMEBODY

by Charles Gordone (Samuel French)

Synopsis: Set in a West Greenwich Village bar in New York City that is owned by an African-American man named Johnny Williams. This play feels a lot like *The Time of Your Life* by William Saroyan. An assortment of street characters of all colors, hookers, racketeers, and pot smokers, frequent the bar, and each has a story to tell. The central plot line is thin: Will Johnny go into the rackets or play it legal?

Analysis: A snapshot of street-level black-and-white race relations in 1969. Full of rage, wit, and dignity. All levels.

Scenes/Monologues: Male/Female Scenes (1)

NORMAN CONQUESTS, THE—TABLE MANNERS

by Alan Ayckbourn (Samuel French)

Synopsis: Sarah and her husband, Reg, arrive in the country to take over the mother-nursing duties from Reg's sister Annie for a weekend while she goes on a romantic holiday, presumably with her longtime friend, Tom. But Sarah discovers that Annie is actually planning to spend the time with Norman, her charming and romantic brother-in-law, an arrangement that Sarah contends won't do at all. Annie then reluctantly cancels the trip. Soon, however, everyone in the house knows what she and Norman were up to. This discovery adds to family tensions and produces more embarrassment and confusion during the weekend. When Norman's plans with Annie go awry, he makes a play for Sarah. But in the very final moment of the play, he and Annie get back together.

Analysis: *Table Manners* is part of a trilogy of plays called *The Norman Conquests.* The other two parts, *Living Together* and *Round and Round the Garden,* take place during the same weekend in the same house and involve the same cast of characters. Each comedy stands alone. Written in the British vernacular. All levels.

Scenes/Monologues: Male Monologues (2), Female/Female Scenes (1), Male/Female Scenes (1)

NOT ENOUGH ROPE
by Elaine May (Samuel French)

Synopsis: Edith wants to borrow some rope from Claude, her new neighbor across the hall, so that she can hang herself. Apparently nonplused by this request, he gives her some twine instead. Edith then goes back to her apartment and ties herself up. Once she is standing on the chair ready to make the fatal jump, however, she changes her mind and calls for Claude to rescue her, which he is in no hurry to do. He finally cuts her down, however.

Analysis: A silly 1964 one-act play that can be loads of fun for acting students because the premise is so outrageous. All levels.

Scenes/Monologues: Male/Female Scenes (1)

NUTS
by Tom Topor (Samuel French)

Synopsis: After Claudia's marriage broke up, she became a high-priced call girl for a few months. Then she killed an abusive customer and was charged with manslaughter. Examined by court psychiatrists, she was found incompetent to stand trial. The action of this drama centers around Claudia's sanity hearing. She believes she acted properly and wants to be found sane so that she can face charges. Her mother and stepfather, on the other hand, want her found incompetent; then they won't be forced to balance her values against their own.

Analysis: A couple of Claudia's monologues invariably curl the audience members' hair. Set against a world of prostitution, this play is appropriate for sophisticated actors only.

Scenes/Monologues: Male Monologues (2), Female Monologues (4)

ODD COUPLE, THE (FEMALE VERSION)
by Neil Simon (Samuel French)

Synopsis: When Florence's husband leaves her after 14 years of marriage, she moves in with her good friend, Olive. This new living arrangement quickly degenerates into a situation in which Florence's compulsive cleanliness and worrying drives Olive, a toss-cares-to-the-wind type of person, to distraction.

Analysis: A fun reversal of the male version of the same comedy. This interpretation doesn't work quite as well, however, because it is basically more humorous to have two men playing house. All levels.

Scenes/Monologues: Female/Female Scenes (3)

ODD COUPLE, THE (MALE VERSION)
by Neil Simon (Samuel French)

Synopsis: Oscar and Felix, both recently separated from their wives, are polar opposites. Oscar is a cigar-smoking slob who can't cook a frozen dinner, and Felix is compulsively clean and a gourmet cook. When they decide to share Oscar's eight-room Riverside Drive apartment in New York City, Felix drives Oscar to utter distraction within three weeks.

Analysis: This 1965 comedy is almost an industry in itself, having been turned into a successful movie, television series, and continual revivals around the United States. The roles of Oscar and Felix were originally created by Walter Matthau and Art Carney. All levels.

Scenes/Monologues: Male/Male Scenes (4), Three-Person Scenes (1)

OF MICE AND MEN

by John Steinbeck (Dramatists Play Service)

Synopsis: George and Lennie are migrant farm workers, always close to broke, and always dreaming of a place of their own. George calls the shots and watches after his physically powerful but childlike friend. Their last job near Weed, California, ended abruptly when Lennie innocently tried to feel the pretty fabric of a woman's dress. She panicked, ran to the law, and cried rape, causing the men to have to flee. The pair's current job is on a ranch in southern California, but this situation turns into even more of a disaster than the preceding one. Lennie accidentally kills the flirtatious wife of the boss's jealous son. Certain that Lennie will be lynched by a mob, George decides to kill him first, as an act of pity and love.

Analysis: Gritty 1937 drama about the struggles of migrant Americans. All levels.

Scenes/Monologues: Male/Male Scenes (1), Male/Female Scenes (1)

OH DAD, POOR DAD, MAMMA'S HUNG YOU IN THE CLOSET AND I'M FEELIN' SO SAD

by Arthur Kopit (Samuel French)

Synopsis: Jonathan's mother shields him from the outside world, so he occupies himself with his large coin and stamp collections, and constructs a telescope, hoping that he'll see things far away. As the curtain rises, he and his mother are arriving in a Caribbean resort city, bringing with them enough luggage to occupy an entire squad of bellboys. In addition, Madame Rosepettle, as usual, carries with her the corpse of her late husband, neatly stuffed and ready to be hung inside the closet. A few days later, Rosalie, an attractive young woman who house sits for an absentee couple across the way visits Jonathan. When she turns seductive, Madame Rosepettle kicks her out.

Meanwhile, she is courted by Commodore Roseabove, the owner of a very long yacht. By the end of this insane comedy, Jonathan kills Rosalie rather than accept her invitation to accompany her into the outside world. Madame Rosepettle continues to shield him, and her husband's corpse keeps falling out of the closet.

Analysis: Written in the Absurdist tradition, this 1962 comedy is fun for actors who are willing to jump directly into the deep end of the pool. All levels.

Scenes/Monologues: Male Monologues (1), Male/Female Scenes (1)

OLD TIMES

by Harold Pinter (Evergreen)

Synopsis: Kate and Deeley spend an evening with Kate's friend, Ann, whom she hasn't seen for 20 years. As is typical of many Harold Pinter plays, it is unclear exactly what the relationships are among the three of them. Perhaps Kate and Ann used to be lovers. Perhaps Deeley and Ann were lovers before he married Kate.

Analysis: Harold Pinter's work can be something of a puzzle for actors because he toys with reality. As soon as you think you know where the characters are coming from, they move. When you consider all the famous pauses in Pinter's scripts, keep in mind that a pause is something, not merely silence. All levels.

Scenes/Monologues: Male/Female Scenes (2)

OLEANNA

by David Mamet (Dramatists Play Service)

Synopsis: John is a successful, published university professor who, on the eve of receiving tenure, is accused of sexual harassment by Carol, a female student. Subsequently, his tenure is denied, he can't afford the house he and his wife were going to purchase with the anticipated salary increase, and his career is put into reverse. The play poses several questions. Was John treated fairly? Did he actually harass Carol, or did she misinterpret the fumbling efforts of a concerned teacher to comfort and encourage her? In the final moments of the play, John discovers that Carol, now being advised by an unnamed group of radical feminists, is planning to press criminal rape charges unless he makes certain concessions to her and the group. He becomes enraged by this and hits her, barely restraining himself from doing her great bodily harm. More difficult questions arise after the final curtain falls.

Analysis: *Oleanna* was a big 1993 Broadway hit for David Mamet. During a December 1992 appearance at the Dramatists Guild in New York City, he explained the play's title: "'Oleanna' was the title of a song about a utopia of that name in western Pennsylvania, a planned community set up in the post-Civil War period by a Norwegian singer who had made a lot of money and wanted to make a beautiful community for Norwegians to come and live in. His name was Ole and his wife's name was Anna, so he called it *Oleanna*. It failed, and everybody went bust. *Oleanna* is a play about failed utopia, in this case the failed utopia of academia." All levels.

Scenes/Monologues: Male Monologues (1), Female Monologues (1), Male/Female Scenes (1)

ON GOLDEN POND
by Ernest Thompson (Dramatists Play Service)

Synopsis: Norman and Ethel, who have been married for 46 years, have spent many summers in their house on Golden Pond. This year, however, it is clear that age is catching up with Norman, so the sojourn takes on an added air of poignancy. The summer becomes a time of taking stock and reassessing life and relationships, particularly those Norman, Ethel, and their daughter, Chelsea, share.

Analysis: *On Golden Pond* ran on Broadway in 1979 and then was made into a wonderful movie starring Henry Fonda, Jane Fonda, and Katharine Hepburn, which won several Academy Awards in 1981. All levels.

Scenes/Monologues: Male/Male Scenes (1), Female/Female Scenes (1)

ONLY GAME IN TOWN, THE
by Frank D. Gilroy (Samuel French)

Synopsis: Fran and Joe live and work in Las Vegas, she as a dancer at the Tropicana, he as a lounge singer. Both are trying to overcome addictions, Joe to gambling and Fran to Tom Lockwood, a wealthy married man with whom she has carried on a 10-year affair. Joe moves in with Fran, and they form a convenient sexual relationship in which they're mutually supportive but emotionally undemanding. When Tom shows up unexpectedly and says that he is finally ready to marry Fran, she refuses him because she has fallen in love with Joe—although she won't say so out loud.

Joe and Fran continue to live together for two more years, each of them keeping their emotional distance, each afraid of deeper commitment. Then, in a touching scene that comes at the end of a traumatic day and night during which Joe starts gambling again, he tells her for the first time that he loves her and asks her to marry him. Fran resists at first but eventually says yes.

Analysis: Although this play is a soap opera, it is good for scene work. All levels.

Scenes/Monologues: Male Monologues (1), Male/Female Scenes (2)

ON THE OPEN ROAD
by Steve Tesich (Samuel French)

Synopsis: Set in the burned-out, post-Civil War landscape of some future time, Al and Angel gather precious paintings and art treasures from gutted churches and museums. They intend to barter their way into the Land of the Free. Captured by the coalition government, they're guaranteed freedom in exchange for carrying out one task. They must murder Jesus Christ, who is in the midst of His second coming.

Analysis: This 1992 play is darkly satirical, frequently horrific, and always philosophical. Presents excellent scene challenges for intelligent, physical actors.
Scenes/Monologues: Male/Male Scenes (2)

OPEN ADMISSIONS
by Shirley Lauro (Samuel French)
Synopsis: Calvin, an 18-year-old African-American sophomore in New York State's university system, has a fifth-grade reading level. He has been passed along from year to year with a "B" average even though he isn't learning anything. Ginny, one of Calvin's teachers, is a well-intentioned, overworked woman with her own personal problems. Both people are victims of an inflexible educational system, and by the final curtain, they manage to come to a deeper understanding of each other's situation. In the last scene, Ginny sits down with Calvin and quietly begins to teach him on a level he can grasp, intent on giving him an education at last.
Analysis: A "message" drama with some explosive scenes. All levels.
Scenes/Monologues: Male/Female Scenes (3)

ORPHANS
by Lyle Kessler (Samuel French)
Synopsis: Treat, who is streetwise, violent, and continually in trouble with the law, has raised Phillip, his childlike, reclusive younger brother, since their mother's death. Their father deserted the family long ago. Treat gets by primarily through robbing people and committing petty crimes in North Philadelphia. One night, he brings home Harold, a well-dressed drunk he met in a bar, and decides to hold him hostage. Harold, who is an orphan, can't be restrained, however, and the next morning takes over the household, becoming something of a father figure.

Harold evidently has a great deal of money, but it comes from murky, unexplained sources, probably from the Chicago underworld. He buys the brothers clothes, encourages the younger one to expand his horizons, teaches him how to read maps so he'll never be lost again, and hires Treat as his personal body guard. Then during a walk with Treat, some mysterious men from Chicago show up, forcefully take Harold aside, and mortally wound him. He finds his way back to the house and dies, leaving the brothers alone again.
Analysis: This drama has a David Mamet feel and plenty of subtext. Actors need to be comfortable with "street" dynamics and slang. All levels.
Scenes/Monologues: Male Monologues (1), Male/Male Scenes (2)

OTHER PEOPLE'S MONEY
by Jerry Sterner (Samuel French)
Synopsis: Garfinkle wants to take over conservatively run New England Wire and Cable because the company's parts are worth more than its present stock quote. In other words, he wants to buy it, dismantle it, and sell it off piece by piece. The play pits the values of a "green-mailer" against those of an old-school businessman.
Analysis: Well written. Made into a 1991 movie starring Danny DeVito. All levels.
Scenes/Monologues: Male Monologues (2), Female/Female Scenes (1), Male/Female Scenes (2)

OTHERWISE ENGAGED
by Simon Gray (Samuel French)
Synopsis: Simon Hench settles in to listen to his new recording of Wagner's *Parsifal*. But before he can begin enjoying it, the upstairs border drops by; followed by Simon's brother, Stephen, who is anxious about a job promotion; and then Simon's friend, Jeff, who wants to discuss the complications in his love life. In short order, Jeff is followed by Davina, who displays no apparent modesty as she lounges topless while her blouse is drying. Next, Bernard Wood

appears to find out if Simon has in fact seduced his fiancée (he has). Then Simon's wife, Beth, comes home from a tryst and asks for a divorce. All of this happens in about an hour and a half. Simon never does get to listen to "Parsifal."

Analysis: Biting, frequently mean comedy. Written in the British vernacular. All levels.

Scenes/Monologues: Female Monologues (1), Male/Male Scenes (1), Male/Female Scenes (1)

OUR LADY OF THE TORTILLA

by Luis Santeiro (Dramatists Play Service)

Synopsis: Dolores finds an image of the Virgin Mary in a slab of tortilla dough, bringing excitement and notoriety to the home she shares with sister, Dahlia, and her sons, Eddy and Nelson. Nelson is embarrassed by the implications of the discovery because his very non-Hispanic college girlfriend is visiting. Eddy, on the other hand, wants to exploit the event to make a quick buck.

Analysis: This good-natured comedy, with its cast of appealingly eccentric Hispanic characters, has been widely produced since it first appeared in 1987. All levels.

Scenes/Monologues: Three-Person Scenes (2)

PAINTING CHURCHES

by Tina Howe (Samuel French)

Synopsis: Artist Margaret (Mags) Church comes home to Boston to paint a portrait of her elderly parents, Fanny and Gardner. Her father is becoming senile, so he and Fanny are packing to move from their large old house to a small, more manageable cottage. Against this background of packing and painting, the three family members come to see each other in new, more respectful terms.

Analysis: This gem is beautifully written. Unfortunately, it doesn't contain any two-character scenes involving the daughter. Fanny does, however, have one lovely monologue. All levels.

Scenes/Monologues: Female Monologues (1)

PHILADELPHIA STORY, THE

by Philip Barry (Samuel French)

Synopsis: Tracy Lord, of the Philadelphia Lords, married and quickly divorced C. K. Dexter Haven last year, and is going to marry successful, self-made businessperson George Kittredge this weekend. A gossip magazine sends a reporter and a female photographer to cover the society wedding, and Tracy winds up in a moonlit romantic encounter with the reporter. The next morning, which is the day of the wedding, everything gets worked out: Tracy and her fiancé decide to call off their marriage, the reporter proposes, Tracy demurs at first, and—surprise of surprises—Tracy remarries Dexter!

Analysis: The moral of this play is that the rich are as decent as the rest of us. This was, of course, a major vehicle for Katharine Hepburn. *The Philadelphia Story* ran for more than 400 performances on Broadway and, in 1940, was turned into one of Hollywood's most famous comedies. All levels.

Scenes/Monologues: Male/Female Scenes (1)

PIANO LESSON, THE

by August Wilson (Plume)

Synopsis: The action is set in Pittsburgh, 1936. Boy Willie wants to buy the land down south that his ancestors used to work as slaves, but he needs to first sell the old, ornately carved family piano to raise the initial investment. But Boy Willie's sister, Berniece, has possession of the instrument and won't hear of selling it. She points out that there is too much family history in those carvings, and that if you don't have history, you don't have anything.

Analysis: Winner of the 1990 Pulitzer Prize. The entire cast is African American. All levels.

Scenes/Monologues: Male Monologues (4), Male/Female Scenes (1)

PICK UP AX
by Anthony Clarvoe (Broadway Play Publishing)
Synopsis: The action of this play is set in the early 1980s against the background of the California's Silicon Valley software industry. *Pick Up Ax* is about Keith, a brilliant "Deadhead" computer nerd, and his business partner, Brian. They transformed their company from a garage-type operation into a multimillion-dollar corporation, but now it is falling apart. Keith's brain seems to be slowing down, Brian's business acumen is failing, they can't compete with the Big Boys for the limited availability of microchips, and their prospects look quite dim.

Then Nick shows up. Thinking that he has a couple of suckers on the line, he befriends Keith and Brian. Nick convinces them to bribe the microchip suppliers into delivering the goods. But when he tries to take over Keith and Brian's company, he gets a big surprise. It turns out that Keith knows a thing or two about intrigue and trickery from playing the game "Dungeons and Dragons."
Analysis: This 1990 comedy/drama is unusual because of its milieu. It was developed in San Francisco at the old Eureka Theatre, the same place that developed *Angels in America*. All levels.
Scenes/Monologues: Male Monologues (1), Male/Male Scenes (3), Three-Person Scenes (1)

PICNIC
by William Inge (Dramatists Play Service)
Synopsis: On the day of the big Labor Day picnic in a small Kansas town, Madge Owens is swept off her feet by Hal Carter, a handsome, earthy drifter. Suddenly, her picture-perfect life, complete with plans to marry the town's most eligible bachelor, is turned upside down; at the final curtain, she leaves home to follow Hal into an uncertain future. Against the same background, single schoolteacher Rosemary Sydney finally succeeds in getting Howard Bevens to agree to marry her.
Analysis: Winner of the 1953 Pulitzer Prize and later adapted for a movie, William Inge's play is romantic and poetic. All levels.
Scenes/Monologues: Male/Female Scenes (2)

PIZZA MAN
by Darlene Craviotto (Samuel French)
Synopsis: Julie and Alice are frustrated by their careers and romantic lives. In a moment of misguided impulse, they decide to pick a man, any man, and rape him. They select the pizza-delivery guy as a good victim and begin an awkward seduction. When that doesn't work, Julie and Alice turn more violent, tying up the man. Finally, after much back-and-forth discussion about the respective options for men and women in this world, the women release the man unharmed.
Analysis: Rape is rough subject matter to build a comedy on, and Darlene Craviotto's effort might not be justified. Still, she has created some interesting possibilities for scene work, and the larger issues of violence and power are worth examining on their own merits. For sophisticated actors.
Scenes/Monologues: Female Monologues (1), Female/Female Scenes (1) Three-Person Scenes (1)

PLAY MEMORY
by Joanna M. Glass (Samuel French)
Synopsis: The sad plot of *Play Memory* is offset by a deft, frequently humorous and skillful theatrical presentation. A family in Saskatoon, Saskatchewan, Canada, is torn apart by the husband's stubborn refusal to rebuild his life after he is betrayed by three friends in 1944. He goes into an alcoholic decline for 10 years, moving steadily from prosperity to poverty, and dragging his wife, Ruth, and their young daughter, Jean, with him. The relentless descent finally ends when Ruth and Jean leave the husband in 1955, moving to a safe, nonviolent home.

After they go, he trades the kitchen stove for more liquor, locks the front door, and proceeds to drink himself to death. The women become adult survivors. This play, which is about memory, is told in flashback sequences. So when the audience first meets Ruth and Jean, they've developed a sense of humor about their lives.

Analysis: Hal Prince's 1984 production was nominated for a Tony. For sophisticated actors.

Scenes/Monologues: Male Monologues (2), Female Monologues (1), Male/Female Scenes (2)

PORCH

by Jeffrey Sweet (Samuel French)

Synopsis: Amy has traveled from New York City to her small midwestern hometown to be with her widower father when he undergoes exploratory surgery. Their conversation on the front porch of the old house quickly exposes the reasons why she has stayed away all these years. Amy is a disappointment to her father. He reflects on the untimely death of his only son 10 years ago and voices regret that Amy won't carry on the small family business or have children.

Then Sam, Amy's high-school flame, drops by unexpectedly. As she quickly surmises, her father arranged this get-together in the hope that those long-cold sparks might fly again, resulting in perhaps a grandchild for him. Even though Sam still has feelings for Amy, she has no interest in taking up with him again. Furthermore, Amy still believes that her decision to have an abortion after Sam made her pregnant while they were in school was the right one.

Analysis: Not much physical action in this 1979 one-act play, but Jeffrey Sweet writes terrific dialogue with plenty of emotional subtext. All levels.

Scenes/Monologues: Female Monologues (1), Male/Female Scenes (3)

PRELUDE TO A KISS

by Craig Lucas (Broadway Play Publishing)

Synopsis: A very old man, living out the final chapter of his life and distressed by the recent death of his wife, happens upon Rita and Peter's wedding. The man joins the festivities, kisses Rita, and, magically, his spirit moves into her body, and her spirit into his. Peter then goes on his honeymoon with the woman who looks like Rita but who is suddenly behaving like the old man. By the time they return home, Peter has figured out that a switch has taken place. So he orchestrates another meeting between Rita and the old man, hoping that the transformation can be reversed. Success! Their spirits are switched back, and the young couple begin their marriage all over again. The old man, meanwhile, faces his mortality with dignity.

Analysis: The reversal-of-bodies theatrical device is one of the most unusual you'll ever encounter. Having a young woman's personality in an old man's body, and vice versa, leads to some charming and funny encounters. Most scenes are quite short. Nominated for a Tony Award in 1990 and turned into a 1992 movie starring Alec Baldwin and Meg Ryan. All levels.

Scenes/Monologues: Male Monologues (1), Male/Female Scenes (1), Three-Person Scenes (2)

PRIMARY ENGLISH CLASS, THE

by Israel Horovitz (Dramatists Play Service)

Synopsis: Debbie Wastba attempts to teach English as a foreign language to a roomful of adult students who not only don't understand a word she is saying, but also don't understand each other. Members of the class include a Polish man, an Italian man, a French man, a German man, a Chinese woman, and a Japanese woman. Only Wastba speaks English, and her modus operandi is to teach English by "total immersion." This means that she refuses to speak any language except English to her students. The result: a comedy based on confusion.

Analysis: This 1976 play is actually a comment on the insensitivity of Americans to other cultures. Hysterically funny, but no scene possibilities. All levels.

Scenes/Monologues: Female Monologues (1)

PRISONER OF SECOND AVENUE, THE

by Neil Simon (Samuel French)

Synopsis: Mel is having a midlife crisis. He has high blood pressure; takes valium to relax; hates living in New York City with its endless labor strikes, irate neighbors, and general hassles; and hates the small, overpriced apartment on Second Avenue he shares with his wife, Edna. And when Mel can't find a new job after being fired from the ad agency he works for, he suffers a nervous breakdown. Expensive therapy doesn't help him recover, nor do well-intentioned visits from his brother and sisters. Finally, however, Mel decides to fight back against the system, to no longer be a victim. At the final curtain, the audience knows that he and Edna will survive, but they still seem beleaguered.

Analysis: An in-your-face, one-liner, zinger comedy hung on a simplistic plot. In other words, vintage Neil Simon: good material for actors who want to work on comedy. The play received the customary slew of Tony nominations in 1972, and Mike Nichols won for Best Director. All levels.

Scenes/Monologues: Male/Female Scenes (1)

PRIVATE LIVES

by Noël Coward (Samuel French)

Synopsis: Elyot and Sybil are on their honeymoon in the south of France. The terrace of their hotel room overlooks the water, moonlight pours in—the perfect picture of bliss. Then Elyot discovers that his ex-wife, Amanda, and her new husband are honeymooning in the adjacent hotel room. Naturally, all hell breaks loose. Amanda and Elyot fall into one another's arms, admitting they never should have broken up in the first place. They unceremoniously abandon their respective new spouses and head for Paris and an even-more-romantic reunion. For a while, it is touch and go, with Elyot and Amanda reverting to their former love/hate relationship. Then their respective ex-newlywed spouses show up in Paris, and all hell breaks loose all over again. In the end, however, Elyot and Amanda decide to stay together forever.

Analysis: Noël Coward is at his best in this 1930 honey of a comedy. He and Gertrude Lawrence became the toast of two continents for their portrayals of Elyot and Amanda. Appropriate for all levels, but novice American actors, particularly those at the high-school or university level, may have trouble with the worldliness of the characters, the high-comedy tone, and the sharp repartee.

Scenes/Monologues: Male/Female Scenes (4)

PROMISE, THE

by José Rivera (Broadway Play Publishing)

Synopsis: Set in the backyard of Guzman's working-class home in Patchogue, New York, the central events in this delightfully theatrical play involve Lilia's wedding to a man she doesn't love and her father's commitment to winning independence for Puerto Rico. Mainly, however, *The Promise* is a mélange, mixing pageantry, magic, superstition, possession by spirits, and religion; the playwright refers to this style as "magical realism."

Analysis: A striking work by an increasingly important playwright, *The Promise* unfortunately contains no scene work. Two monologues, however, are excellent for scene-study work. All characters are Hispanic. All levels.

Scenes/Monologues: Male Monologues (1), Female Monologues (1)

PROPOSAL, THE

by Anton Chekhov [*The Sneeze, Plays and Stories* by Anton Chekhov, translated and adapted by Michael Frayn (Samuel French)]

Synopsis: Lomov has finally gotten up enough nerve to ask Natalya Stepanovna to marry him. He puts on his finest suit and makes the trip to the neighboring farm that she lives on.

Alone with his beloved, Lomov begins his proposal with an itemized list of his assets, primary among which is Ox Lea Meadows, the property he lives on. Natalya points out that the property isn't really his, that in fact it belongs to her family. He begs to differ and before you know it, they're involved in an argument and the proposal is no longer on the table.

Natalya's father joins the fray, Lomov storms out, everyone calms down, and Lomov comes back to try again. This time, however, he and Natalya start arguing about who has the better hunting dog. Finally, Lomov faints dead away from the sheer anxiety of it all. This alarms the father, who presumes that Lomov is actually dead. Suddenly, Lomov revives and before anything else can go wrong, Natalya's father urges the disoriented lovers to make the leap into marriage. They kiss. Curtain.

Analysis: Anyone who thinks that Anton Chekhov can't be funny needs to read this hysterical one-act play. All levels.

Scenes and Monologues: Male/Female Scenes (1), Three-Person Scenes (1)

P. S. YOUR CAT IS DEAD

by James Kirkwood [revised edition (Samuel French)]

Synopsis: Vito, a bisexual burglar with a good sense of humor, breaks into Jimmy's apartment in New York City's Greenwich Village on New Year's Eve—the very night that his girlfriend, Kate, has chosen to leave him. Surprised by Kate and Jimmy's return to the apartment, Vito hides under the bed and eavesdrops on their problems. After Kate leaves, Jimmy discovers Vito, overpowers him, and ties him up. All of this is the setup for the two men to get to know one another. By the final curtain, Jimmy and Vito have become friends and potential lovers.

Analysis: This very offbeat comedy is quite black at times. Playwright James Kirkwood says that it is "a play about two losers who meet at a certain crucial time in their lives. Will they help each other?" Sal Mineo played Vito in his last role. For sophisticated actors.

Scenes/Monologues: Male Monologues (1), Male/Male Scenes (1), Male/Female Scenes (1)

RAINMAKER, THE

by N. Richard Nash (Samuel French)

Synopsis: A con man named Starbuck arrives in a drought-stricken western town one August and promises to make it rain. The Curry family pays him $100 to do just that, and within the next 24 hours, he makes believers of everyone. In the process, Starbuck teaches the Currys' plain daughter, Lizzie, to believe in herself. This new relationship also deeply affects Starbuck, and after a night of lovemaking, he admits to Lizzie that he is a con artist.

Analysis: A wonderful 1954 romantic comedy. The roles are bold and colorful; the play, an actor's delight. All levels.

Scenes/Monologues: Male Monologues (1), Male/Female Scenes (3)

RAISIN IN THE SUN, A

by Lorraine Hansberry (Samuel French)

Synopsis: Big Walter Younger worked hard all his life to keep his insurance premiums paid, and now that he is dead, the members of his family are torn about how to spend the $10,000 payout. This was a significant amount of money in 1958. Walter Lee, Big Walter's son, sees himself becoming a big businessperson by investing the money in a liquor store. Mama, Big Walter's widow, would rather escape the Chicago ghetto by making a down payment on a nice home somewhere. With the money left over, she wants to pay for daughter Beneatha's college education. Walter's wife, Ruth, favors getting the house, primarily so that their son, Travis, can have a better life. Naturally, Beneatha wants the money to go toward her education so she that can serve humanity by becoming a doctor.

After acrimonious debate, Mama secretly makes a down payment on a house in a white neighborhood. When Walter finds out what she has done, he drinks himself into a stupor. Seeing his reaction, Mama has misgivings about her actions and entrusts the rest of the money to him. She tells him to go ahead and buy the liquor store, but to be sure to save part of the money for Beneatha. Walter gives the money to his would-be partner, who promptly skips town with it. Just as suddenly as the money appeared, it is gone. The only part the family still has is the amount Mama used for the down payment on the house.

Then Karl Lindner, a representative from the white community where the house is located, arrives. He offers the Youngers a bribe not to move into his neighborhood. At first Walter is tempted to accept the bribe but when the family unites against the offer, he stands up to Karl, telling him that the Youngers will move in anyway.

Analysis: *A Raisin in the Sun,* the first Broadway play written by an African-American woman, was also the first to be directed by an African-American man, Lloyd Richards. It won the 1959 New York Drama Critics Circle Award for Best Play and was made into a movie with Sidney Poitier, who also portrayed Walter Lee on stage. All levels.

Scenes/Monologues: Male Monologues (3), Male/Female Scenes (1), Three-Person Scenes (1)

RED COAT, THE

by John Patrick Shanley [*Welcome to the Moon and Other Plays* (Dramatists Play Service); *13 by Shanley* (Applause)]

Synopsis: Although 17-year-old John is at a festive party, he still feels lonely. He goes outside to sit in the light of the full moon. Mary, who is 16, arrives, and they talk. Their conversation quickly becomes an exultant declaration of mutual love.

Analysis: John Patrick Shanley is best known as the author of the 1987 film comedy *Moonstruck,* and the same kind of moon magic is at work here. Very innocent. All levels.

Scenes/Monologues: Male/Female Scenes (1)

REDWOOD CURTAIN

by Lanford Wilson (Hill & Wang/Noonday)

Synopsis: Seventeen-year-old Geri Riordan was born in Vietnam to a Vietnamese woman and a white American man but was adopted and reared by a wealthy couple in California. Thoroughly American and highly educated, Geri is a music prodigy on her way to Juilliard for advanced training and then recording contracts. She longs for her natural father, however, and spends each summer wandering through the northern California redwoods where thousands of Vietnam veterans have taken refuge. The play revolves around her meeting with one of these men.

Analysis: A well-intentioned 1993 near-miss. Although the play is too metaphoric for scene work, there is an excellent monologue for an Asian-American actress. All levels.

Scenes/Monologues: Female Monologues (1)

REUNION

by David Mamet (Samuel French)

Synopsis: A father and daughter reunite after a 20-year separation. During this mostly quiet and tentatively probing conversation, which takes place in Bernie's apartment, they try to fill in the blanks. He is no longer drinking, but alcoholism has taken a terrible toll on his life; Carol is married to a man who has two children from an earlier marriage. Bernie regrets missing his brother's funeral, and Carol is close to her half-sister. Bernie has settled into a blue-collar restaurant job and is about to remarry; Carol smokes too much, and her sex life isn't great.

Analysis: A deceptively simple 1976 one-act play that will stick with you. David Mamet has captured the essence of the father-daughter relationship. All levels.

Scenes/Monologues: Male/Female Scenes (2)

ROAD TO NIRVANA

by Arthur Kopit (Samuel French)

Synopsis: Arthur Kopit extends satire to its grotesque extreme as he takes viewers into a world where a common locker-room vulgarity ("I'd give my left ball for a piece of that deal") becomes the literal price of doing business in Hollywood. Al and Lou, former producer/partners, reunite to produce the filmed autobiography of rock's biggest female star, Nirvana (who is a ringer for Madonna). What Jerry doesn't know is that Nirvana's loyalty test—and her price for anchoring the deal—is whether or not he'll give up a testicle, or preferably both of them. Al, as it turns out, gave her one of his just to get the option, which is actually a recopied, erotic version of Melville's *Moby Dick*.

Analysis: With this plot, Arthur Kopit was courting censorship trouble from the start, and he got it. *Road to Nirvana* has met with extremes of both protest and praise wherever it has played. Kopit, a serious and consistent contributor to American theater and arguably one of its finest playwrights, is the author of such works as *Oh Dad, Poor Dad, Mamma's Hung You in the Closet and I'm Feelin' So Sad, Indians, Wings,* and *End of the World.* Be warned that every scene in this play contains graphic images and plenty of vulgarity. All levels.

Scenes/Monologues: Male/Male Scenes (3), Male/Female Scenes (1)

ROSENCRANTZ AND GUILDENSTERN ARE DEAD

by Tom Stoppard (Samuel French)

Synopsis: Turning *Hamlet* upside down, Tom Stoppard has made stars of two minor characters and supporting players of Hamlet, Gertrude, Claudius, Polonius, Ophelia, Laertes, and the rest. Most of the time, Rosencrantz and Guildenstern don't know where they are or why they are there. All they understand is that they were "sent for" because they are Hamlet's old school chums. After the players act out *The Murder of Gonzago* and Hamlet kills Polonius, the hapless pair escort him to England, where he presumably will be executed. Then they discover that the letter they're carrying to the King of England demands their own immediate execution. Rosencrantz and Guildenstern don't realize that Hamlet has switched it in order to escape his own death. The events are all predetermined, and Rosencrantz and Guildenstern have no say in the matter.

Analysis: Clever is too modest a word for this 1967 delight, which immediately placed Tom Stoppard on the map as a major talent. The philosophical floor of the play is best summed up by one of the players: "Uncertainty is the normal state." All levels.

Scenes/Monologues: Male Monologues (2), Male/Male Scenes (2)

SAN ANTONIO SUNSET

by Willy Holtzman [*The Best Short Plays of 1988–1989,* edited by Ramon Delgado (Applause)]

Synopsis: Set in 1936, an era of 78 RPM records. Mr. Stone, a white talent scout for a big-city record company, checks into a San Antonio hotel to record Mr. Johnson, a local African-American blues singer. The resulting record sells well up north (although Johnson gets almost none of the profits), so Stone returns the following year to record another one. By the third year of their partnership, Stone is ready to take Johnson to New York for a Carnegie Hall performance. When Stone arrives, however, he discovers that Johnson has been killed in a barroom fight.

Analysis: This very short three-scene play was part of Manhattan's Working Theatre 1987 One-Act Festival. Good regional feel to the dialogue; two different worlds looking at each other. All levels.

Scenes/Monologues: Male/Male Scenes (1)

SCENES AND REVELATIONS

by Elan Garonzik (Samuel French)

Synopsis: The drama opens in 1894 on a Pennsylvania farm as four sisters are about to depart for England and Uncle Jacob's inheritance rather than follow the popular western migration.

In 19 short scenes, the action covers the preceding years and finally returns to the farm in 1894. Along the way, the women fall in love, decide whether or not to pursue careers, and have children. When Uncle Jacob dies, leaving them a fortune in British textile mills, they head for the boat.

Analysis: Innocent, earnest dialogue and scenes, kind of like a dramatic *Oklahoma!* without the music. All levels.

Scenes/Monologues: Female Monologues (1), Male/Female Scenes (3)

SCENES FROM AMERICAN LIFE

by A. R. Gurney, Jr. (Samuel French)

Synopsis: Spanning the years from 1930 to 1970, the play tracks generational changes in an upper-class WASP family in Buffalo, New York. Most of the scenes are very short and flow into one another, with actors playing multiple roles.

Analysis: A. R. Gurney, Jr. takes potshots at hypocritical attitudes and behavior in America in this breezy offering, which is really a series of unrelated scenes from American life united under a single title. As always, he is a master when it comes to writing dialogue. All levels.

Scenes/Monologues: Female Monologues (2), Female/Female Scenes (1)

SEA GULL, THE

by Anton Chekhov [a new version by Jean-Claude Van Itallie (Dramatists Play Service)]

Synopsis: Playwright Anton Chekhov described *The Sea Gull* as "a comedy with three female parts, six male, a landscape, much talk about literature, little action, and tons of love." A modern reader will have difficulty understanding how this play, in which Konstantine, one of the central characters, commits suicide could be called a comedy at all. Indeed, nothing seems to encourage laughter. It is important to understand that the comedy is that of posturing, a study of tedious people who don't know they're being tedious.

Analysis: First produced in 1889, *The Sea Gull* made both Anton Chekhov and the Moscow Art Theatre famous. It was his first attempt at a play of "indirect action," in which the psychology of the characters takes precedence over the action. The complex characters were a perfect marriage for Stanislavski's new acting techniques, which were designed to find "inner truth, the truth of feeling and experience." All levels.

Scenes/Monologues: Male Monologues (2), Female Monologues (1), Male/Female Scenes (1)

SEA HORSE, THE

by Edward J. Moore (Samuel French)

Synopsis: Gertrude Blum is the owner/proprietor of The Sea Horse, a small-town saloon on the California coast. It is a rough place, catering to seamen only—not to their women. Gertrude herself is a big woman, weighing some 200 pounds, fat but firm. She runs the bar with an iron hand, laughing and cussing with the best of them and taking the occasional favorite upstairs for the night. For the past year, she has been sharing her bed with Harry Bales whenever he is in port. Harry has come to adore her and wants to marry her. The play explores their evolving relationship and attempts at intimacy.

Analysis: Originally written as an exercise in Uta Hagen's New York City acting class, *The Sea Horse* went on to be published and to win the 1974 Vernon Rice Drama Desk Award for Outstanding New Playwright. All levels.

Scenes/Monologues: Male Monologues (1), Female Monologues (1), Male/Female Scenes (2)

SEXUAL PERVERSITY IN CHICAGO

by David Mamet (Samuel French)

Synopsis: A fast-moving, one-act play that explores the deceits of the dating game. Danny and Bernard are very much into women, but their methods with them are radically different.

Danny, an assistant office manager, is a nice guy who treats women with respect while his buddy and co-worker Bernard thinks the way to women's hearts is to "treat 'em like shit." The action of the play takes place during a couple of months when the men are dating two roommates, Joan and Deborah. Bernard may think he is hip and knows all the moves, but it is nice-guy Danny who winds up connecting, if only for a brief sexual moment, with Deborah. In the end, the men return to girl-watching, and the women continue as roommates.
Analysis: This dark 1974 comedy with its rough language is vintage Mamet. It is interesting to note how this hugely talented writer's treatment of women has evolved since this early effort brought him fame. The scenes are short. All levels.
Scenes/Monologues: Male/Male Scenes (2), Male/Female Scenes (1)

SHADOW BOX, THE
by Michael Cristofer (Samuel French)
Synopsis: The action occurs in three cottages on the grounds of a large hospital in California. Terminally ill patients are allowed to use the cottages for visits with their families. Joe is using Cottage Number One to spend some time with his wife and 14-year-old son. Brian is living with his lover, Mark, in Cottage Number Two and receives an unexpected visit from his ex-wife. Felicity and her daughter are in Cottage Number Three. The play explores the complex relationships that become more complex—or simpler—as death approaches.
Analysis: This beautiful drama won both the 1977 Tony Award and Pulitzer Prize for Best Play. All levels.
Scenes/Monologues: Male Monologues (1), Female Monologues (3), Male/Female Scenes (4)

SHIRLEY VALENTINE
by Willy Russell (Michelin House, London)
Synopsis: Shirley Valentine, a 42-year-old Liverpool housewife with two grown children and a complacent husband goes on an impulsive fortnight vacation in sun-drenched Greece, has a romance with a Zorba-like tavern owner, and decides not to return home. In the process, she takes stock of her life, marriage, and unrealized dreams.
Analysis: Shirley is the only character in this insightful and touching comedy. *Shirley Valentine* won England's Olivier Award for Best Comedy, and Pauline Collins won a Tony for Best Actress during the 1989 Broadway run. Written in the British vernacular. All levels.
Scenes/Monologues: Female Monologues (2)

SHIVAREE
by William Mastrosimone (Samuel French)
Synopsis: Chandler is a hemophiliac living in seclusion, protected from the world by his domineering mother. Shivaree, a southern belly dancer, sublets an apartment in the building across the way and strikes up a relationship with Chandler, much to his mother's chagrin.
Analysis: The very talented Mastrosimone must have been in a strange place when he wrote this odd comedy. Like *Oh Dad, Poor Dad, Mamma's Hung You in the Closet and I'm Feelin' So Sad,* the characters have little direct conflict, and the transitions are difficult to justify. Overall, not a good choice for scene work, but Shivaree's monologue is excellent. All levels.
Scenes/Monologues: Female Monologues (1)

SIGHT UNSEEN
by Donald Margulies (Dramatists Play Service)
Synopsis: On the occasion of his first major exhibit outside of North America, artist Jonathan Waxman looks up his former lover, Patricia, who is now married and living with her archaeologist husband, Nick, in Norfolk, England. Although 15 years have passed, Jonathan finds that

Patricia is still smarting from the way he dropped her, and that Nick has no use for him at all, professionally or personally. Jonathan's visit with Patricia provides a platform for revisiting their early days together, going over the reasons why they broke up, including the incompatibility between his Jewish heritage and her Gentile background. Jonathan is also forced to defend his artistic integrity and financial success when attacked by Nick and, later at the exhibit, by a German art critic/interviewer.

Analysis: Winner of the 1992 Obie Award for Best New American Play, *Sight Unseen* works on several levels and is structurally very clever. It is a broad, intellectual debate about the merits of art, set against a background of a failed love affair and mixed with questions about Jewish assimilation. All levels.

Scenes/Monologues: Male Monologues (3), Male/Male Scenes (1), Male/Female Scenes (2), Three-Person Scenes (1)

SIGN IN SIDNEY BRUSTEIN'S WINDOW, THE
by Lorraine Hansberry (Samuel French)

Synopsis: The evolution of Iris and Sidney's relationship is the spine of this play even though it has plot lines involving politics, publishing, and prostitution. Sidney is a committed and arguably naive liberal. Iris is an aspiring actress, coming to terms with the reality that she has, at best, average talent. In the end, although they break up, there is a possibility that they'll get back together.

Analysis: Playwright Lorraine Hansberry was probably trying to do too many things with this drama, which closed on Broadway on January 12, 1965, the day she died. Dated now, the play is kind of an afterthought of 1950s intellectualism and the Beat Generation, complete with such expressions as "dig," "hipster," and "chick"; however, the scenes still ring true and are excellent for workshop study. All levels.

Scenes/Monologues: Male Monologues (1), Female Monologues (1), Male/Female Scenes (3)

SILENT NIGHT, LONELY NIGHT
by Robert Anderson (Samuel French)

Synopsis: Katherine and John first meet in a New England inn on Christmas Eve when they discover that they occupy adjoining rooms. She is distressed because her husband, who is in England on a business trip, has been having affairs. John is sad because his wife has been institutionalized for insanity for the last five years. Both of them are lonely, needing to be held and loved, and near dawn they finally give in to this yearning. The next day, Katherine leaves for England with her son, and John returns to the vigil he keeps with his wife. No regrets.

Analysis: In the end, this lovely 1959 play, which starred Henry Fonda, evokes a poetic, adult mood. The main characters are the kind of vaguely well-off, educated people that seem to populate a number of plays from the 1950s. Viewers get the sense that the characters spend a great deal of time gazing reflectively out the picture window at the freshly fallen snow as they sip a Scotch and water. All levels.

Scenes/Monologues: Male/Female Scenes (2)

SISTER MARY IGNATIUS EXPLAINS IT ALL FOR YOU
by Christopher Durang (Dramatists Play Service)

Synopsis: The title of this play says it all. Sister Mary Ignatius, a Catholic nun, lectures the audience on the pros, cons, and history of the world from a Catholic perspective. Some of her former students appear to talk about how the nun's teachings have affected them, but the focus of the play is the Sister's lectures.

Analysis: Wonderful one-act satire of Catholicism. All levels.

Scenes/Monologues: Female Monologues (1)

SIX DEGREES OF SEPARATION
by John Guare (Dramatists Play Service)
Synopsis: Paul, a young, charming African-American man, maneuvers his way into the lives of Louisa and Flanders Kittredge and two other high-living, white New York families, masquerading each time as the son of famous actor Sidney Poitier. In each case, once Paul's deception is discovered and he has disappeared, no one can figure out what possible motive he could have had for carrying out such a charade because he didn't steal any valuable property. The mystery deepens when Paul befriends Rick and Elizabeth, a couple of aspiring actors, this time pretending to be Flanders Kittredge's illegitimate son.

In short order, Paul seduces Rick, who has never before had a homosexual experience and cons him out of all the money he and Elizabeth saved, $250. When Rick realizes he has been duped, he commits suicide. After Paul's escapades show up in a newspaper article, he telephones the Kittredge residence, claiming remorse and saying that he wants to go straight. Even more, he wants Flanders to be his mentor, training him to buy and sell fine art. Louisa and Flanders agree to help Paul, but when they go to meet him at a prearranged location, he isn't there. They never see him again.
Analysis: This clever, fast-moving comedy-drama is crammed with metaphor, ultimately becoming a comment on identity, pretension, and America's supposed classless society. The plot is presented in flashback, narrated by Louisa and Flanders, one quick scene melding into another on an open stage. Playwright John Guare based the work on an actual New York episode. For sophisticated actors.
Scenes/Monologues: Male Monologues (1), Female Monologues (1)

SNOWANGEL
by Lewis John Carlino [*Cages* (Dramatists Play Service)]
Synopsis: Connie is a prostitute, so she presumes that John wants to have sex when he shows up at her shabby hotel room on the Lower East Side at 4 A.M. Soon, however, she discovers that he longs for more than that. John wants true romance and affection, and he expects her to reenact the first meeting he had years ago with the only woman he ever loved. Connie resists this charade, drinking heavily as he continues to elaborately set the stage. Finally, the fantasy falls apart as she turns on John, demanding that he honor her memory of the first time she was in love. He then begins to reenact her fantasy.
Analysis: A poetic, frequently moving 1963 one-act drama. Good material for sophisticated actors.
Scenes/Monologues: Female Monologues (1), Male/Female Scenes (2)

SOCIAL EVENT, A
by William Inge [*Eleven Short Plays by William Inge* (Dramatists Play Service)]
Synopsis: Randy and Carole, two up-and-coming Hollywood actors, consider it imperative that they be "seen" at the funeral of a star even though they didn't care very much about him. They've been trying unsuccessfully to get an invitation to the funeral when they discover that their very own maid has been invited. They use double talk to get the sweet woman to let them go to the funeral with her.
Analysis: A delightful trifle, all of 10 pages long, from William Inge. Actors will recognize that industry pretensions are timeless. All levels.
Scenes/Monologues: Male/Female Scenes (1)

SOCIAL SECURITY
by Andrew Bergman (Samuel French)
Synopsis: Sophie, who is 70 years old, has been passed from one daughter to another and currently resides with Barbara and her husband in their fancy Fifth Avenue apartment in New York City. Barbara and David are successful art dealers with their own gallery, and they run with

the heavy hitters. Unpretentious Sophie, meanwhile, would be happiest with the Long Island oldsters. Sophie unexpectedly falls for one of their elderly artist friends, becoming youthful and lusty again in the process. As the play ends, they are about to move to Paris.

Analysis: A lightweight 1986 comedy, directed by Mike Nichols, aimed squarely at the Wednesday matinee crowd. All levels.

Scenes/Monologues: Female/Female Scenes (1)

SORROWS OF STEPHEN
by Peter Parnell (Samuel French)

Synopsis: Stephen loves Christine, and Christine loves Stephen. Christine also loves William, Stephen's best friend. In the end, Christine marries William, leaving Stephen to read Balzac instead of Goethe. All characters are contemporary, upwardly mobile, educated, witty New Yorkers.

Analysis: From today's not-so-innocent perspective, this 1980 comedy is actually kind of sweet because of the way the characters fall into and out of bed so easily. All levels.

Scenes/Monologues: Male/Male Scenes (1), Male/Female Scenes (4)

SPEED OF DARKNESS, THE
by Steve Tesich (Samuel French)

Synopsis: Joe is a successful South Dakota businessperson who is about to be named Man of the Year. His old Vietnam buddy Lou visits unexpectedly, bringing to the surface 20 years of buried war horrors. Lou winds up committing suicide, and Joe comes to terms somewhat with his demons and his family.

Analysis: A strange and uncomfortable play that has many symbols and hidden secrets. For example, Joe's daughter Mary carries around a bag of dirt as part of a school project, pretending that it is a baby. She and her boyfriend name the "baby" after Lou. Joe, however, isn't actually Mary's father. But Steve Tesich has quite a good ear for dialogue. All levels.

Scenes/Monologues: Male Monologues (1), Male/Male Scenes (1), Male/Female Scenes (1)

SPEED-THE-PLOW
by David Mamet (Samuel French)

Synopsis: Bobby Gould, the head of production for a big Hollywood movie studio, listens favorably to a pitch his longtime friend Charlie Fox is making. The proposed movie, designed for hot star Doug Brown, is sure to make money. Also on Bobby's desk is a book by a serious East Coast writer that deals with radiation, the end of civilization, and eroding values. He gives the radiation book to Karen, his sexy temp, to read, asking for her private and personal recommendation. (Actually, Bobby just wants to sleep with her. Surprise, surprise.) She reads it and convinces Bobby to give the green light to the radiation book rather than the Doug Brown project. Karen then sleeps with Bobby. Charlie flips out when he discovers his pet project is dead. After a violent confrontation with Bobby and a scene with Karen, the projects revert again. At the end, Karen is out, and Charlie is back in with the Doug Brown vehicle.

Analysis: A comic sendup of the Hollywood movie industry. All levels.

Scenes/Monologues: Male/Male Scenes (2), Male/Female Scenes (2)

SPLENDOR IN THE GRASS
by William Inge [adapted by F. Andrew Leslie (Dramatists Play Service)]

Synopsis: Deanie Loomis and Bud Stamper are young lovers whose passions and ambitions are thwarted continually by the prejudices and ignorance of their elders. The action takes place in a small oil-boom town in Kansas during the 1920s.

Analysis: William Inge's popular screenplay makes it to the stage in this adaptation. There is a bang-up scene between Bud and his father, Ace. All levels.

Scenes/Monologues: Male/Male Scenes (1)

SPLIT SECOND
by Dennis McIntyre (Samuel French)
Synopsis: Val Johnson is an African-American cop in New York City. he has a chip on his shoulder and a great deal of resentment toward white society. When a white car thief he has captured and handcuffed begins to spew racial epithets, Val snaps and kills the man, shooting him cleanly through the heart. Then, realizing what he has done, he restages the event to make it look like a case of self defense. Subsequently, Val has scenes with his wife, who urges him to continue with the deception rather than risk jail; his father, a retired cop, who wants him to tell the truth; his buddy, who confesses that he also once killed a man in cold blood; and the investigating officer, who knows Val is lying but can't prove it. At the official hearing (and on the very last page of the script), Val hesitates only briefly, considers changing his story, and then stands by his lie.
Analysis: This 1980 drama has some powerful scenes, even though the basic situation is a dramatic contrivance. Playwright Dennis McIntyre's dialogue rings true. All levels.
Scenes/Monologues: Male/Male Scenes (2), Male/Female Scenes (2)

SPOILS OF WAR
by Michael Weller (Samuel French)
Synopsis: Set in the mid-1950s in New York City, the action in this play centers on 16-year-old Martin's efforts to orchestrate a reconciliation between his parents, who have been separated for 10 years. Before World War II, Elise and Andrew were part of the very active political left, so when he joined the Army and went off to fight, Elise felt betrayed and abandoned. When Andrew returned, he was a changed man in her eyes and part of the "system." She then left with their young son to follow a bohemian way of life. Since then, Andrew has bounced from one vocational pursuit to another, making a pretty good living and grazing in low-commitment romantic relationships. Martin manages to get his parents together at a party, but the meeting turns disastrous. These two ships will continue to pass in the night.
Analysis: If you think you know Michael Weller's work (*Loose Ends, Moonchildren*), this 1989 drama might surprise you. Finely tuned relationships, an interesting backdrop, plenty of passion. Excellent for scene work. All levels.
Scenes/Monologues: Female/Female Scenes (1), Male/Female Scenes (3), Three-Person Scenes (1)

STEEL MAGNOLIAS
by Robert Harling (Dramatists Play Service)
Synopsis: Shelby Eatenton-Latcherie is the prettiest young woman in Chinquapin, Louisiana. She marries the most eligible young man around, and her life would be perfect if she didn't have diabetes. Against her doctor's advice, Shelby has a baby; a short while later, her body begins to fail. Ultimately, she has to have a kidney transplant, and her own mother is the donor. The operation is unsuccessful, and Shelby dies. This is the core plot line that holds *Steel Magnolias* together.
Analysis: The comedy is set in the town beauty parlor and is chock full of southern humor and wisdom, as well as several stereotypical southern women. This play by actor/writer Robert Harling was later made into a successful big-budget 1989 movie, starring Olympia Dukakis, Sally Field, Darryl Hannah, Shirley MacLaine, Dolly Parton, Julia Roberts, and Tom Skerritt. All levels.
Scenes/Monologues: Female Monologues (1), Female/Female Scenes (1)

STILL LIFE
by Emily Mann (Dramatists Play Service)
Synopsis: A 1981 documentary-style play that is unusual in several respects, not the least of which is that the actors don't look at each other until the very final moment. The rest of the time, they individually address the audience, telling overlapping stories about the Vietnam

War and its effects on them. The playwright attempts to connect the violence of the war with violence in our society. Cheryl and Mark are married, and Nadine is his mistress.
Analysis: Although there have been a number of plays about the Vietnam War and its aftermath, many of which attempt to capture the emptiness, futility, and wastefulness associated with the war, *Still Life* is one of the most disturbing and effective. All levels.
Scenes/Monologues: Male Monologues (2), Female Monologues (1)

STRANGE SNOW
by Steve Metcalfe (Samuel French)
Synopsis: Megs and Dave were in Vietnam together and share a deep secret. One day when they were to be dropped by helicopter into a battle, Dave froze in terror, jumped badly, and broke both ankles. Megs was hit by enemy fire when he jumped. Their buddy Bobby came to their aid and was killed. Both men still feel guilty. While Dave has become an alcoholic, Megs has dealt better with his guilt, coming to terms with himself, Bobby, and the war.

One day, years after the war has ended, Megs unexpectedly shows up at the house Dave shares with his sister Martha, explaining he and Dave have a long-established date to go fishing. Martha and Megs are immediately attracted to each other, and Dave just wishes Megs would go away. They work everything out, however, and at the final curtain, the audience knows that Dave will finally emerge from the shadow of his nightmares and that Megs and Martha will be together romantically.
Analysis: One of the better post-Vietnam dramas. Made into the 1989 low-budget movie *Jackknife* starring Kathy Baker, Robert De Niro, and Ed Harris.
Scenes/Monologues: Male/Male Scenes (1), Male/Female Scenes (2)

STRANGEST KIND OF ROMANCE, THE
by Tennessee Williams [*The Theater of Tennessee Williams,* Volume 6 (New Directions)]
Synopsis: A man, referred to throughout the play as "The Little Man," takes a room in a seedy rooming house in the Midwest, and the lonely landlady wants him to satisfy her sexually because her husband is an invalid. The man forms a closer bond, however, with a cat left behind by the last border. A few months after moving in, the man has a nervous breakdown and is hospitalized. When he gets out, he discovers that the woman has rented his room to a new man and, much worse, gotten rid of the cat.
Analysis: An early, thoroughly odd one-act play from Tennessee Williams. Interesting seduction scene. For sophisticated actors.
Scenes/Monologues: Male Monologues (1), Male/Female Scenes (1)

STREETCAR NAMED DESIRE, A
by Tennessee Williams (Dramatists Play Service)
Synopsis: An aging Blanche DuBois, having lost the family plantation and all her money, arrives in New Orleans to visit her younger sister, Stella, who is pregnant and happily married to a crude and forceful working-class man named Stanley Kowalski. Hiding her destitution and the details of her sexually sordid past behind a happy façade and illusions of southern gentility, Blanche immediately has conflicts with Stanley, who sees through her pretensions. She is simultaneously horrified by and attracted to his base ways and animal magnetism, and he is repulsed by her false airs and deceits.

Blanche then sees a last hope for emotional refuge in Stanley's good-hearted co-worker, Harold Mitchell, and sets about seducing the bachelor. Mitch falls hard for Blanche and speaks of marriage but, before that can happen, Stanley unravels the truth about her sexual past. This disclosure destroys her relationship with Mitch and catapults her into an emotional breakdown. After a final confrontation with Stanley that turns sexual, Blanche retreats totally into her fantasy life and must be institutionalized.

Analysis: Tennessee Williams's crown jewel, the best of the best. Winner of the 1948 Pulitzer Prize. All levels.
Scenes/Monologues: Female Monologues (1), Female/Female Scenes (2), Male/Female Scenes (3)

SUBJECT WAS ROSES, THE
by Frank D. Gilroy (Samuel French)
Synopsis: After being discharged from the Army in 1946, Timmy returns to the Bronx apartment where he grew up and where his parents still live. The folks are glad to see him and are grateful that he wasn't killed or injured as so many other soldiers were, so they launch into a round of family parties, dinners out, and visits with relatives. On the surface, the play is the perfect picture of a happy family reunion, but old currents run strong and deadly underneath. Timmy's father, John, is an emotionally distant, penny-pinching, self-made man who exists in a sexless marriage. Nettie, Timmy's mother, is a long-suffering woman whose affection is reserved for her own mother and her cousin. Both parents continually struggle for their son's loyalty. Over the course of the first weekend at home, all of this erupts, culminating with an honest acknowledgement of love and Timmy's decision to move out on his own.
Analysis: This 1964 drama is a dandy. Martin Sheen rose to stardom after playing the son in the 1965 Broadway production, which won a Tony Award for Best Play. All levels.
Scenes/Monologues: Female Monologues (1), Male/Male Scenes (2), Male/Female Scenes (2)

SUBSTANCE OF FIRE, THE
by Jon Robin Baitz (Samuel French)
Synopsis: Issac, a refugee of Nazi-occupied Europe, owns a publishing house in New York City, printing "serious" literary works. Increasingly out of step with the public's fast-food tastes, Kreeger/Geldhart Publishers is on the verge of bankruptcy when Issac's children pool their stock in order to take control and publish more popular material.
Analysis: Urban, ethnic, chic, caustic drama from a bright young playwright. The characters tear at each other with literary references. All levels.
Scenes/Monologues: Male Monologues (2), Male/Female Scenes (1)

SUMMER AND SMOKE
by Tennessee Williams (Dramatists Play Service)
Synopsis: The play is set in Mississippi during the early 1900s. Alma, the town minister's prim and proper daughter, has always loved John, the womanizing, hell-raising son of the local doctor, but she has never declared or acted on her feelings. John goes away to college, returning with a medical degree and is still intent on sowing wild oats and having fun. Ultimately, he is transformed into a caring and talented physician, partly because of Alma's example and partly because his irresponsibility contributes to his father's death. Alma finally decides that her lifestyle of fanatical purity isn't healthy, declares her love to John, and agrees to go to bed with him, but it is too late. He already plans to marry Nellie, a sweet, practical, carefree local woman, formerly one of Alma's piano students. This turn of events changes Alma's life forever.
Analysis: A Tennessee Williams classic that puts the soul and the body into conflict. Alma is smoke, while John is the heat of summer. All levels.
Scenes/Monologues: Female Monologues (2), Female/Female Scenes (1), Male/Female Scenes (3)

SUMMER BRAVE
by William Inge (Dramatists Play Service)
Synopsis: This 1962 work is the final revised edition of William Inge's successful play *Picnic*. Set in Kansas, this is the exact same story about Madge and her romance with Hal, a handsome rogue. The only differences between *Summer Brave* and *Picnic* is that this later play is a bit more cinematic in style.

Analysis: William Inge, like Tennessee Williams, enjoyed tinkering with his plays long after they were produced. In the case of *Summer Brave*, Inge was clearly influenced by the film adaptation of his original play and tried to incorporate some of the elements that worked in the movie. However, he was only moderately successful. All levels.
Scenes/Monologues: Male/Male Scenes (1)

SWAN SONG

by Anton Chekhov [*The Sneeze, Plays and Stories* by Anton Chekhov, translated and adapted by Michael Frayn (Samuel French)]
Synopsis: The acting company has left the theater for the evening when Svetlovidov, an elderly comic actor, wakes from a nap and walks out onto the stage. The only other person remaining in the building is the prompter. The two men discuss the life of an actor.
Analysis: One of Anton Chekhov's first popular successes in the theater, adapted from one of his own short stories, *Calchas*. Charming and ultimately moving. Like all of Michael Frayn's adaptations of Chekhov, this is glorious. All levels.
Scenes/Monologues: Male Monologues (2)

SWEET BIRD OF YOUTH

by Tennessee Williams (Dramatists Play Service)
Synopsis: Chance Wayne still has his chorus-line good looks even though he is in his late twenties. The aspiring actor and sometime gigolo arrives in his hometown of St. Cloud as the "escort" of Princess Kosmonopolis, better known to the world as the aging actress Alexandra Del Lago. Chance plans to parlay Alexandra's Hollywood influence into important introductions out west and a ticket out of Louisiana for his true and only love, Heavenly Finley. But her father, a corrupt segregationist politician, has put word out to kill or castrate Chance if he is caught because he infected Heavenly with venereal disease during an earlier visit.

Although time has passed by most of the characters in this play, they continue to grasp for success. It is too late for Chance to be a star, too late for Alexandra to make a true comeback, and too late for Heavenly to have children or happiness. For all of them, the sweet bird of youth has flown away. At the end of the play, Chance refuses to run any more. He stands awaiting castration at the hands of Boss Finley's henchmen as Alexandra departs for Hollywood.
Analysis: Despite some structural weaknesses, primarily the fact that Alexandra barely appears in the second act at all, the play drew kudos from the critics and has become a staple of American theater. The original 1960 Broadway production starred Paul Newman as Chance Wayne and Geraldine Page as Alexandra. Bruce Dern made his Broadway debut in a small role. All levels.
Scenes/Monologues: Male Monologues (1), Female Monologues (2), Male/Male Scenes (1), Male/Female Scenes (1)

TAKEN IN MARRIAGE

by Thomas Babe (Dramatists Play Service)
Synopsis: Annie is getting married tomorrow, so her various female relatives are gathered for the rehearsal and wedding in this New Hampshire church. No plot line per se, just a character study. Ultimately, the wedding is called off.
Analysis: Very A. R. Gurney-esque in style. Upper-class, bloodless, repressed characters finding moments of truth as they expose the skeletons in their closets. All levels.
Scenes/Monologues: Female Monologues (1)

TALKING WITH . . .

by Jane Martin (Samuel French)
Synopsis: A compilation of 11 monologues for women, all credited to Jane Martin. There is no plot or obvious theme.

Analysis: These well-written monologues are appropriate for class but probably too awkward for audition purposes. Most require props of one kind or another and are too long to fit the standard three-minute-monologue format. All levels.
Scenes/Monologues: Female Monologues (11)

TASTE OF HONEY, A
by Shelagh Delaney (Grove Press)
Synopsis: Jo moves into a slummy flat in Salford, Lancashire, with her bar-hopping, whorish mother. Almost immediately, the mother moves out to marry a younger boyfriend, and Jo takes up with a black sailor. Their romance is intense and brief, leaving her pregnant and alone once he ships out. A gay student then moves in, caring for Jo as her pregnancy progresses. Late in her ninth month, Jo's mother comes back after her marriage falls apart, so the good-hearted student is forced out. At the final curtain, Jo is going into labor for a home delivery.
Analysis: Unsentimental and powerful, this perceptive drama is a modern classic. Shelagh Delaney wrote it in 1959 when she was only 18 years old.
Scenes/Monologues: Female/Female Scenes (1), Male/Female Scenes (3)

TENTH MAN, THE
by Paddy Chayefsky (Samuel French)
Synopsis: Everything is in an uproar at the tiny orthodox synagogue of the Congregation Atereth-Fifereth Yisroel in Mineola, a Long Island town. Not only is the sexton facing the usual trouble of finding a tenth Jew for morning prayer, Foreman has just shown up with his schizophrenic granddaughter and announced that she is, in fact, possessed by a dybbuk. This is a migratory soul that lands in the body of another human being in order to return to heaven. Foreman suggests an exorcism. After some debate, the sexton agrees to conduct the service, and preparations get underway. By the end of the play, when the exorcism takes place with some very surprising results, the granddaughter has fallen in love, a Jew who is grabbed from the street to make the quorum finds salvation, and the elders' faith is strengthened.
Analysis: Funny, poignant, and instructive, this 1959 comedy still delivers. All levels.
Scenes/Monologues: Male Monologues (2), Female Monologues (1), Male/Female Scenes (1)

THAT CHAMPIONSHIP SEASON
by Jason Miller (Samuel French)
Synopsis: The 1952 Pennsylvania High School Basketball champions are having their annual reunion at the coach's house. Plenty of liquor and horseplay only temporarily cover explosive tensions and violence among the men. No longer a close team under the strict but loving guidance of their leader, it is now every man for himself in the game of life.
Analysis: This stunning drama was the winner of the 1973 Tony Award for Best Play. Two glorious monologues for the coach. All levels.
Scenes/Monologues: Male Monologues (2)

TIME OF YOUR LIFE, THE
by William Saroyan (Samuel French)
Synopsis: In 1939 Nick's saloon, a waterfront honky-tonk bar in "the lousiest part" of San Francisco, is a gathering place for eccentric characters. Joe is a fellow bent on finding the good and gentle in people; he is trying to live a life in which he doesn't hurt anyone. There are also two young lovers, an aspiring comic, a piano player, a cop who doesn't like his work, a prostitute with the proverbial heart of gold, and a few men who aren't nice at all. In the end, good conquers evil, at least for now and at least in spirit, and love promises to prevail.
Analysis: *The Time of Your Life* was awarded both the 1940 New York Drama Critics Circle Award and the 1940 Pulitzer Prize. The scenes in this play are gentle and evocative, and the

play reflects William Saroyan's personal slant on life more than it centers on a plot line. The characters are, for the most part, endearing eccentics. All levels.

Scenes/Monologues: Male Monologues (3), Male/Female Scenes (1)

TO GILLIAN ON HER 37TH BIRTHDAY

by Michael Brady (Broadway Play Publishing)

Synopsis: Gillian was killed in a boating accident two years ago, and her husband, David, is still in mourning. It seems that everyone he knows, including Rachel, his 16-year-old daughter, is angling to bring him back into the sunlight, but he is still having moonlit conversations with the Gillian he remembers. Finally, after a summer introduction to Kevin, a delightful woman with an unusual man's name, David emerges from the shell.

Analysis: Gentle, frequently whimsical 1984 drama. No fireworks, but a great deal of wit and honesty. All levels.

Scenes/Monologues: Male/Female Scenes (3)

TOP GIRLS

by Caryl Churchill (Samuel French)

Synopsis: After Marlene is promoted to manager at the Top Girls Employment Agency, she hosts a celebration lunch that is attended by six women from the history pages: Isabella Bird (1831–1904), Lady Nijo (born 1258), Dull Gret (subject of a Brueghel painting), Pope Joan (thought to have been Pope between 854–856 while disguised as a man) and Patient Griselda (a character from *The Canterbury Tales* by Chaucer). There are toasts and lunch and much talk about how these various women fared in their lifetimes.

In subsequent scenes, the actresses who play the six historical figures now play office co-workers and Marlene's relatives. What the audience learns, finally, is that Marlene has ripped herself from her upbringing in order to achieve success in a man's world and, in the process, she has acquired the worst traits of successful men. The Top Girls Employment Agency coaches its job-seekers using these same tactics. In the last scene of the play, it becomes clear that the ultra-ambitious Marlene went so far as to abandon her own offspring, giving the child, who is now 16 years old, to her sister Joyce to raise.

Analysis: This script plays much better than it reads. Double-casting, making historical figures live in the present moment, and overlapping dialogue present a challenge. Still, this is a devastating indictment of conservative politics, both British and American, and some pertinent questions are raised about women's roles in relation to men. All levels.

Scenes/Monologues: Female Monologues (1), Female/Female Scenes (1)

TOUCH OF THE POET, A

by Eugene O'Neill (Random House/Modern Library)

Synopsis: Cornelius Melody, to the Irish manor born, has wound up struggling to make ends meet in a small Massachusetts tavern late in life. Although he was once a military hero in the Napoleonic Wars, he can now only relive those distant glories during an annual party during which he puts on his old officer's uniform and holds court for the local low life and his own embarrassed family.

The events of this story take place on such a day, and there is no major plot. As Eugene O'Neill does in other dramas, such as *Long Day's Journey Into Night,* the central character is presented at a point of revelation and, in a few short hours, his life changes forever. In this case, Melody schemes to see his daughter marry the wealthy son of a neighboring landowner. When the young man's parents respond by threatening to cut off his inheritance and by offering Melody a bribe to move away, he turns violent. Forced to confront the fact that he has become a shell of a man, Melody goes into a dark, drunken rage and shoots his prized mare, a symbol of his aristocratic origins and self-deception.

Analysis: This play was published after Eugene O'Neill's death and didn't reach Broadway until 1958. The language is rich, the literary references are many, and the dialogue is challenging. Best suited for serious, literate actors.

Scenes/Monologues: Female Monologues (1), Male/Female Scenes (3)

TOYER

by Gardner McKay (Samuel French)

Synopsis: This two-character potboiler centers on the question of whether or not a male intruder in a woman's home in the Hollywood Hills is a rapist, a voyeur, an actor, or a serial mutilator— or all of the above. The woman, a psychiatrist at a local hospital, is at first convinced that she is facing a voyeur, so she uses her knowledge of scopophilia to neutralize the potentially dangerous situation.

But then the situation turns deadly as the intruder admits to being the notorious Toyer, a serial mutilator who gives women an animal tranquilizer and then severs their spinal cords, rendering them his "toys." After terrorizing the psychiatrist with this possibility for a while, he suddenly turns jovial and says he is actually an actor practicing his character work. She is relieved, disoriented, and emotionally drained. They then drink some liquor and head for the bedroom. The next morning, however, she learns that he is the Toyer after all. When he tries to drug her, she turns the tables on him and at the final curtain, she has him tied up and is about to cut his spinal cord.

Analysis: This play was originally published as a novella and inspired a movie of a different name. Tony Richardson directed Kathleen Turner and Brad Davis in a production at the Kennedy Center in Washington, DC, and there was a production at the Actors Studio. For intense, advanced actors who want to delve into the darkest psychological wilderness within, this tightly written psychological thriller is ideal. Some scenes include justified nudity.

Scenes/Monologues: Male/Female Scenes (5)

TOYS IN THE ATTIC

by Lillian Hellman (Dramatists Play Service)

Synopsis: Julian Berniers, brash and full of bravado, arrives in New Orleans one day in the 1940s for a visit with his budget-minded, simple-living sisters, bringing with him the wonderful news that he has struck it rich. It turns out, however, that he is involved in a romantic affair with Charlotte Warkins, a woman who helped him arrange a crooked real-estate deal in order to get money from Cyrus, her rich, ruthless husband. Julian intends to leave his clinging young wife, Lily, to marry Charlotte, but before that can happen, Lily tells Cyrus about his wife's extramarital romance. Outraged, Cyrus arranges for a vicious retaliation against Julian and Charlotte.

Analysis: A sprawling three-act drama—the kind no one writes anymore—*Toys in the Attic* opened on Broadway in 1960 and ran for more than a year, garnering Tony nominations for Anne Revere, Jason Robards, Maureen Stapleton, and Irene Worth. Revere won a Tony Award for her portrayal of Anna, and Lillian Hellman was nominated for the script. All levels.

Scenes/Monologues: Female/Female Scenes (1)

TRIBUTE

by Bernard Slade (Samuel French)

Synopsis: Wisecracking, fun-loving Scottie Templeton is diagnosed with a form of leukemia at the age of 51 and told to get his affairs in order. He decides to keep the diagnosis a secret and, without any appeal for pity, tries to salvage the strained relationship he has with Jud, his 20-year-old son. As this relationship evolves, Scottie also comes to a deeper appreciation of his former wife and the true meaning of friendship. The dramatic device in the play is a tribute to Scottie, which is being given at a downtown theater by friends from all over the country. The action moves back and forth between the stage of that theater and Scottie's apartment.

Analysis: A lovely comedy, guaranteed to make audience members cry. Jack Lemmon portrayed Scottie on Broadway in 1978 and in the subsequent movie. Robert Picardo, later one of the stars of the television show "China Beach," played Lemmon's son on stage, and Robbie Benson did so in the movie. All levels.

Scenes/Monologues: Female Monologues (1), Male/Male Scenes (1), Male/Female Scenes (1)

TRIP BACK DOWN, THE

by John Bishop (Samuel French)

Synopsis: The play is set in Mansfield, Ohio, where most folks work at the Westinghouse plant. Bobby Horvath escaped all of that to become a bigtime stock-car driver on the southern circuit. Now, eight years later, it is clear that he'll never be "number one" as a driver, so he has returned to his hometown in order to reestablish ties with the wife and child he left behind.

Analysis: Ran briefly on Broadway in 1977 with John Cullum. The best part of the play is the stock-car/factory-town/blue-collar milieu. John Bishop's dialogue rings true. All levels.

Scenes/Monologues: Male Monologues (1), Male/Female Scenes (1)

TRUE WEST

by Sam Shepard (Samuel French)

Synopsis: Austin is housesitting near Los Angeles for his mother who is on vacation in Alaska. Because he is a successful screenwriter, he is using the time to cement a new deal with movie producer Saul Kimmer. Then Austin's older brother Lee shows up, a vagabond and petty thief. The usual air of tension between these dissimilar men becomes even more highly charged when Lee decides to pitch a movie idea of his own to Saul and, wonder of wonders, Saul buys it.

Analysis: Probably Sam Shepard's most accessible play and a favorite in scene-study workshops. All levels.

Scenes/Monologues: Male/Male Scenes (3), Three-Person Scenes (1)

TWENTY-SEVEN WAGONS FULL OF COTTON

by Tennessee Williams [*The Theater of Tennessee Williams,* Volume 6 (New Directions)]

Synopsis: Jake is a sharecropper whose income has been hurt by the encroaching syndicate. In retaliation, he secretly burns down the syndicate's big cotton gin and then innocently makes himself available to gin all that cotton that is sitting around after the fire. Silva Vicarro, the superintendent of the Syndicate Plantation where the fire occurred, comes to Jake's place to give him the gin business. Left alone with Jake's child-like wife, Silva quickly discovers who set the fire and then responds by cruelly seducing the woman. Later, Jake gloats about all this newfound business, oblivious to his wife's disheveled, sexually ravaged appearance. She tells him that Silva is planning to come back with loads of cotton (and presumably plans for more seduction) all summer.

Analysis: An early one-act play from Tennessee Williams that is realistic and gritty. You can almost feel the perspiration and smell the dust on these rural, uneducated southern people as they do one another in. For sophisticated actors.

Scenes/Monologues: Male/Female Scenes (1)

TWICE AROUND THE PARK

by Murray Schisgal (Samuel French)

Synopsis: These two one-act plays were a showcase for Anne Jackson and Eli Wallach. In the first, *A Need For Brussels Sprouts,* Leon is an actor practicing loudly for an audition as an opera singer. His upstairs neighbor complains to no avail. Then a police officer shows up to give him a summons for disturbing the peace. It turns out the officer is Margaret, the upstairs neighbor Leon has never seen; she is actually a very nice widow with two teenagers. Leon is currently single, having been married three times before. In short order, a love affair is born.

The second one-act play, *A Need For Less Expertise,* involves a married couple, Gus and Edie, who are having sexual problems. Edie is neck-deep in therapy, self-help groups, and counselors, but Gus only grudgingly cooperates. Viewers first discover the couple comically trying to follow the recorded instructions of sex counselor Dr. Oliovsky; each of his exercises is designed to lead couples one step closer to the bedroom. After several embarrassing stops and starts, Gus admits that he has had a number of affairs, all one-night stands, but that this behavior is all over. Edie gets mad, leaves, and then comes back. As the curtain falls, they begin to carry out Dr. Oliovsky's foot-massage exercises.

Analysis: New York Jewish humor, very funny at times. All levels.

Scenes/Monologues: Female Monologues (1), Male/Female Scenes (3)

TWO ROOMS

by Lee Blessing (Dramatists Play Service)

Synopsis: Michael Wells was kidnapped from the university where he was teaching in Beirut. As the play opens, he has been in captivity for a year, and his wife, Lainie, has constructed a shrine to him in her home in the United States. The room is as identical as she can make it to the prison in which he is being held, with only a mattress on the floor. Ellen Van Oss, a State Department representative, often visits Lainie, imploring her to remain silent, not to go to the press with her story, to let the government do what it has to do to free Michael. Walker Harris, on the other hand, is a reporter who believes Lainie's best option is to go to the media. He prevails, but in the end, it makes no difference because Michael's captors execute him.

Analysis: This tense 1988 drama too frequently feels like a college lecture, but it contains a couple of powerful and challenging short scenes. All levels.

Scenes/Monologues: Female/Female Scenes (1), Male/Female Scenes (1)

TWO SMALL BODIES

by Neal Bell (Dramatists Play Service)

Synopsis: Two young children disappear from their bedroom during the night, and Lieutenant Brann is assigned to the case. He suspects that Eileen, their mother, who is a cocktail hostess in a strip joint, killed them, but this turns out not to be true. From the beginning, there is a strong personal chemistry between the officer and Eileen. As the investigation of the crime deepens, their relationship becomes overtly sexual, taking on aspects of masochism and religious guilt.

Analysis: Adult material, plenty of subtext, sexually loaded, frequent rough language. This well-written 1977 play evolved from readings at the Playwrights Conference of the Eugene O'Neill Memorial Theater Center and had early productions at Playwrights Horizons in New York City. For experienced actors.

Scenes/Monologues: Male/Female Scenes (4)

VALUE OF NAMES, THE

by Jeffrey Sweet (Dramatists Play Service)

Synopsis: New York City-based actress Norma Silverman arrives in Hollywood to appear in a play and to visit with her elderly father, Benny. When the play's director suffers a stroke, Norma is put in an awkward position by his replacement, Leo Greshen, the man who named her father as a communist sympathizer in testimony before the House UnAmerican Activities Commission during the 1950s. Out of respect for her father, Norma feels that she can't continue in the show without his blessings. Leo visits Benny's home to meet with Norma and to try to reconcile with Benny. They heatedly kick the subject of "naming names" back and forth, arriving at no satisfying conclusions. In the end, Norma proceeds with the play, but Benny doesn't forgive Leo for what he did. Some wrongs, he contends, can never be undone.

Analysis: Originally commissioned by the Actors Theatre of Louisville in 1982, the first production of this drama was directed by Emily Mann, herself a prolific and talented playwright. All levels.
Scenes/Monologues: Male Monologues (1), Male/Female Scenes (2)

VIEUX CARRÉ
by Tennessee Williams (New Directions)
Synopsis: For part of 1938, Tennessee Williams lived in a French Quarter rooming house in New Orleans. *Vieux Carré* is more of a tableaux of the sad but colorful occupants of that house than it is a play. Nightingale is an aging, gay, tubercular painter; Mrs. Wire, a demented, opportunistic landlady; Tye McCool, a drug-addicted barker at a strip-show joint; his lover, Jane Sparks, a fashion illustrator from up north whose leukemia is at first in remission but then returns. These and other characters move in and out of the house, their stories being narrated by a young writer, a role clearly based on Williams himself.
Analysis: This play is useful for actors in search of powerful scenes and monologues, but it doesn't hold together as a complete work. In fact, it closed after only five performances on Broadway in 1977 and is rarely revived. Best suited for advanced actors.
Scenes/Monologues: Male Monologues (1), Female Monologues (1), Male/Male Scenes (1), Male/Female Scenes (1)

VIEW FROM THE BRIDGE, A
by Arthur Miller (Dramatists Play Service)
Synopsis: Eddie Carbone is a longshoreman of Italian descent, working the docks from the Brooklyn Bridge to the breakwater. He helps two of this wife's cousins immigrate illegally from Sicily to the United States, putting them up in the small apartment he and Beatrice share with her beautiful orphaned niece, Catherine. The older of the immigrant brothers turns out to be hardworking and dependable, but the younger one is evidently cut from a different cloth. Rodolpho sings and cooks, and can even repair a dress, skills that make him suspect in Eddie's eyes.

Then when Rodolpho and Catherine fall in love, Eddie is driven almost crazy with repressed jealousy. In his efforts to break up the couple, he accuses Rodolpho of being gay, of courting Catherine only to gain American citizenship. When it becomes clear that Catherine will marry Rodolpho, Eddie turns the brothers in to the Immigration Bureau. Before being deported, Marco, the older brother, seeks out Eddie and kills him. Rodolpho ultimately marries Catherine.
Analysis: In his autobiography, *Time Bends,* Arthur Miller explains that he wrote this famous drama originally as a one-act companion piece to *A Memory of Two Mondays.* The playwright found the 1955 production unsatisfactory because Van Heflin didn't have a seat-of-the-pants feel for the character of Eddie Carbone, but the 1965 Off-Broadway revival was excellent because of the presence of Robert Duvall and Jon Voight as the immigrant brothers. All levels.
Scenes/Monologues: Male/Male Scenes (1), Female/Female Scenes (1), Male/Female Scenes (4)

VISIT, THE
by Friedrich Dürrenmatt [translated by Patrick Bowles (Grove Press)]
Synopsis: Claire Zachanassian, the richest woman in the world, returns to her Central European hometown, which is suffering from economic depression and disrepair. She offers a million pounds to the town and its residents on one condition: that they murder beloved local citizen Alfred Ill, the man who done her wrong all those many years ago. The offer alone makes the town prosperous, as the citizens begin to purchase goods on credit. In the end, murder is rationalized in the name of justice, and poor Alfred dies from fright.

Analysis: Written by a major German dramatist, this parable is a vicious indictment of the power of greed. All levels.

Scenes/Monologues: Male/Male Scenes (1), Male/Female Scenes (1)

VITAL SIGNS

by Jane Martin (Samuel French)

Synopsis: The play is a series of short monologues performed by six young women, sometimes relating to one another or to one of the two men who assist them, and sometimes to the audience. There is no discernible plot or theme except an effort to figure out, or comment on, colorful or poignant life situations. One woman talks about working as a waitress in an all-nude diner, another supervises unruly children at a playground, and still another describes a fun but rare excursion to Coney Island with her father.

Analysis: For actresses who like to use cute stories as monologue material, *Vital Signs*, which was born at the Actors Theatre of Louisville, is a gold mine because it has 39 of them. Only a few, however, contain obvious conflict or tension.

Scenes/Monologues: Female Monologues (2)

WAITING FOR LEFTY

by Clifford Odets (Grove Press)

Synopsis: The year is 1935, and a group of taxi drivers are gathered in a smoke-filled room to vote on whether or not to go on strike. As they wait for their leader, Lefty, to show up, the men take turns going to center stage to tell their stories. These episodes dramatize families being torn apart, economic hardship, and corruption in the business place, and constitute the body of the drama. In the end, word comes that Lefty has been murdered, and the workers finally unite, demanding with one voice, "Strike! Strike! Strike!"

Analysis: This kind of political theater (sometimes known as agitprop, a combination of "agitation" and "propaganda") was common during and after the Great Depression. Clifford Odets wrote *Waiting for Lefty*, a five-scene, one-act play, intending for it to be performed in labor halls as well as theaters. It was an immediate success, putting him and the Group Theatre firmly on the map. Odets and Sanford Meisner jointly directed that first production.

Scenes/Monologues: Male Monologues (1), Male/Female Scenes (2)

WAITING FOR THE PARADE

by John Murrell (Talonbooks, Canada)

Synopsis: A group of women in Calgary, Canada, do their part to support the men, young and old, who are overseas fighting in World War II. In 24 scenes presented in a single act spanning three years, they cope with the pressures of war at home, sometimes with humor, sometimes with tears.

Analysis: Even though the play is set in Canada and makes many references to that country's government and local scene, much of the material can be adapted for workshops anywhere. The play contains a couple of excellent monologues. All levels.

Scenes/Monologues: Female Monologues (2), Female/Female Scenes (1)

WAIT UNTIL DARK

by Frederick Knott (Dramatists Play Service)

Synopsis: Susy and Sam Hendrix unwittingly get caught up in a murder mystery after Sam meets a woman in a Canadian airport and agrees to deliver a doll she owns to a person in New York City. It turns out the doll is stuffed with $50,000 worth of heroin, and before Sam can deliver it, the doll disappears from the apartment. Mike Talman, Sergeant Carlino, and Harry Roat, Jr., are criminals who conspire to locate the doll, arrange for Sam to be called away on business, and then proceeding to trick Susy, who is blind, into hunting for it. They make her think that her

husband is somehow involved in a murder. In a cliffhanger ending, the criminals kill one another off, leaving her safe. The doll was in the hands of a neighbor child who lives upstairs all along.
Analysis: Susy's blindness presents an unusual acting challenge. All levels.
Scenes/Monologues: Male/Female Scenes (1)

WARM PENINSULA, THE
by Joe Masteroff (Samuel French)
Synopsis: Ruth Arnold is finally getting married. But first, the audience needs to go back to the months she spent in Florida, "the warm peninsula," rooming with the former Miss Utah and aspiring performer, Joanne DeLynn. Ruth was romantically mixed up with a guy who turned out to be a gigolo, and Joanne's fellow surprised her by announcing he was already married. But everything worked out fine. Joanne's boyfriend turned out to be married in name, but not in spirit, and Ruth's gigolo friend was the impetus for her march into maturity. Now she is back in Milwaukee, about to marry David, who had been there all the time, if only she had noticed him. Joanne got on a plane headed for Tampa, in pursuit of her friend who has gone off by himself to heal his emotional wounds. She is determined to put up a fight for true love.
Analysis: This innocent 1959 comedy starred Julie Harris. Back then, some women actually liked men whistling at them and pursuing a man was a major occupation. A movie ticket cost $1.10, and popcorn was 35 cents. In short, the play is about a social and political atmosphere that existed a long time ago. Taken on its own terms, it delivers some good scenes. All levels.
Scenes/Monologues: Female Monologues (1), Male/Female Scenes (3)

WASH, THE
by Philip Kan Gotanda (Dramatists Play Service) [*Between Worlds, Contemporary Asian-American Plays* (Theatre Communications Group)]
Synopsis: After 42 years of marriage, at the age of 67, Masi Matsumoto left her husband, Nobu, 13 months ago. The play tracks them as they attempt to live alone or with new lovers, and try to redefine their relationships with their adult children. Masi and Nobu are both Nisei, second-generation Japanese Americans, and divorce is very unusual among these people.
Analysis: Well-written drama that shines a light on generational differences in the Japanese-American culture. All levels.
Scenes/Monologues: Male Monologues (2), Female Monologues (1), Male/Female Scenes (1)

WATERMELON BOATS
by Wendy MacLaughlin [*Twenty-Five Ten-Minute Plays from Actors Theatre of Louisville* (Samuel French)]
Synopsis: In the course of three short scenes covering just 6½ pages, friends Kitty and Kate age from 11 to 21. All of the action takes place on the bank of a lake as they watch their self-made watermelon boats—dug-out watermelon rinds with candles for masts—blow across to the other side. The trip becomes a metaphor for their aging.
Analysis: Very charming little playlet. Challenging for the age-adjustment requirements and the analysis of a shifting friendship. All levels.
Scenes/Monologues: Female/Female Scenes (1)

WHAT I DID LAST SUMMER
by A. R. Gurney, Jr. (Dramatists Play Service)
Synopsis: During the summer of 1945, 14-year old Charlie is happily under the influence of Anna the Pig Woman, a local free spirit and self-styled mentor who is determined to develop his very hidden talents. Maybe he is a sculptor? A painter? None of the above?

Charlie's mother, Grace, meanwhile, who was herself once under Anna's influence, is threatened by this laissez-faire philosophy. She would rather he join the country-club set and pursue a more conventional life path. The matter finally comes to a head when Grace and Anna decide to let Charlie choose for himself. He opts for Anna, moving into her barn. The arrangement is short-lived, however, because he soon wrecks her car, which he is too young to be driving. This event leads to legal and financial problems for Anna, and she is forced to sell her home and move into a trailer. This ends her time with Charlie. He then leaves for boarding school, his apprenticeship to Anna a fond memory.

Analysis: If you liked the movie *Harold and Maude,* you're going to love this play. Anna the Pig Woman is a lovable eccentric, the kind of person who disregards just about every rule and guideline society has to offer so that she can march along in her unorthodox but highly moral fashion. Clearly, A. R. Gurney, Jr. is suggesting that everyone would be better off with a little bit of what Anna has. All levels.

Scenes/Monologues: Female/Female Scenes (1)

WHEN YOU COMIN' BACK, RED RYDER?

by Mark Medoff (Dramatists Play Service)

Synopsis: Stephen and Angel work in a diner in a one-horse town on the edge of a New Mexico desert. He dreams of escaping to Baton Rouge, but she'll probably spend her entire life in the area. Their very predictable existence is interrupted by the arrival of Teddy, a crazed Vietnam War vet who is running from the law. He takes over the diner, taunting and humiliating customers and staff, and finally leaves. At the end of the play, Stephen hitches a ride for Baton Rouge, and Angel cleans up the place for tomorrow's customers.

Analysis: Mark Medoff's 1974 drama is full of lost people trying to find their way after the mind-numbing 1960s. He has an excellent ear for regional speech, and there is always an air of underlying tension. All levels.

Scenes/Monologues: Male/Female Scenes (1)

WHO'S AFRAID OF VIRGINIA WOOLF?

by Edward Albee (Dramatists Play Service)

Synopsis: George came to teach history at a small New England university 23 years ago and shortly afterward married Martha, the college president's daughter. As George's prospects for academic prominence dimmed, however, their relationship, while remaining vivid and loving in its own way, has become cloaked in illusion and perverse game playing. The action takes place between 2 A.M. and 5 A.M. one Sunday morning after a faculty reception at Martha's father's house. George and Martha "entertain" Nick, the new, young, handsome biology professor and Honey, his simpering wife.

Everyone is slightly drunk as the curtain goes up, and a continual flow of alcohol fuels round after round of vicious game playing, truth telling, deception, seduction, and verbal brutality. Martha tries to seduce Nick, but he is too drunk to perform; Honey spends most of her time throwing up and sleeping in the bathroom; and George retaliates against Martha in an unexpected game where he "kills" their imaginary 21-year-old son.

Analysis: George and Martha, probably the most famous couple in modern drama, continually lash out at each other, cutting away layer after layer of façade, exposing raw nerve. All scenes require extreme honesty and vulnerability. The play walked off with almost all the Tony Awards when it premiered on Broadway in 1963, including Best Actress for Uta Hagen as Martha. Sophisticated, demanding material that is appropriate for advanced actors.

Scenes/Monologues: Female Monologues (1), Male/Male Scenes (2), Male/Female Scenes (4)

WHOSE LIFE IS IT ANYWAY?

by Brian Clark (Dramatic Publishing Company)

Synopsis: Ken Harrison, sculptor and art teacher, suffered a spinal-cord injury in a car accident and is paralyzed from the neck down. After learning that the damage is permanent, he announces to the hospital staff that he would rather die than live this way. The physician in charge of the intensive-care ward contends that it is his duty to keep injured people alive and refuses to facilitate a suicide. A court hearing to determine Ken's sanity is conducted, after which the judge orders the hospital to let him die if he wants to. Dignity begins not with life, but with choice.

Analysis: Tom Conti first played the role of Ken Harrison in London and then won a Tony Award for Best Actor in the 1979 Broadway production. Richard Dreyfuss starred in an excellent 1981 movie version. The script is written in the British vernacular but can easily be adapted to standard American usage. All levels.

Scenes/Monologues: Male/Male Scenes (1), Male/Female Scenes (2)

WILD HONEY

by Michael Frayn [adapted from an early, untitled play by Anton Chekhov (Samuel French)]

Synopsis: Anton Chekhov's original play, discovered in a Moscow safe-deposit box after his death, would, in Michael Frayn's estimate, run "over six hours" and has too many sprawling plot lines and characters. Taking a great deal of liberty with the original manuscript, he has centralized the story on a premise that would later show up in *The Cherry Orchard,* namely the pending loss of a family estate. The primary subject of the moment, however, is love. Set during the first balmy days of summer, romance is in the air, and all manner of intrigue is woven throughout. Everyone here is madly in love with someone who loves or is married to someone else, creating delicious comedic scenes.

Analysis: Unlike Anton Chekhov's major plays, no one will argue that this modern adaptation is anything but a comedy. Michael Frayn has cleverly managed to maintain the spirit of Chekhov's style while adapting with a very light touch. All levels.

Scenes/Monologues: Male Monologues (1), Male/Female Scenes (4)

WOMEN, THE

by Clare Boothe Luce (Dramatists Play Service)

Synopsis: Sweet and trusting Mary is shocked to discover that her wealthy husband, Stephen, is having an affair with Crystal Allen, a sales clerk at Saks. Mary's gossipy friends spread the word all over town and, finally, a Reno divorce results. Two years later, Crystal, now married to Stephen, is bored and begins an affair with yet another man. Mary finds out about it and having learned how to survive in the female jungle, helps sabotage their marriage. At the final curtain, Crystal and Stephen have divorced, and Mary and Stephen are reuniting.

Analysis: No one writes plays like this anymore. *The Women,* with its massive 44-character, all-female cast, would cost a fortune to stage professionally today. Still, it is a claws-out gem and a delight for scene-study purposes. All levels.

Scenes/Monologues: Female/Female Scenes (3)

WOOLGATHERER, THE

by William Mastrosimone (Samuel French)

Synopsis: Cliff is stuck in Philadelphia overnight while he waits for repairs on his big-rig truck. He starts talking with Rosie, a candy-counter clerk at a local five-and-dime store. When they wind up at her apartment, Cliff expects that they're going to have sex. But he soon realizes that Rosie is a bit odd, that she has no intentions of sleeping with him, and that she collects men's sweaters. He leaves at the end of Act I but returns later in the night, drawn by some kind of unnamed attraction. At this point, Cliff discovers that Rosie has an entire closetful of men's sweaters and, in fact, has never recovered from an earlier nervous breakdown. She prefers a fantasy love life to the risks of involvement with real flesh-and-blood men. The play ends with Rosie beginning to have another breakdown and Cliff comforting her.

Analysis: William Mastrosimone, who also wrote *Extremities*, has a wonderful way with working-class language and manners. This strange play is very funny at times. All levels.

Scenes/Monologues: Male Monologues (1), Female Monologues (1), Male/Female Scenes (2)

YANKEE DAWG YOU DIE

by Philip Kan Gotanda (Dramatists Play Service)

Synopsis: Two actors in Hollywood continually cross paths at parties, auditions, and acting classes. Vincent Chang has made a career of playing stereotypical Asian-American roles in movies and on television, but he takes pride in having survived in the cold entertainment industry. Bradley Yamashita, young and ambitious, regards Vincent with disdain because he is a bad role model. Each encounter brings the men to a greater understanding of one another and growing mutual animosity toward the faceless people who produce films and television shows.

Analysis: Biting satire that captures the frustration Asian-American actors face. The entire cast is Asian American. All levels.

Scenes/Monologues: Male Monologues (4), Male/Male Scenes (4)

ZOOMAN AND THE SIGN

by Charles Fuller (Samuel French)

Synopsis: Reuben and Rachel's 12-year-old daughter was killed in urban-gang crossfire as she sat on the front porch of her home. Although it is likely that several neighbors witnessed the tragedy, no one comes forward to identify the killer. So Reuben hangs a large sign over the front of his house that reads, "The Killers of our daughter Jinny are free on the streets because our neighbors will not identify them." The sign becomes a subject of disagreement in the family and the object of anger in the neighborhood. Finally, the same hoodlum who shot Jinny comes to the house to rip down the sign and is killed by Uncle Emmett. Another death, however, doesn't bring Jinny back or solve anything.

Analysis: As tragic as today's headlines, this well-written drama was first presented in 1980 at New York City's Negro Ensemble Company. All of the characters are African American. All levels.

Scenes/Monologues: Male Monologues (2), Female Monologues (1)

ZOO STORY, THE

by Edward Albee (Dramatists Play Service)

Synopsis: Peter is enjoying a warm afternoon in New York City's Central Park when a stranger walks up and announces that he has been to the zoo. Peter and Jerry get into a conversation that begins on friendly terms but soon takes on overtones of dominance and control. Jerry becomes increasingly volatile, finally drawing a knife. Then he inexplicably tosses the knife to Peter and, once when Peter tries to defend himself with it, Jerry lunges, impaling himself on the knife and committing suicide.

Analysis: This play premiered in Berlin in 1959 and has been much discussed ever since. It is about animals, both human and four-legged, as well as communication, both verbal and physical. All levels.

Scenes/Monologues: Male/Male Scenes (1)

Part Two
Male Monologues

ABSENT FRIENDS
by Alan Ayckbourn (Samuel French)
Comedy: Act I, p. 29; Colin (30s).
Colin's former friends have invited him to a tea party to cheer him up after the untimely death of his fiancée. At the very end of Act I, he delivers this exquisitely sensitive and touching speech about how much he loved the woman, how happy he is to have her memory, and how much he appreciates this group of good friends. As they listen to him, they descend into abject depression and tears. Fun for workshops, but less suitable for auditions. Depending on the delivery, this monologue is either very funny or very sad. Start: "It's a funny thing about somebody dying— you never know, till it actually happens, how it's going to affect you." End: "I just want you to know that, despite everything that happened, in a funny sort of way, I too am very happy."

ABSURD PERSON SINGULAR
by Alan Ayckbourn (Samuel French)
Comedy-Drama: Act II, pp. 41–44; Geoffrey (30s).
Oblivious to the fact that his wife, Eva, is trying to commit suicide at the precise moment he is talking to her, Geoffrey, an unrepentant womanizer, suggests that they legally separate. She sits at the kitchen table, clinging to her partially written suicide note and staring blankly at him the whole time. For audition use, excerpt the section that deals specifically with the separation. For workshops, it is probably more interesting to work on Geoffrey's transitions, starting with his entrance and initial complaints about his job, then moving to the couple's marriage trouble, and finally getting into the imminent arrival of their Christmas-party guests. Written in the British vernacular. Start: "God, I need a drink. You want a drink?" End: "What I lack in morals, I make up in ethics."
Comedy-Drama: Act III, pp. 79–80; Ronald (40s).
On the surface, this monologue doesn't look like much, just a man explaining to his friends that he doesn't understand women. To do it justice, an actor needs to address issues of mortality, life changes, and shifting expectations. As Ronald speaks on this apparently cheerful Christmas eve, his second wife is sitting upstairs in alcoholic isolation, and his business has fallen apart. Written in the British vernacular. Eliminate Geoffrey's lines here. Start: "You seem to have got things pretty well organized on the homefront." End: "Couldn't do without them, could we, I suppose. . . ."

AFTER THE FALL
by Arthur Miller (Dramatists Play Service)
Drama: Act I, pp. 38–39; Quentin (40s).
Quentin tells Louise about meeting a young woman in the park. He was fascinated by her because she "wasn't defending anything, upholding anything, or accusing—she was just there." Start: "I sat by the park for a while." End: "This city is full of lovers."

AH, WILDERNESS!
by Eugene O'Neill (Samuel French)
Comedy: Act III, Scene 2, pp. 106–108; Richard (16).
As Richard waits on a moonlit beach for his true love to sneak out of her home and join him, he carries on a dialogue with himself. He kicks himself for stupidities, recites some poetry, and declares his most ecstatic love. Probably not the best choice for auditions, but this is a charming theatrical moment—excellent workshop material for a young actor working on self-stimulation and the uses of imagination. Start: "Must be nearly nine. . . . I can hear the Town Hall clock strike, it's so still tonight." End: "Let her suffer for a change!"
Comedy: Act IV, Scene 3, pp. 124–126; Miller (50).
A father/son lecture about the birds and the bees, circa 1906. Dad bumbles and mumbles his way through it, illuminating nothing. Start: "But listen here, Richard, it's about time you and I had a serious talk." End: "I never had anything to do with such women, and it'll be a hell of a lot better for you if you never do!"

ALL MY SONS
by Arthur Miller (Dramatists Play Service)
Drama: Act I, pp. 30–31; Chris (32).
Trying to explain why he is having trouble committing himself fully to Annie, Chris recalls his experiences in the war and his dedication to his brother. Omit Annie's lines at the beginning of Chris's speech. Start: "You remember, overseas, I was in command of a company? . . . Well, I lost them. . . . Just about all of (them). . . . It takes a little time to toss that off." End: "I didn't want to take any of it. And I guess that included you."

AMADEUS
by Peter Shaffer (Samuel French)
Drama: Act II, pp. 72–73; Mozart (25–30).
Baron Van Swieten is horrified to learn that Mozart wants to write an opera based on the play *The Marriage of Figaro*. Mozart blasts the Baron and his contemporaries for their loftiness and artistic pretensions, arguing in favor of "flesh and blood" opera, stories of real people, not gods and goddesses. Start: "I don't understand you! You're all upon perches." End with either: "and turn the audience into God" or "my tongue is stupid. My heart isn't."

AMEN CORNER, THE
by James Baldwin (Samuel French)
Drama: Act II, p. 52; David (18).
David talks to Luke, his musician father who is on his deathbed. David explains how the prospect of being a professional musician has drawn him away from his mother's church. The space that used to be filled by God is now filled by music. Eliminate Luke's line. Start: "A few months ago some guys come in the church and they heard me playing piano and they kept coming back all the time. Mama said it was the Holy Ghost drawing them in. But it wasn't." End: "And I was trying to find some way of preparing Mama's mind."
Drama: Act II, pp. 52–53; Luke (40–50).
Luke, on his deathbed, tells his son that it is okay to be a professional musician. He tells David that it wasn't music that messed up his life. Start: "you got to wondering all over again if you wanted to be like your daddy and end up like your daddy. Ain't that right? . . . Well, son, tell you one thing. . . ." End: "So don't you think you got to end up like your daddy just because you want to join a band."
Drama: Act III, p. 88; David (18).
After a traumatic confrontation with his mother, David tells her why he has to leave home and be his own man. Great monologue. Start: "And if I listened—what would happen? What

do you think would happen if I listened?" End with either: "Mama—you knew this day was coming" or "I ain't going to be hanging around the house. I'll see you before I go."

AMERI/CAIN GOTHIC
by Paul Carter Harrison [*Totem Voices, Plays from the Black World Repertory,* edited by Paul Carter Harrison (Grove Press)]
Drama: Act II; I. W. Harper (mid-30s).
Cass and Harper met in a seedy Memphis motel room yesterday and surprised themselves by making explosive love. In the afterglow, Harper tells Cass that she shouldn't get the wrong idea about what happened and that he doesn't intend to stick around. Cass guesses that he is married, and he admits that he used to be but no longer is. She then presses him to talk about his ex-wife. Start: "I did everything in my power to win that woman's respect, and she showed me no more appreciation than a common whore!" End: "I grabbed her in the throat! . . . And kissed her!"

AMERICAN PLAN, THE
by Richard Greenberg (Dramatists Play Service)
Drama: Act I, Scene 6, pp. 34–35; Nick (20s).
Eva, the mother of Nick's fiancée, confronts him with the litany of untruths he has told her daughter during their courtship. In this very stark and well-written speech, Nick explains how his father lost his fortune, suffered a nervous breakdown, and committed suicide. At this point in the play, Nick's homosexuality is still a secret. Start: "After my mother died, my father more or less lost control of things." End: "Well. This has been a marvelous party, you've been a perfect hostess, and I've had a splendid time."

ANDERSONVILLE TRIAL, THE
by Saul Levitt (Dramatists Play Service)
Drama: Act II, Scene 1, p. 69; Chipman (31).
Chipman implores the military court to address questions of moral responsibility, not merely the technical matter of conspiracy. Start: "General, I do not enter that area of my own free will." End: "Let us have a human victory in this room."

ANOTHER ANTIGONE
by A. R. Gurney, Jr. (Dramatists Play Service)
Drama: One-act play, pp. 17–18; Henry (40–50).
Outraged that one of his students is persisting in writing an anti-war adaptation of the Greek classic *Antigone,* Henry defends his opposition and explains his concept of tragedy in this wonderful speech delivered to the Dean of Humane Studies. Eliminate Diana's single line. Start: "Do you know what tragedy is, Diana? . . . I don't think you do." End: "That is just troublemaking. And I cannot give her credit for it."

AUTUMN GARDEN, THE
by Lillian Hellman (Dramatists Play Service)
Drama: Act III, pp. 93–94; Ned Crossman (46).
Years ago, Ned Crossman would have jumped at the chance to marry Constance Tuckerman, but she was holding a secret flame for her first love, Nick Denery, who married another woman a long time ago. A moment earlier, in sadness and despair, Constance asked if Ned would have her at this late date. Struck speechless at first, this monologue is his answer. The speech comes at the very end of the play and carries heavy subtext. It could be a rich selection for an actor willing to fully explore it. Cut Constance's few lines that interrupt the speech. Start: "I live in a room and I go to work and I play a game called getting through the day." End: "And I've never liked liars—least of all those who lie to themselves."

BALTIMORE WALTZ, THE
by Paula Vogel (Dramatists Play Service)
Comedy: One-act play, Scene 1, pp. 9–10; Carl (25–35).
The pink triangular badge that Carl wears announces to the world that he is gay and proud. Perhaps because of this forthright expression of his sexual orientation, he has been harassed by his straight boss at a branch of the San Francisco library and, in fact, was recently laid off from his job. In this very funny, very angry monologue, Carl leads a group of children in an irreverent going-away sing-along. Start: "Good morning, boys and girls. It's Monday morning, and it's time for 'Reading Hour with Uncle Carl.'" End: "In a language you might understand, up-ay ours-yay!"
Comedy-Drama: One-act play, Scene 16, pp. 30–31; The Little Dutch Boy at Age 50 (50).
Complete with corny Dutch accent, The Little Dutch Boy at Age 50 tells the story of how he faced death by putting his thumb in the dam. This truly is a dark-humored speech, and you'll have to cut and paste a bit, eliminating Anna's lines. Start: "It was kermis-time, the festival in my village." End: "I was stupid. Wrong place, wrong time."

BEAR, THE
by Anton Chekhov [*The Sneeze, Plays and Stories* by Anton Chekhov, translated and adapted by Michael Frayn (Samuel French)]
Comedy: One-act play, pp. 52–53; Smirnov (45–55).
Smirnov arrives at the widow Popova's home in order to collect a debt owed to him by her late husband. When she is unable to pay him, Smirnov goes into a rage but at the same time, he finds himself to be attracted to the widow Popova. In this speech, he tells her how awful all women are. Start: "Oh, but this is amazing! How do you want me to talk to you?" End: "Tell me, in all honesty—have you ever in your life seen a woman who could be sincere and constant and true? You haven't!"

BEDROOMS, FIVE COMEDIES
by Renée Taylor and Joseph Bologna (Samuel French)
Comedy: "David and Nancy," pp. 7–8; David (35–45).
David is the nervous father of the bride. In the middle of the night, he wakes Nancy up to tell her that he has changed his mind about allowing her to marry. Although father and daughter embrace at the end, this speech is basically a crazed monologue. For a cute audition-length excerpt, start mid-speech. Start: "Look, Nancy, I can't see how you can really be in love with this guy." End: "Nancy, I beg you. Don't marry Melvin."

BOYS' LIFE
by Howard Korder (Dramatists Play Service)
Comedy: Scene 6, pp. 31–32; Phil (late 20s).
Phil confides in his best friend, Jack, how much he needs this woman he has been seeing for the last few weeks and why he is afraid of being alone. They have a lot in common, hit it off on the first date, and talked about God for three hours straight once. This is the perfect relationship—except she isn't reciprocating. Even worse, when Phil declared his need for her after a couple of intense weeks, she was repulsed. She claimed that no one should ever need anyone else that much. Start: "I would have destroyed myself for this woman." End: "Plus, my hair is falling out, that really sucks."
Comedy: Scene 8, pp. 40–41; Don (late 20s).
Lisa is furious and ready to leave after discovering that Don recently slept with another woman. In an attempt to charm her and calm her down, he tells about this very strange dream. Start: "Okay . . . okay . . . now . . . I was . . . flying. In a plane, I mean a rocket." End: "And we died. And the ocean ate our bones."

BREAKING THE CODE
by Hugh Whitemore (Samuel French)
Drama: Act II, Scene 2, pp. 71–72; Knox (60).
Concerned about Turing's homosexuality and unorthodox work practices, Knox, his boss at the Government Code and Cipher School, admonishes him in this speech. Knox quotes the philosopher Wittgenstein, drawing a comparison between the limits of science and those of humanity. Eliminate Turing's single line. Start: "All right! Let me give you an example." End: "'the problems of life remain completely unanswered.'"

BUCK
by Ronald Ribman (Theatre Communications Group) [*New Plays USA, 1983* (Theatre Communications Group); *The Rug Merchants of Chaos and Other Plays by Ronald Ribman* (Theatre Communications Group)]
Drama: Act I, Scene 4; Buck (late 30s).
Buck tells his co-worker Charlie about his child custody dilemma and how he misses his son. Excellent monologue. Start: "They got me back in the playground again, Charlie. The same cruddy playground across the street from the apartment I spent five years of my life in with Kenny." End: ". . . scared that no matter what I do I'm gonna lose him anyway."

BURN THIS
by Lanford Wilson (Hill & Wang/Noonday; HarperCollins London Ltd.)
Comedy-Drama: Act I; Pale (36).
Pale's entrance. He is angry about a guy who wanted the same parking space outside. This monologue is full of profanity and is appropriate only for an actor willing to go full-tilt. Definitely not for the timid. Start: "Goddamn this fuckin' place." At the end of this passage, pick up again with, "I mean no personal disparagement of the neighborhood in which you have your domicile, honey, but this street's dying of crotch rot." End: "Trans Am and go beep-beep, you know?"

CHERRY ORCHARD, THE
by Anton Chekhov [*Chekhov, The Major Plays,* translated by Ann Dunnigan (Signet Books)]
Drama: Act III; Lopakhin (40–50).
Born to serfs, Lopakhin is a self-made man. He surprises everyone by purchasing at auction the very estate that his father and grandfather were slaves on. Start: "I bought it. Kindly wait a moment, ladies and gentlemen, my head is swimming." End: "Music! Strike up!"

CHILDREN OF A LESSER GOD
by Mark Medoff (Dramatists Play Service)
Drama: Act II, pp. 67–68; James (30).
In the final moments of the play, James and his deaf wife, Sarah, have a huge argument over whether or not she is playing a control game by refusing to try to speak; she is willing to communicate only by signing. In this speech, James sums up his position, demanding that she speak. Very powerful material that absolutely must be delivered with love. Start: "You think I'm going to let you change my children into people like you who so cleverly see vanity and cowardice as pride? You're going nowhere, you're achieving nothing." End: "Now come on! I want you to speak to me. Let me hear it. Speak! Speak! Speak!"

COASTAL DISTURBANCES
by Tina Howe (Samuel French)
Comedy: Act II, Scene 2, pp. 63–65; Leo (28).
Leo the lifeguard tells Holly a humorous, fantastic story about Juanita Wijojac, a girl with six fingers he knew in school. Start: "I was thirteen and she was eleven." End: "I'll tell you one thing—

she could have given one hell of a back rub." For monologue purposes, cut Holly's lines and Leo's direct responses to them.

COLD STORAGE
by Ronald Ribman (Samuel French)
Drama: Act II, pp. 58–60; Landau (mid-40s).
Landau has just finished explaining how he was separated from his parents in Nazi Germany and never saw them again. He speaks now of the last moments, when they walked away and he couldn't follow them. Then he tells of being in a New York City apartment not long ago, an apartment that reminded him of his childhood home in Munich. This is a wonderfully reflective monologue, perhaps a bit long for audition purposes. Start: "They walked down an alley and they went away." End: ". . . so what I've been doing that's very interesting since April is that I've been trying to figure out where my bedroom was."

COLORED MUSEUM, THE
by George C. Wolfe (Broadway Play Publishing)
Drama: "A Soldier with a Secret"; Junie Robinson (20s).
Junie, a young soldier, tells a horrific story about dying on the battlefield and coming back to life. Since then, he was able to see the future hurt in people's faces, so he has been giving them the hypodermic needle to prevent their pain. Do the whole speech for class work; shorten it for audition purposes. Start: "Pst. Pst. Guess what? I know the secret. The secret to your pain." End: "The secret to yours, and yours. Pst. Pst. Pst. Pst."

CROSSING DELANCEY
by Susan Sandler (Samuel French)
Comedy-Drama: Act II, pp. 66–67; Sam (early 30s).
Sam is wooing Isabelle and in this lovely monologue speaks of the value in simple virtues. He tells her how fortunate she is to have an elderly, wise grandmother like Bubbie. Then Sam tells Isabelle that he would like to be with her in an open, honest fashion. His intentions are clear. Not much conflict here and probably not the most dynamic choice for audition purposes, but plenty of mood and texture. Excellent for workshops. Cut and paste at the beginning, eliminating Isabelle's line. Start: "This is the most wonderful thing you can do for yourself, Isabelle, to be with her like this." End: "...I want very much to show you the best I got, Isabelle. Please let me do that. Maybe I talked too much—but I been saving up."

DANCE AND THE RAILROAD, THE
by David Henry Hwang (Dramatists Play Service)
Comedy-Drama: Scene 4, pp. 29–30; Ma (18).
Looking for proof of his dedication to be a dancer, Lone has left Ma alone in the woods to crouch and imitate a locust all night. At some point during the night, he delivers this mono-logue directly to the audience. Ma talks about Second Uncle, whose life was ruined by locusts, and the revenge he took against grasshoppers. Start: "Locusts travel in huge swarms, so large that when they cross the sky, they block out the sun." End: "But then again, Second Uncle never tortured actual locusts, just weak grasshoppers." Remember, you're supposed to deliver this speech while crouching to imitate a locust.

DARK AT THE TOP OF THE STAIRS, THE
by William Inge (Dramatists Play Service)
Drama: Act II, pp. 48–49; Sammy (16).
Reenie's blind date, a Jewish boy from Hollywood, tells her family how he has spent his whole life living in military academies. Although Sammy tries to be cheerful, the audience sees how

sad and lonely he really is. Later this evening, Sammy will commit suicide. Cut Reenie's line at the top of Sammy's speech. Start: "I've never been to many parties, have you?" End: "I guess I've bored you enough, telling you about myself."
Drama: Act III, pp. 72–73; Rubin (36).
Rubin, an uneducated, sincere man, tells his wife, Cora, why he feels like a stranger in his own town, a man out of place and time. Cut Cora's lines and Rubin's direct responses to them. Start: "Goddamn it! What have I got to give 'em?" End: "How can I feel I've got anything to give to my children when the world's as strange to me as it is to them?"

DAY IN THE DEATH OF JOE EGG, A
by Peter Nichols (Samuel French)
Drama: Act II, pp. 62–63; Bri (33).
Bri and Sheila's spastic daughter had a major seizure, and though Bri delayed seeking medical help in the hope that the child would die peacefully, she survived. In this monologue, delivered directly to the audience, Bri describes the hectic trip to the hospital and Joe's later return home. He says that, at last, his marriage to Sheila is over, that he is leaving. Written in the British vernacular. Start: "Sheila and I went with Joe in the ambulance." End: "Want a nice slow job—game-warden—keeper at Regents Park—better still, Kew Garden. Well, cheers."

DEATH OF A SALESMAN
by Arthur Miller (Dramatists Play Service)
Drama: Act II, pp. 58–59; Willy (over 60).
Willy begs for his job by telling his young boss, Howard, why he has spent his life being a salesman. Cut Howard's single line. Start: "Business is definitely business, but just listen to me for a minute." End: "They don't know me any more."

DIVISION STREET
by Steve Tesich (Samuel French)
Comedy: Act I, pp. 26–27; Sal (30s).
Dianah's Legal Aid lawyer, Sal, tells her how rotten his life has been and how she should show pity by paying attention to him. But she isn't even listening. Start: "You are looking at a desperate, homeless, friendless creature, Dianah." End: "This is the single longest uninterrupted speech I have ever made, Dianah, and I hope it moved you."
Comedy: Act I, pp. 28–29; Chris (37).
Chris tells his ex-wife, Dianah, that he no longer cares about 1960s causes and that he isn't interested in being a radical leader any longer. Cut Dianah's lines and Chris's direct responses to them. Start: "We're not we, Dianah." End: "I want it now!"
Comedy: Act I, pp. 37–38; Roger (mid-30s).
Roger tells Chris, a former leader of the 1960s radical movement, how he has sold out and that he is full of shame for deserting the revolution. Omit Chris's lines and Roger's direct responses to them. Start: "You should spit on me!" End: "If I had an orgasm I'd give it to them just so they'd leave me alone!"

DOES A TIGER WEAR A NECKTIE?
by Don Petersen (Dramatists Play Service)
Drama: Act II, Scene 2, pp. 64–65; Bickham (20).
A bitter, violent speech in which Bickham tells the staff psychiatrist at the detention center about how, after a long search, he found his father—and brutally beat him. Rough material. Start: "I was sick to my stomach. He made me puke . . . Just like you do. That lousy sono-fabitch!" End: "You cured me, doctor, and now I belong to you."

DRESSER, THE
by Ronald Harwood (Samuel French)
Drama: Act I, pp. 13–14; Norman (35–45).
Sir is an elderly actor in the Old School tradition, and his big role is King Lear, which he has played hundreds of times in the provinces. Tonight, however, as curtain time approaches, Sir is confined to a nearby hospital in a state of emotional collapse. It appears that for the first time, a performance will have to be canceled. In this poignant monologue, Norman, Sir's longtime dresser, lovingly tells Her Ladyship how he came to be in the actor's employ. Written in the British vernacular. Start: "Sixteen years. I wish I could remember." End: "Next day he asked if I'd be his dresser."
Drama: Act II, p. 68; Norman (35–45).
Norman is concerned that Sir is becoming overly excited by Irene's flirtations and that this may be bad for his health. Alone with Irene, Norman insists that she tell him precisely what she has been doing with the old actor. She tries to pull away from Norman, threatening to tell Sir if he doesn't let go of her arm. He scoffs, telling her how very well he knows his boss and how futile it is for her to make such a threat. Start: "Tell Sir? On me? I quake in my boots." End: "I have to know all he does."
Drama: Act II, pp. 61–62; Sir (about 60).
Tired and increasingly philosophical, Sir explains to Her Ladyship why he identifies with King Lear. Start: "I thought tonight I caught sight of him." End: "I'll see a locked door, a sign turned in the window, closed, gone away, and a drawn blind."
Drama: Act II, pp. 79–80; Norman (35–45).
The final speech in the play. Norman is drunk, and Sir has been dead only a few moments. Norman reflects on his relationship with the actor, bemoaning the fact that it was "always a back seat." Start: "He never once took me out for a meal." Continue to the end of the play.

DYLAN
by Sidney Michaels (Samuel French)
Drama: Act I, pp. 42–43; Dylan (38).
Midway during his final American lecture tour, Dylan Thomas is tiring of the constant adoration. At a party given in his honor, he retreats to a bedroom where he hears a child crying. Dylan gets the boy to go back to sleep as another poet comes in to discover him sitting quietly by the crib. He explains that he lulled the child to sleep by reciting his favorite poem, "Baa, Baa, Black Sheep." Then he explains what the poem means to him personally. Dylan speaks with an English accent. Start: ". . . one of my favorite poems and the story of my life." End as he recites the poem a second time: "'And one for the little boy who lives down the lane.'"

END OF THE WORLD WITH SYMPOSIUM TO FOLLOW, THE
by Arthur Kopit (Samuel French)
Drama: Act III, pp. 87–89; Stone (60s).
Stone recalls what it was like to witness nuclear testing on Christmas Island before World War II. After the explosion, flying birds that were nearby caught on fire. Start: "In any event, there we were on this ship, this battleship, not too far from where the detonation was to take place." End: "And I thought: This is what it will be like at the end of time. And we all felt . . . the thrill of that idea."
Drama: Act III, pp. 89–91; Trent (35–45).
Trent remembers picking up his newborn son in his arms and being tempted to throw him from the apartment window. It was a seductive moment, and he was drawn to that window—but he resisted. In telling the story, he makes the point that countries with nuclear power deal with the threat of war the same way. Start: "Now I know where we met! . . . It was at our place." End: "If doom comes . . . it will come in that way."

EVILS OF TOBACCO, THE

by Anton Chekhov [*The Sneeze, Plays and Stories* by Anton Chekhov, translated and adapted by Michael Frayn (Samuel French)]
Comedy: One-act play, pp. 61–66; Nyukhin (50–55).
Nyukhin sets out to lecture young female students on the evils of using tobacco, but he gets off the track easily. The more he talks, the more the girls learn about his private life. Nyukhin has been married for 33 years to a domineering woman who has borne him seven daughters who don't appreciate him. Toward the end of this speech, he hears his wife approach and abruptly brings himself back to the assigned topic. This monologue isn't good for auditions, but it is wonderful for class work. For advanced actors. Start: "Ladies and, if I may say so, gentlemen." End: "That is all I have to say, and I am very pleased to have had the opportunity to get it off my chest."

FENCES

by August Wilson (Samuel French)
Drama: Act I, Scene 1, pp. 16–17; Troy (53).
Troy tells Rose and Bono about the time he wrestled with "Mr. Death" and won in 1941. Omit Rose and Bono's lines and Troy's direct responses to them. Start: "I looked up one day and Death was marching straight at me." End: "He's gonna have to fight to get me. I ain't easy."
Drama: Act I, Scene 3, pp. 39–40; Troy (53).
In this short monologue, Troy tells his young son, Cory, that it is his responsibility to take care of the boy and that he doesn't do it because he likes Cory. Start: "Like you? I go out of there every morning . . . bust my butt." End: "You understand what I'm saying, boy?"

FIRST BREEZE OF SUMMER, THE

by Leslie Lee (Samuel French) [*Black Thunder, An Anthology of Contemporary African American Drama* (Mentor/Penguin)]
Drama: Act I, SF pp. 20–21; Sam (20s).
The setting: the deep south in the late 1920s. Sam, an African-American, got into a confrontation with a white man at the train station when he came to the defense of an elderly porter who had dropped the man's bags. Rather than being grateful to Sam, the porter began to apologize to the traveler, thereby humiliating Sam. That was two days ago, and he walked off the job on the spot. Now he is telling his girlfriend, Lucretia, about the event as he prepares to move on to the next town. Begin midway through Sam's speech. Start: "Colored people weren't ready for colored doctors, or maybe colored doctors weren't ready for colored people." End: "Baby, I'm so miserable, it's funny . . . miserable."

FOB

by David Henry Hwang (Dramatists Play Service)
Comedy: Act II, p. 35; Dale (20s).
In this short speech at the top of the act, delivered directly to the audience, Dale describes the differences between himself and his very Chinese parents. Start: "I am much better now." End: "I'm making it in America."

FOX, THE

by Alan Miller [based on D. H. Lawrence's short novel of the same name (Samuel French)]
Drama: Act III, Scene 1, p. 61; Henry Grenfel (20s).
Henry Grenfel, a mysterious young soldier, has been a guest at Nellie and Jill's farm for only one day and has already asked Nellie to marry him. Jill feels threatened by this turn of events and has been warning Nellie to be wary of Henry. He realizes that Jill is his enemy and, in this speech, presses Nellie hard for a commitment. Henry ultimately ends up killing Jill. She was

right to be suspicious. You'll have to cut and paste, eliminating Nellie's lines. Written in the British vernacular. Start: "What's holding you in, Nellie, say what's on your mind!" End: "You want the feel of me. You need it! Say you'll have me, Nellie. Say it!"

FRANKIE AND JOHNNY IN THE CLAIR DE LUNE
by Terrence McNally (Dramatists Play Service)
Drama: Act II, p. 60; Johnny (46).
Johnny tells Frankie that he is her Prince Charming. Very nice monologue in which a man who isn't great with words finds eloquence. Start: "You don't want to hear anything you don't already know." End: "I know this thing, Frankie."

GLASS MENAGERIE, THE
by Tennessee Williams (Dramatists Play Service)
Drama: Act I, Scene 3, p. 24; Tom (21).
Tom is furious with his mother, Amanda, for prying into and controlling his life. Start: "I'm going to opium dens." End: "You ugly—babbling old—witch."
Drama: Act II, Scene 8, p. 68; Tom (21).
At the end of the play, Tom talks to the audience, revealing that he hasn't been able to separate himself from his sister, Laura. Start: "I didn't go to the moon." End: "Blow out your candles, Laura—and so good-bye."

GLENGARRY GLEN ROSS
by David Mamet (Samuel French)
Drama: Act I, Scene 3, pp. 27–29; Roma (40s).
Super salesperson Roma sets up a sucker. He is going to sell him some Florida swampland. Cut Lingk's few lines and Roma's direct responses to them. Start: "all train compartments smell vaguely of shit." End: "It's been a long day."
Drama: Act II, pp. 43–44; Levene (50s).
Levene made a big sale last night, or so he believes: eight units of property for $82,000 to an unsuspecting couple. Here, he gloats about how he put it over on them. What he doesn't realize is that this same couple regularly signs contracts to buy property but doesn't have any money. Cut Roma's few other lines and Levene's direct responses to them. Start: "What we have to do is admit to ourself that we see that opportunity. . . ." End: ". . . and we toast. In silence." Roma's line, "Always be closing . . ." can be spoken by Levene. Both of these monologues from *Glengarry Glen Ross* are too long for audition purposes but are good for workshops.

HELLO AND GOODBYE
by Athol Fugard (Samuel French)
Drama: Act II, p. 50; Johnny (late 20s).
Johnny tells his sister about the day years ago when he left home to go to railroad school, got as far as the bridge, and turned back to be with his father. Having a career wasn't important, but being devoted to his father was. Johnny is a white Afrikaner, so an accent is appropriate. Start: "Yes, I wanted to go. They are the most beautiful things in the world!" End: "I sweep, I wash, I wait . . . it was me. What I wanted."

HOUSE OF BLUE LEAVES, THE
by John Guare (Samuel French)
Comedy: Act II, Scene 1, pp. 35–37; Ronnie (18).
Ronnie is building a bomb in order to blow up the Pope while telling the audience about the terrible humiliation he felt when Artie's Hollywood producer buddy visited six years ago. Start: "My father tell you all about me?" End: "I'll show you all. I'll be too big for any of you."

HOUSE OF RAMON IGLESIA, THE
by José Rivera (Samuel French)
Drama: Act I, Scene 1, pp. 14–15; Ramon (49).
Ramon has just returned from Puerto Rico where he tried to locate Doa Prez, the legal owner of his Long Island home. The family is hanging on Ramon's every word as he first leads them on, suggesting that Doa Prez is dead, and then delightedly admits that he found her and had the papers signed. You have to piece this monologue together, cutting out the other characters' responses to Ramon's story, but it works. Start: "When I landed in San Juan, I took a bus to Adjuntas." End: "They think she can fly and bring the dead come to life! They are always making stories about her!"

HURLYBURLY
by David Rabe (Samuel French)
Comedy-Drama: Act I, Scene 2, pp. 49–50; Mickey (mid-30s).
Feeling caught in a romantic triangle, Mickey tells Eddie and Darlene that they should continue their relationship without him. Start: "You know what I'm going to do?" End: "Am I totally off base here, Eddie, or what?"
Drama: Act I, Scene 3, pp. 67–69; Phil (30s).
Edging close to a nervous breakdown, Phil describes for Eddie how he sees Los Angeles and the world from his moving car. An intense monologue, full of haunting, stark imagery. Start: "Eddie, for god's sake don't terrify me." End: "I got to stay married. I'm lost without her."
Drama: Act II, Scene 1, pp. 116–117; Eddie (mid-30s).
Eddie, who is very drunk, has been engaging in some truth-telling repartee with his good friend, Phil. Eddie then abruptly announces that he is depressed by the news about the neutron bomb in today's paper. His speech is a drunken harangue, but there is a sad logic to it. Start: "The aborigine had a lot of problems." End: ". . . we have emptied out the heavens and put oblivion in the hands of a bunch of aging insurance salesmen whose jobs are insecure."

HUSBANDRY
by Patrick Tovat (Samuel French)
Drama: One-act play, Scene 2, pp. 19–20; Harry (37).
Harry tries to get his wife, Bev, to understand the plight of the American farmer in general and his parents in particular. Start: "I am absolutely pissed off about . . . and feeling shit worthless about a whole lot of stuff." End: ". . . and there are mysteries, by God, not yet penetrated by Purdue University."

I HATE HAMLET
by Paul Rudnick (Dramatists Play Service)
Comedy: Act II, Scene 2, p. 67; Andrew (27–34).
Andrew tells Barrymore (actually, the ghost of Barrymore) about a brief moment of inspiration during the performance the night before, a moment in which he transcended himself and "became" Hamlet. In order to really pull this off, an actor needs to be able to play Shakespeare. He has to perform five lines of the "To be or not to be" section, and he must do it well to make the point. You might want to add even a few more lines of that famous speech. Start: "Last night, right from the start, I knew I was bombing." End: "And only eight thousand lines left to go."

I NEVER SANG FOR MY FATHER
by Robert Anderson (Dramatists Play Service)
Drama: Act II, p. 62; Gene (40).
The final speech in the play, very moving and introspective. Gene summarizes the final years of his father's life and the complex relationship they had. He discovers that death ends a life but

not a relationship. Start: "That night I left my father's house forever." End: "But, still, when I hear the word Father . . . It matters."

IN PERPETUITY THROUGHOUT THE UNIVERSE
by Eric Overmyer (Broadway Play Publishing)
Drama: Part I; Lyle (30s).
Lyle tells Dennis about how he gets moments of "runaway impulse," during which he experiences an overwhelming urge to do something that, while innocent, might not be socially acceptable. For example, the other day when he was riding on the New York City subway, a beautiful young Asian woman was standing in front of him and he had an urge to run his hand up her leg. Start: "I was on a train coming down. Packed ass to forehead as usual." End: "And I realized you can throw your life away. Like that. In an instant."
Drama: Part II; Dennis (30s)
Dennis describes the frustration of being Asian in America. Asian people think that he is American, and American people think that he is vaguely Asian. Japanese? Chinese? Cambodian? Start: "My life is a mystery to me." End: "I count in Chinese . . . Nowhere at home." For a shorter audition version, start: "I came to this country when I was twelve." End at the same place.

IN THE BOOM BOOM ROOM
by David Rabe (Samuel French)
Drama: Act II; Al (30s).
Al, a low-life, violent man, tells Chrissy about the relationship he had with a "hundred-buck-a-night hooker" when he was 18. Very graphic and sexual language. Start: "My first wife was a beauty." End: "I knew it cold—if I looked an' met their eyes, they was gonna take me right outa my shoes." (This monologue doesn't appear in the latest, two-act version of the play, but it can be found in the earlier, three-act versions.)

I OUGHT TO BE IN PICTURES
by Neil Simon (Samuel French)
Comedy: Act II, Scene 3, pp. 61–62; Herb (45).
After learning that his daughter, Libby, has a job working as a parking valet and that she is promoting herself as an actress by writing her name and number on the back of the valet-parking tickets, Herb tells her why this is a dumb idea. Cut Libby's lines and Herb's direct responses to them. Start: "Libby, can I ask you a serious personal question?" End: "I'll contact her first thing in the morning and hope and pray that someone else with spareribs in their teeth didn't get to her before me!"

JOE TURNER'S COME AND GONE
by August Wilson (Samuel French)
Drama: Act I, Scene 4, pp. 72–73; Bynum (60s).
Bynum is a "conjure man" who is pretty wise in the ways of women. Here, he advises young Jeremy, who is intent on chasing women, to look a little deeper than surface beauty. Good speech. You can probably make two monologues out of this text with some editing. Start: "You just can't look at it like that. You got to look at the whole thing." End: "You got to learn how to come to your own time and place with a woman."
Drama: Act II, Scene 2, pp. 106–107; Bynum (60s).
Another wise speech from the conjure man, having to do with how a man needs to find his own "song" in life. Cut and paste the monologue, eliminating Loomis. Start: "Mr. Loomis done picked some cotton. Ain't you, Herald Loomis? You done picked a bunch of cotton." End: "That's why I can tell you one of Joe Turner's niggers. 'Cause you forgot how to sing your song."

Drama: Act II, Scene 2, pp. 108–109; Loomis (32).
Loomis tells Bynum and Seth how he came to be incarcerated on Joe Turner's chain gang, lost his wife, and came to be traveling these past four years in search of her. Start: "Joe Turner catched me when my little girl was just born. Wasn't nothing but a little baby sucking on her mama's titty when he catched me." End: "When I find my wife that be the making of my own."

JOINED AT THE HEAD
by Catherine Butterfield (Dramatists Play Service) [*Women Playwrights—Best Plays of 1992* (Smith & Kraus)]
Drama: Act II, DPS pp. 59–60; Jim (late 30s).
Jim addresses the audience for the first time in the play, explaining in calm detail his emotional reactions to his wife's progressive cancer and her imminent death. This is a crusher of a speech, breathtakingly poignant, and the playwright explicitly advises that actors don't give in to maudlin impulses when playing it. Start: "Here's what you won't hear from them about me. You won't hear about the nights I lie awake looking at Maggy." End: "I just thought you should know."

K-2
by Patrick Meyers (Dramatists Play Service)
Drama: One-act play, pp. 21–22; Harold (mid-30s).
After listening to Taylor expound on his rather racist view of the world, Harold levels him with this monologue. Harold describes an American society obsessed with the production and sale of gizmos. Cut Taylor's lines and Harold's direct responses to them. Start: "Let me tell you who you really do it for . . . You do it for the gadgets." End: "That's all part of the Gizmo plan, baby. It's all a part of the Gizmo plan."

KEY EXCHANGE
by Kevin Wade (Dramatists Play Service)
Comedy: Scene 5, p. 24; Michael (late 20s).
Newly married and bitter because his wife has walked out on him, Michael tells Philip how he sought revenge by putting tiger balm in her contraceptive-jelly tube. Don't rush to use this selection for audition purposes; it has been used a great deal. Cut Philip's few lines. Start: "I can't believe it. We're in bed." End: "I figure I'd give them something to remember me by."

LADY AND THE CLARINET, THE
by Michael Cristofer (Dramatists Play Service)
Comedy: Act I, pp. 32–33; Jack (40s).
Jack's mistress is pressing him to separate from his wife, Marge. In a spasm of self-disclosure, he suddenly acknowledges that he is a stranger in his own life, that he doesn't recognize himself. You'll have to cut and paste this speech. Just eliminate Luba's lines. Start: "I don't feel anything about them any more. The kids. I look at them—they're bright." End: "I'm telling you they're wrong, because that isn't me! It isn't! It isn't me!"
Comedy: Act I, pp. 35–36; Jack (40s).
Jack finally got up enough nerve to leave his wife. Now he stands in the living room of his astonished girlfriend and gives her a blow-by-blow description of the Grand Farewell. He tells her how Marge helped him pack and how, before that, they got the giggles and made the best love ever. He is still trembling from the excitement of it all, in fact. Start: "Well, I did it. It's done. Finished. I finished it. I did it. Jesus." End: "And then, after, we went upstairs, she helped me pack, I picked the suitcase, kissed her good-bye, and here I am."

LANDSCAPE OF THE BODY
by John Guare (Dramatists Play Service)
Comedy: Act I, pp. 25–26; Raulito (35–45).
Raulito, an opportunistic and flamboyant Cuban refugee, is the owner/operator of a small New York City travel agency. He tells Betty, the sister of his former employee/lover, how he came to be what he is today—and why he happens to be wearing a gold lamé dress over his business suit. Start: "That is exactly what your sister Rosalie said to me the first time we met." End: "Then she would let me sleep with her after and dreams would come out of our heads like little Turkish moons."

LAST OF THE RED HOT LOVERS
by Neil Simon (Samuel French)
Comedy: Act I, pp. 29–30; Barney (47).
Barney brings Elaine to his mother's apartment and tells her why he wants to have a one-day fling. Because the complete monologue is too long for audition purposes and arguably too long for class, you should shorten it. Start: "I started getting the urge about five years ago." End: "for once I didn't just exist—I lived!"

LAUGHING WILD
by Christopher Durang (Dramatists Play Service)
Comedy: One-act play, Scene 2, pp. 21–22; A Man (any age).
The man talks directly to the members of the audience, telling them about a violent encounter he recently had with a strange woman at the supermarket. A short (about 1^1/2 minutes long), intense monologue excerpt from a very long speech. It is funny because it is outrageous. Start: "I was in the supermarket the other day about to buy some tuna fish when I sensed this very disturbed presence right behind me." End: "It makes me want to never leave my apartment ever ever again."

LONG DAY'S JOURNEY INTO NIGHT
by Eugene O'Neill (Yale University Press)
Drama: Act IV; James Tyrone (65).
James tells his drunk son, Edmund, about his glory days as a young actor and how he sold out his artistic integrity by purchasing a vehicle-play for himself. This role became his trademark, a fate he accepted because of the money. Now he is full of regret. Start: "Yes, maybe life overdid the lesson for me, and made a dollar worth too much." End: "What the hell was it I wanted to buy, I wonder, that was worth—well, no matter. It's a late day for regrets."
Drama: Act IV; Edmund (23).
Edmund tells his very drunk father about some "high spots" in his memory, specifically the times he spent at sea; these were the moments when he came closest to finding God. Start: "You've just told me some high spots in your memories." End: "I will always be a stranger who never feels at home."

LOU GEHRIG DID NOT DIE OF CANCER
by Jason Miller [*Three One-Act Plays by Jason Miller* (Dramatists Play Service)]
Drama: One-act play, pp. 55–56; Victor (32).
Victor gives a personal treasure, a baseball autographed by Lou Gehrig, to Barbara with instructions that she is to pass it on to her young son. While Victor gives it to her, he recounts how the ball came to be autographed by the great player, how he and his father experienced that particular day at the ball park so many years ago. Start: "You're a strong woman . . . a little strange but strong." End: ". . . give this ball to Jeffrey . . . I've had it too long."

LOVERS AND OTHER STRANGERS
by Renée Taylor and Joseph Bologna (Samuel French)
Comedy: "Mike and Susan," pp. 24–26; He (Mike, 30s).
Four days before his wedding, Mike gets cold feet. He comes to Susan's apartment at about
4 A.M. to call it off. After Mike delivers an impassioned monologue that she casually ignores,
they continue with their wedding plans as before. Start: "What do you expect me to do, carry
on a long conversation at four in the morning?" End: "That's it. It's all over. Goodbye. I'm
sorry. That's it." For a shorter version, start: "India's overpopulated! We'll all be sterilized
soon." Continue to the same end.

LOVE SUICIDE AT SCHOFIELD BARRACKS, THE
by Romulus Linney (Dramatists Play Service) [one-act version; *Seventeen Short Plays by
Romulus Linney* (Smith & Kraus)]
Drama: DPS pp. 13–14; Ruggles (45–50).
Ruggles, an old-school, blood-and-guts Army sergeant major, testifies about his in-your-face
relationship with the general and the last meeting they had before the general and his wife
committed suicide. He is on the stand for a couple of pages, so you can construct monologues
from his dialogue in various ways. One choice is to begin toward the end, when Ruggles starts
talking about nostalgia. He hits emotional peaks, describing how his son died. The language is
graphic, too rough perhaps for audition purposes, but it rings true. Start: "Nostalgia. Maybe
he thought that would be safe." End: "And that was the end of the interview."
Drama: DPS pp. 31–34; Roundhouse (50s).
A former university president and now a restaurant owner, Roundhouse testifies about his
close friendship with the general. He tells how his own homosexuality led to his downfall in
the American educational system, and how the general helped him pick up the pieces of his
life. This beautifully written speech is too long for most audition purposes but perfect for
class. Start: "I was President of two American universities." End: "In an age where everyone
else is innocent, Michael chose the terrible right to be guilty." For a shorter, audition-length
excerpt, start: "So here I am, better off than ever, a closet queen midwestern college president."
Continue to the same end.

LUV
by Murray Schisgal (Dramatists Play Service)
Comedy: Act I, pp. 11–12; Harry (late 30s).
Just moments ago, Milt discovered his old classmate, Harry, preparing to jump from a bridge
and talked him down. Harry explains that the really big issues in life are troubling him. He
believes that everything is summed up in one episode: a dog walked up to him one day in the
park and lifted its leg on his pants leg. As he tells it, you can see that Harry is a haunted man
and has reached the point where he is seeing significance in absolutely everything around him.
You'll have to cut and paste a lot, completely eliminating Milt's lines, but it works. Start: ". . . I'm
at the end of the line. Everything's falling apart . . . . The world, Milt. People. Life . . . ." End:
"I became aware . . . aware of the whole rotten senseless stinking deal. Nothing mattered to me
after that. Nothing."

MA RAINEY'S BLACK BOTTOM
by August Wilson (New American Library)
Drama: Act I; Toledo (45–55).
Toledo is the only person in the recording studio who can spell "music" so when he wins a
dollar from Levee in a spelling test, no one is impressed. Trying to get the others to see how
ludicrous their ignorance is, Toledo tells this story about the Lord's Prayer. Start: "Alright.

Now I'm gonna tell you a story to show just how ridiculous he sound." End: "Only 'cause I knowed how to spell music, I still got my dollar."
Drama: Act I; Cutler (35–45).
Cutler tells the other musicians how Slow Drag got his nickname during a dance contest when his dance partner's boyfriend walked in with a knife. Omit Slow Drag and Levee's interruptions. Start: "Slow Drag break a woman's back when he dance." End: "The women got to hanging around him so bad after that, them fellows in that town ran us out of there."
Drama: Act I; Toledo (45–55).
Toledo gives the other musicians a brief lesson in black history, humorously comparing black people to leftovers from a stew on a white person's table. Start: "Now I'm gonna show you how this goes . . . Where you just a leftover from history." End: "So go on and get off the plate and let me eat something else." If you use this selection for an audition, it might be more effective to end the monologue a line earlier in midsentence. End: "He'll tell you he done ate your black ass."
Drama: Act I; Levee (32).
Stung because the other musicians believe he is sucking up to the white record producers, Levee launches into this impassioned defense of his independence and integrity. He describes how, as a child, he tried to save his mother from being raped by a gang of white men. Start: "Levee got to be Levee!" End: "You all just leave Levee alone about the white man." To shorten this monologue for audition purposes, begin halfway through the speech. Start: "My mama was frying up some chicken."
Drama: Act II; Toledo (45–55).
Toledo starts talking about how many ways he has been a fool during his life, particularly with women. Start: "Now, I married a woman. A good woman." End: "So yeah, Toledo been a fool about a woman. That's part of making life."

MARCO POLO SINGS A SOLO
by John Guare (Dramatists Play Service)
Comedy: Act I, p. 16; Stony (36).
Stony explains that he is sensitive to the needs of plants and can hear their anguished cries. He concludes that people are really plants, not animals. A thoroughly odd and wonderful monologue, good for class. Stony's twisted logic is fun to work on. Start: "Theory? You call scientific fact theory?" End: "My plant nature. I celebrate that."
Comedy: Act I, p. 27; Stony (36).
Stony shares his very revisionist take on the plot of Henrik Ibsen's *A Doll's House*. His view is that Nora doesn't really leave at the end of the play, that her husband keeps building new rooms to contain her. As always, Stony marches to a different drummer; he has a frenetic inner rhythm and sees things that others don't. A challenging and fun monologue. Start: "Nora never left." End: ". . . her closet crammed with clothes, her possessions, her life sat waiting for her in a rocking chair."

"MASTER HAROLD" . . . AND THE BOYS
by Athol Fugard (Samuel French)
Drama: One-act play, pp. 32–34; Hally (17).
Hally delightedly relives the day that Sam built a crude kite. When they took it up on a hill, it actually flew! Cut Sam's lines and Hally's responses to them. Start: "You went a little distance from me down the hill." End: "I had a stiff neck the next day from looking up so much."
Drama: One-act play, p. 56; Hally (17).
Distressed because he has just learned that his alcoholic, abusive father is coming home from the hospital, Hally turns on Sam and Willy. He yells at them for having unrealistically rosy expectations about the human race. Cut Sam's lines and Hally's responses to them. Start: "Do you

want to know what is really wrong with your lovely dream, Sam?" End: "And guess who I think is going to be this year's winner?"
Drama: One-act play, pp. 62–64; Sam (mid-40s).
Hally has just spat in Sam's face, ordering him to be subservient to all white men. Furious at first and then sad, Sam delivers this devastating monologue. For workshop purposes, do the whole monologue. For audition purposes, stop at the halfway mark. Cut Hally's line and Sam's response to it. Start: "You don't know all of what you've just done . . . Master Harold." End: ". . . you're going to be sitting up there by yourself for a long time to come, and there won't be a kite in the sky." South-African accents are appropriate for all of these monologues.

MATCHMAKER, THE
by Thornton Wilder (Samuel French)
Comedy: Act I, pp. 18–19; Horace Vandergelder (60).
Horace Vandergelder is a self-made, blustery old fool who intends to remarry. In this speech to the audience, he outlines his amusingly parental views about the other sex. Remember, this play is set in the 1880s. Start: "Ninety-nine per cent of the people in the world are fools and the rest of us are in great danger of contagion." End: "Yes, like all you other fools, I'm willing to risk a little security for a certain amount of adventure. Think it over."
Comedy: Act II, pp. 47–48; Cornelius (33).
Cornelius is the head clerk in Vandergelder's Yonkers store. He has snuck out to have some fun and has fallen hard for Miss Molloy, the owner of the hat shop. Cornelius is a very innocent man; at 33, he has never even been kissed. In this speech, delivered to the audience, he is ecstatic about the wonders of women, particularly Miss Molloy. Start: "Isn't the world full of wonderful things? There we sit cooped up in Yonkers." End: "Even if I have to dig ditches for the rest of my life, I'll be a ditch digger who once had a wonderful day."

MEDAL OF HONOR RAG
by Tom Cole (Samuel French)
Drama: One-act play, pp. 36–38; Jackson (23).
Dale Jackson is an African-American soldier who has been awarded the Congressional Medal of Honor. In this speech, he tells how he almost cracked up at the Washington, DC, ceremonies over the hypocrisy of it all. Omit Doc's lines and the voice of Lyndon Johnson. Start: "I been home eight, nine months. Then I get this call." End: "It was weird!"

MIDDLE AGES, THE
by A. R. Gurney, Jr. (Dramatists Play Service)
Comedy: Act II, pp. 44–45; Charles (60s).
Charles, a distinguished, upper-class WASP defends the virtues of a private men's club, comparing its very civilized service to the treatment men receive in public places. Start: "Barney, I want you to go down to the pool, and ask your friends to put on their clothes." End: "That's what Barney wants apparently. And I'm sorry."

MISS JULIE
by August Strindberg [*Six Plays of Strindberg,* translated by Elizabeth Sprigge (Doubleday/Anchor)]
Drama: One-act play; Jean (30).
Jean tells Miss Julie about the time he hid in the Count's privy on the castle grounds where she lived. Not knowing the purpose of the building, he had snuck in to look at the opulent interior. When people approached, he had only one escape, through the opening used for excrement. Finally safe again, Jean hid in a nearby hedge of raspberry canes and, for the first time, caught sight of Miss Julie, practically the vision of a young angel. He subsequently watched her from afar and because a romance between them was impossible, he attempted suicide.

Keep in mind that Jean might be lying about everything. At this point in the play, he is intent on seducing Julie, and the anecdote may be seen as a device to endear himself to her. Start: "One time I went into the Garden of Eden with my mother to weed the onion beds." End: "There was no hope of winning you . . . you were simply a symbol of the hopelessness of ever getting out of the class I was born in."

MISS LONELYHEARTS
by Howard Teichmann [adapted from Nathanael West's novel of the same name (Dramatists Play Service)]
Drama): Act II, Scene 4, p. 71; Miss Lonelyhearts (26).
In this strong, brief speech, Lonelyhearts speaks of his father, a preacher who brought no love to his own home. Then he tells his employer, the very cynical Mr. Shrike, that he despises him. Start: "My father stood in the pulpit every Sunday." End: "Two things I don't want: to be like him, to be like you."

MISTER ROBERTS
by Thomas Heggen and Joshua Logan (Dramatists Play Service)
Drama: Act I, Scene 6, p. 41; The Captain (40–50).
The Captain tells Mister Roberts why he hates know-it-all college guys and how much he wants to be a full commander in the Navy. Start: "I think you're a pretty smart boy." End: "Now get out of here!"

MOON FOR THE MISBEGOTTEN, A
by Eugene O'Neill (Samuel French)
Drama: Act III, pp. 88–90; Tyrone (early 40s).
Tyrone has a secret. While escorting his mother's body cross country a year ago, he spent his time drinking heavily and sleeping with the trashiest whore he could find on the train. In this painful monologue, Tyrone confesses his sins to Josie, seeking her forgiveness. Only experienced actors should attempt this challenging speech. You'll have to edit this monologue a bit, but it works. Start: "When mama died, I'd been on the wagon for nearly two years. Not even a glass of beer." End: "I suppose I had some mad idea she could make me forget—what was in the baggage car ahead."

NERD, THE
by Larry Shue (Dramatists Play Service)
Comedy: Act II, pp. 49–50; Willum (34).
Burnt out from hassling with Rick, his unwanted house guest, for a week, Willum tells a horror story about an airplane trip the two of them took together. Start: "Six days. Has it been just six days?" End: "I think he only escaped because the ones who really had the grounds didn't want to stand up."

NORMAN CONQUESTS, THE—TABLE MANNERS
by Alan Ayckbourn (Samuel French)
Comedy: Act I, Scene 2, pp. 21–22; Norman (30s).
Everyone in the family knows that Norman intended to take his wife's sister, Annie, away for a romantic weekend, so he is being ostracized at breakfast. After making repeated efforts to get someone to talk to him, he resorts to reading their minds. This excerpt, which is written in the British vernacular, begins after Norman reads aloud from the Puffa Puffa Rice cereal box. Start: "Hang on, I've got another game. Mind reading. I'll read your minds." End: "I knew you wouldn't come. You didn't have the guts."

Comedy: Act I, Scene 2, pp. 22–23; Norman (30s).
This excerpt comes later in the breakfast speech discussed above. Everyone except Reg has left the table at this point, so Norman talks to him as Reg glumly eats his cereal in silence. The speech is touching and funny. Norman describes his marriage, one that is efficient but unromantic. Start: "I suppose you think I'm cruel, too, don't you? Well, I've damn good cause to be, haven't I?" End: "... The real me. Look at me...."

NUTS
by Tom Topor (Samuel French)
Drama: Act II, p. 46; Arthur Kirk (60s).
Arthur Kirk is a self-made, no-nonsense millionaire whose stepdaughter, Claudia, has been arrested for prostitution and murder. Testifying on the stand during her sanity hearing, Arthur succinctly puts forth his philosophy on love, marriage, and the propriety of getting "a little something on the side." Start: "Let me finish would ya." End: "As far as I'm concerned, a man can chase sheep, just so long as he comes home and takes care of his family. Bill didn't. Bill took a walk."
Drama: Act II, p. 53; Arthur Kirk (60s).
Testifying on the stand, Arthur Kirk has just been asked why it is so important to him that his stepdaughter be found incompetent to stand trial. In response, he lashes out at the entire legal system and denies that Claudia is a prostitute. To his way of thinking, that is impossible; she must be mentally ill. Start: "We're thinking about a trial." End: "You get that straight."

OH DAD, POOR DAD, MAMMA'S HUNG YOU IN THE CLOSET AND I'M FEELIN' SO SAD
by Arthur Kopit (Samuel French)
Comedy: Act I, Scene 2, pp. 19–20; Jonathan (17–25).
Jonathan, a fellow with no social skills, is smitten with Rosalie, the pretty young woman who baby-sits for the absentee couple in the penthouse across the way. He has been watching her through his homemade telescope. In this speech, Jonathan haltingly but excitedly tells her how to make such a telescope. Eliminate Rosalie's single line. Start: "Well, I made it out of lenses and tubing. The lenses I had because Ma-Ma-Mother gave me a set of lenses so I could see my stamps better." End: "Even if I didn't see anything else, I did see you. And—and I'm—very glad."

OLEANNA
by David Mamet (Dramatists Play Service)
Drama: Act II, pp. 33–34; John (35–45).
John is a college professor facing sexual-harassment charges. As his exasperation grows, he tries to explain to Carol, the student accusing him of harassment, what communication really is. You'll have to cut and paste the dialogue a bit, but it works. Start: "Wait a second, will you, just one moment. Nice day today." End: "I don't think we can proceed until we accept that each of us is human. And we still can have difficulties."

ONLY GAME IN TOWN, THE
by Frank D. Gilroy (Samuel French)
Drama: Act II, Scene 2, pp. 69–70; Joe (30–35).
Joe asks Fran to marry him. When she hesitates, he levels her with this monologue, accusing her of being afraid of making a deeper commitment. Start: "For two years, I've slinked through these corridors as the villain in Apartment 2C." End: "Do I perceive the hint of a smile—the trace of a tear? ... Say it."

ORPHANS

by Lyle Kessler (Samuel French)

Drama: Act II, Scene 1, pp. 50–51; Harold (40–50).

Harold gives the boys a lecture about the value of moderation. He tells a story from his boyhood. Cut Treat and Phillip's lines and Harold's direct responses to them. Start: "You know who you remind me of, Treat?" End: ". . . How far a man will go for financial gain."

OTHER PEOPLE'S MONEY

by Jerry Sterner (Samuel French)

Comedy-Drama: Act II, pp. 63–64; Garfinkle (40–45).

Kate has just offered Garfinkle $20 per share "greenmail" if he'll cease his efforts to take over New England Wire and Cable. Garfinkle scoffs at the offer, setting his price at $25 per share and claiming that he would rather talk about Kate's good looks. As it becomes evident that Kate isn't authorized to pay $25, her mood sinks. He considers her for a moment and then delivers this short, cynical monologue. Cut Kate's single interruption of the speech. Stage directions indicate that Kate exits in the middle of Garfinkle's monologue and he keeps talking, presumably to the audience. For audition purposes, he should continue speaking directly to Kate; eliminate her exit.

Comedy-Drama: Act II, pp. 86–88; Garfinkle (40–45).

Garfinkle addresses stockholders of the company he is taking over. Start: "You just heard the prayer for the dead, and fellow stuckholders (sic), you didn't say 'Amen' and you didn't even get to sip the wine." End: "Now that is a funeral worth having."

PIANO LESSON, THE

by August Wilson (Plume)

Comedy-Drama: Act I, Scene 1; Doaker Charles (47).

During the 27 years Doaker Charles has worked for the railroad, he has made some keen observations about all of the travelers he has seen coming and going. After Boy Willie butters him up by suggesting that women are always waiting for him at every depot down south, Doaker starts talking about what he has seen and learned over the years. You'll have to cut and paste. Start: "I'm cooking now, but I used to line track." End: "It'll come back every time."

Comedy-Drama: Act I, Scene 1; Avery Brown (38).

Avery Brown migrated north and got a job running the elevator in a skyscraper downtown. He also became a preacher and has been trying to raise the money to start his first church. In this speech, Avery tells a very skeptical Boy Willie, who used to work alongside him picking cotton, how he came to be a preacher in the first place. Start: "It came to me in a dream." End: "So I became a preacher."

Comedy-Drama: Act I, Scene 2; Boy Willie (30).

Boy Willie explains that he intends to sell the family's piano, an heirloom, because he wants to purchase the land his ancestors worked on as slaves. His sister Berniece is adamantly opposed to this plan. Start: "Now, I'm gonna tell you the way I see it." End: "But that's why I'm gonna take this piano out of here and sell it."

Comedy-Drama: Act II, Scene 1; Wining Boy (56).

Wining Boy just sold Lymon his "all-silk" suit for $3, as well as a sharp pair of Florsheim shoes for $3. As Lymon happily goes upstairs to get dressed so he and Boy Willie can go downtown and find some women, Wining Boy muses about how he almost was Lymon's daddy; he had that close a relationship with the young man's mother. Start: "That's all Lymon thinks about is women." End: "Fellow walked in and shot him thinking he was someone else."

PICK UP AX
by Anthony Clarvoe (Broadway Play Publishing)
Comedy-Drama: Act I, Scene 6; Mick (mid-30s).
Mick is a corrupt wheeler-dealer intent on taking over a failing software company. He tells the two computer-nerd, acid-head owners how he intimidated some microchip people into delivering some goods. Start: "I swear to God this is a kindergarten industry." End: "He won't be grateful, they never are. You work, you do your best."

PLAY MEMORY
by Joanna M. Glass (Samuel French)
Drama: Act II, pp. 61–62; Cam (late 50s).
Cam is evidently determined to drink himself to death and to drag his wife and young daughter, Jean, down with him. A few moments ago, Jean came home from school and told him that she longs for a normal life. In this speech, which is tinged with self-pity, Cam defends his life choices. Rather than seeing his stubborn nature as a liability, he considers it an asset. You'll have to cut and paste a little. Start: "You know what normal is? Normal is where nothing happens." End: "And when they go to bed at night they say, 'God, when will you stop me? When will you send someone in to stop me?'"
Drama: Act II, p. 66; Cam (late 50s).
Cam is in the process of rejecting his sponsors from Alcoholics Anonymous. They accuse him of having a superiority complex, and he responds by justifying his behavior, claiming to have higher standards than everyone else. You'll have to cut and paste, eliminating Ross's lines. Start: ". . . I'm trying like hell to hold onto something. And I've realized that all I've got to hold onto is what I carry around in my head." End: "The sound of their coats, turning. And I will never recover from that!"

PRELUDE TO A KISS
by Craig Lucas (Broadway Play Publishing)
Comedy: Act II; The Old Man (60s).
Rita's soul is in the Old Man's body, and she has learned a great deal from the experience. Here, the Old Man (really Rita) tells Peter what life means to him/her in very existential terms. In portraying the Old Man, actors shouldn't make any effort to speak in a woman's tone or style. Start: "You know . . . if you think how we're born and we go through all the struggle." End: "So we might as well have a good time while we're here, don't you think?"

PROMISE, THE
by José Rivera (Broadway Play Publishing)
Comedy-Drama: Act II, Scene 2; Guzman (about 40).
Guzman encourages Hiberto, a sickly, fearful, awkward—but quite possibly wealthy—man to marry his daughter, Lilia. Guzman promises to make a gift of his book, *Tales of Marcario*, which contains stories of magical happenings in the small Puerto Rican town. It might be effective to precisely mime the book when using this speech for audition purposes. Start: "You marry her, my friend, and tonight you touch her." End: "This book will come in handy when you liberate Puerto Rico for me."

P. S. YOUR CAT IS DEAD
by James Kirkwood [revised edition (Samuel French)]
Comedy: Act II, pp. 60–61; Jimmy (38).
Jimmy has let Vito talk him into sharing some marijuana and is completely stoned. Jimmy tells his prisoner about a recent commercial audition that was awful. Start: "Now get this scene:

Nine men and three women glued together behind this long conference table. . . ." End: "'No, you see, there was a little speck of shit in the pool—you!'"

RAINMAKER, THE
by N. Richard Nash (Samuel French)
Drama: Act I, pp. 41–42; Starbuck (30s).
Starbuck tells the skeptical Curry family precisely how he intends to make it rain. He is a spellbinding orator, and utterly charismatic. Omit Lizzie and Noah's interruptions. Start: "What do you care how I do it, sister, as long as it's done!" End: "And me? I'm ridin' right through that rainbow!—Well, how about it? Is it a deal?"

RAISIN IN THE SUN, A
by Lorraine Hansberry (Samuel French)
Drama: Act II, Scene 2, pp. 87–88; Walter (35).
When Ruth and Mama discover that Walter hasn't been at his work for the past three days, they ask him what he has been doing instead. He tells them that, basically, he has been driving around Chicago and getting drunk at the Green Hat. Start: "Mama—you don't know all the things a man got leisure can find to do in this city." End: "You can just sit there and drink and listen to them three men play and you realize that don't nothing matter worth a damn, but just being there."
Drama: Act II, Scene 2, pp. 90–91; Walter (35).
Walter tells his 10-year-old son, Travis, what life is going to be like in about seven years, at which point he plans to be a big business executive. Start: "You know what, Travis? In seven years you going to be 17 years old." End: "You just name it, son . . . And I hand you the world."
Drama: Act III, pp. 123–124; Walter (35).
Walter's "friend" and would-be business associate has disappeared with all of Walter's money. As he reflects on the tragic turn of events, he discovers a hard lesson in life. In this short and extremely bitter monologue, Walter tells Mama about the difference between "the takers and the 'tooken.'" Start: "You all always telling me to see life like it is." End: "He's taught me to keep my eye on what counts in this world. Yeah—thanks, Willy!"

ROSENCRANTZ AND GUILDENSTERN ARE DEAD
by Tom Stoppard (Samuel French)
Comedy: Act II, pp. 54–55; Rosencrantz (20–30).
Up to this point, Rosencrantz has been bewildered about where he is and why he is there. He just wants to go home, but he can't because he and Guildenstern were "sent for." Here, Rosencrantz grapples with whether it is possible to conceive of one's own death. You'll have to cut and paste this amusing speech a bit. Start: "Do you ever think of yourself as actually dead, lying in a box with a lid on it?" End: "Eternity is a terrible thought. I mean, where's it going to end?"
Comedy: Act II, pp. 55–56; Rosencrantz (20–30).
This monologue is actually a continuation of the "dead in a box" speech discussed above, but you can treat it as a separate monologue. Rosencrantz tells a couple of bad jokes as he tries to understand the meaning of time, consciousness, and death. He orders someone in the wings to come out, but no one does. So he then orders the person to keep out, and no one enters. In this way, Rosencrantz gains control of the situation. Start: "Two early Christians chanced to meet in Heaven." End: "Keep out, then! I forbid anyone to enter! . . . That's better."

SEA GULL, THE
by Anton Chekhov [a new version by Jean-Claude Van Itallie (Dramatists Play Service)]
Drama: Act I, p. 8; Treplev (25).
Treplev, an aspiring playwright and the son of a famous actress, talks about the difference between his view of theater and his mother's. In this speech, he tells his uncle how frustrating

it has been to live in her shadow and how much he disagrees with her conventional attitudes toward the theater and acting. Start: "You see, my mother doesn't love me. Why should she?" End: "I imagined I could read their thoughts, and I was going through agonies."
Drama: Act II, pp. 25–27; Trigorin (late 30s).
Trigorin tells Nina, who adores him, how difficult it is to be a famous writer. This long speech is good for class work. Eliminate Nina's interruption and Trigorin's response. Start: "I hear you talk about fame and happiness and a bright interesting life, but to me these are words which if you'll forgive me are about as meaningful as sugar plums." End: "Oh how horrible that all was. It was really torture."

SEA HORSE, THE
by Edward J. Moore (Samuel French)
Drama: Act I, pp. 15–16; Harry (late 30s).
Harry has spent his life as a sailor. In this lovely monologue, he tells Gertrude about his dream of a son, a home, and his own boat. Start: "A while back . . . I get relieved of the midwatch." End: "And he'll have a great mom! . . . Well . . . what do ya think?!"

SHADOW BOX, THE
by Michael Cristofer (Samuel French)
Drama: Act II, pp. 68–69; Mark (25–30).
Mark tells Beverly about how he was selling his ass on Market Street when he first met her ex-husband, Brian. Mark's love for Brian is apparent. Cut Beverly's lines. Start: ". . . when I met Brian, I was hustling outside a bar in San Francisco." End: "And he never stopped talking. Never."

SIGHT UNSEEN
by Donald Margulies (Dramatists Play Service)
Drama: Act I, Scene 1, pp. 16–17; Jonathan (35–45).
Jonathan tells Patricia about how his father, who died last week, covered an entire wall of the family home with photographs, stapling them right to the wall. Eliminate Patricia's lines and Jonathan's direct responses to them. Start: "I went to pack up his house the other day?" End: "That's all gone now. It's all gone."
Drama: Act II, Scene 6, p. 48; Jonathan (35–45).
Trying to answer the question "What is good art?", Jonathan tells an interviewer why he was disgusted by the huge turnout for the Van Gogh exhibit in New York. Start: "Okay, let me ask you something: When we talk about good art, what are we talking about?" End: "The art was just a backdrop for the real show that was happening. In the gift shop!" You can extend the monologue a bit more. Cut Grete's lines. End: "'cause the media told them so!"
Drama: Act II, Scene 6, pp. 49–50; Jonathan (35–45).
Now a famous and wealthy painter, Jonathan tells an interviewer how basically stupid his fame really is. He points out that eight years ago, he was painting houses, not canvas. Start: "What I am today? What am I today?" End: "The work loses its importance, the importance becomes 'Waxman.'"

SIGN IN SIDNEY BRUSTEIN'S WINDOW, THE
by Lorraine Hansberry (Samuel French)
Drama: Act II, Scene 3, pp. 88–89; Alton Scales (27).
Alton Scales just discovered that the woman he intends to marry is a prostitute, not a fashion model as she has claimed. In this bitter speech, he tells his friend Sidney about his lowly origins and swears he won't accept the "white man's trash." Start: "The white man done wrapped his trash in tinsel, and give it to the nigger again, huh, Sidney?" End: "I don't want white man's leavings, Sidney. Not now. Not ever."

SIX DEGREES OF SEPARATION
by John Guare (Dramatists Play Service)
Drama: One-act play, p. 50; Rick (early 20s).
Rick is an aspiring actor in New York City, recently having arrived from Utah with his girl-friend. He falls under Paul's spell and winds up depleting his bank account for the con man and having sex with him. This monologue, delivered directly to the audience, reveals Rick's embarrassment, disillusionment, and shame. A short time after this speech, he commits suicide by jumping from a building. Start: "He told me he had some of his own money and he wanted to treat me." End: "My father said I was a fool and I can't have him be right. What have I done?"

SPEED OF DARKNESS, THE
by Steve Tesich (Samuel French)
Drama: Act II, Scene 6, pp. 81–83; Joe (mid-40s).
Joe's teenage daughter, Mary, has discovered that he isn't her natural father. In this anguished speech, he tells her how he was sterilized when Agent Orange was dropped on him while he was fighting in Vietnam. Joe also reveals that after the war, he and his buddy Lou sought revenge against the United States when they got jobs dumping toxic wastes for upstanding American companies. Full of bitter, graphic images and a lot of venom, this piece is best for experienced actors. Start: "You see, Mary. I fell in love with your mom the first night I met her." End: "I wanna take it back and I don't know how."

STILL LIFE
by Emily Mann (Dramatists Play Service)
Drama: Act III, Scene 6, p. 45; Mark (28).
Mark, a burned-out Vietnam vet, observes that criminals on the evening news go to jail for doing what he did legally during the war. A short, powerful speech. Start: "I don't know. I just don't know." End: "I need to tell them what I did."
Drama: Act III, Scene 7, pp. 46–47; Mark (28).
In an anguished, deeply introspective confession, Mark reveals how he executed an entire Vietnamese family. He is haunted and tortured by his act. Very difficult material, well written. Unfortunately, this speech is too long for audition purposes. Start: "I killed three children, a mother and father in cold blood." End: "I'm shell shocked."

STRANGEST KIND OF ROMANCE, THE
by Tennessee Williams [*The Theater of Tennessee Williams,* Volume 6 (New Directions)]
Drama: Scene 3; Old Man (65–75).
Tennessee Williams describes this character named The Old Man as looking like Walt Whitman. The character is the lonely boarding-house landlady's father-in-law, and he visits one of the boarders. In a striking speech, he talks about visiting the plant where he used to work and demanding a job. This short piece is good audition material. Start: "The day before yesterday, I went down to the plant." End: "The Superintendent . . . said, 'Hush up, be still! I'll send for the wagon!'"

SUBSTANCE OF FIRE, THE
by Jon Robin Baitz (Samuel French)
Drama: Act I, pp. 32–33; Martin (late 20s).
Martin tells his family how books have ruined his life. Start: "Poison! You want to talk about poison?" End "I hear the book chains are now selling preemptive strike video games, so why bother anyway? I'm out." The challenge for actors is to avoid a one-note harangue. Martin is angry and is summing up a lifetime of frustration in his too literary family.

Drama: Act II, pp. 64–65; Issac (60s).
Issac tells Marge, a psychiatric social worker sent by his sons to determine his mental competence, about the memories he has of his family in an apartment. Start: "Listen to me. You come here with an agenda." End: "The silence, Miss Hackett. The silence. Pointless."

SWAN SONG
by Anton Chekhov [*The Sneeze, Plays and Stories* by Anton Chekhov, translated and adapted by Michael Frayn (Samuel French)]
Comedy: One-act play, pp. 73–75; Svetlovidov (68).
An elderly comic actor wearing a clown costume wakes from a liquor-induced nap to discover that everyone has left the theater except Nikita the prompter and himself. Before Svetlovidov realizes that anyone else is there, he talks to himself. Start: "Well, here's a fine how-do-you-do! Here's a fine state of affairs!" End: "I'm not fit to be seen! Better go and get dressed."
Comedy: One-act play, pp. 77–78; Svetlovidov (68).
Svetlovidov tells Nikita how consistently actors are ostracized by the public, remembering a romance that ended years ago when he refused to give up his profession. This is a very touching speech. Start: "When I was a young actor, when I was just starting to get my teeth into it, I remember there was a woman who loved me for my art." End: "Don't trust them an inch!"

SWEET BIRD OF YOUTH
by Tennessee Williams (Dramatists Play Service)
Drama: Act I, Scene 2, pp. 28–30; Chance (29).
Chance is an aging Adonis with a good body. He is still clinging to the hope of Hollywood success, but he makes his money by sleeping with wealthy women. In this very honest speech, Chance tells one of them about his life and aspirations. Cut Princess's lines and his direct responses to them. Start: "Here is the town I was born in." End: "And that was when Heavenly became more important to me than anything else." For a shorter audition version, start: "I'm talking about the parade."

TENTH MAN, THE
by Paddy Chayefsky (Samuel French)
Comedy-Drama: Act I, pp. 13–14; Foreman (60s).
Foreman has surprised the other elderly Jews who are gathered in the tiny synagogue for morning prayers by showing up with Evelyn, his schizophrenic granddaughter, who is currently waiting in the rabbi's office. Clearly in a state of high anxiety, he composes himself and then tells the amazed men that his granddaughter is possessed by a dybbuk, a spirit, and that the voice of a woman he dishonored years ago has come out of her throat. Start: "She is possessed, Alper. She has a dybbuk in her." End: "May God strike me down on this spot, Alper, if every word I tell you is not true."
Drama: Act II, Scene 1, pp. 45–46; Arthur (30s).
During a moment of lucidity in between schizophrenic departures, Evelyn has been talking to Arthur about her illness. Then, in a remarkably introspective speech, he tells her about himself, explaining why life is unsatisfactory for him, why he'll probably commit suicide one day even though he has enjoyed all the accouterments of success. Toward the end of the speech, Arthur is on the verge of tears. Start: "Life is merely dreary if you're sane, and unbearable if you are sensitive." End: "As you see, I have quite a theatrical way when I want to."

THAT CHAMPIONSHIP SEASON
by Jason Miller (Dramatists Play Service)
Drama: Act II, p. 26; Coach (60s).
The coach implores his boys to stop squabbling, not to fall apart on him now. He says he never got married because coaching basketball was more than a profession—it was a vocation.

A strong monologue. Start: "Booze and women. I tried to protect you from it." End: "You, boys, are my real trophies, never forget that. Never."
Drama: Act III, pp. 46–47; Coach (60s).
In one devastating speech in the final moments of the play, the coach sums up his life, remembering the innocent optimism of childhood and the agony of the stock-market crash, and blaming the Jews. His team, his pathetically glorious championship high-school basketball team, is his life, but a memory of greatness is all that is left. This monologue is long but stunning. Start: "We don't need them, boys . . . It's history now." End: "I made you winners. I made you winners." For audition purposes, start: "Jesus, I can still see buckets of ice cream. Great red slabs of beef."

TIME OF YOUR LIFE, THE
by William Saroyan (Samuel French)
Comedy: Act II, p. 68; Harry (20s).
Harry is an energetic comic and dancer who most people don't find funny. Here, he tries one of his routines on a patron of Nick's Saloon. Start: "This is it. I'm up at Sharkey's on Turk Street. It's a quarter to nine." End: "I turn around. Everybody's behind the eight ball!"
Comedy: Act II, pp. 74–76; Kit Carson (58).
Probably the most colorful character in the play, Kit Carson is a throwback to the American West, and he tells fantastic tales, most of which aren't true. In the end, he does something very heroic. This particular anecdote, which you'll have to cut and paste, deals with his outrageous adventures in Gallup. Start: "I don't suppose you ever fell in love with a midget weighing thirty-nine pounds?" End: "I don't suppose you ever had to put a dress on to save your skin, did you?"
Drama: Act V, pp. 99–100; Joe (25–35).
Joe tells his friend Tom about money, where it comes from and what it does to people. Start: "Now don't be a fool, Tom. Listen carefully." End: "Now, don't ever bother me about it again."

TRIP BACK DOWN, THE
by John Bishop (Samuel French)
Comedy: Act II, pp. 75–76; Chuck (24).
Chuck has a big case of hero worship and is beside himself when he gets a chance to talk to stock-car driver Bobby Horvath. Excited, Chuck describes in detail the very first time he saw Bobby race. You'll have to eliminate the other characters' lines and piece this speech together, but it works well. Start: "You know you was in the first stock car race I ever saw." End: "man, what a race."

VALUE OF NAMES, THE
by Jeffrey Sweet (Dramatists Play Service)
Drama: One-act play, p. 41; Leo (late 60s).
Late in this one-act play, Leo complains about how everyone wants him to prove he is repentant for having named names before the House Un-American Activities Committee. Although he considers what he did to be wrong, he doesn't think public apologies will help anything. Start: "Look, I've been though this before." End: "And believe me, you're about the only reason I'd think of doing it."

VIEUX CARRÉ
by Tennessee Williams (New Directions)
Drama: Part I, Scene 2; Writer (28).
In the preceding scene, Nightingale goes to the writer's rooming-house cubicle to comfort him after hearing sobs. They talk of loneliness, death, and love and then have sex. As the

lights fade on that scene, the writer steps out and speaks to the audience as the play's narrator. In an extraordinarily poetic speech, he says that, as he lay in his bed with Nightingale, a vision of his grandmother as a saint, appeared to him. He muses about her reaction to the two entwined men. Start: "When I was alone in the room, the visitor having retreated beyond the plywood partition between his cubicle and mine." End: "An almost invisible gesture of . . . forgiveness? . . . through understanding? . . . before she dissolved into sleep. . . ."

WAITING FOR LEFTY
by Clifford Odets (Grove Press)
Drama: Scene III, "The Young Hack and His Girl"; Sid (25–35).
Sid tells his girlfriend, Florrie, why he is disgusted with the 1935 American system of government and economics. He claims that the cards are stacked against the little guy and that, in the end, the big guys with the money just want those on the bottom to go fight wars. A speech full of moral outrage and passion. Start: "We worked like hell to send him to college—my kid brother, Sam, I mean—and look what he done—joined the navy!" End: "They'll teach Sam to point the guns the wrong way, that dumb basketball player!"

WASH, THE
by Philip Kan Gotanda (Dramatists Play Service) [*Between Worlds, Contemporary Asian-American Plays* (Theatre Communications Group)]
Drama: Act I, Scene 3, DPS p. 12; Sadao (65).
Sadao, a widower, is seeing Masi, who is recently separated after 42 years of marriage. She is making coffee for them when he suddenly tells this very personal story. During a visit with a group of widows, one of them asked Sadao why he was still wearing a wedding ring since his wife was dead and he was actively trying to meet a new woman. He broke down and cried, and then off took the ring. Start: "We were all sitting around in somebody's living room, when someone said, 'How come you're still wearing your wedding ring?'" End: "'Because you're not married any more.'"
Drama: Act II, Scene 2, DPS pp. 35–36; Sadao (65).
Sadao and Masi lie in bed together. He speaks of his deceased wife, the challenges of aging, and how fortunate he is to have a second chance at romance. Start: "She just slept all the time." End: "Can you imagine what the kids are thinking?"

WILD HONEY
by Michael Frayn [adapted from an early, untitled play by Anton Chekhov (Samuel French)]
Comedy: Act I, Scene 2, pp. 44–45; Platonov (28–32).
Back in their university days, Sofya and Platonov were idealistic lovers. Today, married to different partners, they meet unexpectedly, and the old flames still burn. But Sofya wounds Platonov when she asks why he hasn't done more with his life. In this speech, he responds and then attacks her choice of a husband. Eliminate Sofya's lines. Start: "Is every man you meet really such a threat to your Sergey?" End: "What in all the wide world made you marry that man?" For an audition-length excerpt, start: "Why haven't I done better? The first thing you asked me!"

WOOLGATHERER, THE
by William Mastrosimone (Samuel French)
Comedy-Drama: Act I, pp. 36–37; Cliff (25–35).
Cliff tells Rosie about the awful life of a trucker. This long monologue runs 4 1/2 pages. For audition purposes, begin about three pages into the speech with Cliff. Start: "You swear this is your last run." End: "Lose touch. Lose yourself in the road."

YANKEE DAWG YOU DIE
by Philip Kan Gotanda (Dramatists Play Service)
Comedy: Act I, Scene 2, pp. 19–20; Bradley (20s).
Bradley meets Vincent in the waiting room at an audition and performs his monologue for him. In this strange piece, a fellow is driving his car when a Neil Sedaka song comes on the radio. He happily mistakes the name "Sedaka" for Japanese. The idea is that when legitimate hero-models are missing, a person will just make them up. This monologue is excellent for workshops and under the right circumstances, could work as an audition piece. The problem is that taken out of context, the point might not be clear to an auditor. Good speech, though, and fun to do. Start: "It was night. It was one of those typical summer nights in the valley." End: "Neil Sedaakaa! I knew. I just knew for once, where ever I drove to that night, the road belonged to me."
Comedy-Drama: Act I, Scene 3, pp. 25–26; Vincent (60s).
Vincent yells at Bradley for his lack of sensitivity, explaining that movies didn't always depict "Asian Americans," that the term used to be "Orientals." He recalls the days he and others worked on the "chop suey circuit" playing Chinatowns and Little Tokyos around the country as "hoofers, jugglers, acrobats." This is a terrific monologue! Start: "That's all there was, Bradley. That's all there was! But you don't think I wouldn't have wanted to play a better role than that bucktoothed, groveling waiter?" End: "Who remembers? Who appreciates?"
Comedy-Drama: Act II, Scene 1, pp. 38–39; Bradley (20s).
In an effort to teach Bradley how to perform Shakespeare, Vincent asks him to relive his first LSD trip. As such, this thoroughly odd speech is all about friendly cows that Bradley sees as human. And then they pretend to be cows again. As with Bradley's earlier monologue, you might have trouble with this in audition because, out of context, it might confuse an auditor. For workshop use, however, it is excellent. Eliminate Vincent's few lines. Start: "I am walking. There is a tightness I feel in the back of my neck." End: "They slowly lumber away, stupid and dumb. Moo, moo. It's a true story."
Comedy-Drama: Act II, Scene 4, p. 50; Vincent (60s).
This short speech comes in the final moment of the play, and it could be a hair-raiser. Vincent begins reenacting a scene from a movie in which he plays a stereotypical Japanese soldier. Then, gradually, he drops the accent, but the action continues. Start: "Remember this?" End: "Why can't you hear what I'm saying? Why can't you see me as I really am?"

ZOOMAN AND THE SIGN
by Charles Fuller (Samuel French)
Drama: Act II, pp. 46–48; Zooman (18).
Zooman, the inner-city gang member who accidentally killed Jinny, has been hiding from the police ever since. Throughout the play, he represents a street-level counterpart to the civility and basic decency of the victim's family. He delivers all five of his monologues directly to the audience; these are rough stuff, full of violent, graphic images. The following excerpt is fine for special audition purposes. In it, Zooman talks about what it is like to be on the run. Start: "It kin be fun being on the run." End: "Niggahs can't be heroes, don't he know nothin'?"
Drama: Act II, p. 58; Victor (15).
Victor's 12-year-old sister, Jinny, was accidentally killed three days ago when caught in inner-city-gang crossfire. In this short speech, he tells the audience about the special relationship they shared. Start: "They always tell me that I've got a better education than they had." End: "I know it, but I'll never tell them!"

Part Three
Female Monologues

ABDICATION, THE

by Ruth Wolff [*The New Women's Theatre* (Random House)]
Drama: Act I; Christina (28–35).
Christina complains to Cardinal Azzolino about being isolated as the Queen of Sweden and of being expected to sexually submit to men she doesn't love in order to provide an heir to the throne. Christina then tells the Cardinal that she desires him. A superb monologue, found at the very end of Act I. Cut Oxenstierna's lines. Start: "I am Queen of Sweden. By reason of my exalted rank and privilege, I am allowed anything I want." End: "I will never give myself to a man—unless it is you."
Drama: Act II; Christina (28–35).
In this flashback sequence, Christina decides to give up the throne. She is being torn in two by her sexual longings and is unhappy with herself as a woman. Start: "I am unfit for this occupation. The months go by, I don't know where they're going." End: "I'm being torn apart! I must give up the crown . . . I want . . . not to be a woman. I want to tear out the feminine parts of me!"

ABSENT FRIENDS

by Alan Ayckbourn (Samuel French)
Comedy: Act II, p. 41; Diana (30s).
Diana begins this speech by recalling a pretty red coat she owned as a child. She liked red because she wanted to join the Canadian Royal Mounted Police, but then she found out that "girls don't do that kind of thing." They type and knit and marry and have babies. So Diana married and had babies, but now she sees how empty all of this is and wishes that she could have joined the Royal Mounted Police anyway. At the end of the speech, she breaks into sobs. A very unusual monologue that could be a show stopper at an audition. Written in the British vernacular. Start: "I'd seen it in the window of this shop when I walked to school. It was red." End: "I know I should have joined the Mounted Police. (Starts to sob) I want to join the Mounted Police. Please."

AGNES OF GOD

by John Pielmeier (Samuel French)
Drama: Act I, Scene 4, pp. 19–20; Agnes (21).
Agnes tells her court-appointed psychiatrist where she believes "good" and "bad" babies come from. This is an interesting speech, full of inner conviction and logic that is apparent only to Agnes. Start: "Well, I think they come from when an angel lights on their mother's chest and whispers into her ear." End: "God loves you! . . . God loves you."

Drama: Act I, Scene 10, pp. 48–49; Mother Superior (50s).
It is becoming clear that the psychiatrist intends to probe Agnes's mind more deeply, and the Mother Superior feels threatened. In this reflective speech, she describes her adult life as a time of pointless drifting. After joining the convent, she didn't find meaning . . . until the night she heard Agnes singing in an upstairs room. Suddenly, Mother Superior felt connected to God. She asks the doctor not to jeopardize her faith. Start: "When I was a child I used to speak with my guardian angel." End: "Those years after six were very bleak."

AMEN CORNER, THE
by James Baldwin (Samuel French)
Drama: Act III, pp. 87–88; Margaret (35–45).
Margaret begs her son not to pursue the life of a professional musician, not to turn out like his daddy. A short, strong speech. Eliminate Odessa's line. Start: "David, I'm older than you. I done been down the line." End: "You think I want you one day lying where your daddy lies today?"

AMERI/CAIN GOTHIC
by Paul Carter Harrison [*Totem Voices, Plays from the Black World Repertory*, edited by Paul Carter Harrison (Grove Press)]
Drama: Act I; Cass (30s).
Cass is a reclusive woman who lives in a Memphis rooming house across the street from the motel where Martin Luther King will soon stay. As history will show, he'll also die there. In this haunting speech, Cass tells I. W. Harper, who has been sent to check out the motel for King, why she is afraid that someone is pursuing her. Start: "I was leaving that department store on Main Street where the old Gayoso Hotel used to be." End: "When I awoke, a man's hand was around my throat."

ANNA CHRISTIE
by Eugene O'Neill (Vintage Books)
Drama: Act III; Anna (20).
In an impassioned speech, Anna confesses to Mat and her father, who believe that she was reared an innocent farm girl, that she has in fact been a prostitute. You'll have to piece together the monologue a bit, but it works. Cut the men's few lines and Anna's direct responses to them. Start: "It was one of them cousins that you think is such nice people—the youngest son—Paul—that started me wrong." End: "Like hell you will. You're like all the rest."

ANOTHER ANTIGONE
by A. R. Gurney, Jr. (Dramatists Play Service)
Drama: One-act play, pp. 37–39; Judy (early 20s).
Judy Miller is a college senior who has written a modern anti-war adaptation of the Greek drama *Antigone*, but the Professor of Classics has refused to accept it for grading. In defiance, she has mounted a campaign for a university production of her play, causing factions for and against her to form on campus. In the scene leading to this monologue, Judy learned from Diana Eberhart, the Dean of Humane Studies, that the professor has agreed to give her a "C," which will enable her to graduate on time.

Judy won't accept this, however, opting for a stand on the principle of the issue. When Diana tells Judy that if she doesn't graduate, she'll lose the Wall Street job that is awaiting her, Judy lashes into the older woman with this speech. In it, Judy attacks feminist values in general and the Dean personally, positioning herself against what she perceives to be a feminist stereotype. Start: "What's a job anyway? Is it the most important thing in the world?" End: "And now here I am, about to graduate, or rather not graduate, because I've come up with the first vaguely unselfish idea I've ever had in my life, and this place, this institution—in which my family has invested at least seventy thousand dollars—won't give me credit for it."

APPROACHING ZANZIBAR
by Tina Howe (Samuel French)
Comedy: Act II, pp. 108–110; Olivia (81).
Olivia is a famous avant-garde artist living in Taos, New Mexico. She delivers this speech on her deathbed to her 9-year-old great-niece. Olivia is a crusty old woman, full of life, energy, and fun, and this definitely isn't a last-gasp kind of monologue. At the end of the speech, Olivia and the girl start jumping up and down on the bed. Start: "I was on a train somewhere between Paris and Tangier." End: "I thought my heart would burst. Zanzibar!"

BAD HABITS
by Terrence McNally [1990 revised edition (Dramatists Play Service)]
Comedy: "Dunelawn," pp. 24–25; Dolly (late 20s).
Dolly tells Dr. Pepper why she and her husband, Harry, have been trying to kill each other. According to Dolly, Harry is compulsive, worries too much, reads road signs out loud, and follows her around with coasters. Start: "His hobby is tropical fish. I hate tropical fish." End: "That incident with the lawn mower was just the straw that broke the camel's back."

BETWEEN DAYLIGHT AND BOONVILLE
by Matt Williams (Samuel French)
Comedy: Act I, pp. 35–36; Marlene (30s).
Trying to prove that she and Big Jim have bigger fights than Carla and Larry, Marlene describes one humdinger they had when they wound up throwing every stick of furniture out in the yard. Start: "This one time, before the kids were born, Big Jim was workin' construction before goin' to work for the company." End either: "Left everything in the yard and went up and went to bed." or: "Don't never go to bed angry."
Comedy: Act I, p. 39; Marlene (30s).
Marlene explains why it is so important to come up with just the right name for the baby she is carrying, especially if it is a girl. After all, as she explains, just imagine how life might have turned out for Farrah Fawcett-Majors if she'd been named Carol or something. You'll have to cut and paste. Good short, contemporary, comic monologue for the right occasion. Start: "You can't just name a girl anything. Boys you can name about anything. They always end up with nicknames anyway." End either: "Don't sound right without the Majors. All in the name." or: "You're goin' to be her godmother, so I want you to like the name I pick."

BLUE WINDOW
by Craig Lucas (Samuel French)
Drama: Scene 3, pp. 62–65; Libby (33).
Libby tells Norbert about the accident in which she and her husband fell from a seventh-floor balcony. She was seriously injured, and he was killed. You'll have to piece together the monologue, but it works fine. Cut out the other characters' lines. Start: "When I first came to New York?" End: "I'm thirty-three years old. I can't have anybody hold me. I can never be held."

BORN IN THE RSA
by Barney Simon and the cast [*Woza Afrika! An Anthology of South African Plays,* edited by Duma Ndlovu (George Braziller, Inc.)]
Drama; Mia (35–45).
Mia, a white South-African lawyer, speaks of her involvement in the anti-apartheid movement. Here, she recounts an argument she had with a white government prosecutor. The short

speech is located about halfway through the play. Start: "The other day I had this conversation, no, no—argument—with this prosecutor . . . umm ah . . . agh forget his name." End: "Listen, and, if you're counting barbarians—we're the first in line."
Drama; Mia (35–45).
In this short speech, located about five pages from the end of the play, Mia bitterly advises people not to believe the South-African government when it announces that apartheid is dead. Start: "They say we haven't even begun to feel the force of the government. That there are mountains full of arms and mine shafts full of fuel." End: "I swear I wanted to pray—I wish I believed in God."
Drama; Thenjiwe (30s).
A black trade unionist and mother, Thenjiwe was jailed on trumped-up charges. Inside the prison, she was forced to stand for prolonged periods of time. In this speech, which you'll have to patch together a bit, she talks about being left alone with a white police officer. He makes sexual overtures, but she is almost delirious from standing so long that her mind leaps to fantasies of gunning everybody down with the man's pistol. You'll find this monologue near the halfway point in the play. Start: "Early one morning, there was a loud bang." End: "I think we were equally disappointed." A South-African accent is appropriate for all three monologues.

BUCK

by Ronald Ribman [*New Plays USA, 1983* (Theatre Communications Group); *The Rug Merchants of Chaos and Other Plays by Ronald Ribman* (Theatre Communications Group)]
Drama: Act II; Shirley (mid-20s).
Shirley tells Buck, the producer of a small-time cable-television station, about her experiences as a stripper in Texas and how much she wants to be an actress. This very graphic material isn't suited for inexperienced actresses. If done well, the monologue could be a heart stopper. Start:" Do you think I could be an actress? I mean if I went to one of those acting classes and had lessons and really worked at it?" End: "I was the first one there to actually use words, or tell a story."

BURN THIS

by Lanford Wilson (Hill & Wang/Noonday; HarperCollins Canada Ltd.)
Comedy-Drama: Act I; Anna (32).
Anna tells Larry what a disaster Robbie's wake was, especially since no one in Robbie's family seemed to know that he was gay and presumed that she was his girlfriend. And then, to top it off, she had to sleep in a bedroom that contained a collection of butterflies pinned to the wall. Cut Larry's lines and Anna's direct responses to them. Start: "In about eight seconds I know they have no idea that Robbie's gay." End: "There's these two bag ladies yelling at each other, apparently they're rivals. I fit right in."

CAMERAS

by Jon Jory [*Twenty-Five Ten-Minute Plays from Actors Theatre of Louisville* (Samuel French)
Drama: One-act play, pp. 245–246; Young Woman (18–30).
Several professional photographers dispassionately discuss what comprises the perfect shot and the relationship between a photograph and the person who looks at it. Then a young woman walks on stage and describes a horrible car accident in which a motorist ran into a working road crew. Bodies were strewn all around, and a person was screaming silently inside the car. Passersby tried to get him out while a photographer stopped and took pictures of the scene. What if the photographer had put down the camera and helped with the rescue? Would the person have lived? Start: "I was driving through West Virginia and ahead of me I saw where this car had lost control." End: "I'd like to be wrong, but I don't think I am."

CANDIDA
by George Bernard Shaw (Signet)
Comedy-Drama: Act III; Candida (33).
This speech, in which Candida chooses between her husband and the lovesick young poet, Marchbanks, comes at the end of the play. In it, she firmly establishes herself as a strong, fiercely independent woman. She decides that she'll stay with her husband, "the weaker of the two," not out of duty and obligation, but out of free choice. You'll have to cut and paste the speech a bit, but it will make an excellent workshop monologue. Start: "I give myself to the weaker of the two." End: "I am mixing up your beautiful cadences and spoiling them, am I not, darling?"

CHAPTER TWO
by Neil Simon (Samuel French)
Comedy-Drama: Act II, Scene 7, pp. 119–121; Jennie (32).
Jennie tells off George for putting her in the untenable position of having to compete with the memory of his deceased wife, Barbara. This is a very strong, stop-you-in-your-tracks kind of speech. Start: "You know what you want better than me, George." End: "Sometimes I don't know when to stop talking. For that I'm sorry, George, and I apologize. I am now through!"

CHEATERS
by Michael Jacobs (Samuel French)
Comedy: Act I, Scene 2, pp. 15–16; Grace (50).
Grace and Sam met in a movie theater earlier tonight, felt electricity, and have guiltily made their way to a motel room, complete with X-rated movies on the television. They begin an affair, the first for each of them. Here, Grace recalls the first time she ever went to bed with a man. Actually, she is stalling because she is quite anxious about cheating on her husband. Begin with Grace singing "Amazing Grace" or start: "I was remembering the first time I ever went to bed with a man—I was almost twenty years old." End: "What could I tell them? I didn't feel a thing."

COASTAL DISTURBANCES
by Tina Howe (Samuel French)
Comedy: Act I, Scene 5, pp. 54–55; Holly (24).
Holly exuberantly fantasizes about what the world would have been like if dolphins had legs and behaved like people. The more she talks, the more amused she becomes with herself. Cut Leo's lines and Holly's direct responses to them. Start: "You know what I read in a book? That the island of Atlantis was really inhabited by dolphins." End: "Boy, do I feel weird . . . I'm so light-handed all of a sudden . . . I mean, headed."

COLORED MUSEUM, THE
by George C. Wolfe (Broadway Play Publishing)
Comedy-Drama: "The Party"; Topsy Washington (20–30).
Topsy comes on funky, dancing. She describes a wild party she went to uptown the other night and how that party is always going on in her brain. Whenever she walks down the street, she sashays all over the place "'cause I'm dancing to the music of the madness in me." This is a truly stunning, show-stopping speech for the right actress. Start: "Yoho! Party! Party!" End: "So, hunny, don't waste your time trying to label or define me 'cause I'm not what I was ten years ago or ten minutes ago. I'm all of that and then some. And whereas I can't live inside yesterday's pain, I can't live without it."
Comedy-Drama: "Lala's Opening"; Lala (30–45).
Lala is a famous opera singer and something of a flamboyant character. A good monologue for an actress who can do a French accent and sing a bit—just a bit. The actress doesn't have to

be an opera singer. Fine audition material in the right hands, not for beginners. Start: "Yes, it's me! Lala Lamazing Grace!" End: "I am going away."

COME BACK, LITTLE SHEBA
by William Inge (Samuel French)
Drama: Act II, Scene 4, pp. 75–76; Lola (39).
In this moving speech, which comes at the very end of the play, Lola tells her husband about a dream she had last night in which he was a hero and their dog, Little Sheba, died. Eliminate Doc's lines and Lola's direct responses to them. Start: "You know what, Doc? I had another dream last night." End: "We got to go on.' Now isn't that strange?"

COME BACK TO THE 5 & DIME, JIMMY DEAN, JIMMY DEAN
by Ed Graczyk (Samuel French)
Drama: Act II, pp. 67–71; Mona (30s).
As she has done many times before, Mona tells the story of how she came to make love with James Dean on the set of the movie *Giant* 20 years earlier. This is a fantasy, of course, but she has embroidered it and believes in it deeply. You'll have to cut, paste, and alter some lines to make the speech work, but the result is worth the effort. Wonderfully poetic. Start: "It was like a regular parade. People from all over these parts headed for Marfa, bumper to bumper, to be in that movie." End: "We spent that whole entire night together . . . until the sun started to peek out from over the edge of the earth, turnin' the sky into the brightest red I ever saw." For a shorter, audition-length excerpt, start: "That night, I laid there in the back seat of the Buick and kept thinkin' about how I was chosen above all them thousands of others." End in the same place.
Drama: Act II, pp. 82–83; Joanne (30s).
At this point, everyone knows that Joanne is really Joe, who has undergone a sex-change operation. In this speech, which you'll have to cut and paste, Joanne talks about an interlude she had with Lester T. a couple of years earlier. Turns out he'd abandoned his lover, and Joanne's friend, Sissy because she had a mastectomy. Start: "I went there with the intention of seeing you . . . I had heard you were living there and thought I would show up on your doorstep." End: ". . . one day the watermelons just disappeared . . . went away, and . . . so did (he)."

COMMANCHE CAFE
by William Hauptman (Samuel French)
Comedy: One-act play, pp. 10–11; Mattie (40s–50s).
Mattie gently tells Ronnie, who is younger and very unsophisticated, what it is like to make love with a man who is special to you. Drawing on a finely etched memory, she describes her most loving adventure in precise detail. Cut Ronnie's lines and Mattie's direct responses to them. Start: "When we started driving that morning." End: "You're still young. But one day everything's happened. Then the night's no different from the day."
Comedy: One-act play, pp. 12–13; Ronnie (mid-20s).
Ronnie has a humorously distorted idea of what the world is like because she has never left her small Oklahoma town. In fact, she has gotten all of her information from movie magazines and cheap tabloids. In this very funny speech, Ronnie tells Mattie about the strange and wonderful places she intends to visit. Start: "I'll never be like you . . . There's a whole mysterious country out there." End: "Just let me go anyplace but here—in Oklahoma."

CROSSING DELANCEY
by Susan Sandler (Samuel French)
Comedy-Drama: Act II, p. 69; Bubbie (80s).
Bubbie is a Jewish grandmother who lives on the Lower East Side of New York but still has one foot in the old country. She has employed a matchmaker to cook up a romance between

her granddaughter, Isabelle, and Sam the pickle-maker. After some false starts, the romance has taken off, and this very sweet speech is directed toward Sam. Bubbie tells him how she came to marry Shiah, a tailor's son, and that she intends to dance at Sam's wedding. Start: "You're some big-time operator, Sammy." End: "You'll buy the schnapps. We'll have a good time."

DANNY AND THE DEEP BLUE SEA
by John Patrick Shanley (Dramatists Play Service) [*13 by Shanley* (Applause Books)]
Drama: One-act play, Scene 2, DPS pp. 26–27; Roberta (31).
Roberta tells Danny about a dream she once had while under the influence of opium. She dreamed of the deep blue sea and whales jumping out of the water all around her. Then they stopped, and the sea was calm. Start: "There's boats right up by Westchester Square." End: ". . . 'cause I knew it had all them whales in it."

DAY IN THE DEATH OF JOE EGG, A
by Peter Nichols (Samuel French)
Drama: Act I, pp. 28–29; Sheila (35).
While speaking about Josephine, her spastic daughter, Sheila tells the audience about something that took place nine years ago. This event caused Sheila and her husband, Bri, to believe that their daughter had a will of her own. The celebration was brief, however, because Josephine had another grand-mal seizure and regressed. A lovely speech that illustrates a mother's love. Start: "I join in these jokes to please him." End: "Perhaps it's being a woman."

DEATH AND THE MAIDEN
by Ariel Dorfman (Penguin)
Drama: Act II, Scene 1; Paulina (40).
Paulina tells her husband, Gerardo, what kind of revenge she seeks against Roberto for raping and torturing her. Cut Gerardo's lines and Paulina's direct responses to them. Start: "When I heard his voice last night, the first thought that rushed through my head, what I've been thinking all these years." End: "That's what I want."

DEATH OF A SALESMAN
by Arthur Miller (Dramatists Play Service)
Drama: Act I, pp. 40–42; Linda (late 50s).
Linda tells her sons why their father is a good man, why she loves him. To construct this monologue, omit Biff and Happy's lines and Linda's direct responses to them, and then rewrite around them. This can be a powerful monologue if you patch it together the right way. Start: "I don't say he's a great man. Willy Loman never made a lot of money." End: "When does he get a medal for that?"

DELICATE BALANCE, A
by Edward Albee (Samuel French)
Drama: Act III, pp. 81–82; Agnes (late 50s).
Family friends Harry and Edna have moved into an upstairs bedroom, apparently intending to live here permanently, an intrusion that has brought Agnes's family to the edge of hysteria and violence. Here, she contends that Harry and Edna have brought "the plague" with them, a "disease" to which only a few are immune. Powerful speech. You'll have to piece it together, cutting out the other characters' lines, but it works. Start: "Thank you, Claire; I was merely waiting—until I'd heard, and thought a little, listened to the rest of you." End: "Or shall we burn them out, rid ourselves of it all . . . and wait for the next invasion. You decide, my darling."

DIVISION STREET
by Steve Tesich (Samuel French)
Comedy; Act I, p. 25; Dianah (30s).
Dianah, still marching after all these years, tells her adoring Legal Aid lawyer, Sal, how exciting her ex-husband, Chris Adrian, used to be when he led the protest movement. In her eyes, he was a cross between Che Guevara and Chuck Mangione, smelling of mimeo ink and Cuban cigars, standing like a titan with a bullhorn in his hands. According to Dianah, Chris was beautiful. This is a difficult comic monologue but can be a show stopper if played full tilt. Cut Sal's lines and Dianah's direct responses to them. Start: "We met in Chicago." End: "I let his spark die . . . The flame of the rebel became a charcoal lighter on the Bar-B-Que Pit of History."

DREAM GIRL
by Elmer Rice (Dramatists Play Service)
Comedy: Act I, pp. 12–14; Georgina (23).
As Georgina dresses for work and puts on her makeup, she talks to herself in the mirror, assessing her life, her physical assets, the status of her unpublished novel, and the possibility that she is too much of a daydreamer. Start: "All right, Mother. I'm practically dressed." End: "Well, if I'm going to play with fire, I may as well look my best. So here goes."

DUET FOR ONE
by Tom Kempinski (Samuel French)
Drama: Act I, Session 2, p. 13; Stephanie (33).
Stephanie is a world-famous violinist whose career was cut short by multiple sclerosis. She tells her psychiatrist, Dr. Feldmann, how she met her husband, who is a prominent composer. She happily describes the evening he approached her after one of her concerts and they played an impromptu Beethoven duet back stage. Stephanie relates the story through rose-colored glasses, however, and the last line is a leveler. Omit Feldmann's one-line interruption. Written in the British vernacular. Start: "It was lovely, actually. I was at the B. B. C." End: "The papers called it a fairy story, but it wasn't . . . Fairy stories don't happen, do they?"

ECCENTRICITIES OF A NIGHTINGALE, THE
by Tennessee Williams (Dramatists Play Service)
Drama: Act I, Scene 2, p. 17; Alma (25–29).
Alma itemizes for her father the many community services she performs. Start: "Father, I do all I can. More than I have the strength for. I have my vocal pupils." End: "Oh, I've had to bite my tongue so much it's a wonder I have one left!"
Drama: Act II, Scene 3, p. 41; Alma (25–29).
It is 2 A.M., and Alma is having a panic attack. Her feelings were hurt by John's earlier departure from her "group," where he was an invited guest. She knows now that he left on a false pretense. A moment ago, John told her that she is lonely, a diagnosis that made her angry. In this speech, Alma accuses him of avoiding her and her "eccentric" friends and of planning to marry a "Northern beauty" someday. This is a difficult speech because Alma is distraught. Eliminate John's lines. Start: "Oh, how wise and superior you are! John Buchanan, Junior, graduate of Johns Hopkins, magna cum laude!" End: "But everything perfect and regular as the tick of that—clock!"
Drama: Act III, Scene 1; Alma (25–29).
In what is probably the most significant monologue in the play, Alma confesses to John that she has always loved him and that she has fantasized about being intimate with him. You'll have to cut and paste, eliminating John's lines. Start: "I always say too much or say too little. The few young men I've gone out with have found me" or start: "Look. My ring has cut my finger. No! I shall have to be honest! I can't play any kind of a game!" End: "Would I have

sprung from my seat, or would I have stayed?" (This monologue doesn't appear in the DPS acting edition. You can, however, find it in earlier library compilations.)
Drama: Epilogue, pp. 54–55; Alma (25–29, playing mid-to-late 30s).
John is long gone from Alma's life, and she has turned into a lonely woman, seeking comfort from the occasional involvement with traveling salesmen. In this speech, she describes the landmarks in Glorious Hill. Each one Alma mentions has particular meaning to her at this point in her life, which is the key to playing the piece. When she tells one salesman about that part of the city known as "Tiger Town," she is making a thinly veiled proposition. You'll have to cut and paste a bit, eliminating the man's lines. Start: "Sit down and I'll point out a few of our historical landmarks to you." End: "Tiger Town, it's the part of town that a traveling salesman might be interested in. Are you interested in it?" or end: "Oh!—There goes the first sky-rocket! Look at it burst into a million stars!"

ECHOES
by N. Richard Nash (Samuel French)
Drama: Act I, pp. 23–24; Tilda (20–25).
Tilda and Sam share a room in a mental institution. In this speech, she tells him how she first started inventing imaginary friends and how the doctor ("The Person") caused her to drive them away. Omit Sam's single line. Start: "When I first came here, there was nobody here." End: ". . . and one day I opened my eyes a little . . . and you were there . . . and you've never hurt me . . . and never gone away."
Drama: Act II, pp. 51–52; Tilda (20–25).
Afraid that Sam is edging too close to sanity, Tilda passionately warns him about the doctor's therapeutic tricks and the false values that await him outside. Start: "Now listen to me, Sammy. Don't you see what the technique is?" End: "And you'll be right back there, where you started from . . . playing a part that somebody assigned you . . . making other people's motions because you're too frightened to be still."

EDUCATING RITA
by Willy Russell (Samuel French)
Comedy-Drama: Act I, Scene 7, pp. 31–32; Rita (26).
Frank invited his student Rita to a dinner party at his place last night, but she was embarrassed by her lower-class origins and didn't show up. This morning, during their regular session, she explains what happened and makes a new commitment to improve herself. Written in the lower-class British vernacular, which is important to Rita's portrayal. Cut Frank's single line. Start: "I'm all right with you, here in this room; but when I saw those people you were with, I couldn't come in." End: "and that's why I came back. And that's why I'm staying."

EFFECT OF GAMMA RAYS ON MAN-IN-THE-MOON MARIGOLDS
by Paul Zindel (Bantam)
Drama: Act I; Beatrice (30s).
Although this telephone conversation doesn't strictly qualify as a monologue, it presents unique challenges and is particularly good. Beatrice is talking to and flirting with Mr. Goodman, her daughter's high-school science teacher. Start: "Hello. Yes it is. Who is this? . . . I hope there hasn't been any trouble at school." End: "It's been a true pleasure speaking with you. Goodbye."
Drama: Act I; Beatrice (30s).
Another telephone conversation between Beatrice and Mr. Goodman. She is concerned about the radiation-exposed marigold seeds her daughter brought home. Start: "Hello—Mr. Goodman, please . . . How would I know if he's got a class? . . . You know, really, our schools need more exciting young men like you, I really mean that. Really. Oh, I do. Goodbye, Mr. Goodman."

Drama: Act I; Beatrice (30s).
Beatrice has just quieted her daughter from a violent nightmare, and they're talking about Beatrice's childhood. You'll have to do some cutting and pasting, but the result is a very textured monologue. Eliminate Ruth's lines. Start: "My father made up for all the other men in this whole world, Ruth. If only you two could have met." End: "I see the face of my father and my heart stands still."

EMPRESS OF CHINA
by Ruth Wolff (Broadway Play Publishing)
Drama: Act I; Tsu-Hsi (60s).
In this short speech, Tsu-Hsi tells the concubine Li Lien-Ying how she came to seize the reins of power; she started out as a dutiful wife but found it necessary to take charge because of her ineffectual husband. Start: "When I first came to the palace, I was ready to be the perfect feminine complement to my masculine lord." End: "Where are the women today who would dare what I dared? They do not exist!"
Drama: Act II; Tsu-Hsi (60s).
Having elevated herself to the throne, Tsu-Hsi refuses to receive the British ambassador because she hates all that Britain stands for. In an unusual charade carried out with a costumed actor, she demonstrates for Li Lien-Ying, the Chief Eunuch, and General Jung Lu how she would speak to the ambassador if she were to see him. Playing out the scene with actor Shen Tai, who is dressed as Sir Claude Macdonald, she blasts the British for their imperialistic ways in China. Start: "White Christians! What you are saying is we should become prejudiced, intolerant and despotic—like you." End: "We were here long before you existed, and long after you are gone we shall remain."

EQUUS
by Peter Schaffer (Samuel French)
Drama: Act II, Scene 23, p. 69; Dora (37–43).
Dora implores the psychiatrist to understand that parents aren't merely instigators of psychological problems in their children. She is confused by and ashamed of her young son's awful actions, but she loves him deeply. A very powerful and moving selection. Start: "Look, Doctor: you don't have to live with this" End: "I only know he was my little Alan, and then the Devil came."

FATHER'S DAY
by Oliver Hailey (Dramatists Play Service)
Comedy-Drama: Act I, p. 17; Louise (30–35)
In her black-humor style, Louise tells Marian and Estelle how awful her marriage was, how she and Tom tried to kill each other all the time, and why they got a divorce. Eliminate the brief interruptions by Marian and Estelle. Start: "Marian, I'm going to explain divorce to you one more time." End: "When I say that is why we get divorced!"
Comedy-Drama: Act II, pp. 60–61; Estelle (25–30).
At the end of the play, Estelle sums up her philosophy on family life and vows not to hate Harold, even though he is remarrying. Start: "I admire Marian very much." End: "Marian doesn't hate. I'm not going to either. I wish you wouldn't."

FENCES
by August Wilson (Samuel French)
Drama: Act II, Scene 1, pp. 67–68; Rose (43).
After Troy tells Rose that he made another woman pregnant, she tells him why she has stayed with him for 18 years. Start: "I been standing with you! I been right here with you, Troy." End: "You take . . . and don't even know nobody's giving!"

Drama: Act II, Scene 5, pp. 90–91; Rose (43).
When Cory informs his mother that he doesn't intend to go to Troy's funeral, Rose tells him why he should respect his father and why she loved him. Start: "You can't be nobody but who you are, Cory." End, "And if the Lord see fit to keep up my strength . . . I'm gonna do her just like your daddy did you . . . I'm gonna give her the best of what's in me."

FOB
by David Henry Hwang (Dramatists Play Service)
Comedy: Act I, Scene 2, pp. 33–34; Grace (20).
Grace, a first-generation Chinese American, describes her unsuccessful childhood efforts to blend in with the white children. Start: "Yeah. It's tough trying to live in Chinatown." End: "So I drove home."

FOX, THE
by Alan Miller [based on D. H. Lawrence's novel of the same name (Samuel French)]
Drama: Act III, Scene 2, p. 71; Jill (29).
Jill tries to talk Nellie out of marrying the strange young soldier who has come to live with them. Written in the British vernacular, but you may want to convert it to American English. Start: "Listen to me, Nellie, please." End: "Call it off. Call it off before it's too late!"

FRANKIE AND JOHNNY IN THE CLAIR DE LUNE
by Terrence McNally (Dramatists Play Service)
Drama: Act II, pp. 43–44; Frankie (40).
Frankie tells Johnny about when she was a young girl and how her grandmother would come into her room and close the blinds at night. A truly lovely speech. Frankie can speak Johnny's line: "It's supposed to make them romantic." Cut Johnny's second line that interrupts the speech. Start: "I've always been very suspicious of what moonlight does to people." End: "I just want my Nana back."

GETTING OUT
by Marsha Norman (Dramatists Play Service)
Drama: Act I, pp. 9–10; Arlie (20s).
Arlie is southern, tough, streetwise, and recently out of prison. Here, she talks about the time she and her young friends threw another child's pet frogs at cars. Start: "So, there was this little kid, see, this creepy little fucker next door." End: "I never had so much fun in one day in my whole life."

GINGERBREAD LADY, THE
by Neil Simon (Samuel French)
Comedy-Drama: Act II, pp. 52–54; Toby (40).
Toby tells Jimmy and Evy that her husband wants a divorce, that he isn't interested in her sexually any more. Then she recites her impressive sexual resumé. Cut Jimmy and Evy's lines and Toby's direct responses to them. Start: "Martin has grown accustomed to my face . . . accustomed to my voice." End: "Then let him get out, I don't need him!"
Comedy-Drama: Act III, p. 68; Toby (40).
Evy arrived back in her apartment a few moments ago, hungover and sporting a black-and-blue eye. Her daughter, Polly, and her good friend, Toby, were anxiously waiting for her. Relieved in the knowledge that Evy is at least safe, Toby lashes into her for being so self-destructive, and for not owning up to who and what she really is. Cut Evy's line. Start: "Damn you, Evy. Damn you for being so God-damned honest all the time. Who needs the truth if this is what it gets you?" End: "That's the first time in my entire life I ever told anyone off. I think I'm going to be sick."

GLASS MENAGERIE, THE
by Tennessee Williams (Dramatists Play Service)
Drama: Scene 6, pp. 43–44; Amanda (40s).
Amanda enters, wearing "a girlish frock of yellowed voile with a blue silk sash . . . carrying a bunch of jonquils," all in preparation for the arrival of Laura's gentleman caller. In this monologue, Amanda tells Laura the history of the dress. Start: "Now, Laura. Just look at your mother." End: "I hope they get here before it rains."

HEIDI CHRONICLES, THE
by Wendy Wasserstein (Dramatists Play Service)
Comedy: Act II, Scene 4, pp. 59–62; Heidi (playing 37).
The occasion is a 1986 luncheon for Miss Crain's School East Coast Alumnae Association at the Plaza Hotel in New York City, and Dr. Heidi Holland, a prominent art historian, is the featured speaker. She talks extemporaneously about how the women's movement has fragmented. This monologue is far too long for audition use, but it is so succinct, intelligent, and well-constructed that it is wonderful for workshops. Start: "Hello. Hello." End: "Thank you."

HELLO AND GOODBYE
by Athol Fugard (Samuel French)
Drama: Act II, pp. 46–47; Hester (late 30s).
Hester tells her brother how frightened their mother was and then she recalls what it was like to see the mother's body in a casket. You'll have to piece together this monologue a bit, eliminating Johnny's lines. Hester is a white Afrikaner, so an accent is appropriate. Start: "What did you know about her? You wasn't even five years when she died." End: "There was something I wanted to do, but it was too late."

HOOTERS
by Ted Tally (Dramatists Play Service)
Drama: Act II, Scene 6, pp. 64–65; Cheryl (25).
This monologue is probably the redeeming moment in *Hooters*. Cheryl has been running from adulthood and all it implies. She allowed herself to be picked up and taken to bed by a hot and horny 19-year-old guy at the beach, who, after the lovemaking, told her he loved her. Now he is asleep on Cheryl's arm, and she talks to him even though he can't hear her. With true insight, she speaks of her history as a sex object and says she intends to stop being one. For audition purposes, wake the other actor up. Talk to someone who can hear you. Start: "Hey, Clint. You file your shirts in the closet?" End: "So hey! . . . Welcome to the top."

HOUSE OF BLUE LEAVES, THE
by John Guare (Samuel French)
Comedy: Act I, pp. 9–10; Bunny (late 30s).
Bunny, who tends to talk nonstop, tells Artie about the wonderful excitement along the parade route where the Pope will travel. Start: "Oooo, it's freezing out there. Breath's coming out of everybody's mouth like a balloon in a cartoon." End: ". . . like a burglar's torch looking all through the sky—Everybody's waiting, Artie—everybody!"
Comedy: Act I, pp. 12–13; Bunny (late 30s).
Bunny happily tells Artie how she plans to get the Pope's attention as he passes by in the parade. Start: "Miss Henshaw's saving us this divine place by the cemetery so the Pope will have to slow down." End: "And nobody'll believe it. Oh, Artie, tables turn."

HURLYBURLY
by David Rabe (Samuel French)
Comedy-Drama: Act II, Scene 1, pp. 93–95; Bonnie (late 30s).
Bonnie talks about a phone conversation she had earlier in the day with a strange guy. Building on the theme that cocaine is superior to EST as a mood enhancer, she says she finally hung up on the man. This impassioned, mentally frenetic monologue would be wonderful for auditions if EST and cocaine weren't so passé. Still, it is a toot to work on. Start: "I'm telling this guy on the phone that drugs are and just have been as far as I can remember, an ever-present component of my personality." End: ". . . and slam down the phone and hang it up."

HUSBANDRY
by Patrick Tovat (Samuel French)
Drama: One-act play, Scene 2, pp. 27–28; Dee (55).
Dee gets a little tight and tells her son, Harry, that his aging father is having a tough time running the family farm. You'll have to change or cut a line here and there, but the monologue works. Eliminate Harry's lines, and connect Dee's speeches. Start: ". . . Les and I had a humdinger of a fight." End: "I think this one more year business is the silliest thing I ever heard."

IN THE BOOM BOOM ROOM
by David Rabe (Samuel French)
Drama: Act I, pp. 39–40; Susan (25–35).
Susan, who is a lesbian, tells Chrissy about the time she shot her high-school football-hero boyfriend. Start: "All through my sophomore year in high school, I was in love with a boy and we were sleeping together." End: "It's somethin', though, how once you shoot a man, they're none of them the same any more, and you know how easy, if you got a gun, they fall down."
Drama: Act II, p. 104; Chrissy (early 20s).
Chrissy, a very unsophisticated young woman, summons up her courage and tells her abusive husband, Al, that she thinks she is going crazy. The tension escalates as she accuses him of being a lousy sex partner. Short, venomous, graphic sexual language. Start: "Listen to me what I'm saying!" End: "Am I making myself clear, Big Al?"

I STAND BEFORE YOU NAKED
by Joyce Carol Oates [*12 Plays by Joyce Carol Oates* (Plume Drama)]
Drama: "Little Blood Button"; Girl (20s).
A prostitute addresses the audience, complaining about the blood blister on her lip, a result of too-intense lovemaking last night. About midway into this sexually graphic speech, she shifts into a provocative one-to-one mode, presumably talking to the man who did this to her. For sophisticated actresses. Start: "One of you's to blame—I could name which!" End: "That's the God's honest truth, guaranteed. Says so on the label."
Drama: "The Boy"; Woman (30s).
A substitute public-school teacher addresses the audience, telling about the romance she struck up with a teenage boy. She took him to a motel, they drank, and she got turned on, but he was impotent. This sexually graphic speech is appropriate for sophisticated actresses. Start: "This boy named Kit—soon as I started subbing for his class he pestered me with love, called out 'Hey, good-lookin' on the street, eyeing me every chance he could." End: ". . . he was laughing too, maybe he was crying, nose running like a baby's, and I just lay there thinking, All right, kid, all right, you bastards, this is it."

IT HAD TO BE YOU

by Renée Taylor and Joseph Bologna (Samuel French)

Comedy: Act I, pp. 9–11; Theda (28–35).

Rushing late into a commercial audition, Theda nervously rambles through her life story, crying, laughing, dancing, and singing. This monologue can be a show stopper if you play it full out. Very New York. Start: "I had to get up early to go to a funeral this morning." End: "I have the power to make my dreams come true. It's not too late for me."

JOE TURNER'S COME AND GONE

by August Wilson (Samuel French)

Drama: Act II, Scene 1, pp. 95–97; Molly (22).

Molly tells Mattie why she doesn't trust men. You'll have to cut and paste, but this mono-logue is very good. Eliminate Mattie's lines, and adapt a few others. Start: "I don't trust none of these men. Jack or nobody else." End: "That's why I don't trust nobody but the good Lord above, and I don't love nobody but my mama."

Drama: Act II, Scene 3, pp. 111–112; Bertha (40s).

Bertha gives Mattie a pep talk about men and spiritual advisers. Start: "If I was you, Mattie, I wouldn't go getting all tied up with Bynum in that stuff. That kind of stuff, even if it do work for a while, it don't last." End: "You got your time coming. You watch what Bertha's saying."

JOINED AT THE HEAD

by Catherine Butterfield (Dramatists Play Service) [*Women Playwrights—Best Plays of 1992* (Smith & Kraus)]

Drama: Act I, DPS pp. 9–11; Maggie (late 30s).

This play takes the form of a narration by Maggie, as she steps into and out of the action. You'll have to paste together this speech, which is in two pieces. In a very reflective mood, Maggie recalls a walk down a crowded Boston street and how overhearing snippets of the conversations of passersby prompted a philosophical revelation. This isn't a passionate, show-stopper kind of speech, simply an introspective, straightforward, and beautifully written monologue. Start: "I was walking down Newbury Street in Boston on a very brisk, very clear day, late afternoon." Cut from the end of this speech directly to the beginning of Maggie's next speech, eliminating the comments of the passersby. Continue with: "Fragments of conversations. Who knows where they were meant to lead?" End: "And convinced that, really, deep down in the truest part of life, we are nobody's backdrop."

KATHY AND MO SHOW, THE: PARALLEL LIVES

by Mo Gaffney and Kathy Najimy (Dramatists Play Service)

Comedy: "Hank and Karen Sue," pp. 100–101; Karen Sue (28–35).

Set in a country-and-western bar, Hank has been coming on to Karen Sue as he always does, telling her how pretty she is and asking her when she is going to give up that other guy and marry him? Then Hank passes out face down on the bar. At this point, Karen Sue tells the waitress how she would have married him if she thought he was serious. Hell, she would do anything to get her life off the dime. Start: "Yeah, I'd marry him—if I thought he meant a goddam word of what he was sayin'." End: "I think a nut job is what you call it, Adele. Oh, turn this song up. I love it."

KEELY AND DU

by Jane Martin (Samuel French)

Drama: One-act play, Scene 8, pp. 26–27; Keely (early 30s).

Keely has responded to her antiabortion captor by remaining silent—until now. In this emotional speech, she tears into Du, the grandmotherly woman assigned to care for and guard her; Du has just finished quoting some scripture as justification for Keely's imprisonment. Cut Du's

lines and Keely's responses to them. Start: Hey, I didn't choose to have this baby." End: "You're criminal filth, and I will see to it that you get yours. Now, leave me alone."
Drama: One-act play, Scene 13, p. 40; Keely (early 30s).
Keely is no longer yelling at her captor, Du, though she is still hoping to escape from her basement prison. After Du graphically describes the horrors of abortion, Keely responds with this quiet, intense speech, trying to explain why she shouldn't be made to carry this baby to term. Start: "I can't raise this baby." End: "So I guess it's me or the baby, so I guess that's crazy, but you don't . . . I don't show you . . . just how . . . how angry I really am. I don't. I don't."

KEY EXCHANGE
by Kevin Wade (Dramatists Play Service)
Comedy-Drama: Scene 3, p. 18; Lisa (late 20s).
Lisa tells her friend Michael about her mother's death from cancer. This isn't as macabre a story as it sounds. After relating it, Lisa cracks a joke. Start: "When I was very young, my mother got cancer." End: "It was a long time before I could even give a decent kiss without somewhere asking myself whether or not this guy would stand outside my window for six months while I died."

LARK, THE
by Jean Anouilh [adapted by Lillian Hellman (Dramatists Play Service)]
Drama: Act I, pp. 6–7; Joan (18).
Joan is being tried as a heretic. In this speech to the court, she recalls her simple origins, tending sheep in the field. She also explains how she began to hear "voices," instructions from God to raise an army and fight the British. The speech runs about 1 1/2 pages, but you can easily shorten it. Eliminate Warwick and Cauchon's lines. Start: "Then I'll start at the beginning. It's always nicer at the beginning." End: "And that was the day I was saddled with France. And my work on the farm."
Drama: Act II, p. 54; Joan (18).
Now in her prison cell, Joan recants her confession, knowing as she does so that she'll face death by burning at the stake. Start: "And I will wear cast-off brocade and put jewels in my hair and grow old. I will be happy that few people remember my warrior days." End: "Call your soldiers, Warwick. I deny my confession."

LAST OF THE RED HOT LOVERS
by Neil Simon (Samuel French)
Comedy: Act I, pp. 26–27; Elaine (late 30s).
Barney brought Elaine to his mother's apartment to have sex. Instead, she tells him off. In this speech, Elaine angrily defends her basic philosophy of life. Start: "You hypocrite!" End: "If you can't taste it, touch it or smell it, forget it!"

LATER
by Corrine Jacker (Dramatists Play Service)
Drama: Act I, Scene 1, pp. 24–25; Molly (55–65).
Molly's husband, Malachai, died a year ago, and she and her daughters are gathered at the Rhode Island summer place. Here in the moonlight on the beach, Molly sits alone, deeply in pain, remembering the day he died as well as happy times and the distinctive birthmark on his shoulder. She misses Malachai terribly, can't get him out of her mind. Start: "There's no privacy in this house." End, "Well, he's in the ground. I won't see it again."
Drama: Act I, Scene 2, pp. 35–36; Laurie (35).
Laurie has just finished washing her hair, laughing with her mother. Alone now in the bathroom, she reflects on how hard it is to sleep now that her father, Malachai, is dead. She tells of lying awake in the night, next to her husband, Norm, listening to him snore and trying to sleep.

Then, just as Laurie dozes off, Malachai's face looms before her, his lips stitched shut, just as she remembers seeing him in the mortuary—and she is awake again. Start: "Hell no . . . It wouldn't hurt." End: "His equipment is definitely no more than half the size of mine."
Drama: Act II, pp. 37–38; Kate (37–40).
Kate is an expert sailor, thanks to her father, Malachai. She came close to being the boy that her father secretly wanted, and they shared a different kind of bond than he did with her sisters. Kate and Malachai did things that were almost father/son is spirit, such as sailing. Here, she sits quietly in her anchored sailboat and reflects on the relationship she had with her dad and how she felt after he died. Start: "I can sail." End: Well . . . Katey's a girl after all."

LAUGHING WILD
by Christopher Durang (Dramatists Play Service)
Comedy: One-act play, Scene 1, pp. 5–6; A Woman (any age).
The woman talks directly to the audience, telling them about a violent encounter she recently had with a man in the supermarket aisle. A short—perhaps $1^1/2$ minutes in length—intense excerpt from a very long speech. The monologue is funny because it is outrageous. Start: "I want to talk to you about life." End: "I'll take a taxi to the Metropolitan Museum of Art. I need to be surrounded with culture right now, not tuna fish."

LES BELLES SOEURS
by Michel Tremblay [translated by John Van Burek and Bill Glassco (Talonbooks, Canada)]
Comedy-Drama: Act I; Des-Neiges Verrette.
Des-Neiges Verrette has fallen in love with a door-to-door brush salesperson and defensively explains to her friends how that came to happen, confessing how much she needs someone to love. Start: "The first time I saw him I thought he was ugly." End: "If he goes away, I'll be all alone again, and I need . . . someone to love . . . I need a man."
Comedy-Drama: Act II; Angeline Sauv (59).
Angeline reveals, to the horror of the other women, that she has been frequenting a nightclub (read: den of iniquity) for four years. She turns to the audience, justifies these simple pleasures, and then promises not to behave this way anymore. Start: "It's easy to judge people." End: "I guess the party's over."
Drama: Act II; Rose (44).
A bitter, venomous speech in which Rose condemns men for the way they exercise power over women. According to her, life isn't like a pretty French movie. In reality, women get pregnant and are lost for life. Rose hates her sex-craving husband, her marriage, all of it. Start: "Life is life and no Goddamn Frenchman ever made a movie about that." End: "They get grabbed by the throat, and they stay that way, right to the end!"

LIPS TOGETHER, TEETH APART
by Terrence McNally (Dramatists Play Service)
Comedy-Drama: Act II, pp. 44–45; Chloe (40).
Chloe is the kind of person who is always being helpful, refilling your cup and checking to see if you are okay. Her husband just told her to "shut up" and not to talk for six hours. Embarrassed in front of their friends, she defends herself in this speech and then exits into the house. Start: "Before I go into my six-hour exile." End: ". . . we'll have bugs galore. Pussy Galore! Remember her?"

LITTLE FOXES, THE
by Lillian Hellman (Dramatists Play Service)
Drama: Act III, pp. 58–59; Birdie (40).
High-strung Birdie has had just enough of Addie's elderberry wine to loosen her tongue. She recalls her first big party 22 years ago, the one where she met her future husband,

Oscar. Mama didn't like Oscar from the start, she remembers, and perhaps she should have listened to her mother. Cut Addie's interruption of the speech. Start: "Mama used to give me elderberry wine when I was a little girl. For hiccups." End: "And so she had. They were all gone."

LONG DAY'S JOURNEY INTO NIGHT
by Eugene O'Neill (Yale University Press)
Drama: Act III; Mary (54).
In a morphine-induced reverie, Mary tells her maid, Cathleen, what it was like to be young and in love with a famous actor like James Tyrone. As she tells the story, the audience gets a glimpse of the innocent young girl Mary once was. Start: "If you think Mr. Tyrone is handsome now, Cathleen." End: "It has made me forgive so many other things."

LOOK HOMEWARD, ANGEL
by Ketti Frings [based on Thomas Wolfe's novel of the same name (Samuel French)]
Drama: Act III, pp. 80–81; Laura (23).
For reasons of her own, Laura didn't tell Eugene that she is engaged to a man in another town, perhaps because she hoped against hope that her relationship with Eugene would work out even though he is too young for her. Their romance blossomed and, less than an hour ago, he asked her to marry him. Believing that she has accepted, Eugene runs off to pack, but Laura knows that she can't do it. In this speech, she tells Eugene's irate mother that she won't marry him and is, in fact, leaving on the afternoon train. Eliminate Eliza's few lines at the beginning of this scene. Start: "Mrs. Gant, I am not marrying Eugene. I'm not." End: "Some day you're going to have to let him go, too. Good-bye, Mrs. Gant."

LOSS OF ROSES, A
by William Inge (Dramatists Play Service)
Drama: Act II, Scene 2, p. 74; Lila (32).
Lila's prospects as an actress are dim, and she has agreed to go to Kansas City and perform in blue movies with her boyfriend. As she prepares to depart, she shares with Helen, who knows nothing of Lila's future plans, a memory of her first day in the first grade. Lila recalls how she approached the event with childlike innocence and joy, only to be jerked into reality when the teacher slapped her. It was her first major lesson in life. Start: "I remember my first day of school." End: "There's so many things I still want back."

LOST IN YONKERS
by Neil Simon (Samuel French)
Drama: Act II, Scene 2, pp. 83–84; Bella (35).
Bella grew up with an unnamed learning disability and, in some ways, is childlike. Still, love has found her, and she wants to marry an usher at a local movie theater. She finally gets the courage to ask her stern mother and other family members for their approval. When they respond badly, Bella yells at them, telling them how much she longs to be in love with someone who will love her back. A very touching speech, not funny at all. Start: "You think I can't have healthy babies, momma?" End: "Hold me . . . Somebody please hold me."

LOVERS AND OTHER STRANGERS
by Renée Taylor and Joseph Bologna (Samuel French)
Comedy: "Bea, Frank, Richie and Joan," p. 40; Bea (45–55).
Bea's son and his wife have surprised everyone by announcing their separation. To head off this catastrophe, Bea takes Joan to the bedroom for a mother-in-law/daughter-in-law chat.

This is the funniest of a couple of monologue possibilities. Start: "And Joan, of all the pictures in your wedding album, my favorite is this one." End: ". . . and they're still together."

LOVE SUICIDE AT SCHOFIELD BARRACKS, THE
by Romulus Linney (Dramatists Play Service) [one-act version; *Seventeen Short Plays by Romulus Linney* (Smith & Kraus)]
Drama: One-act play, DPS pp. 28–30; Mrs. Bates (34).
In a remarkable monologue that is too long ($1^1/2$ pages) for most auditions, Mrs. Bates tells the court how she first met the late general and his wife, how they saved her life, rescued her from a life of prostitution, and introduced her to her current husband. She is grief-stricken by their joint suicide. Start: "I met them first outside Miami, in a place called Slim's, on Route One." End: "That's what they mean to me, the General and his wife."

LUDLOW FAIR
by Lanford Wilson [*Balm in Gilead and Other Plays* by Lanford Wilson (Hill & Wang/Noonday)]
Comedy: Agnes (20s).
At the very end of this 16-page one-act play, Agnes talks to her roommate, who falls asleep in the middle of the speech. After that, she sort of talks to herself and to an imaginary dinner date. Agnes is concerned about the sad state of her love life, and she is trying to get over a bad cold. Fun for class work. A great deal of detail and subtext. If you are ambitious, you can do the entire 2-page monologue. Start: "I don't know why you should worry any more about Joe than you did about whoever it was before." For a shorter monologue, start: "You know what Charles looks like? He looks like one of those little model men you make out of pipe cleaners." End: "I've got to quit saying that."

LUV
by Murray Schisgal (Dramatists Play Service)
Comedy: Act I, pp. 29–30; Ellen (early 30s).
In this gloriously dark speech, Ellen explains her dilemma to her new husband, Harry. On one hand, she has a cold, calculating mind that frightens men away and, on the other, she is a woman, warm and passionate. You'll have to cut and paste quite a bit, eliminating all of Harry's lines and adjusting Ellen's responses. Start: "I was lonely, Harry; I was always lonely." End: ". . . She loses her dream and . . . It makes an animal of her, a vicious little creature who thinks only of scratching and biting and getting revenge."

MARCO POLO SINGS A SOLO
by John Guare (Dramatists Play Service)
Comedy: Act I, p. 29; Diane (30s).
In this wild and woolly monologue, Diane tells Tom about her childhood music training, by now hopelessly interlaced with surreal erotic fantasy. Start: "I really started cookin' when I was eight." End: "Diane de la Nova and her Massage Parlor of Melody."

MATCHMAKER, THE
by Thornton Wilder (Samuel French)
Comedy: Act IV, pp. 109–110; Dolly Levi (40–50).
Dolly Levi has the unsuspecting Horace Vandergelder just about ready to pop the question. Before the big moment, however, she stops alone on stage to talk privately to the spirit of her late husband, explaining to him that she is going to marry for money and that she doesn't want to remain a recluse. They don't write them like this anymore. Start: "Ephraim Levi, I'm going to get married again. Ephraim, I'm marrying Horace Vandergelder for his money." End: "Anyway, that's the opinion of the second Mrs. Vandergelder."

MISS MARGARIDA'S WAY
by Roberto Athayde (Samuel French)
Comedy-Drama: pp. 9–13; Miss Margarida (30–50).
This is a one-woman, two-act play in which the theater audience is treated like an undisciplined, rather stupid eighth-grade class. Miss Margarida instructs, harangues, seduces, and berates the audience members. You can draw excerpts from almost any place. One choice is to start at the top of the play when she introduces herself and continue for about 2¹/₂ pages. Start: "Good evening to all of you." End: "There is a very nice nursery rhyme that goes: 'The deserving ones, who are they?/They are those who obey.'"

Another option is to begin where the first selection ends (pp. 13–15), just after Miss Margarida writes the following on the blackboard: "The deserving ones, who are they? They are those who obey." Her very next line is: "I want to take advantage of this first class." Continue for about 1¹/₂ pages. End: ". . . any Holy Ghosts in class? None, right? Fuck you then! You can go to hell."

MRS. CALIFORNIA
by Doris Baizley (Dramatists Play Service)
Comedy: Act 1, pp. 7–8; Dot (25–35).
Dot is Mrs. Los Angeles, competing in the 1955 Mrs. California contest. Here, she is rehearsing the very dramatic story of her "proudest moment," telling how she transmitted radio signals to convoys at sea during World War II. Start: "It was the winter of 1943. I was an ensign." End: "I was the whole U.S. Navy that night. The whole U.S.A."
Comedy: Act I, pp. 24–25; Babs (25–35).
Babs gives her friend, Dot, a locker-room pep talk. You'll have to cut and paste the text, eliminating Dot's lines, but it is worth it. An excellent comical speech. Start: "You want to win this thing or not?" End: "You're gonna win this thing if it kills me!"
Comedy: Act II, p. 42; Dot (25–35).
Mrs. Los Angeles presents her "Family Fun" speech, telling how she successfully fills each and every season and holiday with family fun. Start: "I guess you could say our Family Fun begins when the girls and I bake the pies for Back to School Jamboree." End: "by the time we're finished with all the thank-you notes, it's Back to School again!"
Comedy: Act II, p. 48; Mrs. San Francisco (25–35).
Mrs. San Francisco proudly shares her recipe for her "Christmas Ice Angel." Start: "My husband calls it our Frozen French Bombshell." End: "crushed and forced through a strainer. I call it her heart."

MRS. WARREN'S PROFESSION
by George Bernard Shaw (Signet)
Drama: Act IV; Mrs. Warren (40–50).
Once Vivie learned that her mother is still operating a chain of brothels, she refused to accept any more money from her. Mrs. Warren visits her daughter and tells Vivie that her Cambridge-education values are false. Omit Vivie's single line and Mrs. Warren's direct response to it. Start: "Vivie, listen to me. You don't understand. You've been taught wrong on purpose." End: "Can't you see that you're cutting your own throat as well as breaking my heart in turning your back on me?"

NATURE AND PURPOSE OF THE UNIVERSE, THE
by Christopher Durang (Dramatists Play Service)
Comedy, One-act play, pp. 24–25; Elaine (25–45).
God has sent Elaine to impersonate the census taker who lambastes Eleanor for leading a "lousy life," suggesting that she consider suicide. A very funny speech because it is so off-the-wall

and demented. Point by point, Elaine tells Eleanor why her life is such a failure. Start: "You phony liar. Your oldest son pushes dope and is a pimp." End: "Why do you continue living, Mrs. Mann!? Why don't you do yourself a favor!?"

Comedy, One-act play, pp. 28–29; Elaine (28–29).

Elaine, formerly the census taker and Sister Annie De Maupassant, the radical nun of Bernardsville, is the Pope now. In this speech, she stands on a table top and speaks in a grand and holy fashion, sharing her thoughts and insights on the subject of death. Start: "Death comes to us all, my brothers and sisters in Christ." End: "For we are the little people of the earth, and His is the power and the glory, and never the twain shall meet. Hubb-ba, hubb-ba, hubb-ba."

NEVIS MOUNTAIN DEW
by Steve Carter (Dramatists Play Service)
Drama: Act II, pp. 33–34; Zepora (43).

Zepora tells Ayton she wants him to leave the woman he has lived with for a number of years and marry her. He says he would if she would move out of this house, where she cares for her older brother who is confined to an iron-lung machine and who rules with an iron hand. Anyway, Ayton believes he isn't good enough for Zepora, that he isn't educated enough, is too rough, and too black in color. In this short, sexually honest speech, Zepora tells him that she has loved him since he was a child, that he is a good man and that, when he is with her, he can't be black enough. Zepora has a West-Indian heritage, so a slight accent is appropriate. Start: "Ayton, think back! I've known you . . . ever since I could see." End: ". . . with every stroke, I'm thinking . . . 'Blacker!' 'Blacker!' 'Blacker!' I'll be thinking it tonight! Leave her, Ayton. Leave her and let me dream, 'Blacker!' 'Blacker!' 'Blacker!' just any damned night I want to."

'NIGHT, MOTHER
by Marsha Norman (Dramatists Play Service)
Drama: One-act play, p. 50; Jessie (37–43).

Jessie tells her mother why suicide is the best option, explaining how she has lost her identity somewhere along the way. Start: "I am what became of your child." End: ". . . so there's no reason to stay, except to keep you company, and that's . . . not reason enough because I'm not . . . very good company. Am I?"

NIGHT OF THE IGUANA, THE
by Tennessee Williams (Dramatists Play Service)
Drama: Act III; Hannah (39).

Hannah is an unusually perceptive sketch artist who supports her poet grandfather and herself in a hand-to-mouth existence as they travel from tourist resort to tourist resort. In this haunting and poignant speech, she tells Shannon of the beauty—and evidence of God—she has seen in the eyes of the dying in Shanghai. She also mentions that she has recently begun to see that same expression in the eyes of her grandfather. Start: "You see, in my profession I have to look hard and close at human faces in order to catch something in them before they get restless and call out, 'Waiter, the check, we're leaving!'." End: "Lately my grandfather's eyes have looked up at me like that." (This monologue doesn't appear in the DPS acting edition. You can, however, find it in earlier library compilations.)

NUTS
by Tom Topor (Samuel French)
Drama: Act II, pp. 43–44; Rose (60s).

Although her daughter is the accused, Rose behaves as if she were on trial. She is defensive about her record as a mother. In this monologue, she begins by telling the court how lovely Claudia's wedding was. Then she goes into a venomous attack on her former husband, who

cheated on her. Cut Claudia's few lines and Rose's direct responses to them. Motivate the transitions internally. Start: "Your honor, I know it's a terrible thing to hear a mother say her daughter is." End: "That's how much he loved me: six dollars and thirty-one cents worth."
Drama: Act III, pp. 75–76; Claudia (early 30s).
Claudia faces the court and graphically outlines her fee structure for various prostitution services. Explicit sexual language. Appropriate for sophisticated actresses. Start: "I get a hundred for a straight lay, a hundred for a hand job." End: "Do you all get what I'm telling you?"
Drama: Act III, pp. 82–83; Claudia (early 30s).
In answer to the question, "Do you love your mother?", Claudia tells the court what she thinks about love. An insightful monologue. Start: "When I was a little girl, I used to say to her, I love you to the moon and down again and around the world and back again." End: "It's too much and not enough."
Drama: Act III, pp. 83–84; Claudia (early 30s).
The final speech in the play is a blast furnace of a monologue. Cut the judge's lines and Claudia's direct responses to them. Start: "Wait a second, wait one goddamn second. What is this?" End: "Get it straight: I won't be nuts for you. Do you get what I'm telling you?"

OLEANNA
by David Mamet (Dramatists Play Service)
Drama: Act III, pp. 39–40; Carol (20).
Carol accused her professor of sexual harassment, and his flourishing career subsequently has been put on hold. Now the student becomes a demanding teacher as she lectures him on his transgressions. Start: "The issue here is not what I 'feel.' It is not my 'feelings,' but the feelings of women." End: "You worked twenty years for the right to insult me. And you feel entitled to be paid for it."

OTHERWISE ENGAGED
by Simon Gray (Samuel French)
Comedy-Drama: Act II, p. 36; Beth (30s).
Beth has just discovered that her husband, Simon, has known for months that she has been having an affair, and that rather than enjoy her guilt, he opted for silence. In this terrific monologue, she tells him what she thinks of his deceit. What Simon doesn't know is that Beth is pregnant, but she doesn't know who the father is. Written in the British vernacular. Start: "You know the most insulting thing, that you let me go on and on being unfaithful without altering your manner or your behaviour." End: "Damn. Damn you . . . Oh, damn . . . So you might as well listen to your Wagner."

PAINTING CHURCHES
by Tina Howe (Samuel French)
Drama: Act II, Scene 1, pp. 72–73; Fanny (60s).
Fanny tells her daughter, an artist, that if she is going to paint the family, do it truthfully. Start: ". . . and to you who see him once a year, if that . . . what is he to you?" End: "If you want to paint us so badly, you ought to paint us as we really are. There's your picture."

PIZZA MAN
by Darlene Craviotto (Samuel French)
Comedy-Drama: Act II, Scene 2, pp. 75–76; Julie (late 20s).
Julie has become frustrated by her efforts to rape a man. This started as a kind of misdirected lark, but it has turned ugly, almost violent. She complains to her roommate and their potential victim that fairy tales don't, in fact, exist and that life is a kick in the teeth. Then Julie continues in a bittersweet fashion, describing how she learned that a pretty smile isn't

enough to get you through. Start: "I'm unemployed. I've had ten jobs in the last eight years. I live in a crappy one-bedroom apartment." End: "But can you see what a nice smile it used to be? Can you see how nice things used to be?"

PLAY MEMORY
by Joanna M. Glass (Samuel French)
Drama: Act II, pp. 76–77; Jean (20).
Jean's father is an unrepentant alcoholic, evidently intent on destroying his life along with his family's. Here, Jean tells him how much she loved him when she was a young girl, how much she adored going on a business trip with him. They drove places, saw wild horses, met people, and ate candy. In the context of the play, the actress is actually in her early teens when she makes this speech. The material can, however, work very well for actresses in their mid-20s. A very touching, beautiful monologue. You'll have to cut and paste a bit, omitting Cam's lines and references to the horses being sold for dog food. Start: "I remember the first time I knew I loved you." End: "I haven't been able to love you since then, because you're making me sick."

PORCH
by Jeffrey Sweet (Samuel French)
Drama: One-act play, p. 34; Amy (early 30s).
Amy resents her widower father for pressuring her to marry and have a family and for continually comparing her unfavorably to the memory of her late brother. In this poignant speech, she talks about the decision she made to have an abortion, how that affected her relationship with her father, and why she resents her brother for dying. Start: "My father's daughter. That sounds so possessive." End: "Christ, talk about selfish!"

PRIMARY ENGLISH CLASS, THE
by Israel Horovitz (Dramatists Play Service)
Comedy: Act I, pp. 28–29; Debbie Wastba (25–40).
Facing a classroom filled with students who know no English, Debbie tries to introduce herself and explain what is going to happen in class. She has no sensitivity at all to other cultures, and that is what makes this speech funny. A blackboard is a desirable prop, but you can get by without it. Start: "Listen, now, I'll just go really slow. My name is Debbie Wastba." End: "Now then: Questions?"

PROMISE, THE
by José Rivera (Broadway Play Publishing)
Comedy-Drama: Act II, Scene 8; Lilia (18).
Lilia's father, now old and feeble and on his way to a nursing home, listens as she declares her independence from him. She tells him that because he robbed her of the only man she ever loved, she'll make sure he never knows his future grandchildren. Start: "I talked to the home. You're getting the one-bedroom on the first floor." End: ". . . a broken promise makes us free of each other. You set me free."

REDWOOD CURTAIN
by Lanford Wilson (Hill & Wang/Noonday)
Drama: Scene 2; Geri (17).
Geri Riordan is a music prodigy. In a powerful speech, she tells her aunt why she has abruptly decided to abandon the art and why she isn't going to Juilliard. She is tired of being thought of as that "adorable Vietnam war bastard." Start: "I'm not appreciated. I'm 'special.'" End: "I don't want to be special."

SCENES AND REVELATIONS
by Elan Garonzik (Samuel French)
Drama: Scene 10, pp. 35–36; Helena (25).
It is 1893, and Helena is feeling romantic toward her new farm manager, Samuel. After a scene during which they dance around the questions of commitment and marriage, he asks why she so often sits on the back porch steps with that air of longing about her. In response, she delivers this speech, telling him about a former love and how he vanished from her life during the period when her father was dying. Helena admits that this took the air right out of her. Start: "There are some things in life, Samuel, that are so private. Things that should . . . shouldn't be said to just anyone." End: "And am as you find me today: Sitting on the back porch. Pulling stems off blades of grass."

SCENES FROM AMERICAN LIFE
by A. R. Gurney, Jr. (Samuel French)
Comedy: Act I, pp. 32–33; Woman (50 plus).
A nervous resident of an expensive neighborhood addresses a neighborhood-council meeting, protesting the potential construction of a fence around the area. The character, an older woman, isn't used to public speaking and refers frequently to 3 × 5 cards throughout her speech. Good contemporary, comic material for a WASP-y actress in her fifties. Start: "Um. I want to make three quick points about this whole business of the fence." End: "I mean, I'm just not sure a fence is the best solution."
Comedy: Act II, p. 51; Mrs. Hayes (50 plus).
A woman explains to her pianist why she has taken up singing at this late age. Interesting monologue material for the actress who can effectively create the illusion of the pianist. Start: "Before we begin, you probably want to know, don't you, why I'm taking up singing lessons at my age." End: "I'm singing my heart out!" You can also try to sing a bar or two and end: "I'm terribly sorry. I'm terribly, terribly sorry."

SEA GULL, THE
by Anton Chekhov [a new version by Jean-Claude Van Itallie (Dramatists Play Service)]
Drama: Act IV, pp. 51–52; Nina (21).
Nina, nervous and hungry, has appeared unexpectedly in Treplev's study. Ecstatic to see her, he declares his love once again. Nina, however, tells Treplev that she is here for only a moment and that she has accepted a winter acting engagement in a distant province. Suddenly, hearing Trigorin's voice in the next room, she pulls back and, in this monologue, tells Treplev that she is still in love with Trigorin even though he abandoned her. Nina then explains how she'd lost faith in herself after Trigorin treated her so badly, but now she has found her true self on the stage—and in acting. Somehow, though, her words sound hollow and desperate. Start: "Why did you say you kiss the ground I walk on?" End: "When I think about my work I'm not so afraid of life any more."

SEA HORSE, THE
by Edward J. Moore (Samuel French)
Drama: Act II, pp. 51–52; Gertrude (late 30s).
Gertrude describes the events surrounding her father's death when she was a little girl, her subsequent upbringing, and how she came to own and run The Sea Horse saloon. Although in the context of the play, this role must be played by a "big woman," but the actress's size doesn't matter for this isolated monologue, particularly when used for audition purposes. Start: "I was sitting on the pier one day, doing my homework." End: ". . . and I didn't need . . . anyone . . . anymore."

SHADOW BOX, THE
by Michael Cristofer (Samuel French)
Drama: Act II, pp. 71–72; Beverly (mid-30s).
Beverly is disgusted by Mark's self-serving tone as tells he tells her how he and her ex-husband, Brian, became lovers. When Mark continues to enumerate in graphic and putrid detail the way he has had to care for the dying man these last few months, Beverly levels him with this impassioned speech. Start: "Let me tell you something, as one whore to another." Cut Mark's line and Beverly's direct response to it. End: "My God, why isn't that ever enough?"
Drama: Act II, pp. 77–78; Maggie (38–45).
Maggie pleads with Joe, her husband, to come home from the hospital, knowing full well he can't. Cut Joe's line and Maggie's direct response to it. Start: "For Christ's sake, don't make me say things I don't understand." End: "I want you to be there because I want you to come home." or end: "Come home. That's all. Come home."
Drama: Act II, pp. 58–60; Agnes (44–50).
Agnes's mother, Felicity, seemed to cross over suddenly into old age the day word came that her daughter Claire had been killed in an accident. Felicity's health deteriorated as she became increasingly despondent. After many months of emotional and financial decline, she began to fantasize that Claire was still alive. That was when Agnes began to write fictitious letters to Felicity, signing Claire's name to them, hoping they would lift the woman's spirits. In a poignant speech, Agnes tells the offstage Interviewer why she has deceived her mother. Once you cut and paste, eliminating the Interviewer's lines, you'll have a wonderful monologue. Start: "We were very close. Our whole family." End with Agnes's admission that she has been writing the letters. Rework her lines and the interviewer's so that the material reads: "So . . . So I've been writing these letters for almost two years . . . You're not angry with me, are you?"

SHIRLEY VALENTINE
by Willy Russell (Michelin House, London)
Comedy: Act I, Scene 1; Shirley (42).
Since *Shirley Valentine* has only one character, the entire play is a monologue, much of which is literally addressed to the walls in Shirley's kitchen. For the most part, Shirley talks about past events and although they still affect her, the speeches don't have enough tension for auditions. Still, this is wonderfully rich material, frequently touching. Written in the British vernacular.

You have many excerpts to choose from. You can do the last part of Shirley's story about having tea with Marjorie Majors. This section begins on a light note and takes an introspective, perhaps tearful turn at the end. Start: "The waitress was just puttin' the tea an' cakes on the table." End: ". . . who turned me into this? I don't want this." For a touching excerpt, try beginning immediately after this point. Start: "Do you remember her, wall? Remember Shirley Valentine? She got married to a boy called Joe." End: "I've always wondered why is it that if somebody says 'I love you' it seems to automatically give them the right to treat you worse."
Drama: Act I, Scene 2; Shirley (42).
This is the only section in the play when Shirley is in the throes of a dilemma in the present moment. As such, it arguably makes the best material for audition purposes. She is waiting in her kitchen for her friend Jane to pick her up to go to the airport and fly to Greece. Start: "Guess where I'm going?" End: "and keep Joe safe. Please." For a longer excerpt, continue to this point: ". . . got hold of a pen an' wrote, across the wall, in big letters—GREECE."

SHIVAREE
by William Mastrosimone (Samuel French)
Comedy: Act I, pp. 33–34; Shivaree (20s).
Shivaree tells Chandler how she makes a living as a belly dancer. This character is southern to her toes, apparently rural, displays a sophisticated vocabulary, and is bright, sassy, sexy, very

much in her own orbit, a free spirit. Start: "Well, sport, you can dance for dance and get a flat rate, or you can dance for tips." End: "And that's m'story bub, now where's this wine?"

SIGN IN SIDNEY BRUSTEIN'S WINDOW, THE
by Lorraine Hansberry (Samuel French)
Drama: Act I, Scene 2, pp. 45–46; Iris (29).
Iris is experiencing an episode of serious self-doubt about her ability to succeed as an actress. In this often-performed monologue, she tells her husband, Sidney, what it is really like at an audition. Start: "You don't know what it's like though." End:"Oh, Jesus, do I ever feel twenty-nine!"

SISTER MARY IGNATIUS EXPLAINS IT ALL FOR YOU
by Christopher Durang (Dramatists Play Service)
Comedy: One-act play, pp. 30–31; Sister Mary Ignatius (40–60).
This funny play contains a couple of possible monologues, but this is the best because it includes some outrageous Catholic doctrine. The actress should wear a traditional nun's habit. Start: "I have your questions here on little file cards." End: "If you die instantaneously and are unable to say a good act of contrition, you will go straight to hell."

SIX DEGREES OF SEPARATION
by John Guare (Dramatists Play Service)
Drama: One-act play, p. 45; Ouisa (43).
Ouisa has just discovered how the young intruder managed to learn so many personal details of her private family life. This causes her to reflect on how "everybody on this planet is separated by only six other people. Six degrees of separation." Start: "Can you believe it? Paul learned all that in three months. Three months!" End: "Six degrees of separation between me and everyone else on this planet. But to find the right six people."

SNOWANGEL
by Lewis John Carlino [*Cages* (Dramatists Play Service)]
Drama: One-act play, pp. 24–25; Connie (mid-to-late 30s).
As dawn approaches and the liquor heightens her reverie, Connie, a prostitute, tells her john about her first love, a Mexican laborer named Paco. He was a gentle man with a special smile. Start: "He came to me while I was workin' in a house in Stockton." End: "That's what I remember, mister. That's what I imagine."

STEEL MAGNOLIAS
by Robert Harling (Dramatists Play Service)
Drama: Act II, Scene 2, pp. 66–67; M'Lynn (50ish).
M'lynn tells her friends about the final hours of her daughter's life. The monologue is peaceful, accepting, and loving—not a crying scene. Start: "No, I couldn't leave my Shelby." End: "It was the most precious moment of my life thus far."

STILL LIFE
by Emily Mann (Dramatists Play Service)
Drama: Act III, Scene 4, p. 42, "The Spaghetti Story"; Cheryl (28).
On the surface, this is simply the funny story of a wife trying to cope with her husband's wild and wacky yearly spaghetti feast for 40 close friends. But underneath the surface lies the disturbing edge and manic quality of a woman who is just barely hanging on. The following excerpt is appropriate for audition purposes. Start: "I hate to cook. Probably because he likes to cook." End: "I can't take it."

STREETCAR NAMED DESIRE, A
by Tennessee Williams (Dramatists Play Service)
Drama: Act II, Scene 2, pp. 67–68; Blanche (early 30s).
A romance between Blanche and Mitch is blossoming, but he doubts his feelings for Blanche because his mother views the union with skepticism. Returning from a date, the lovers flirt in the dim lantern light. Suddenly, Mitch asks Blanche exactly how old she is; this is a dangerous question because Blanche is several years older than she has led him to believe. Afraid that he might be slipping from her clutches, Blanche goes into this story about her long-ago marriage to a boy who turned out to be gay. His ultimate suicide made her very needy for someone exactly like Mitch. Blinded by love, Mitch buys Blanche's story completely. Start: "He was a boy, just a boy, when I was a very young girl." End: "And then the searchlight which had been turned on the world was turned off again and never for one moment since has there been any light stronger than this kitchen candle. . . ."

SUBJECT WAS ROSES, THE
by Frank D. Gilroy (Samuel French)
Drama: Act II, Scene 3, p. 64; Nettie (45).
Nettie tells her son how she came to marry his father. Tinged now with bitterness and regret, she still can remember the appeal her husband had as a young man. A good monologue, with plenty of subtext. Start: "I think it was his energy . . . a certain wildness. He was not like my father at all." End: "The baker from Paterson was all tongue-tied outside, but in the home he would have been beautiful . . . Go to bed now."

SUMMER AND SMOKE
by Tennessee Williams (Dramatists Play Service)
Drama: Part I, Scene 1, pp. 17–18; Alma (25–29).
Alma has been in love with John since childhood, but they've evolved into radically different kinds of adults. She is shy, proper, and nervous, while he is something of a hell raiser and a rogue. In this speech, motivated by her feelings of unrequited love, Alma blasts John for wasting his considerable talents and his life. Start: "I'm afraid you and I move in different circles." End: "You know what I call it? I call it a desecration!"
Drama: Part II, Scene 5, p. 73; Alma (25–29).
Alma has come to John's office to tell him that she'll sleep with him and that she loves him. When she kisses him, however, he pulls back, explaining that what he now feels for her is spiritual, not physical. In this emotional speech, Alma tells John that she has loved him since childhood. Start: "But I don't want to be talked to like some incurably sick patient you have to comfort." End: "Why did you come almost close enough—and no closer?"

SWEET BIRD OF YOUTH
by Tennessee Williams (Dramatists Play Service)
Drama: Act I, Scene 1, pp. 19–20; Princess Kosmonopolis (50–60).
The princess tells her lover, Chance, about the disastrous screening of her "comeback" film. People laughed in the wrong places, and she fled from the theater. Cut Chance's lines and the princess's direct responses to them. Rewrite around Chance this way: "If I could paint deserts and nomads, if I could paint . . . smoke . . . but you come after the comeback. Start: "Stars in retirement sometimes give acting lessons." End: "Flight, just flight, not interrupted until I woke up this morning."
Drama: Act I, Scene 1, pp. 25–26; Princess Kosmonopolis (50–60).
Princess Kosmonopolis tells Chance that she can't be blackmailed, but that she'll give him money in exchange for sex. You'll have to cut and paste, eliminating Chance's lines and

rewriting around him. Start: "You are trembling and sweating . . . you see this part doesn't suit you. . . ." End: "I'm sending a young man down with some travelers' checks to cash for me. . . ."

TAKEN IN MARRIAGE
by Thomas Babe (Dramatists Play Service)
Comedy: Act I, pp. 19–20; Ruth (late 50s).
At the rehearsal for Annie's upcoming wedding, her various female relatives chat about what marriage and love actually mean. In this crusty speech, Annie's aunt Ruth explains to Annie and the others why she stayed with her late husband for 25 years, despite his infidelities. Loyalty, you see, is the key. Start: "I may seem the smallest part of a fool, and Anne and Andrea may think worse, but I'm not." End: "I want you to remember that, Anne."

TALKING WITH . . .
by Jane Martin (Samuel French)
Comedy-Drama: "Fifteen Minutes," pp. 7–10; Actress (any age).
An actress spends the final moments before going on stage putting on her makeup and talking to the audience about how strange it is to be part of a theatrical transaction.
Comedy-Drama: "Scraps," pp. 13–16; Actress (35).
A housewife lives a fantasy life as the Patchwork Girl of Oz, from the seventh Oz book. Each day, after her husband leaves for work and her daughter goes off to high school, she dresses up in her colorful patch-quilt outfit and cleans the house. In this monologue, she tells the audience why this escape is necessary for her sanity.
Drama: "Clear Glass Marbles," pp. 19–22; Actress (20–30).
A woman talks about the final days of her mother's life. During this monologue, she drops marbles, one at a time, on the floor, symbolizing the passing of each day.
Comedy: "Audition," pp. 25–27; Actress (late 20s).
An actress goes on stage to audition. She brings a cat on a leash with her. The more she talks, the stranger she seems. She threatens to kill the cat right there if she doesn't get the job.
Comedy-Drama: "Rodeo," pp. 31–34; Actress (late 20s).
A woman named Lurlene, former rodeo rider, complains about modern-day merchandising of the rodeo. During this speech, the actress works on a piece of tack.
Comedy-Drama: "Twirler," pp. 37–40; Actress (20–30).
A young woman wearing a spangled one-piece swimsuit and carrying a baton talks about the glories of being a twirler. She elevates the twirler to the rank of deity.
Drama: "Lamps," pp.43–45; Actress (65).
Surrounded by lamps, perhaps a dozen or so, a woman talks about old age. She turns off the lamps one at time until, finally, there is darkness.
Comedy: "Handler," pp. 49–52; Actress (20–30).
Here, a rural woman discusses the pros and cons of religious snake handling.
Drama: "Dragons," pp. 55–57; Actress (20–30).
This woman is nine months pregnant and in labor as she speaks. Prenatal tests indicated that her baby is abnormal, but she is having it anyway.
Comedy: "French Fries," pp. 61–63; Actress (60s).
A bag lady rambles on in a funny touching manner about how wonderful it would be to actually live in a McDonald's fast-food restaurant. In the middle of her long speech, there is a nice 1 1/2-minute excerpt that is appropriate for auditions. Start: "I saw a man healed by a Big Mac." End: "Healed by a Big Mac. I saw it."
Comedy: "Marks," pp. 67–69; Actress (early 40s).
A woman talks about all of the tattoos on her body. They represent various people and events in her life.

TENTH MAN, THE
by Paddy Chayefsky (Samuel French)
Comedy-Drama: Act II, Scene 1, pp. 43–44; The Girl (Evelyn, 18).
This speech begins in a lucid fashion, but midway through the girl stops making sense. She starts by talking about life in the mental institution and shifts into descriptions of her secret life as a movie actress. Probably not a wise choice for auditions. Start: "I'm being institutionalized again. Dr. Molineaux's Sanitarium in Long Island. I'm a little paranoid." End: "He's really Mr. Hirschman the Cabalist. He's making a golem. You ought to come here, Rabbi."

TOP GIRLS
by Caryl Churchill (Samuel French)
Comedy-Drama: Act I, Scene 1, p. 27; Lady Nijo (30s).
Lady Nijo is one of the historical guests at Marlene's celebration lunch. Born in 1258, Nijo was the emperor's concubine and later a Buddhist nun. In this short speech, she tells how she was impregnated by her young lover before she became a concubine. The emperor thought she was four months pregnant when she was actually in her sixth month. When the baby was born, Nijo's lover, Akebono, cut the cord and took the baby away. Nijo told the emperor that she miscarried. Start: "I too was often in embarrassing situations, there's no need for a scandal." End: "Then I told the Emperor that the baby had miscarried because of my illness, and there you are. The danger was past."

TOUCH OF THE POET, A
by Eugene O'Neill (Random House/Modern Library)
Drama: Act IV; Nora (40).
Nora's husband stormed off hours ago, bent on defending his honor in a duel. Now, at midnight, she is worried that a terrible fate might have befallen him. She confides to her daughter that perhaps this is God's way of punishing the family. The speech requires a slight Irish brogue. A good dramatic monologue for an actress of power and intelligence. Start: "Don't tell me not to worry. You're as bad as Mickey." End: "Oh, if I only had the courage!"

TRIBUTE
by Bernard Slade (Samuel French)
Comedy: Act I, pp. 28–29; Hilary (30s).
Hilary, a former call girl who is now a successful travel agent, speaks to the audience about her affection for and relationship with Scottie Templeton, who has been diagnosed with a terminal disease. She explains how he arranged for her former clients to raise the money so that she could start her own travel agency. Start: "Okay, maybe it's about time I introduced myself." End: "I'm here for the same reason you are. I love him."

TWICE AROUND THE PARK
by Murray Schisgal (Samuel French)
Comedy: "A Need For Brussels Sprouts," pp. 26–28; Margaret (40s).
Margaret is a New York City cop who is mad because her downstairs neighbor plays his opera music too loud. After complaining to him on the telephone to no avail, she puts on her uniform and knocks on his door to issue a summons for disturbing the peace. It turns out he is a widower, and since she is a single mother, they hit it off in an insulting kind of way. In a very funny speech, she tells him about her awful marriages. This is a very good monologue for an actress who has a feel for New York Jewish humor. You'll have to cut and paste, eliminating Leon's lines. In its entirety, the speech is probably too long for most audition purposes, but it is easy to cut. Start: "Three short marriages, huh? You think that's funny?" End: ". . . and that, Mr. Rose, is the story of two short marriages that were not so funny!"

VIEUX CARRÉ
by Tennessee Williams (New Directions)
Drama: Part II, Scene 9; Jane (20s).
The story Jane relates in this speech may or may not be true. What Tye doesn't know is that Jane's blood count has "taken a turn for the worse," signaling a return of leukemia, and she is deeply depressed. In the preceding scene, Jane has ordered the low-life Tye out because he has begun shooting heroin again. Then she begins this speech, telling him how she came to meet a wealthy Brazilian in a bar—a man she is expecting momentarily, and a man who will pay for her services. You'll have to cut and paste a bit, omitting Tye's lines. Start: "I know what I said, I said a buyer to look at my illustrations, but what I said was a lie." End: "The bed bit is finished between us. You're moving out today."

VITAL SIGNS
by Jane Martin (Samuel French)
Drama, pp. 57–58: "Abortion Lawyer"; Woman (25–40).
Vital Signs is composed of more than 30 monologues for women on a variety of contemporary topics. One particularly intense speech focuses on the abortion issue. A female prosecutor is being replaced by a male in an abortion-clinic-protest case. In this speech, she demands that she be the one to try it. Start: "Suitable? No, actually that doesn't seem 'suitable' to me." End: "You can't do anything about number one and you are cordially invited to number two, my treat. How about it?"
Drama, p. 79: "Endings"; Woman (25–40).
This monologue is also quite compelling. Here, a woman takes her bag out to the car, intending to leave her companion while he is sleeping. But she can't do it. Instead, she returns to the house and climbs into the bed with him. Maybe she'll leave next time. Start: "I sat in the chair by the bed watching him sleep until I ached from sitting and then went out to the tool shed where I had hidden the suitcase." End: "And as I fell asleep I thought, well, that's all right, it's going on then. It's going on."

WAITING FOR THE PARADE
by John Murrell (Talonbooks, Canada)
Drama: Scene 14; Catherine (early 30s).
Earlier today, Catherine received word that Billy, her husband, is missing in action in World War II, and she has been hitting the bottle a little heavy ever since as other women try to comfort her. In this touching speech, she recalls the fights she and Billy had in the early days of their marriage and how those are her most vivid memories. Eliminate Margaret's line. Start: "When Billy and I were first married—we fought all the time." End: "Losing him—a little at a time."
Comedy-Drama: Scene 20; Margaret (mid-to-late 50s).
As she draws a stocking seam up her leg with an eyebrow pencil, Margaret talks about the sadness of getting old, as well as the fact that her imprisoned youngest son didn't want to see her the last time she visited him in jail. Finally, she cries out in pain against it all, resolving to overcome the bad thoughts. Because of the eyebrow pencil, this might not be the best piece for audition purposes, but it is excellent for workshop use.

WARM PENINSULA, THE
by Joe Masteroff (Samuel French)
Comedy: Act II, pp. 67–68; Iris (60).
Iris is a former movie queen, now retired in Florida, but she is still quite the party gal. In this brief speech, she tells her young friend Ruth about her career and the fact that Rudolph Valentino was in love with her. The audience hears just a hint of regret that she is getting older.

At the end, Iris sheds a tear. You'll have to cut and paste this sweet monologue a bit, eliminating Ruth's lines. Start: "What time is it? . . . I'm so depressed today, I refuse to wind my watch." End: "Is my mascara afloat?"

WASH, THE
by Philip Kan Gotanda (Dramatists Play Service) [*Between Worlds, Contemporary Asian-American Plays* (Theatre Communications Group)]
Drama: Act II, Scene 7, DPS p. 44; Masi (67).
Masi tells her adult daughters why she left their father after 42 years of marriage. She confesses that he didn't find her sexually desirable. Furthermore, he considered her to be stupid. She is now very happy with a new man, Sadao. An excellent monologue. Start: "here are things you kids don't know." End: "I like Sadao. I like Sadao very much."

WHO'S AFRAID OF VIRGINIA WOOLF?
by Edward Albee (Dramatists Play Service)
Drama: Act III, p. 88; Martha (52).
Martha took the new biology teacher to her bedroom, but he was unable to have sex with her because he was too drunk. Now, back in the living room, she tells him that all men except her husband are flops, describing the futile seductive dance she has endured so many times. Rough material, appropriate for advanced actresses. By this point in the play, Martha has been drinking steadily for many hours and is seeing through an alcoholic veil. Start: "You're all flops." End: "There is only one man in my life who has ever . . . made me happy. Do you know that? One!"

WOOLGATHERER, THE
by William Mastrosimone (Samuel French)
Drama: Act I, p. 28; Rosie (mid-20s).
Rosie is tortured by the memory of hoodlums viciously breaking the legs of the pretty cranes in the zoo. Here, she tells Cliff about the circumstances. The terror is still real. Start: "You may think it's funny but I was the last one to see them last summer." End: "They can't make the birds come alive again."

ZOOMAN AND THE SIGN
by Charles Fuller (Samuel French)
Drama: Act II, pp. 33–34; Rachel (mid-30s).
Still in mourning over the violent death of her 12-year-old daughter, Rachel describes the step-by-step deterioration of this formerly safe neighborhood. this is a powerful monologue. Start: "What is it about men, they won't let well enough alone?" End: "I just want to move."

Part Four
Male/Male Scenes

AMEN CORNER, THE
by James Baldwin (Samuel French)
Drama: Act II, pp. 49–54; Luke (40–50) and David (18).
David hasn't seen his father, Luke, for 10 years, ever since the day his mother took him and walked out on the man. But like his father, David is born to be a musician. It is in his blood, and he has identified with his father from afar. Until last week, however, David always thought his father left his mother, not the other way around. It makes a difference. Luke is dying, and the father/son relationship is more important than ever. In this wonderful scene, Luke tells David that it is possible to be a good musician without screwing up your life the way he has. Both characters have good monologues. Start, Luke: "Hello there." End, Luke: "Oh yes."

AMERICAN BUFFALO
by David Mamet (Samuel French)
Drama: Act I, pp. 5–10; Don (late 40s) and Bob (30–40).
Bob's job was to tail the man with the coin collection and not to let him get out of sight. When the man went into a building, however, Bob lost him and came slinking back to the junk shop to report his failure to Don, the mastermind behind the coin heist. Don is worried that Bob's failure to follow instructions to the letter might jeopardize the entire caper, so he tries to teach Bob the principles of successful street survival. Start, Don: "So? . . . So what, Bob?" End, Don: "Well, we'll see."
Drama: Act I, pp. 22–32; Don (late 40s) and Teach (35–45).
Teach presses Don for details of his plan to steal the coin collection. When Teach finds out that the heist might result in a great deal of money, he maneuvers to cut Bob out of the picture. Start, Teach: "So what is this thing with the kid?" End, Teach: ". . . you can take your 90 dollars for the nickel, shove it up your ass—the good it did you—and you want to know why? (And I'm not saying anything. . . .) Because you didn't take the time to go first class."
Drama: Act II, pp. 54–60; Don (late 40s) and Teach (35–45).
Teach and Don make last-minute plans for pulling off the coin-collection robbery. Ultimately, however, they don't go through with it. The entire scene between the men is too long for most workshops. The entire scene runs 18 pages, which is too long for most scene-study workshops. Try this excerpt, which begins after Bob's exit. Start, Don: "Fuckin' kid." End, Teach: "Because I got the balls to face some facts? You scare me sometimes, Don."

AMERICAN PLAN, THE
by Richard Greenberg (Dramatists Play Service)
Drama: Act II, Scene 2, pp. 44–49; Nick (20s) and Gil (28–35).
When Gil kisses Nick briefly on the mouth in this scene, the moment shocks audience members because, up until this point, they thought that both men were heterosexual. The truth is that

Gil and Nick are lovers, and Gil has followed Nick to a Catskills resort in an effort to rekindle their romance. Complex characters. This is a good scene for the right actors. Start, Gil: "I sat at the bar through last call. This woman in a grey beehive kept ordering Brandy Alexanders." End, Nick: "I'm a man who crosses moats."

ANDERSONVILLE TRIAL, THE
by Saul Levitt (Dramatists Play Service)
Drama: Act I, Scene 2, pp. 47–49; Chipman (31) and Hosmer (30–45).
Two weeks into the trial of Confederate Army officer Henry Wirz, Colonel Chipman still isn't sure that he made a good case for the charge of conspiracy. More to the point, he wants to find a way to get the court to address the broader question of moral responsibility. In this scene, Chipman and Hosmer, the assistant judge advocate, consider whether or not to call a witness both men suspect is lying. His testimony will help convict Wirz, but the men wonder if they'll be compromising their principles by calling him? Start, Hosmer: "Don't you see what he's trying to do? Provoke you into playing the idealist here?" End, Hosmer: "Sometimes, you make me feel so old."

ANGELS IN AMERICA: A GAY FANTASIA ON NATIONAL THEMES, PART I: MILLENNIUM APPROACHES
by Tony Kushner (Theatre Communications Group)
Drama: Act I, Scene 4; Louis (about 30) and Prior (30).
Louis and Prior are longtime lovers. After the funeral service for Louis's grandmother, they sit on a bench and talk about being Jewish and being gay. Then Prior shows Louis a Kaposi's sarcoma lesion on his arm, an irrefutable sign of the progression of AIDS. Start, Louis: "My grandmother actually saw Emma Goldman speak. In Yiddish. But all Grandma could remember was that she spoke well and wore a hat." End, Louis: "Then I'll come home."
Drama: Act II, Scene 7; Joe (early 30s) and Louis (about 30).
Joe and Louis meet by accident on the steps of the Hall of Justice. Louis is depressed because his longtime lover is dying of AIDS, and Joe is tormented by his shifting sexual preferences and crumbling marriage. As the men talk about values during the Reagan era, their conversation increasingly takes on sexual undertones. Start, Joe: "Can I . . . ?" End, Louis: "You're scared. So am I. Everybody is in the land of the free. God help us all."

BABY DANCE, THE
by Jane Anderson (Samuel French)
Comedy-Drama: Act II, Scene 1, pp. 50–56; Richard (30s) and Ron (30–50).
Richard and his wife, Rachel, have purchased the as-yet-unborn child of Wanda and Al, a dirt-poor Louisiana couple. Wanda has gone into labor, so Richard and Rachel have come to the hospital to witness the birth of "their" baby. Al shows up, however, and tries to ask for more money. Here, Richard and Ron, his lawyer, discuss tactics. Start, Richard: "Hello? Oh . . . yes, I'm trying to dial out." End, Richard: "I agree, my friend, I agree."

BENT
by Martin Sherman (Samuel French)
Drama: Act I, Scene 4, pp. 36–43; Max (34) and Rudy (30).
Hiding from the Gestapo, Max and Rudy pitch a tent in a camp near Cologne. Although they're broke and desperate, they still have their love. (At the very end of this scene, the off-stage voice of a police officer orders Max and Rudy to surrender. It interrupts their song, riveting them. It would be effective to include that moment if possible.) Start, Rudy: "Cheese! Max!" End, Max and Rudy: "Will you forget me? Was I ever really there?"

Drama: Act I, Scene 6, pp. 51–57; Max (34) and Horst (30–40).
Max becomes friends with Horst in the camp. The audience learns that Max, a non-Jew, has managed to get a yellow star, which permits the wearer more camp privileges, instead of a pink star, which indicates a homosexual, by providing entertainment for the Nazi guards. Max made love to a young woman who had only recently died. Begin with Max's entrance as he crawls up next to Horst. Start, Max: "Hi. . . . Here." Continue until the end of the scene. End, Max: "One. Two. Three. Four. Five. Six. Seven. Eight. Nine. Ten."

Drama: Act II, Scene 2, pp. 68–77; Max (34) and Horst (30–40).
Max and Horst are assigned to rock detail, which consists of moving a pile of heavy rocks from one place to another. After they move the pile, they must move it back to its original position. Then they do it again—all day, every day, with a three-minute break every two hours, during which they must stand at attention. This scene begins with Max and Horst moving the rocks and continues into the break. While at attention, they verbally go through an entire act of lovemaking. Very graphic and sexual material. Start, Horst: "It's so hot." End, Max: "Do it in three minutes."

Drama: Act II, Scene 3, pp. 78–84; Max (34) and Horst (30–40).
As the men move rocks from one place to another, and back, Horst tells Max that he has fallen in love with him. Start, Horst: "I'm going crazy. I'm going crazy." End, Horst: "Poor you, you don't love anybody. It's getting cold. Winter's coming."

BETRAYAL
by Harold Pinter (Dramatists Play Service)
Drama: One-act play, Scene 2, pp. 12–16; Jerry (30s) and Robert (30s).
Jerry is guilt ridden because Emma, his longtime lover, informed her husband, Robert, who is also Jerry's best friend, about their now-defunct affair. He asked Robert to drop by his home this evening for a private chat. During the scene, Robert discloses that he knew about the affair for years but opted to maintain a discreet silence. He tells Jerry that, at any rate, his marriage to Emma is on the rocks. Start, Jerry: "It's good of you to come." End, Jerry: "The Lake District."

BORN YESTERDAY
by Garson Kanin (Dramatists Play Service)
Comedy: Act I, pp. 34–37; Harry Brock (40s) and Ed Devery (50s).
Self-made millionaire and con man Harry Brock is worried that his dumb-but-beautiful girlfriend will embarrass him as he tries to wine and dine the Washington, DC, elite in an attempt to get them to pass legislation that is in his own best interest. Against the advice of his alcoholic lawyer, Ed Devery, Harry decides to hire the serious-minded journalist who lives down the hall to tutor the woman, to show her the ropes in Washington. Start, Brock: "She's gonna be in the way, that dame." End, Brock: "I don't believe in nothin' on no friendly basis."

BREAKING THE CODE
by Hugh Whitemore (Samuel French)
Drama: Act I, Scene 6, pp. 39–46; Turing (39) and Ron (20).
Turing picked up a young man, brought him home for a tryst and, this morning, discovers that he wants to be paid for his services. Start, Ron: "What's the time?" End, Turing: "Down the road, turn left."

Drama: Act I, Scene 8, pp. 55–60; Turing (39) and Ross (30–50).
Detective Sergeant Ross is investigating a minor burglary at Turing's home. He has learned that the pieces of Turing's story about the event don't hold together and figures that Turing must be lying to protect someone. In this scene, Turing reluctantly admits he was trying to conceal a homosexual relationship. Ross immediately responds to this new information by telling Turing that he has committed a crime by having sex with another man. Start, Turing:

"Sergeant Ross." End, Turing: "Anyway . . . all right. . . . Yes, I'll make a statement. You'll want me to go to the police station. I'd better get dressed."

BUTLEY

by Simon Gray (Samuel French)
Comedy-Drama: Act I, pp. 15–22; Ben (35–40) and Joey (mid-20s).
Ben's jealousy plays close to the surface in this confrontation with his lover/student, Joey. The scene is quite long, but this excerpt captures the flavor and underlying tensions of their relationship. Start, Ben: "You're in trouble, Joey." End, Joey: "That's right, he's a butcher."
Comedy-Drama: Act II, pp. 48–52; Ben (35–40) and Joey (mid-20s).
After a big argument with Anne, his estranged wife, Ben turns his hostility on his student/lover, Joey. Start, Ben: "If it's Anne you were hiding from, she's gone. If it's Edna, she hasn't arrived." End, Joey: "It doesn't matter. Let it go."
Comedy-Drama: Act II, pp. 57–66; Ben (35–40) and Reg (mid-30s).
Reg, Joey's new lover, has come to Ben's office to explain that Joey will be moving out of Ben's flat and in with him. What Reg doesn't know is that Ben has just learned that his wife, Anne, has announced that she's moving in with a new man, too. In fact, as Reg enters the scene, Ben is completing a mischief-making telephone call to Kent Vale Comprehensive, the school where his wife's new lover works. The scene bristles with jealousy. Start, Ben: "Come." End, Reg: "It's worked out quite well though, hasn't it?" For a shorter version of the dialogue, end the first time they toast each other. End, Reg: "Cheers."

CANDIDA

by George Bernard Shaw (Signet)
Comedy-Drama: Act III; Marchbanks (18) and Morell (40).
Morell's wife, Candida, has just left the room. Marchbanks and Morell get into a full-tilt argument about which of them is the better man for her. Finally, Marchbanks proposes that Candida choose. This is a dynamic 5-page scene. Start, Morell: "Well?" End, Marchbanks: "Send for her, Morell. Send for her and let her choose between us."

CAT ON A HOT TIN ROOF

by Tennessee Williams (Dramatists Play Service)
Drama: Act II, pp. 47–59; Brick (27) and Big Daddy (65).
Brick tells Big Daddy why he drinks so much. For workshop purposes, try this excerpt from the act-long confrontation between the men. Eliminate the lines of the various family members who come and go. Start, Big Daddy: "What makes you so restless?" End, Brick: "I'm sorry, Big Daddy."

CAT'S-PAW

by William Mastrosimone (Samuel French)
Drama: Act I, pp. 7–13; Victor (25–40) and David Darling (35–50).
David Darling, a low-level employee of the Environmental Protection Agency, has been taken captive by urban guerrillas who are intent on exposing the imminent dangers of water pollution and the government's role in permitting this to happen. David and his captor discuss the terms of his imprisonment, and then Victor administers an injection of truth serum. Start, David: "Excuse me. If it's all the same to you, might I have beef?" End, David: "Bye."

CHAPTER TWO

by Neil Simon (Samuel French)
Comedy-Drama: Act I, Scene 9, pp. 59–68; George (42) and Leo (40).
George surprises Leo, his brother, with the news that he is marrying Jennie after a two-week courtship. Leo is very worried and tries to talk George into waiting. Update Leo's reference to

Jimmy Carter. Start, Leo: "George, will you let somebody else in New York use the phone?" End, Leo: "I don't know what the hell I'm doing in publicity. I was born to be a Jewish mother."

CHASE, THE
by Horton Foote (Dramatists Play Service)
Drama: Act II, Scene 1, pp. 33–37; Sheriff Hawes (40–45) and Damon (40–45).
The outlaw everyone is hunting for broke into Damon's store last night, ripping up clothes and trashing the place. Damon is scared and angry, and he accuses Sheriff Hawes of not properly protecting him. Hawes pleads for patience and says he'll get the criminal. Using a Texas accent is helpful but not essential. Start, Damon: "Did you see my store?" End, Damon: "All right."
Drama: Act II, Scene 1, pp. 38–40; Sheriff Hawes (40–45) and Edwin (early 30s).
Edwin Stewart, the nervous, high-strung, son of the town banker, wants the sheriff to guard his house, but Hawes can't spare anyone. Edwin threatens to reject Hawes's loan application. Omit the reference to Ruby. Start, Edwin: "Hello, . . . Hawes." End, Edwin: "And my wife has a lot of friends, and every one of them is gonna hear of your treatment of us."

COLD STORAGE
by Ronald Ribman (Samuel French)
Comedy-Drama: Act II, pp. 43–50; Landau (mid-40s) and Parmigian (mid-60s).
Landau and Parmigian, two patients in a cancer ward, discuss philosophy. This scene is funnier than you might think. Parmigian makes his ultimate existential point: There is no point at all to life. Landau is frustrated with this explanation and doesn't agree. A heated philosophical thrust and parry. Start, Parmigian: "You ever make a mistake with what you're doing, Landau?" End, Parmigian: "That's a brilliant perception, Landau. You know what I'm going to do with it as soon as I leave this roof? I'm going to write it down in my book of great sayings of the Western World."

DANCE AND THE RAILROAD, THE
by David Henry Hwang (Dramatists Play Service)
Comedy-Drama: Scene 3, pp. 23–29; Lone (20) and Ma (18).
To pass the time during a labor strike against the railroad, Lone, one of the Asian-American workers, has gone off by himself to practice opera dances. Ma, another worker, watches from the bushes for a while and then asks for instruction. In this scene, Lone tells Ma how much dedication being in the opera requires. Start, Ma: "How long will it be before I can play Gwan Gung?" End, Ma: "If you do, you're crazy. Lone? Come back here."

DEATH AND THE MAIDEN
by Ariel Dorfman (Penguin)
Drama: Act II, Scene 2; Gerardo (45) and Roberto (50).
Gerardo feeds the captive Roberto, who is tied to a chair, and tells him that he is going to have to confess to the crimes Paulina is accusing him of if he wants his freedom. Roberto professes his innocence. Eliminate Paulina's brief appearance in the scene. Start, Gerardo: "You're not hungry, Doctor Miranda?" End, Gerardo: "I'm going to tell her that you need to piss."

DEATH OF A SALESMAN
by Arthur Miller (Dramatists Play Service)
Drama: Act I, pp. 12–18; Biff (34) and Happy (32).
Brothers Biff and Happy are in their bedroom, talking about their aspirations, their relationship with their father, and the past. Start, Happy: "He's going to get his license taken away." End, Biff: "I was the only one he'd let lock up the place."

DIVISION STREET

by Steve Tesich (Samuel French)

Comedy: Act I, pp. 33–39; Chris (37) and Roger (mid-30s).

Roger, dressed as an old bum, complete with gray wig, shows up in Chris's apartment. Full of guilt for selling out, Roger wants Chris to take up the 1960s banner again and lead a new revolution. Chris wants no part of it; he has gone straight and is no longer a radical. Start, Chris: "Who's there? Who are you?" End, Roger: You go right ahead, man . . . Dream on, man!"

DOES A TIGER WEAR A NECKTIE?

by Don Petersen (Dramatists Play Service)

Drama: Act II, Scene 1, pp. 43–51; Winters (35) and Bickham (20).

Of all the inmates, Bickham has the biggest chip on his shoulder and is the one most likely to start a fight. In this scene between Bickham and Pete Winters, the English teacher, the audience discovers that he is also remarkably sensitive and has the makings of a writer. Start, Bickham: "Gimme your wallet, lame, or I'll break your back." End, Bickham: "You know what I really want, Pete? I'll tell ya what I want . . . I want . . . I can't remember."

Drama: Act II, Scene 2, pp. 55–67; Werner (40s) and Bickham (20).

This scene is almost a one-act play in itself. Bickham tells Werner, the staff psychiatrist, how, after a long search, he found his father working in a barber shop and how he came to brutally beat up the man. This emotionally violent, sometimes physical scene definitely isn't suited for novice actors. Start, Werner: "Well? Come in, Bickham." Continue through the end of Act II. End, Bickham: "Ayieeeee!! God! God!" For a shorter version, try this excerpt. Start, Bickham: "You ain't the Great White Doctor you think you are!" Continue to the same end.

END OF THE WORLD WITH SYMPOSIUM TO FOLLOW, THE

by Arthur Kopit (Samuel French)

Comedy-Drama: Act I, pp. 26–32; Trent (35–45) and Stone (60s).

Stone is trying to commission Trent to write a play about the imminent end of the world. Trent is convinced that Stone is crazy and, despite the offer of money, he wants no part of this. You'll need a pistol for this scene, but you don't have to fire it. Start, Stone: "Your agent informs me you have certain reservations about my scenario." End, Stone: "I hope you take this job. Good day."

ENEMY OF THE PEOPLE, AN

by Henrik Ibsen [adapted by Arthur Miller (Dramatists Play Service)]

Drama: Act I, Scene 2, pp. 28–32; Peter (30s) and Thomas (30s).

Peter is convinced that his brother's discovery of local water pollution will lead their small city to financial ruin, carrying him and his political opportunities along with it. Here, Peter orders Thomas to publicly disavow the scientific reports. Thomas refuses, reacting first with surprise and then with fury to his brother's request. Eliminate Catherine's line at the beginning of the scene. Start, Peter: "I received your thesis about the condition of the Springs yesterday." End, Peter: "I forbid you as your superior, and when I give orders you obey."

Drama: Act III, pp. 65–68; Peter (30s) and Thomas (30s).

Peter has succeeded in turning the town against his brother, but he wants to ensure that Thomas doesn't go somewhere else in Norway to publicize his charges of water pollution and corrupt local politics. In this scene, Peter outlines possible criminal charges that can be brought against Thomas if he goes public anywhere at all. Start, Thomas: "Keep your hat on if you like, it's a little draughty in here today." End, Thomas: "Oh, we do, Peter!"

FAR COUNTRY, A
by Henry Denker (Samuel French)
Drama: Act II, Scene 1, pp. 43–51; Freud (37) and Breuer (35–45).
Freud is convinced there are significant similarities between his patient, Elizabeth, and one treated by Dr. Breuer. Freud gets his reluctant friend to fill in the blanks that are missing from his final case report. Breuer is nervous that Freud, already controversial for his hypnotism experiments, will jump to conclusions, go public with them, and discredit both men. Breuer is full of guilt over this particular case because he fell in love with the patient. You'll have to cut and paste a bit at the end, eliminating Martha. Start, Freud: "A schnapps?" End, Freud: "Agreed."

FENCES
by August Wilson (Samuel French)
Drama: Act I, Scene 3, pp. 33–40; Troy (53) and Cory (17).
Troy tells his son, Cory, why he doesn't want him to go to college on a football scholarship, why it is better for him to stay away from sports. Cory, of course, disagrees. Start, Troy: "You just now coming in here from leaving this morning?" End, Troy: "Then get the hell out of my face, and get on down to that A&P."

FOOL FOR LOVE
by Sam Shepard (Dramatists Play Service)
Comedy-Drama: One-act play, pp. 28–34; Eddie (late 30s) and Martin (mid-30s).
May goes into the bathroom to get dressed for her date with Martin, leaving Eddie and Martin alone. Eddie shocks Martin by telling him that May is his half-sister and that they've fooled around. Start, Martin: "She's not mad or anything, is she?" Eliminate all of the Old Man's lines. End, Eddie: "But the second we saw each other, that very second, we knew we'd never stop being in love."

GENIUSES
by Jonathan Reynolds (Samuel French)
Comedy: Act I, pp. 10–16; Jocko (33) and Bart (57).
Bart, the makeup man who is a dead ringer for Ernest Hemingway, pines for the long-gone simple days of movie-making, when men were men and the titles made sense. He thinks he could do a better job on this job than Jocko, the screenwriter, is doing. Start, Jocko: "Started without us, I see." End, Bart: "There's your ending. How about this? He lives . . . but with a big wound."
Comedy: Act III, pp. 61–67; Jocko (33) and Milo (32).
Milo tells Jocko, the screenwriter, about the frustrations of being a star movie director. You'll have to cut and paste a bit. After Milo's line, "Well, we have two choices. Talk her out of pressing charges, or kill her. Just kidding, Jocko," cut to Milo, continuing with: "God, I hate this picture." Then start, Milo: "Now that's what I like to see!" End, Milo: "Which is almost as much fun as making money."

GLENGARRY GLEN ROSS
by David Mamet (Samuel French)
Drama: Act I, Scene 1, pp. 7–15; Williamson (40s) and Levene (50s).
Levene's sales are slumping, so he is trying to get Williamson to give him some hot leads. He offers a bribe, which Williamson takes. Start, Levene: "John . . . John . . . John. Okay. John. John." End, Levene: "Good. Mmm. I, you know, I left my wallet back at the hotel."
Comedy-Drama: Act I, Scene 2, pp. 15–27; Moss (50s) and Aaronow (50s).
Moss tries to con Aaronow, another salesperson, into robbing the company office. Long scene, but David Mamet's dialogue moves quickly. Start, Moss: "Polacks and deadbeats." End,

Moss: "Because you listened." For a shorter version, start, Moss: "Look at Jerry Graff. He's clean." Continue to the end of the scene.

GOOSE AND TOMTOM
by David Rabe (Samuel French)
Drama: Act I, pp. 10–18; Goose (30s) and Tomtom (40s).
When Goose arrives, his friend Tomtom is happy to see him. They show each other their guns, tell each other their nightmares, and talk about Bingo's sister. At this point, the audience doesn't know that she is, in fact, being held captive in a back room. These characters are violent and dangerous, sometimes acting more like animals than humans. For experienced actors only. Start, Goose: "Hey." End, Tomtom: "Hey! How you? 'At's what I been waitin' for. I been onna edge a my chair."
Drama: Act I, pp. 50–56; Goose (30s) and Tomtom (40s).
Lorraine discovered that the jewels have been stolen, and she is very mad. In this scene, Goose and Tomtom develop a plan to steal some money and buy more jewels in order to make Lorraine happy again. Start, Tomtom: "We gotta make a plan!" End, Tomtom: "We thought it was ghosts stealin' our secrets, but it was really Bingo stealin' our treasure."

HAPPINESS CAGE, THE
by Dennis J. Reardon (Samuel French)
Drama: Act II, pp. 77–82; Reese (late 20s) and Doctor Freytag (40–50).
Reese is first admitted to the hospital with only a broken arm. He is then transferred to the terminal-cancer ward, where he discovers that Doctor Freytag is conducting terrible plea- sure/pain experiments. In this scene, Reese wakes up to discover his head bandaged and a metal probe inserted into his brain. Freytag hands him a remote-control device and asks him to deliver his own jolt of pleasure. Reese refuses to cooperate, thereby making the doctor face the reality of what he is doing to an unwilling subject. This challenging scene deals head on with life-and-death issues. Start, Freytag: "Getting your legs back under you now?" End, Reese: "No."

HOOTERS
by Ted Tally (Dramatists Play Service)
Comedy: Act I, Scene 1, pp. 7–12; Ricky (19) and Clint (19).
Clint is home from college on a break, so he and his old high-school buddy Ricky have come to Cape Cod for some hell-raising. In this scene, they're settling into their motel room while they talk about hot babes in very graphic terms. Ricky is excited because he thinks he saw a "10" in the parking lot. Start, Ricky: "Did you see that?" End, Ricky: "An Ab-so-lute Ten."
Comedy: Act I, Scene 4, pp. 28–31; Ricky (19) and Clint (19).
Clint and Ricky have hooked up with a couple of older women and invited them out to dinner. Back in the motel room, the guys are working on a game plan to get the women into bed. Basically, the plan amounts to "surprise, beer, dirty talk, divide and conquer." Start, Clint: "You piece of grunt." End, Clint: "Which one of us is going to walk the dog?"

HURLYBURLY
by David Rabe (Samuel French)
Comedy-Drama: Act I, Scene 1, pp. 9–19; Phil (mid-30s) and Eddie (mid-30s).
Phil arrives to tell a very hungover Eddie that he has had a terrible fight with his wife, during which he hit her with his fist. David Rabe has specific ideas about how this long, 10-page scene should be played: "It is important to note that there is an element of play in this whole scene . . . ; on some level, it is a game, a riff." Start, Phil: "Eddie." End, Eddie: "I wouldn't piss on her if the flames were about to engulf her goddamn, you know, central nervous system!"

Comedy-Drama: Act I, Scene 1, pp. 27–33; Eddie (mid-30s) and Mickey (mid-30s).
Eddie is distressed because Mickey made an apparently successful play for his new girlfriend yesterday. Also, his ex-wife called again, which always puts him in a foul mood. Start, Mickey: "Do you realize, Eddie, that you are now toking up at eight fifty-eight in the morning on top of the shit you already put up your nose?" End, Eddie: "What do you want me to do, abandon my kid in her hands and with no other hope? Forget about it!"
Comedy-Drama: Act I, Scene 3, pp. 61–69; Phil (mid-30s) and Eddie (mid-30s).
When he arrives at the house, Phil is full of manic energy. He tells Eddie that he is returning to his wife because he is lost without her. He also admits that he has been taking some kind of poison in order to ruin his sperm count. Eddie is alternately sympathetic and shocked. Start, Phil: "So, guess what?" End, Phil: "I come here to tell you. I got to stay married. I'm lost without her."

I HATE HAMLET
by Paul Rudnick (Dramatists Play Service)
Comedy: Act I, Scene 1, pp. 23–29; Andrew (27–33) and Barrymore (45–50).
Andrew's temporary New York apartment turns out to be haunted by John Barrymore's ghost, who moves in and out of the proceedings. The ghost tries to help Andrew prepare for the daunting task of playing the title role in *Hamlet*. In this scene, Barrymore gives Andrew some advice on acting and romance. Start, Barrymore: "Dear fellow . . . May I?" End, Barrymore: "You would prefer, perhaps, some form of therapy? Continued discussion? What is the present-day epithet—'communication'?"

IMMIGRANT, THE
by Mark Harelik (Broadway Play Publishing)
Comedy-Drama: Act I, Scene 5; Haskell (20s) and Milton (30).
Haskell Harelik has lived in an upstairs room in Ida and Milton Perry's house for six weeks, paying his way as a banana peddler. In this funny scene, Milton summons Haskell to his office at the bank and advises Haskell on ways to expand his business, including the notion of buying a horse. Milton offers to finance the purchase for Haskell. The language barrier is what makes this dialogue funny. Haskell speaks, at best, broken English with a heavy Russian accent, and Milton is a no-nonsense Texan. The year is 1909. Start, Haskell: "Mr. Perry?" End, Haskell: "At home, yes. You draw very good!"

I NEVER SANG FOR MY FATHER
by Robert Anderson (Dramatists Play Service)
Drama: Act II, pp. 55–62; Gene (40) and Tom (almost 80).
Gene has decided that he wants to remarry and move to California, where his soon-to-be wife already lives and has a medical practice. In doing so, however, he'll be leaving Tom, his elderly father, alone in New York to fend for himself. In this climactic scene, the last one in a remarkable script, Gene tells his father about his decision and asks him to move to California, too. Tom won't hear of it, accusing his son of abandoning him and of being ungrateful. Powerful, primal material. Start, Gene: "You ready to be tucked in?" End, Tom: "Go to hell!"

K-2
by Patrick Meyers (Dramatists Play Service)
Drama: One-act play, pp. 17–23; Harold (mid-30s) and Taylor (38).
Two men are trying to escape from an ice ledge on the side of one of the world's highest mountains. Most of the time, Taylor is in the process of climbing up and down ropes, thereby rendering scene work impractical. This excerpt, when both men are at rest, captures the basic relationship between them; it also highlights their philosophical differences. Harold is a political

liberal given to existential explorations, while Taylor is conservative and pragmatic. Start, Harold: "Taylor . . . I've got an idea." End, Taylor: "Now if you have any helpful suggestions . . . just . . . fucking . . . say . . . so!"

LARGO DESOLATO
by Vaclav Havel [translated by Tom Stoppard (Grove Weidenfeld)]
Comedy-Drama: Scene 4; Bertram (35–45) and Leopold (45–50).
Bertram is an emissary for unnamed intellectuals. He has come to Leopold's flat to see about his mental health and to encourage him to continue to defy the government. Cut Lucy's offstage lines and Leopold's responses. Start, Bertram: "How long is it since you went out?" End, Bertram: "So, I beg you—Be again that brilliant Leopold Nettles whom everybody held on high!"

LAST YANKEE, THE
by Arthur Miller (Dramatists Play Service)
Drama: One-act play, pp. 5–14; Leroy (48) and Frick (60).
Two men meet for the first time in the waiting room of a New York state mental hospital where both of their wives are being treated for depression. Frick is upscale, has money, and is impressed by appearances. Leroy, though a direct descendant of Alexander Hamilton and the son of a lawyer, is a carpenter by trade and cares nothing about appearances. Frick's pretentiousness makes Leroy angry, and this emotion confuses Frick. Do the entire play, which is only 9 pages long.

LIE OF THE MIND, A
by Sam Shepard (Dramatists Play Service)
Comedy-Drama: Act I, Scene 3, pp. 13–18; Jake (28–35) and Frankie (late 20s).
Jake has beaten up his wife again. This time, however, he thinks that he has killed her, so he heads south. In this scene, Jake is holed up in a shabby motel in southern California with Frankie, his younger brother, while he tries to clear his head and sort his options. Start, Jake: "I don't want any goddamn ice! It's cold!" End, Frankie: "I won't."

LIFE AND LIMB
by Keith Reddin (Dramatists Play Service)
Drama: Act I, Scene 8, pp. 27–31; Franklin (mid-to-late 20s) and Tod (mid-to-late 20s).
Franklin applies for a job at Tod Cartmell's prosthetic-device factory. Tod is sadistic, and this very difficult material involves sexual humiliation and isn't for novices. Start, Tod: "How you all doing?" End, Tod: "You got the job."

LISBON TRAVIATA, THE
by Terrence McNally (Dramatists Play Service)
Comedy: Act I, pp. 30–38; Mendy (35–45) and Stephen (25–35).
The entire act is a two-character scene between two gay men in which they discuss their love for opera and their various romantic involvements. You'll need a telephone that rings. For scene-study purposes, begin about halfway through the act. Start, Mendy: "There is only one Tosca." Continue to the end of the act.

LITTLE FOXES, THE
by Lillian Hellman (Dramatists Play Service)
Drama: Act II, pp. 31–34; Oscar (late 40s) and Leo (20).
Father and son test the waters to determine precisely how dishonest each is. When Oscar learns that Leo, his son, has been snooping in his employer's safe-deposit box down at the bank, Oscar raises the prospect of "borrowing" the $80,000 worth of Union-Pacific bonds

kept there. Start, Leo: "The boys in the bank don't know a thing. They haven't had any message." End, Oscar: "People ought to help other people. But that's not always the way it happens. And so sometimes you got to think of yourself."

LONELY IMPULSE OF DELIGHT, A

by John Patrick Shanley (Dramatists Play Service) [*Welcome to the Moon and Other Plays* (Dramatists Play Service); *13 by Shanley* (Applause Books)]
Comedy: One-act play, DPS pp. 35–37; Walter (25–35) and Jim (25–35).
Walter is in love with a mermaid who lives in the lake in New York City's Central Park, and he brings his best friend, Jim, to see her. Jim, understandably, doesn't think it is smart to be in Central Park in the middle of the night, especially since he was enjoying himself at a good party. Sally the Mermaid doesn't appear, and Jim, who has run out of patience, leaves. Walter then sends some more secret signals out across the lake and Sally shows up. Or does she? An offstage actress will have to read one line at the very end. Start, Jim: "What are we doing out here, Walter?" End, Walter: "And I you. My solitary, unprovable, deepest only love."

LONG DAY'S JOURNEY INTO NIGHT

by Eugene O'Neill (Yale University Press)
Drama: Act I; James Tyrone (65) and Jamie (33).
Father and son thrust and parry. James accuses Jamie of spending all his money on whores and liquor and of being a bad influence on his brother, Edmund. Jamie accuses his father of being a miser. Both agree to keep wife/mother Mary calm, hoping she won't start with morphine again—but knowing that she already has. Start, Tyrone: "You're a fine lunkhead!" End, Jamie: "Well, if we're going to cut the front hedge today, we'd better go to work."
Drama: Act II, Scene 1; Jamie (33) and Edmund (23).
After Jamie catches Edmund having a drink, the brothers have a heated discussion about their mother, Mary. This scene exposes the nature of Jamie and Edmund's relationship. Start, Jamie: "Sneaking one, eh?" End: Jamie: "Damn! I wish I'd grabbed another drink.

LUV

by Murray Schisgal (Dramatists Play Service)
Comedy: Act I, pp. 10–17; Milt (late 30s) and Harry (late 30s).
Milt discovers his old college chum Harry trying to commit suicide by jumping off a bridge. Milt talks him out of it and then discovers that Harry is struggling with existential angst. They wind up dueling about who had the worst childhood. The dark humor in this 7-page scene is very funny stuff. Start, Milt: "Is it . . . No. Harry Berlin!" End, Harry: "They were cinnamon donuts!"

MAN FOR ALL SEASONS, A

by Robert Bolt (Samuel French)
Drama: Act I, pp. 45–50; Henry VIII (25–35) and Thomas More (late 40s).
Henry VIII is searching for a legal, Church-approved way to divorce his queen, Catherine, so he can marry Anne Boleyn; he hopes to produce a male heir to the throne with her. In his effort to influence the Catholic hierarchy, he seeks the support of his Lord Chancellor, Sir Thomas More. More is a very respected and influential man, but so far, More has diplomatically resisted the king's entreaties. In this scene, Henry tries once again. Start, Henry: "Listen to this, Thomas. Do you know it?" End, Henry: "I must catch the tide or I'll not get back to Richmond till . . . No, don't come. Tell Norfolk."
Drama: Act I, pp. 60–65; Richard Rich (early 30s) and Thomas Cromwell (late 30s).
Thomas Cromwell, former secretary to the Lord Chancellor, Cardinal Wolsey, lost his position of influence when Wolsey fell from favor and died (or was killed). Now working as an aide to

the king, Cromwell is intent on increasing his influence by toppling Sir Thomas More, the new Lord Chancellor. In this scene, Cromwell bribes Richard Rich, Secretary/Librarian to the Duke of Norfolk and a confidante of more, trading a favored post for incriminating information. Start, Cromwell: "Come on. Yes, it may be that I am a little intoxicated." End, Rich: "You enjoyed that! You enjoyed that! You enjoyed it"!

MEDAL OF HONOR RAG
by Tom Cole (Samuel French)
Drama: One-act play, pp. 33–41; D. J. (23) and Doc (40).
D. J. tells the doctor about the day he was awarded the Congressional Medal of Honor by President Lyndon Johnson. You'll have to cut and paste a bit. After the doctor's line, "Tell me when you actually got the medal," cut to D. J.: "I been home eight, nine months." Omit Johnson's speeches. Start, Doc: "Did you ever tell people at home about any of this? About Dakto, about the truck?" End, Doc: "No, I'm not. I'm looking for you to make a decision about yourself."

MISTER ROBERTS
by Thomas Heggen and Joshua Logan (Dramatists Play Service)
Drama: Act I, Scene 1, pp. 6–9; Roberts (25–32) and Doc (35–40).
While on watch last night, Roberts saw a convoy of American battleships heading for battle, and the sight made him long all the more to get into the action. In this scene, he shows Doc his latest request for a transfer, but Doc tells him that it is futile—that he is only going to succeed in making the captain angrier. Start, Doc: "That you, Doug?" End, Doc: "I wish you hadn't seen that task force, Doug. Well, I've got to go down to my hypochondriacs."
Drama: Act I, Scene 6, pp. 39–42; Roberts (25–32) and the Captain (40–50).
Roberts reluctantly strikes a deal with the Captain in which Roberts agrees to stop being a troublemaker in exchange for a shore leave for his crew. Start, Captain: "Come in, Mister Roberts." End, Roberts: "Listen to those crazy bastards out there. Listen to them."

MODIGLIANI
by Dennis McIntyre (Samuel French)
Drama: Act I, Scene 3, pp. 18–25; Modligliani (31) and Zborowski (30s).
Modigliani's agent, Zborowski, tells Modigliani that he is going to show his work to a prominent gallery owner. Modigliani, however, has his mind on escaping the police who are after him for breaking a restaurant window. Start, Modigliani: "Zbo? Zborowski? . . . Zbo—be home." End, Zborowski: "He'll buy faces."
Drama: Act II, Scene 1, pp. 36–43; Modigliani (31) and Utrillo (33).
Modigliani, on the run from the law, goes to Utrillo to see if he can borrow some money. He discovers that Utrillo, who is always drunk, has signed up to join the army and plans to leave the following morning. But this is an impossible plan because Utrillo is frail and physically unfit. Start, Modigliani: "Maumau?" End, Modigliani: "I won't let you do it! I won't let you ruin it! There's nobody left after Cheron. I won't let you ruin it!"

MURDER AT THE HOWARD JOHNSON'S
by Ron Clark and Sam Bobrick (Samuel French)
Comedy: Act II, pp. 46–54; Paul (40–45) and Mitchell (36).
Arlene has abandoned both Paul and Mitchell in favor of a relationship with her guru. The men are waiting in a room at the Howard Johnson's Motel for her to arrive so they can kill her. They plan to hang Arlene and have built a scaffold in the hotel room. You'll have to be inventive to approximate this set piece. Start, Paul: "You know, I've got six towels from this place already. How are you doing?" End, Paul: "Oh, it's going to be good with her out of the way."

NERD, THE
by Larry Shue (Dramatists Play Service)
Comedy: Act II, Scene 1, pp. 53–57; Willum (34) and Rick (30s).
Willum has tried to tell his unwelcome house guest, Rick, that he should leave but has been unsuccessful. Begin the scene as Willum rehearses what he is going to say to Rick when he arrives. Start, Willum: "Now, Rick. Rick, sit down . . . Put down your tambourine." End, Rick: "Sit there, now—and don't move. I'll be in here heateen' up the salt!"

ODD COUPLE, THE (MALE VERSION)
by Neil Simon (Samuel French)
Comedy: Act I, pp. 30–40; Oscar (43) and Felix (44).
In the name of friendship, Oscar invites Felix, his fastidious friend who is suffering over the breakup of his marriage, to move in with him. The audience learns how very different the men are in this scene. Oscar and Felix's interactions are quite funny, but there isn't a great deal of overt conflict. You'll need a telephone that rings and as much room clutter as you can manage. Start, Oscar: "Ohh, Felix, Felix, Felix, Felix!" Continue to the end of Act I. End, Felix: Good night, Frances."
Comedy: Act II, Scene 1, pp. 47–55; Oscar (43) and Felix (44).
Felix and Oscar have been living together for two weeks and already Felix is driving Oscar crazy with his fanatical cleanliness. Here, Felix reluctantly agrees to a double date with the Pigeon sisters who live in an upstairs apartment. Start, Oscar: "I'd be immensely grateful to you, Felix, if you didn't clean up just now." End, Felix: "Frances. I want to get her recipe for London broil. The girls'll be crazy about it."
Comedy: Act II, Scene 2, pp. 56–59; Oscar (43) and Felix (44).
In this hysterically funny scene, the men await the arrival of their dates. Felix becomes apoplectic because the gourmet meal he has prepared is ruined by Oscar's cavalier attention to a dinner schedule. Start, Oscar: "I'm home, dear!" End, Oscar: "Then smile."
Comedy: Act III, pp. 73–82; Oscar (43) and Felix (44).
This scene has the most head-to-head conflict and is, arguably, the most difficult one to play. It takes place the day after the disastrous date with the Pigeon sisters, and Oscar seems bent on getting Felix to move out. Felix is playing the part of the wounded bird. At the end, Felix takes his suitcase and leaves—and moves in with the Pigeon sisters upstairs. You'll need a vacuum cleaner, a plate of pasta, and an offstage arrangement that will allow you to toss the pasta against the kitchen wall. Begin at the top of Act III. Start, Felix: "All right, how much longer is this gonna go on?" End, Felix: "Oh, come on, Oscar. You're not really interested, are you?"

OF MICE AND MEN
by John Steinbeck (Dramatists Play Service)
Drama: Act I, Scene 1, pp. 7–16; George (30–40) and Lennie (30–40).
In this scene, George and Lennie pitch camp by a river, and audience members get their first glimpse at the men's relationship. Viewers learn that they had to flee from northern California because Lennie was falsely accused of rape, that George is the smarter of the two, and that Lennie is physically powerful but mentally childlike. They talk about the farm they hope to have one day. This 15-minute scene can run half an hour if you aren't careful. Start, George: "Lennie, for God's sake, don't drink so much." End, Lennie: "I'm shutting up, George."

ON GOLDEN POND
by Ernest Thompson (Dramatists Play Service)
Drama: Act I, Scene 3, pp. 39–46; Norman (79) and Bill (45).
Bill has his first encounter with Norman, his lover Chelsea's crotchety dad. The two men discuss the generational morality of premarital sex and define the bottom line of their newly

established relationship. Start, Bill: "So, you're a baseball fan, huh?" End, Norman: "Yes! Please do! Just don't let Ethel catch you."

ON THE OPEN ROAD
by Steve Tesich (Samuel French)
Comedy-Drama: Act I, Scene 4, pp. 23–29; Al (20–35) and Angel (20–35).
This very dark satire is set on the burned-out landscape of some future, post-Civil-War time. Angel and his mentor, Al, have been gathering art treasures from gutted-out museums and churches, hoping to barter their way into the Land of the Free. In this physical and emotionally demanding scene, they are in a church when Angel erupts, attacking Al. Angel demands that Al "open up" and behave in an intimate fashion. Al then pulls a knife, holding Angel at bay. They finally settle down and agree to resume their journey.

As written, Al actually cuts Angel with the knife, drawing blood. The threat will suffice. Also, the scene calls for Al to play the piano a little bit, but you can work around that. Start, Angel: "Do you think this was once a church?" End, Al: "You can love a man, a woman, a child or all of mankind in less than five minutes, and then have the rest of the day to do the things you really like to do. Shall we?"
Comedy-Drama: Act II, Scene 2, pp. 46–50; Al (20–35) and Angel (20–35).
Al and Angel have been captured by soldiers of the provisional government and sentenced to die. Al is then led away for a conference, during which he strikes a deal with the captors: he and Angel will be given their freedom in exchange for carrying out a murder. They have to kill Jesus Christ, who is currently on earth during his second coming. In this remarkable scene, Al returns to Angel, cuts the ropes that restrain him, and explains the deal. Angel is horrified, but he agrees to join with Al because it is either that or face certain death. Start, Angel: "What's going on?" End, Angel: "To the Land of the Free, right?" Al: "Right." Angel: "Alright."

ORPHANS
by Lyle Kessler (Samuel French)
Drama: Act I, Scene 3, pp. 26–34; Phillip (early 20s) and Harold (40–50).
Phillip's older brother, Treat, brought Harold home to their North Philadelphia row house last night after having met him in a bar. Deciding to hold the drunk man hostage, Treat tied Harold to a chair and gagged him. Now Phillip is alone with Harold who, after a fashion, frees himself and befriends the younger man. Begin at the top of Act I, Scene 3. Start, Phillip: "Here comes somebody! Here comes an old man with a cane, got a newspaper under this arm. . . ." End, Harold: "Ahhh ya mutter! Little Dead End Kid!"
Drama: Act II, Scene 1, pp. 45–50; Harold (40–50) and Treat (late 20s).
Harold arrived as Treat's hostage two weeks ago, but in the interim has befriended him and his younger brother, spending money lavishly on them. Now Treat has fancy clothes and is enjoying his new status; however, he still doesn't understand where Harold comes from or how he makes so much money. Begin at the top of Act II, Scene 1. Harold enters singing. Start, Harold: "If I had the wings of an angel. . . ." End, Harold: "You know who you remind me of, Treat? Fred. He didn't believe in moderation either."

OTHERWISE ENGAGED
by Simon Gray (Samuel French)
Comedy: Act I, pp. 19–25; Simon (39) and Wood (40s).
Bernard Wood drops by Simon's house to find out if Simon has, in fact, seduced his daughter. As the scene unfolds, Simon learns that Wood is really an old schoolmate from years ago, a fellow he slept with during his sexual-experimentation period, and the daughter in question is actually Wood's fiancée. Simon's visitor is a sad, rather desperate man, which gives the comedy a mean-spirited edge, particularly when the audience learns that Simon did seduce

the daughter. Written in the British vernacular. The entire scene runs about 20 minutes and covers an act break, so you may not want to do it in its entirety. For a shorter version, stop a couple of pages into Act II. End, Simon: "Is it worth my saying sorry over again, or will my earlier apologies serve?" You can also end, Wood: "I'd like to kill you, Hench. Yes—kill you!"

PICK UP AX
by Anthony Clarvoe (Broadway Play Publishing)
Comedy-Drama: Act I, Scene 2; Keith (late 20s) and Brian (late 20s).
Brian tries to get Keith to understand that their software company is in big trouble. All Keith cares about, however, is that he is in a mental slump. What makes this 6-page scene fun is the fact that Keith is a real computer nerd and acid-head, seemingly disconnected from reality. Audience members find out later that he is more savvy than they think. Brian, also a lover of hard rock, has the business brains. Start, Keith: "Someone said you were in the newspapers." End, Brian: "You see? Complex, exotic, pathetically limited. Get stone ax. Enter. 'Okay.' The stone ax says, 'Command me, O Master.' Now we're happening."
Comedy-Drama: Act II, Scene 11; Keith (late 20s) and Brian (late 20s).
Brian and Keith have just gotten slammed down at their company's board of directors meeting. Unbeknownst to them, Mick, their supposed ally, has been operating behind the scenes, preparing to take over the company. Brian and Keith try to figure out what is happening, and then decide to quit the company. At this point, Keith's brain seems to be pepped up again. Start, Brian: "How dare they ask me questions like that? After all these years?" End, Brian: "You're right. You know? You're right."
Comedy-Drama: Act II, Scene 12; Keith (late 20s) and Mick (mid-30s).
Mick believes that he has engineered the perfect company takeover. Here, he discovers that Keith has outsmarted him. Start, Mick: "I'm telling this new clown the same as I told Prescott, it's getting me nowhere, I look around, you've wandered away." End, Keith: "This is Keith Rienzi. Fix me up a new office. A man can't hear himself think in here. Oh yeah?! Oh yeah?!"

P. S. YOUR CAT IS DEAD
by James Kirkwood [revised edition (Samuel French)]
Comedy: Act I, Scene 2, pp. 34–43; Jimmy (38) and Vito (27).
Jimmy has managed to overpower Vito, the prowler, and has tied him up. Vito is trying to figure out a way to get loose, and Jimmy is getting to know his unwanted guest. This excerpt includes the first time Vito comes on to Jimmy sexually. Begin after Jimmy's wild telephone conversation with Kate. Start, Jimmy: "Vito Antonucci. Hmmm, I never did trust Germans." End, Jimmy: "I'm going to put on my thinkin' cap!"

ROAD TO NIRVANA
by Arthur Kopit (Samuel French)
Comedy-Drama: Act I; Al (35–45) and Jerry (35–45).
This entire act is essentially one prolonged scene, about 40 pages in length, between Al and Jerry. Al's sexy partner/lover, Lou, makes occasional interruptions. Al has summoned his former partner Jerry, who is now producing educational films back East, to his Hollywood home. He wants to entice Jerry into a new partnership to produce the filmed autobiography of rock's biggest female star, Nirvana.

Three excerpts are particularly good for scene work. The first option is to begin after Lou's initial exit (pp. 15–22). Start, Al: "Lou's got like enormous untapped talent." End, Jerry: "To better times." Another choice is the part of the act when Jerry is told about Nirvana's involvement in the deal, and that her autobiography is an erotic version of Herman Melville's

Moby Dick (pp. 48–57). Start, Al: "You do want in?" End, Al: "Now you're coming through." The third option is to begin at the same place as the second excerpt and to continue to the end of Act I (pp. 48–63). Start, Al: "You do want in?" End, Al: "One spoon or you're out."

ROSENCRANTZ AND GUILDENSTERN ARE DEAD
by Tom Stoppard (Samuel French)
Comedy: Act I, pp. 29–34; Rosencrantz (20–30) and Guildenstern (20–30).
Two minor players in *Hamlet* are the stars in this comedy. In this scene, Hamlet, Ophelia, Gertrude, and Claudius have just appeared on stage and then exited, leaving Rosencrantz and Guildenstern more baffled than before. Rosencrantz has had enough and wants to turn back but, of course, they don't know where they came from; they know only that they were "sent for." Stylistically, this scene feels a great deal like those in *Waiting for Godot.* Start, Rosencrantz: "I want to go home." Begin the dialogue with the first time Rosencrantz says this. End, Guildenstern: "What are the rules?"
Comedy: Act II, pp. 43–47; Rosencrantz (20–30) and Guildenstern (20–30).
By now, Rosencrantz and Guildenstern are at the castle and still don't understand the purpose of their visit. Rosencrantz would still like very much to return home, but Guildenstern feels they have a duty to perform as requested—that is, if they could figure out precisely what is being requested of them. Start, Guildenstern: "Hm?" End, Rosencrantz: "No. Double bluff."

SAN ANTONIO SUNSET
by Willy Holtzman [*The Best Short Plays of 1988–1989,* edited by Ramon Delgado (Applause)]
Drama: Scene 2; Stone (30–45) and Johnson (25–45).
Record promoter Stone has returned with his recording machine to a San Antonio hotel room to record blues singer Johnson again. The recording Johnson made last year has become a hit up north, but, of course, he doesn't get any of the money. Start, Johnson (singing): "The last fair deal goin' down. The last fair deal goin' down. . . ." End, Johnson (singing): "Travel on, Poor Bob; Just can't turn you 'round."

SEXUAL PERVERSITY IN CHICAGO
by David Mamet (Samuel French)
Comedy: One-act play, pp. 7–14; Danny (28) and Bernard (30–35).
While sitting in a singles bar, Bernard tells Danny about his night of outrageous sexual adventure with a young woman he picked up in a pancake restaurant. Start, Danny: "So how'd you do last night?" End, Bernard: "Well, alright, then. I'll tell you one thing . . . she knew all the pro moves."
Comedy: One-act play, pp. 49–55; Danny (28) and Bernard (30–35).
In this scene, Danny and Bernard sit on the beach, eyeing the women and discussing them in a vulgar way. Start, Bernard: "Lookit this." End, Bernard: ". . . with tits like that . . . who needs anything?"

SIGHT UNSEEN
by Donald Margulies (Dramatists Play Service)
Drama: Act I, Scene 1, pp. 20–24; Jonathan (35–45) and Nick (40s).
Nick's wife, Patricia, has gone outside to get vegetables for dinner, leaving him alone with her former lover and current house guest, Jonathan Waxman. Nick doesn't like this man at all, neither personally nor professionally. Furthermore, Nick, is jealous of Jonathan's relationship with Patricia. Nick is English and, though an educated man, he comes from a rural blue-collar background, and his accent should reflect those origins. This scene is a tense one, the kind that causes nervous laughter in the audience. Start, Nick: "Oops. You've spotted your painting." End, Nick: "Here we hold on to our overcoats."

SORROWS OF STEPHEN

by Peter Parnell (Samuel French)

Comedy: Act II, Scene 3, pp. 61–66; William (mid-20s) and Stephen (mid-20s).

William is convinced that his fiancée is having an affair, but he never suspects that it is with his best friend, Stephen. William and Stephen discuss the situation over lunch. Eliminate the waitress's lines. Start, William: "I think she's having an affair." End, Stephen: "Yes."

SPEED OF DARKNESS, THE

by Steve Tesich (Samuel French)

Drama: Act II, Scene 2, pp. 54–59; Joe (mid-40s) and Lou (mid-40s).

Joe's old Vietnam buddy, Lou, has shown up unexpectedly. In this rather cryptic scene, the men allude to secrets in their past. Joe tells Lou to leave, to move along and not speak of the past to his family. Start, Lou: "What a lovely girl. And I can tell she loves you very much." Continue to the end of the scene. End, Lou: "The Son of Wall is leaving Sioux Falls tomorrow and I'll be moving on with it."

SPEED-THE-PLOW

by David Mamet (Samuel French)

Comedy-Drama: Act I, pp. 17–26; Fox (40s) and Gould (40s).

Fox pitches a movie project to his friend, Gould, a high-powered Hollywood studio executive. This project will star Doug Brown and is guaranteed to make a great deal of money. Fox is almost beside himself as he smells success. Start, Gould: "I know what you wanted to say, and you're right. I know what you're going to ask." End, Gould: "But it ain't crowded."

Comedy-Drama: Act III, pp. 59–67; Fox (40s) and Gould (40s).

Gould slept with his sexy temp, Karen, last night and has decided, on her recommendation, to give the green light to a movie project based on a gloomy book about the perils of radiation. Fox enters the scene thinking that the Doug Brown project is still a "go" and is shocked to learn that Gould is putting this on the back burner in favor of the new project. Fox and Gould end up having a fistfight in the office. For scene-study purposes, start, Fox: "I'm not upset with you . . . Alright." End, Gould: "Alright—ask it."

SPLENDOR IN THE GRASS

by William Inge [adapted by F. Andrew Leslie (Dramatists Play Service)]

Drama: Act II, Scene 2, pp. 51–54; Bud (18) and Ace (50).

The stock market is crashing, people are jumping out of windows in New York City, and Ace's son is flunking out of Yale. In this brief, multilayered scene, the overbearing, self-made father attempts to understand his drifting and increasingly defiant son, in order to justify all of the meddling he has done in the young man's life and affairs. But there is no understanding, and they end up farther apart than when they began. Start, Ace: "Sell out! What do you mean, sell out?" End, Bud: "I've got to get back to school, Dad. I'll . . . see you later."

SPLIT SECOND

by Dennis McIntyre (Samuel French)

Drama: Act I, Scene 1, pp. 7–16; Val (28–35) and Willis (25–35).

Willis, a white car thief, is captured and handcuffed by Val, an African-American New York City cop. When the prisoner begins to spew racial epithets, the officer loses his temper and shoots Willis right through the heart. Then, realizing what he has done, Val restages the crime scene to make it look like a case of self-defense. This is an extremely difficult scene involving violence and overt racism of the vilest nature. Definitely not for novice actors. You'll need a gun that shoots blanks and a pair of handcuffs. Start, Val: "Freeze, motherfucker! Freeze it!" Continue through the end of Act I, Scene 1. End, Willis: "No difference, man! Get it?!"

Drama: Act I, Scene 2, pp. 17–28; Val (28–35) and Parker (35–45).

Parker interrogates Val about the killing that took place earlier in the evening. Val is lying about the true events, claiming he shot the criminal in an act of self-defense. Actually, Val killed Willis in cold blood. Parker smells a lie, but can't prove it. To play the entire scene, start, Parker: "Nice. Real clean. I'd say just about textbook." End, Parker: "I hope so, Johnson. Unless you get nicked in the line of duty, you're going to be around for a long time." For a shorter version, cut from "wife, 2 kids and a Buick" to "You didn't happen to shoot it out." Continue to the same end.

STRANGE SNOW

by Steve Metcalfe (Samuel French)

Drama: Act I, Scene 1, pp. 23–28; Megs (late 30s) and Dave (late 30s).

The deeply buried shame of cowardice-under-fire is made fresh for Dave when his old Vietnam War buddy Megs unexpectedly shows up. Dave is hungover and, at any rate, doesn't seem too happy to see Megs. Start, Megs: "She's great, your sister, I like her." End, Dave: "Yeah, this trout fishing is a great time."

SUBJECT WAS ROSES, THE

by Frank D. Gilroy (Samuel French)

Drama: Act I, Scene 2, pp. 20–28; John (50) and Timmy (21).

Timmy is home from World War II, and his father has taken him to a baseball game. Back in their Bronx apartment, they share a few beers and try to get to know one another. This is the kind of relationship where neither father nor son has ever expressed his love. Despite a surface appearance of closeness and camaraderie, there is a deep chasm between the two men. Start, John: "I haven't told that one in years." End, John: "My family called her The Lady. To their minds it was an insult. How did we get on this?"

Drama: Act II, Scene 2, pp. 52–59; John (50) and Timmy (21).

It is 10 P.M., and Nettie has mysteriously and uncharacteristically been gone all day. As John and Timmy wait for her and contemplate calling the police, their conversation turns into a session of truth-telling. Timmy recalls how, as a sickly child, he lay in bed at night and dreaded the fights that took place if his father came home. Start, Timmy: "I remember sitting here like this the night she went to have John." End, Timmy: "You pig."

SUMMER BRAVE

by William Inge (Dramatists Play Service)

Drama: Act I, pp. 22–25; Alan (early 20s) and Hal (early 20s).

Alan is surprised when Hal shows up looking for work. He hasn't seen Hal since college, when Hal borrowed his car and took off for California. Now Hal reports that things didn't go so well in Hollywood and even though he managed to get a screen test, he has given up on becoming a movie star. What Hal wants is earnest work, preferably something in management. At first, Alan balks and wants as little contact as possible with Hal. But when Hal becomes emotional and asks for a chance to prove himself, Alan says that he'll get Hal a job. Start, Alan: "Hal! Hal! Come on over." End, Hal: "Yah. That's something I gotta learn . . . patience!"

SWEET BIRD OF YOUTH

by Tennessee Williams (Dramatists Play Service)

Drama: Act I, Scene 1, pp. 7–10; Chance (29) and Dr. Scudder (36).

Dr. Scudder, one of Boss Finley's underlings, tells Chance to get out of town before he gets hurt. Chance is determined not to leave St. Cloud without taking Heavenly Finley with him. Start, Chance: "How did you know I was here?" End, Dr. Scudder: "Heavenly and I are going to be married next month."

TRIBUTE
by Bernard Slade (Samuel French)
Comedy-Drama: Act I, pp. 36–40; Scottie (51) and Jud (20).
Scottie, having been diagnosed with a leukemia, is trying to establish a closer relationship with his son, Jud, who doesn't know that his father is sick. As written, Scottie enters wearing a full-body chicken suit, in an attempt to make Jud laugh. Actors doing class work will somehow have to approximate this or figure out a substitution. Start, Scottie: "Well, it's good to see you can still laugh." End, Scottie: "So do I, son. So do I."

TRUE WEST
by Sam Shepard (Samuel French)
Comedy-Drama: Act I, Scene 4, pp. 25–33; Austin (early 30s) and Lee (early 40s).
Lee proudly dictates his movie scenario to his brother, Austin, who types it up. As a professional screenwriter, Austin can't believe how outrageously bad Lee's story is, but he has promised producer Saul Kimmer that he'll help Austin prepare it. There is an underlying air of tension and competitiveness between the brothers. Start, Lee: "All right, now read it back to me." End, Lee: "And the one who's being chased doesn't know where he's going."
Comedy-Drama: Act II, Scene 5, pp. 34–39; Austin (early 30s) and Lee (early 40s).
Lee returns from his golf game with Saul Kimmer to report that the producer has given him an advance and made a firm commitment to produce his movie idea. Austin is flabbergasted by this turn of events, especially when he learns that Saul is putting everything—including how own movie project—on the back burner so that he can devote all of his energy to selling Lee's idea. You'll need a golf club for this scene. Start, Austin: "He really liked it, huh?" End, Lee: "Relax. We're partners now."
Comedy-Drama: Act II, Scene 7, pp. 43–51; Austin (early 30s) and Lee (early 40s).
Austin, who is drunk and waxing philosophical here, watches Lee sitting at the kitchen table trying to type a screenplay, which he doesn't know how to do. Lee asks for Austin's professional help, but all Austin wants to do now is give it all up, wander in the desert, and perhaps engage in petty thievery—just like Lee does. Austin thinks that if Hollywood will buy a story as bad as Lee's, nothing makes sense any more. After a while, the brothers start talking about their reclusive, drunken father, who also lives in the desert. Start, Austin: "Red sails in the sunset." End, Austin: "Now that's a true story. True to life."

VIEUX CARRÉ
by Tennessee Williams (New Directions)
Drama: Part I, Scene 2; Writer (28) and Nightingale (50s).
This poignant scene begins with sobs and ends with a caress. Nightingale, a tubercular sketch artist, hears the younger man crying in his rooming-house cubicle and comes to comfort him. They speak of "the sound of loneliness," human sorrow, death, and love. The writer tells Nightingale about a recent homosexual encounter, his first, and Nightingale begins to gently pull back the bed sheets. The entire scene runs 10 pages and is appropriate for experienced actors. Start, Nightingale: "I want to ask you something." End, Nightingale: "Shh, walls have ears! Lie back and imagine the paratrooper."

VIEW FROM THE BRIDGE, A
by Arthur Miller (Dramatists Play Service)
Drama: Act I, pp. 33–37; Eddie (40) and Alfieri (50s).
Eddie has come to Alfieri, a lawyer, hoping that something can be done to head off the developing romance between his niece Catherine and the illegal immigrant Rodolpho. Alfieri quickly recognizes that Eddie has more than parental interest in the young woman and advises

him to let the lovers be. Start, Alfieri: "I don't quite understand what I can do for you. Is there a question of law somewhere?" End, Eddie: "I'll see you around."

VISIT, THE
by Friedrich Dürrenmatt [translated by Patrick Bowles (Grove Press)]
Comedy-Drama: Act II; Alfred Ill (64) and Policeman (any age).
Claire Zachanassian, the richest woman in the world, has arrived in her poverty-stricken home town after a 45-year absence. She then offers a million pounds to the residents if they'll murder Alfred Ill, the man who done her wrong all those years ago. The offer alone causes a rise in prosperity because local citizens begin to purchase goods on credit. Of course, the only way they'll be able to pay these bills when they come due is to commit murder. In this scene, Alfred Ill tries to have Zachanassian arrested for threatening his life, but the police officer won't comply with his request. In fact, the cop is wearing new shoes. Omit Zachanassian's interruptions. Also, you'll need a rifle or pistol. Start, Policeman: "Ill. What can I do for you? Take a seat. You're trembling." End, Alfred: "It's me you're hunting down."

WHO'S AFRAID OF VIRGINIA WOOLF?
by Edward Albee (Dramatists Play Service)
Drama: Act I, pp. 17–22; George (46) and Nick (30).
George and Nick, who have been drinking heavily, get to know one another as Martha shows Honey where the bathroom is. Nick isn't accustomed to George's game-playing and becomes defensive as the older man talks about his relationship with his wife, Martha, as well as politics at the college. At one point, Nick threatens to take his wife and leave. Begin after Martha and Honey exit. Start, George: "So, what'll it be?" End, George: "You asked me if I knew women . . . Well, one of the things I do not know about them is what they talk about while the men are talking. I must find out some time."
Drama: Act II, pp. 50–55; George (46) and Nick (30).
Martha is in the kitchen nursing Honey. George and Nick talk about how much money their wives had when they married them. George tells Nick that he'll have to sleep with plenty of faculty wives if he wants to climb the ladder. This excerpt is ideal for workshop use. Begin as Martha leaves the room. Start, George: "No, Martha, I did not clean up the mess I made. I've been trying for years to clean up the mess I made." End, George: "No, baby . . . you almost think you're serious, and it scares the hell out of you."

WHOSE LIFE IS IT ANYWAY?
by Brian Clark (Dramatic Publishing Company)
Drama: Act II; Ken Harrison (35–45) and Dr. Travers (40–55).
After learning that Ken wants to commit suicide, Dr. Travers, the hospital psychiatrist, pays him a visit. The doctor, however, is already predisposed to diagnose Ken as irrational. In this scene, Ken pins Dr. Travers to the wall, philosophically speaking. Start, Dr. Travers: "Mr. Harrison?" End, Dr. Travers: "I'm sorry if I upset you, Mr. Harrison."

YANKEE DAWG YOU DIE
by Philip Kan Gotanda (Dramatists Play Service)
Comedy: Act I, Scene 1, pp. 10–14; Vincent (60s) and Bradley (20s).
Bradley meets well-known-but-fading character actor Vincent Chang at a Hollywood Hills party. They play a game of one-upmanship on the terrace, with Bradley trying to impress the older man and Chang pointing out that he has special billing in a movie playing at local drive-ins. Start, Vincent: "It's a bit warm tonight." End, Bradley: "Make-up a little heavy? Jesus Christ, you had so much hair on your face you looked like a fucking chimpanzee!"

Comedy: Act I, Scene 2, pp. 14–21; Vincent (60s) and Bradley (20s).
The actors meet in the audition waiting room of a theater. Vincent tells Bradley about the old days in Chinatown when he was a song-and-dance man, and Bradley performs his audition monologue for Vincent. Then the two men reenact a scene from Vincent's most famous movie and, as the dialogue ends, a scene from his most famous stage musical. Don't be daunted by the requirement that you sing and dance. This doesn't have to be show-stopping stuff. Start, Bradley: "Yeah, thanks, ten minutes . . . Mr. Chang, I'm sorry." End, Bradley: "What am I doing? What is this shit? You're acting like a Chinese Steppin Fetchit. That's what you're acting like. Jesus, fucking Christ, Vincent."

Comedy: Act I, Scene 3, pp. 23–28; Vincent (60s) and Bradley (20s).
Here, the actors talk after an acting class. Bradley accuses the older man of doing a disservice to his race by playing demeaning roles in movies. Vincent points out a time in a 1950s movie when he actually got the girl, a white girl, and kissed her—on the lips! But, alas, when the film ran on television, that part was cut out. Start, Vincent: "You do not know a thing about the industry. Not a damn thing." End, Vincent: "They edited it out."

Comedy: Act I, Scene 4, pp. 29–32; Vincent (60s) and Bradley (20s).
The actors meet in a bar and mock all of the stereotypical Asian-American roles in famous movies. They fantasize about how they would have played such roles as Robert De Niro's in *Taxi Driver* and Jimmy Stewart's in *Harvey*. Then Vincent and Bradley agree to appear in a play together at the Asian American Theater. This is a fast-moving, 3-page scene. Start, Bradley: "Mr. Chang." End, Vincent: "Let's see what we have here."

ZOO STORY, THE
by Edward Albee (Dramatists Play Service)
Drama: One-act play, pp. 5–15; Jerry (late 30s) and Peter (early 40s).
The Zoo Story is a medium-length, one-act play that is too long for most workshops. As such, you'll have to decide whether to work on the first or second half. Keep in mind, however, that the second part is very physical and violent. The opening moments of the play involve a more interesting game of cat-and-mouse. In this scene, Peter is sitting on a bench in New York City's Central Park, enjoying a free afternoon, when a strange man approaches and strikes up a conversation. Start, Jerry: "I've been to the zoo." End, Jerry: "You do? Good."

Part Five

Female/Female Scenes

ABSENT FRIENDS
by Alan Ayckbourn (Samuel French)
Comedy: Act I, pp. 11–13; Marge (30s) and Evelyn (30s).
Marge asks her friend Evelyn if it is true that she is having a love affair with Diana's husband, Paul. Evelyn says she isn't, which relieves Marge, but then she admits that she and Paul "did it in the back of his car the other afternoon." This is a funny scene because Evelyn then starts elaborating on what a terrible lover the man is, and the women begin to directly insult each other. Start, Marge: "Evelyn, could I have a word with you?" End, Evelyn: "Yes."

AGNES OF GOD
by John Pielmeier (Samuel French)
Drama: Act I, Scene 7, pp. 30–34; Dr. Livingstone (30s) and Agnes (21).
Dr. Livingstone, a court-appointed psychiatrist, probes to see precisely how much Agnes understands about the process of childbearing. Agnes avoids answering directly and steers the conversation toward religion. Start, Agnes: "Yes, Doctor?" End, Agnes: "You should be ashamed! They should lock you up. People like you!"
Drama: Act I, Scene 10, pp. 43–48; Dr. Livingstone (30s) and Mother Superior (50s).
Dr. Livingstone is surprised to learn that the Mother Superior is, in fact, Agnes's aunt. The argument over the young woman's welfare heats up when Livingstone says that she intends to hypnotize Agnes. The conversation then turns into a debate about Catholicism and the doctor's personal background. A good, tense scene. Start, Dr. Livingstone: "What did you find?" End, Doctor: "That's also why I hate nuns." With a bit of cutting and pasting, you can extend this scene to the end of Act I. Eliminate Agnes's offstage singing and the references to it.
Drama: Act II, Scene 2, pp. 59–64; Dr. Livingstone (30s) and Mother Superior (50s).
Under hypnosis, Agnes has remembered the night she gave birth. With her out of the room, Dr. Livingstone and Mother Superior lock horns over the possibility of an immaculate birth. Mother Superior wants to believe in miracles, but the doctor believes that Agnes is the sum of her psychological parts. At the end, the older nun says that she is going back to court to ask that Dr. Livingstone be taken off the case. Start, Mother Superior: "You've formed your opinion about her, haven't you?" End, Mother Superior: "Good-bye, Doctor. Oh, and as for that miracle you wanted, it has happened. It's a very small one, but you'll notice it soon enough."

ALBUM
by David Rimmer (Dramatists Play Service)
Comedy-Drama: Act I, Scene 3, "Ticket to Ride," pp. 23–28; Trish (16) and Peggy (16).
Trish is dying to know if Peggy "did it" during the summer. After some evasion, Peggy acknowledges that she tried, but it didn't work out. In the meantime, Barb, another friend, has

driven off with a guy who throws her out of his car on a beach somewhere when he discovers that she is a virgin. So before long, she is on the telephone asking Trish and Peggy to come get her. This is an appealing scene because of the teenagers' innocent and total obsession with sexual matters. To do this scene right, you'll need some 1960s music. Start, Trish: "Okay! Okay! . . . Haven't you gone yet? . . . God . . . I'll listen as loud as I want!" End, Peggy: "Maybe it's better with pictures."

ALL MY SONS
by Arthur Miller (Dramatists Play Service)
Drama: Act II, pp. 36–38; Ann (26) and Sue (40).
Sue, Ann's next-door neighbor, is supposedly looking for her husband when she and Ann start talking in the yard. The women's exchange is very friendly until Sue gets to the reason for the conversation and makes her point: She would appreciate it if, when Ann and Chris get married, they would go live somewhere else. Start, Sue: "Is my husband . . . ?" End, Sue: ". . . and I'm at the end of my rope on it!"

ANASTASIA
by Marcelle Maurette [adapted by Guy Bolton (Samuel French)]
Drama: Act II, pp. 59–65; Dowager Empress (79) and Anna (20s).
The Dowager Empress interviews a young woman who claims to be Princess Anastasia, the only-surviving daughter of the late Russian tsar Nicholas II. Because a huge fortune is at stake if Anastasia's identity is verified, the empress is skeptical of any claims. As the interview progresses, however, Anna shares many private memories with the older woman, and the empress finally believes her. Start, Dowager Empress: "Yes, I can see why the others have believed, especially my romantic-minded nephew." End, Dowager Empress: "Good night, Anastasia—and please— if it should not be you—don't ever tell me."

AND MISS REARDON DRINKS A LITTLE
by Paul Zindel (Dramatists Play Service)
Comedy-Drama: Act I, pp. 8–13; Ceil (40s) and Catherine (40s).
On the surface, this scene between Ceil and Catherine concerns what to do with their sister, Anna, now that she has had an emotional breakdown and gotten into a great deal of trouble by sleeping with a high-school boy. Their conversation is colored, however, by resentments and competition between the women. Ceil is married to Catherine's former beau and has generally been the overachiever in the family. Start, Catherine: "Well, well, well. I never thought you'd show up. Of course, that's not quite true." End, Catherine: "It isn't bad enough we're paying two hundred bucks a month for a co-op with cockroaches, I have to have a sister who acts as a lifeguard for them."

AUTUMN GARDEN, THE
by Lillian Hellman (Dramatists Play Service)
Drama: Act III, pp. 85–88; Sophie (17) and Nina (40).
Sophie, who is 17 years old, wants enough money so that she can pay for a return trip to her childhood home in France and to repay her mother's debts. Lacking other choices, she opts for blackmail after Nick Denery makes a drunken, fumbling attempt to seduce her. In this scene, she tries to get Nick's wife, Nina, to pay her 5,000 dollars, a tidy sum in 1949. For reasons of her own, Nina is willing to give Sophie the money but wants to call it a "gift," not "blackmail." An excellent scene, with plenty of subtext. The actress playing Sophie should affect a slight French accent. Start, Sophie: "You are a pretty woman, Mrs. Denery, when your face is happy." End, Nina: "How would—how shall we make the arrangements?"

BABY DANCE, THE
by Jane Anderson (Samuel French)
Comedy: Act I, Scene 2, pp. 9–27; Wanda (late 20s) and Rachel (30s).
Rachel and her husband are movie-industry executives who have agreed to purchase the as-yet-unborn baby that Wanda is carrying. This 18-page scene, which takes place in Wanda's Louisiana trailer home, is the first face-to-face meeting between Rachel and the birth mother. Here, Hollywood meets Louisiana, and education meets ignorance. Start, Wanda: "Hello!" End, Rachel: "Sure." For a shorter, 11-page version, begin at the same place and end as Wanda gets the peaches. End, Rachel: "You know what? You don't have to do that. I'll have the Jello." You can try another 11-page option as well. Start, Rachel: "Is everything all right? Did our lawyer send you the check for the air conditioner?" Continue to Al's entrance.

BABY WITH THE BATHWATER
by Christopher Durang (Dramatists Play Service)
Comedy: Act II, Scene 3, pp. 32–35; Principal (35–50) and Miss Pringle (25–35).
Miss Pringle is concerned about the mental stability of her student Daisy, who is actually a boy, but the audience doesn't know that in this scene. Miss Pringle rushes into the principal's office for guidance, but the principal is off on a weird tangent of her own. This is very surreal, black comedy, wonderfully illogical. Actresses should read Christopher Durang's instructions on pp. 60–61; he comments specifically on how to play this scene. Start, Principal: "You can send Miss Pringle in now, Henry." End, Principal: "Who cares if she's dead as long as she publishes? Now, get out of here."

BAD HABITS
by Terrence McNally [1990 revised edition (Dramatists Play Service)]
Comedy: "Ravenswood," pp. 65–70; Benson (late 20s) and Hedges (late 20s).
The broad comedy in this delicious scene between two nurses at a sanitarium demands bold acting choices. Hedges has a giant inferiority complex, and Benson only appears to be the picture of physical and mental health. Start, Hedges: "I admire you so much." End, Hedges: "If you say so, Ruth."

BELL, BOOK AND CANDLE
by John Van Druten (Dramatists Play Service)
Comedy: Act I, Scene 1, pp. 10–14; Gillian (27) and Miss Holroyd (45–55).
Gillian and her aunt, Miss Holroyd, are honest-to-goodness witches who live in New York City. In this scene, Gillian reprimands Miss Holroyd for using her powers to pester the handsome publisher who lives upstairs and makes her promise not to cast spells and such in the building any more. Gillian also confesses that she has a longing to be "normal," to stop being a witch. Start, Miss Holroyd: "So you've met him, after all? Do you still think he's attractive?" End, Gillian: "No. I don't say I wouldn't be tempted, but if I've got a week—I'd like to see how good I am, the other way."

BETWEEN DAYLIGHT AND BOONVILLE
by Matt Williams (Samuel French)
Drama: Act II, pp. 71–76; Carla (26) and Marlene (30s).
Marlene gives Carla some advice she doesn't like, so Carla tells Marlene that her husband, Big Jim, is sleeping with Wanda, the town slut. Marlene, who up to this point has spoken of Big Jim as if he were the perfect man, confesses that she has known about the affair all along and didn't say anything because she is afraid of losing him. You may want to update Burt Reynolds's love life. Start, Marlene: "You think the ghost of Elvis really talked to this woman?" End, Marlene: "Just let me alone."

CHILDREN'S HOUR, THE
by Lillian Hellman (Dramatists Play Service)
Drama: Act I, pp. 18–21; Martha (28) and Lily Mortar (45).
Martha doesn't believe that Lily Mortar is qualified to teach at the school, so she tries to get rid of Lily gently. Martha suggests that Lily take a nice, long ocean cruise. Lily responds angrily, accusing Martha of having unnatural feelings for her niece, Karen, and taking her frustrations out on a blameless aunt. This is a very significant scene because Lily's petulant accusations are overheard by two young girls, one of whom proceeds to start a rumor that Martha and Karen are lesbians. Start, Mrs. Mortar: "I was asked to leave the room." End, Martha: "I want you to leave. And now. I don't wish any delay about it—."
Drama: Act III, pp. 64–67; Karen (28) and Martha (28).
Martha enters this scene with a sense of relief, believing that she, Karen, and Karen's fiancé, Joe, will soon escape local scrutiny and gossip by moving to Vienna. Karen breaks Martha's happy mood by telling her that Joe, like everyone else in this small community, has come to believe they are, in fact, lesbians. Stunned by this final betrayal, Martha becomes gloomy and deeply introspective. She tells Karen that perhaps everyone else is right—perhaps she does love Karen in an unnatural way. When Karen dismisses this as craziness, Martha walks zombie-like into the next room and shoots herself. Start, Martha: "It gets dark so early now. Cooking always makes me feel better." Stop with Martha's exit. End, Karen: "Don't bring me any tea. Thank you. Good night, darling."

COME BACK TO THE 5 & DIME, JIMMY DEAN, JIMMY DEAN
by Ed Graczyk (Samuel French)
Comedy-Drama: Act I, pp. 25–29; Mona (30s, playing late teens) and Sissy (30s, playing late teens).
Mona has unexpectedly returned home, opting not to go to college after all because of her "asthma." In this 4-page flashback scene, she and Sissy, a girlfriend who is fixated on her large bosom and its effect on boys, talk about Joe, who recently disappeared after being fired from his job at the five-and-dime store. Sissy doesn't know that Mona is pregnant with Joe's child. There is no major conflict in the scene, but it is interesting to work on for its character development and subtext. Start, Sissy: "Me an' Joe was gonna get Stella Mae to take your place doin' the McGuire Sisters, but she wouldn't have been as good as you." End, Mona: "It's just 'deceivin' to the eye,' that's all."

COMMANCHE CAFE
by William Hauptman (Samuel French)
Comedy: One-act play, pp. 5–13; Mattie (40s) and Ronnie (20s).
Ronnie has never traveled far from her hometown in southern Oklahoma, but she has big dreams—and a number of misconceptions—about what is out there. Mattie, Ronnie's older co-worker at the Commanche Cafe, is relatively more worldly, having been in love once or twice. They peel potatoes and talk about life in this charming scene. Not much conflict, but plenty of texture. Start, Ronnie: "I don't see why we've got to work on Sunday." End, Ronnie: "And I'm going to see them all. Just let me go anyplace but here—in Oklahoma."

COUPLA WHITE CHICKS SITTING AROUND TALKING, A
by John Ford Noonan (Samuel French)
Comedy: Act I, Scene 3, pp. 21–28; Maude (30s) and Hannah Mae (30s).
Maude, overcome with guilt, confesses that she made love with Hannah Mae's husband, Carl Joe, last night. Surprisingly, Hannah Mae seems to take this news in stride, contending that this just makes their friendship stronger. Maude becomes increasingly exasperated with Hannah Mae's response. Start, Hannah Mae: "A red rose of apology." End, Maude: "Get out!"

CRIMES OF THE HEART
by Beth Henley (Dramatists Play Service)
Comedy-Drama: Act I, pp. 29–32; Meg (27) and Babe (24).
Meg talks to her sister Babe, trying to find out what happened on the day she shot her abusive husband, Zachary. Babe tells Meg about the very satisfying sexual affair she has been having with Willy Jay, a black boy. Start, Meg: "What did Zachary do to you?" End, Meg: ". . . see, 'cause he's gonna be on your side."

DARK AT THE TOP OF THE STAIRS, THE
by William Inge (Dramatists Play Service)
Drama: Act II, pp. 52–57; Cora (34) and Lottie (38).
Lottie tells her sister, Cora, why Cora and her children can't come live with her and Morris; she confesses that they, too, have an unhappy home. Morris hasn't made love to Lottie for three years and has become distant and nervous, occasionally seeking psychotherapy. Seeking psychological help was a big deal during the 1920s. In addition, Lottie says that she never enjoyed sex in the first place. Start, Lottie: "My god, Cora, we can't stay here all night." End, Lottie: "So, don't come to me for sympathy, Cora. I'm not the person to give it to you."

DELICATE BALANCE, A
by Edward Albee (Samuel French)
Drama: Act II, Scene 1, pp. 33–36; Agnes (late 50s) and Julia (36).
This scene is a brief, hostile confrontation between a mother and her adult daughter. Their relationship, which is ordinarily tense, is stretched to the breaking point by the strange presence of Harry and Edna, family friends who have moved into the daughter's upstairs bedroom. Start, Julia: "Do you think I like it? Do you?" End, Julia: "you go straight to hell."

DOLL'S HOUSE, A
by Henrik Ibsen [a new version by Christopher Hampton (Samuel French)]
Drama: Act I, pp. 11–21; Nora (25–35) and Mrs. Linde (25–35).
When Nora's old school friend, Mrs. Kristine Linde, shows up unexpectedly on the day before Christmas, she finds Nora in an ecstatic mood because her husband, Torvald Helmer, has recently been appointed manager of Joint Stock Bank, a politically influential position that carries with it the promise of financial security. This good fortune means even more to Nora because, with the prospect of a hefty increase in family income, she'll be able to pay off a burdensome—and illegal—personal loan that her husband knows nothing about. Mrs. Linde tells Nora that she is a widow now and is close to being destitute. Perhaps Nora could speak to Torvald about a job at his bank? Nora agrees immediately and then confides in Mrs. Linde about her fraudulent loan and how happy she is that it will soon be paid off. Start, Mrs. Linde: "Good morning, Nora." End, Nora: "No, don't. I'm not expecting anyone. I expect it's someone for Torvald."

EFFECT OF GAMMA RAYS ON MAN-IN-THE-MOON MARIGOLDS
by Paul Zindel (Bantam)
Drama: Act I; Beatrice (30s) and Ruth (16).
Beatrice calms her daughter, Ruth, after another violent nightmare, evidently brought on by memories of a former elderly boarder. This is a very interesting, complex scene because Beatrice and Ruth relate not only as mother and daughter, but also as two emotionally troubled souls. Start, Beatrice: "There, now, nobody's after you. Nice and easy. Breathe deeply . . . Did the big bad man come after my little girl?" End, Beatrice: "What's left for me?"

EVERYTHING IN THE GARDEN
by Edward Albee [adapted from the play by Giles Cooper (Dramatists Play Service)]
Drama: Act I, Scene 1, pp. 20–24; Jenny (late 30s) and Mrs. Toothe (50).
Mrs. Toothe, a mysterious English lady, knocks on the door of Jenny's home, which is in a rather fashionable neighborhood. Within minutes, Mrs. Toothe solicits Jenny for a prostitution ring. Jenny is outraged at the proposition, threatens to call the police, and kicks Mrs. Toothe out. After the lady is gone, however, the audience sees that Jenny may very well accept the offer because she and her husband could certainly use the money. Begin after Jack, the flirtatious neighbor, exits. Start, Jenny: "You mustn't believe a thing Jack says, Mrs. . . . ." End, Mrs. Toothe: "What a lovely garden. Do you have a greenhouse?"

FALLEN ANGELS
by Noel Coward (Samuel French)
Comedy: Act II, pp. 36–43; Julia (late 20s) and Jane (late 20s).
Jane and Julia are preparing to entertain their mutual former lover, Maurice, who is a handsome Frenchman. To calm their anxiety, the women drink martinis—and then champagne. As the liquor takes effect, their friendship gives way to competitiveness and, finally, to a full-tilt argument. Jane storms out. Actresses will need someone offstage to ring a telephone several times on cue. Also, Saunders, the maid, moves in and out of the scene, but it is easy to work around her if necessary. Start, Jane: "Julia, what a pretty girl Saunders is." Continue to the end of Act II. End, Jane: "It's true. And I shall go away with him at once, and you and Fred and Willy can go to hell, the whole lot of you!"

FATHER'S DAY
by Oliver Hailey (Dramatists Play Service)
Comedy-Drama: Act I, pp. 25–29; Louise (30–35) and Marian (30–35).
Estelle has just gone inside to prepare lunch, leaving Louise and Marian alone for a moment on the patio. Suddenly, Louise turns uncustomarily serious about her divorce and discloses that her 7-year-old son has chosen to go live with his father in the Midwest. Start, Louise: "I don't like her gazpacho either." End, Marian: ". . . no child should be permitted to."

FOX, THE
by Alan Miller [based on D. H. Lawrence's short novel of the same name (Samuel French)]
Drama: Act II, Scene 2, pp. 42–46; Jill (29) and Nellie (29).
Jill and Nellie invited a young soldier who was passing by to stay with them a few days on their farm, which is in much need of a man's strong back. It becomes clear to Jill that the soldier isn't so innocent; in fact, he is trying to take over the place and to have his way with Nellie. In this scene, Jill tells Nellie that she wants the soldier to leave, but Nellie defends him. Written in the British vernacular. Start, Jill: "Well I can't wait any more." End, Nellie: "Leaving you would be like leaving half my life, how could I do that? Go on up, Jill. Go on."

GETTING OUT
by Marsha Norman (Dramatists Play Service)
Drama: Act II, pp. 46–51; Arlene (early 20s) and Ruby (40s).
Arlene has been out of jail for only a couple of days and is trying to find her way. In this scene, she meets her upstairs neighbor, Ruby, a tough woman who also happens to be an ex-convict. They establish an immediate bond, and Arlene is impressed that Ruby has made a successful transition to outside life, working now as a waitress. Both roles are appropriate for advanced actresses. Start, Ruby: "Candy, I gotta have my five dollars back." End, Ruby: "Mine's the one with the little picture of Johnny Cash on the door."

GINGERBREAD LADY, THE
by Neil Simon (Samuel French)
Comedy-Drama: Act I, pp. 23–29; Evy (43) and Polly (17).
Polly welcomes her mother, Evy, home from 10 weeks of drying out in a sanitarium by announcing that she is moving in with Evy. Start, Polly: "I don't want to get your hopes up, but I have reason to believe I'm your daughter." End, Polly: "Some people have it all."
Comedy-Drama: Act III, pp. 64–69; Evy (43) and Toby (40).
Evy returns home with a black eye after a drunken night with Lou, her old abusive lover. Her friend Toby is waiting for her. Start, Toby: "Well, good morning." Stop just before Polly's entrance. End, Toby: "I have to stop off first and blow up my beauty parlor."

GIRL ON THE VIA FLAMINIA, THE
by Alfred Hayes (Samuel French)
Drama: Act I, pp. 15–18; Lisa (early 20s) and Nina (early 20s).
Facing dire economic circumstances in war-ravaged 1944 Rome, Lisa has agreed to take the same route that many other Italian women have taken. She agrees to be kept by an American soldier, one of the country's liberators. In this scene, Lisa has just arrived at the house where she'll be living with the man, but she is desperately unhappy with the prospect facing her. Nina, who arranged the deal for Lisa, is a pragmatist, contending that a sexual trade is the best option available. In this 3-page scene, Nina tries to prepare Lisa for the imminent arrival of her "husband," but Lisa feels like a prostitute. Both women are Italian, so slight Italian accents are appropriate. Start, Nina: "I'm exhausted. Such a day. Such excitement." End, Nina: "Would you like to bet?"

HEDDA GABLER
by Henrik Ibsen [translated by Christopher Hampton (Samuel French)]
Drama: Act I, pp. 23–29; Hedda (29) and Thea Elvsted (25).
Hedda presses her friend, Thea, to tell the truth about her relationship with Eilert Lovborg. Thea confesses that she despises her much-older husband and has a very close, though not sexual, relationship with Lovborg. He has spent the past three years tutoring her stepchildren and, with her assistance and inspiration, has reformed himself and returned to writing. Start, Hedda: "That is killing two birds with one stone." End, Hedda: "Thea, all this is between you and me."

HOOTERS
by Ted Tally (Dramatists Play Service)
Comedy: Act I; Scene 2, pp. 13–17; Ronda (22) and Cheryl (25).
Cheryl, facing some serious life decisions, has brought Ronda to Cape Cod for a weekend of sun and quiet girl talk. As they check into their motel room, however, they meet a couple of wild-and-crazy 19-year-old post-adolescents. In this scene, the women are watching the guys, who are peering at them through binoculars. You'll need a bed for this scene. Start, Ronda: "I think they're in that last room on the other wing. There's a light on." End, Cheryl: "Good night, Ron."
Comedy: Act I, Scene 5, pp. 31–35; Ronda (22) and Cheryl (25).
To Ronda's dismay, Cheryl has played along with Clint and Ricky, a couple of teenage guys who are obviously interested in little more than getting laid. Cheryl has accepted a dinner date with them, and the women are getting dressed in their motel room. Ronda tells Cheryl she should start acting her age. Start, Ronda: "Where's my bracelet?" End, Ronda: "Right."

HOTHOUSE
by Megan Terry (Samuel French)
Drama: Act I, pp. 30–36; Roz (late 30s) and Jody (19).
Jody longs for her abusive, feuding parents to reconcile. Here, she tries to convince her boozy mother to go to her father's fishing boat, where he is living, and make up with him. Start,

Roz: "Want a night-cap, honey? . . . (singing) 'Amapolla, my pretty little poppy." Continue to the end of the act. End, Roz (singing in fractured German): ". . . and Herr Goebels says dey'll never bomb dis place . . . den ve. . . ."

IMMIGRANT, THE
by Mark Harelik (Broadway Play Publishing)
Comedy-Drama: Act II, Scene 1; Ima (30s) and Leah (20s).
Leah, who is nine months pregnant, is still worried that she is living too far from her Russian-Jewish roots and that the future is too uncertain. In this amusing scene, she and Ima prepare vegetables for a stew and share their respective superstitions. Superstitions are the same the world over, it seems. At the end of the scene, Leah sings a verse of a Russian song in Yiddish as the women dance around the kitchen. She then goes into labor. Start, Ima: "Oh! Leah! You scared me! What is it? Are you feeling all right?" End, Ima: "Well, honey, it's about time."

IMPORTANCE OF BEING EARNEST, THE
by Oscar Wilde (Samuel French)
Comedy: Act II, pp. 58–64; Gwendolen Fairfax (20) and Cecily Cardew (18).
Gwendolen Fairfax has traveled to Mr. Worthing's country home where she unexpectedly meets his pretty young ward, Cecily Cardew. Both women mistakenly believe that they're engaged to marry the same man, whose name is Earnest. Gwendolen and Cecily's proverbial claws come out while they share a very proper tea in this very famous scene. For scene-study purposes, cut Merriman's entrance, lines, and actions. Eliminate the need for a butler by having Cecily serve the tea. Although this may not reflect the propriety of the day, it increases the comic tension between the women. Start, Cecily: "Pray let me introduce myself to you." End, Cecily: "It seems to me, Miss Fairfax, that I am trespassing on your valuable time."

INDEPENDENCE
by Lee Blessing (Dramatists Play Service)
Comedy-Drama: Act I, Scene 1, pp. 14–18; Evelyn (53) and Kess (33).
When Kess, Evelyn's oldest daughter, goes home for the first time in four years, they feel each other out. Evelyn wants to know if Tess is "still homosexual," and Tess tries to determine if Evelyn has recovered from her nervous breakdown. Start, Evelyn: "Have a seat." End, Evelyn: "But it's not true! I am perfectly capable of functioning in a warm and loving universe. Which I try constantly to create!"
Drama: Act I, Scene 3, pp. 26–32; Evelyn (53) and Jo (25).
Evelyn tells Jo, her pregnant daughter, that she intends to give Tess a much-fought-over family heirloom. Then Evelyn really puts the pressure on Jo to live at home after her baby is born. Start, Evelyn: "That takes care of that." End, Evelyn: "It will be a lovely gesture. From the both of us."

IN THE BOOM BOOM ROOM
by David Rabe (Samuel French)
Drama: Act II, pp. 66–73; Chrissy (early 20s) and Susan (25–35).
Susan, who is a lesbian as well as a hardened survivor of strip-club joints, wants to make love to Chrissy, who is unsophisticated, and tells her so. Chrissy does her best to respond gracefully. Start, Chrissy: "You never been interested in astrology, huh?" End, Susan: "No."
Drama: Act II, pp. 78–82; Chrissy (early 20s) and Helen (mid-40s).
Chrissy accuses her mother of not wanting her to be born; she thinks that Helen wishes that she'd had an abortion. This very emotional scene ends with Chrissy sobbing on the floor. Omit Harold's line at the beginning of the scene. Start, Helen: "You been over here talkin' to your father." End, Chrissy: "I gotta stop. I gotta. I'm gonna stop."

ISN'T IT ROMANTIC?

by Wendy Wasserstein (Dramatists Play Service)

Comedy: Act II, Scene 1, pp. 34–37; Lillian (50s) and Tasha Blumberg (50s).
Tasha is the original Jewish mother, and Lillian is her very WASP-y counterpart. They meet through the friendship of their daughters. Lillian and Tasha talk about the travails of motherhood and then agree to have lunch together. In this gently humorous scene, two cultures look at each other, seeking common ground. Start, Lillian: "Mrs. Blumberg?" End, Tasha: "That's why we put out such nice products."

Comedy: Act II, Scene 3, pp. 43–47; Harriet (28) and Lillian (50s).
Mother and daughter have lunch at the posh Four Seasons restaurant in New York City. Harriet asks Lillian for motherly advice on career and family issues, but her successful business-executive mother's answers are unsatisfactory. Start, Lillian: "Everything all right with you?" End, Lillian: "Lovely lunch, Tom. Thank you."

Comedy: Act II, Scene 5, pp. 52–55; Janie (28) and Harriet (28).
Harriet has just surprised everyone by announcing that she is marrying a man she has known for just two weeks. When these two friends are alone, Janie lets Harriet know that she is frustrated with and feels betrayed by this simplistic solution to the career/family puzzle. Janie feels particularly vulnerable because she has just broken up with Paul, the doctor everyone thought was Mr. Right. Start, Janie: "She's in a good mood." End, Janie: "Do you really think anyone ever met someone throwing out the garbage?"

JAR THE FLOOR

by Cheryl West [*Women Playwrights—Best Plays of 1992* (Smith & Kraus)]

Comedy-Drama: Act II; Madear (90) and Raisa (28).
Raisa is an unusual visitor in this African-American household. In this funny and touching scene, she makes the acquaintance of Viola Dawkins, better known as Madear, whose ninetieth birthday is today. Madear is senile but uncommonly wise and a real character. Raisa shows the oldster her mastectomy scar, and Madear shows the younger woman her childbirth stretch marks. They have more in common: the internal scars shared by all women. Start, Raisa: "Where's everybody?" End, Raisa: "You got me on the ropes. And she's down . . . 1-2-3 . . . Wait a minute . . . Wait a minute . . . Slowly but surely, she's getting up . . . up . . . she's up. And the senior Dawkins kicker strikes again . . . Down for the count. . . ."

Drama: Act II, Scene 4; Vinnie (27) and Maydee (47).
Maydee has sacrificed a great deal to see her daughter, Vinnie, graduate from college, but it isn't going to happen. In this emotional scene, mother and daughter finally have it out over Vinnie's aspirations to be a singer. Start, Vinnie: "So. I thought you said all you had to say earlier." End, Maydee: "Well good. Maybe her liking will transport the both of you wherever you plan to go."

JOINED AT THE HEAD

by Catherine Butterfield (Dramatists Play Service) [*Women Playwrights—Best Plays of 1992* (Smith & Kraus)]

Comedy-Drama: Act I, DPS pp. 26–31; Maggy (30s) and Maggie (30s).
Jim has taken his wife, Maggy, and his former high-school lover, Maggie, to dinner in a nice restaurant. By now, Maggie knows that Maggy has cancer and is determined to write, in book form, the story of her courageous struggle. As Maggy and Jim share a romantic moment, Maggie gets up and addresses the audience, sharing her reactions to what has happened. Then, a shock: Maggy gets up from the table, and begins to address the audience, too! Since all of this is happening in Maggie's imagination, Maggy's intrusion is discombobulating.

In addition, Maggy is annoyed that Maggie's version of her story is too maudlin. Embarrassed because the enterprise is getting out of her artistic control, Maggie tries to get Maggy to go

back and sit down. They wind up debating the merits of the story, with the theater audience judging who is right. This is a good scene to work on because of the way it breaks and reestablishes the "fourth wall." The scene works best when an actor sits silently as Jim, but you can do it without him. Start, Maggie: "We looked at our menus. I don't know why, but I was feeling very happy." End, Maggie: "We finished dinner, and Jim went to get the car."
Drama: Act II, DPS pp. 60–65; Maggy (30s) and Maggie (30s).
Maggy is in the hospital for chemotherapy, and everyone knows that she is going to die soon. Maggie visits her. As always, Maggy has a great sense of humor. Start, Maggie: "Maggy?" End, Maggy: "My friend, you absolutely will. 'Bye."

KATHY AND MO SHOW, THE: PARALLEL LIVES
by Mo Gaffney and Kathy Najimy (Dramatists Play Service)
Comedy: Kathy (22–35) and Mo (22–35).
The challenge to performing the 14 comedy sketches that comprise this wonderful play is the need to make quick shifts into radically differing characterizations. In various scenes, the two actresses are called upon to play males, young girls at church, or a couple of angels. None of these scenes is heavyweight, just fun. Five sketches are particularly humorous. In "Period Piece," a menstruating migrant farm worker talks about Lilac Spring Tampons (pp. 25–27). Then two modern women talk about the monthly "curse," theorizing what life would be like if men menstruated. Then they become the men. All of this takes place in two pages. "God" features Teri and Tina, who are five and six years old, respectively (pp. 71–80). The two little girls are in church trying to figure out god, religion, etc.
Some of the sketches focus on the nature of romance. In "Kris and Jeff," a jock takes his girlfriend to a gay hangout for an after-movie snack (pp. 17–22). You may also want to work on "Futon Talk" (pp. 91–94). Here, Jeanine and Bill lie in bed and kick around their relationship. Bill wants to know if sex with him is better than with Jack "Jackhammer," and Jeanine wants to know if she is keeping Bill from moving to Oregon. Another hilarious scene is "Hank and Karen Sue" (pp. 97–103). In a country-western bar, Hank puts his regular moves on Karen Sue, assuring her about 15 times that she is "very very pretty tonight, darlin.'" But he is all hot air, and finally Karen Sue goes home to her children. Play each of the sketches in its entirety.

KEELY AND DU
by Jane Martin (Samuel French)
Drama: One-act play, Scene 15, pp. 44–54; Du (65) and Keely (early 30s).
Keely has been held captive for several months by a Christian antiabortion group intent on preventing her from terminating her pregnancy, which resulted from a rape. She has formed a bond with Du, the woman assigned to be her companion and nurse. Just moments ago, Du's boss, a pastor named Walter, visited Keely for more antiabortion indoctrination. She spit in his face, an act that she and Du simultaneously found very funny. They broke into uncontrolled laughter, and Walter made as dignified an exit as possible.
In this 20-minute scene, the women get to know one another on a deeper level. The scene is interesting not for the overt conflict, but for the way Keely and Du edge toward each other despite their prisoner/guard roles, finding things in common. Begin after Walter exits. Start, Du: "Oh, my." End, Du: "K-K-Katy . . . beautiful lady . . . you're the only g-g-girl that I adore. . . ."

LAST SUMMER AT BLUEFISH COVE
by Jane Chambers (JH Press)
Comedy-Drama: Act I; Eva (early 30s) and Lil (early 30s).
Lil has just told Eva that because of an error made by the rental agent, she is the only straight woman living in Bluefish Cove, which is a lesbian enclave. Eva considers leaving but, frankly,

she is enjoying Lil's company. Furthermore, she has no place else to go since her marriage broke up. Start, Lil: ". . . and to the left, that's the yacht basin. July 4th, they'll race." End, Lil: "Eva, I am your friend, everything's going to be just fine, you'll see. Now, go on. It's freezing out here. Good night."
Comedy-Drama: Act I; Eva (early 30s) and Lil (early 30s).
In this sweet, quiet scene, Eva awkwardly acknowledges being romantically attracted to Lil, who is bemused by the whole situation. Start, Lil: "Who is it?" End, Lil: "This is the first time I've ever taken her advice. Goodnight. Goodnight, Eva."
Comedy-Drama: Act II; Eva (early 30s) and Lil (early 30s).
Eva and Lil have spent the last glorious month together and are planning to share an apartment when they return to New York City. However, Lil still hasn't told Eva that she has inoperable cancer. And, as a result, Eva doesn't understand Lil's reticence. Start, Eva: "How big is your dining room?" End, Lil: "All right, you asked for it."

LATER
by Corrine Jacker (Dramatists Play Service)
Drama: Act I, Scene 1, pp. 5–13; Molly (55–65) and Kate (37–40).
Kate suggests that her mother, Molly, sell the summer place now that her father is dead. She thinks that it is too full of memories. Molly, however, has no intentions of listening to her daughter's advice. Start, Kate: "I don't know what I meant." End, Molly: "We saw the sailboats. They were beautiful. Now. Let's go home."
Drama: Act I, Scene 1, pp. 20–24; Kate (37–40) and Laurie (35).
Sisters Kate and Laurie talk about their sibling rivalry, bicker, laugh, and try to figure out what to do about their mother now that their father is dead. Start, Laurie: "Have you ever had an abortion?" End, Laurie: "Well, you're gonna tell her it's gone, not me."

LAUNDRY AND BOURBON
by James McLure (Dramatists Play Service)
Comedy-Drama: One-act play, pp. 12–19; Hattie (30s) and Elizabeth (30s).
Hattie, seeking a bit of relief from her noisy family, is visiting her friend, Elizabeth. As the two women sit on the porch on a very hot Texas afternoon, Elizabeth admits that her husband hasn't been home for two days and that he doesn't know she is pregnant for the first time. Start, Hattie: "Whew, it's hot out here." End, Elizabeth: "Well, I asked them to send somebody out, but I didn't think they'd send Amy Lee."

LIE OF THE MIND, A
by Sam Shepard (Dramatists Play Service)
Comedy-Drama: Act III, Scene 1, pp. 64–72; Lorraine (50s) and Sally (early-to-mid 20s).
In this 8-page scene, Sally comforts her distressed mother. Lorraine has taken to bed because Sally's brother, Jake, has apparently gone to Montana. He wants to see his wife after beating her up pretty badly recently. Lorraine and Sally talk about the bizarre events surrounding Sally's father's death in Mexico years ago. You'll probably want to use a bed here. Start, Sally: "Rise and shine! It's coffee time!" End, Lorraine: "Pure blue. Pure, pure blue. Wouldn't that be nice?"

LIFE AND LIMB
by Keith Reddin (Dramatists Play Service)
Drama: Act I, Scene 7, pp. 24–26; Effie (20s) and Doina (20s).
Effie tells Doina, her best friend, that she is having an affair but she doesn't love the man. Doina is all for it. You'll need a Christmas tree; a miniature one will do. Also, Doina has a pretty strong New Jersey accent. Start, Doina: "So a very merry Christmas." End, Doina: "You bet."

LOST IN YONKERS
by Neil Simon (Samuel French)
Comedy-Drama: Act II, Scene 3, pp. 88–93; Bella (35) and Grandma (mid-70s).
Bella returns home after a two-day absence and has it out once and for all with her mother, who is known in the play as Grandma. Bella tells Grandma how horrible it was to be raised in a home where no one expressed their love. She then stuns the older woman by admitting that she has slept with a great many boys and men in her life, all because she craves love. This is a beauty of a scene for the right actresses. Grandma has a heavy German accent, and Bella has an unnamed learning disability, making her childlike in some respects. Start, Bella: "Hello, Momma . . . Would you like some tea?" End, Bella: "I think we've both said enough for today . . . don't you?"

LUDLOW FAIR
by Lanford Wilson [*Balm In Gilead and Other Plays by Lanford Wilson* (Hill & Wang/Noonday)]
Comedy-Drama: Rachel (20s) and Agnes (20s).
Rachel is worried that she might have done the wrong thing by turning her boyfriend into the authorities for stealing money from her and Agnes. Agnes thinks that Rachel is overreacting and that the guy had it coming. But all Agnes really wants to do is to get over her cold so she can face the awful lunch she is supposed to have with her boss's son tomorrow. Start, Agnes: "Are you going to take a bath or what?" End, Agnes: "Me? I'm always nursing someone else's broken heart. Just once I'd like a broken heart of my own."
Comedy-Drama: Rachel (20s) and Agnes (20s).
This scene starts precisely where the preceding one ended and continues to the end of the play—if the actress playing Agnes wants to tackle a 2-page monologue. Start, Rachel: "You're great." End, Agnes: "I snore actually. Why don't you go to bed?" For a shorter version, end, Agnes: "No lie, I can't wait till summer to see what kind of sunglasses he's going to pop into the office with. Probably those World's Fair charmers. A double unisphere. Are you going to sleep? . . . Well, crap."

MIDDLE OF THE NIGHT, THE
by Paddy Chayefsky (Samuel French)
Drama: Act II, Scene 1, pp. 32–35; Betty/The Girl (23) and Marilyn/The Girl Friend (early 20s).
Betty's friend Marilyn tries to talk her out of the relationship she has started with a man who is twice her age. Start, The Girl: "Would you close the door please, Marilyn?" End, The Girl Friend: "Yes I do."

MRS. CALIFORNIA
by Doris Baizley (Dramatists Play Service)
Comedy: Act II, pp. 37–41; Dot (25–35) and Babs (25–35).
Dot is Mrs. Los Angeles, competing in the 1955 Mrs. California contest. Babs, her friend, is becoming a liability because she has taken to spying on and sabotaging the other contestants, particularly Mrs. San Bernardino. In this scene, Dot tries to bring Babs into line, but the attempt is futile. Although the subject matter makes this scene funny, keep in mind that these women take themselves very seriously. Start, Babs: "What the hell was that?" End, Babs: "I don't hate you, hon. I don't even know who you are."

MRS. WARREN'S PROFESSION
by George Bernard Shaw (Signet)
Drama: Act IV; Mrs. Warren (40–50) and Vivie (20).
Upon discovering that her mother continues to operate a chain of brothels on the Continent, Vivie banishes her mother from her life forever. Mrs. Warren then challenges the value of

Vivie's university education if it has brought her to a place where she can disown her mother, who has worked very hard all of her life to improve her circumstances. Start, Mrs. Warren: "Well, Vivie, what did you go away like that for without saying a word to me? How could you do such a thing?" End, Vivie: "Good-bye . . . and Good-bye, Frank."

'NIGHT, MOTHER
by Marsha Norman (Dramatists Play Service)
Drama: One-act play; Jessie (late 30s) and Mama (late 50s to early 60s).
In this two-character, one-act, real-time drama, the tension builds steadily until, in the final moments, the daughter commits suicide. The scenes become increasingly difficult to play as the action progresses. Attempting scenes that begin after the play's midpoint is the acting equivalent of trying to jump on a rapidly moving train. Two early scenes capture the situation, the mother/daughter relationship, establish conflict, and are accessible.

The first option begins at the top of play and continues through the references to Jesus committing suicide (pp. 9–17). This section includes the first suggestion that Jessie intends to kill herself, as well as Mama's reaction to the comment. Start, Mama: "Jessie, it's the last snowball, sugar. Put it on the list." End, Mama: "You'll go to hell just for saying that, Jessie!" Jessie: "I didn't know I thought that." The second scene starts a couple of pages after the first excerpt ends (pp. 18–23). The stakes are getting higher, and Mama begins to realize that Jessie is quite serious. Start, Mama: "What's this all about, Jessie?" End, Mama: "We've got a good life here!"

NIGHT OF THE IGUANA, THE
by Tennessee Williams (Dramatists Play Service)
Drama: Act I, Scene 2, pp. 24–27; Maxine Jelkes (40s) and Hannah (39).
Hannah and her 97-year-old grandfather are flat broke, but they still have their pride. As she helps Maxine set the tables for dinner on the verandah, Hannah attempts to barter with her for food and lodging. Maxine, however, wants cash up front. This is a quiet, short, tense scene. Each woman is desperate in her own way. The surface conflict is minimal and is only a mask. Begin at the top of Act II. Start, Maxine: "Miss Jelkes?" End, Maxine: "I do. It gives me the shivers."

NORMAN CONQUESTS, THE—TABLE MANNERS
by Alan Ayckbourn (Samuel French)
Comedy: Act I, Scene 1, pp. 1–7; Sarah (30s) and Annie (30s).
Sarah arrives at the country house to relieve Annie from her mother-nursing duties so that she can take a romantic holiday, presumably with her longtime friend, Tom. However, Annie admits that she is planning to travel with her romantic, charming brother-in-law, Norman. This very rich, comic scene has plenty of texture. Written in the British vernacular. Start, Sarah: "Hallo! We're here." End, Sarah: "What you need is a rest."

ODD COUPLE, THE (FEMALE VERSION)
by Neil Simon (Samuel French)
Comedy: Act II, Scene 1, pp. 47–53; Florence (35–45) and Olive (35–45).
Olive's hormones are raging, so she arranges a double date for herself and Florence with the Spanish men who live upstairs. But Florence, who has been separated from Sidney for only three weeks, isn't in the mood. Start, Florence: "That's something, isn't it, Olive? They think we're lucky." End, Florence: "You didn't tell me his name was Jesus . . . I'll make something simpler. Fish and loaves or something."
Comedy: Act II, Scene 2, pp. 54–57; Florence (35–45) and Olive (35–45).
For tonight's double date with the Spanish guys, Florence has prepared a gourmet meal. No one shows up on time, however, throwing Florence into a compulsive funk. Start, Olive: "Oh, God, it's gorgeous . . . it looks like a Noël Coward play." End, Florence: "I am through."

Comedy: Act II, Scene 3, pp. 73–79; Florence (35–45) and Olive (35–45).
Olive is fed up with Florence after eight months of her compulsive cleanliness and neurotic worrying. The fight in this scene evolves because Florence ruined last night's double date with their upstairs neighbors. This is the most difficult scene in the play because the conflict is more oblique here. Start, Florence: "Alright, how much longer is this going to go on?" End, Olive: "Okay . . . I tried."

ON GOLDEN POND
by Ernest Thompson (Dramatists Play Service)
Drama: Act II, Scene 1, pp. 56–60; Ethel (69) and Chelsea (42).
Chelsea surprises her mother by announcing that she married Bill during her European vacation. In this scene, Ethel and Chelsea also try, unsuccessfully, to discuss the always-strained relationship between Chelsea and her father, Norman. Start, Chelsea: "How." End, Ethel: "Well, he's afraid of you. You should get along fine."

OTHER PEOPLE'S MONEY
by Jerry Sterner (Samuel French)
Drama: Act I, pp. 44–46; Kate (35) and Bea (early 60s).
Bea convinces Kate, her daughter, who is a bright and successful investment banker, to work on behalf of her company in its fight against an attempted takeover. Start, Bea: "How dare you talk to him that way?" End, Kate: "Mom, don't push it."

PIZZA MAN
by Darlene Craviotto (Samuel French)
Comedy: Act I, pp. 31–43; Julie (late 20s) and Alice (mid-20s).
Acting on impulse and unfocused anger at men in general, Julie and Alice agree to pick a man, any man, and rape him. In this somewhat lengthy act, the women make this decision and begin their search. You'll need some dishes to break during this scene, as well as a telephone. Start, Julie: "We shouldn't have to go through any of this. Me getting drunk. You getting fat." End, Julie: "That was not the point of the phone call!"

SCENES FROM AMERICAN LIFE
by A. R. Gurney, Jr. (Samuel French)
Comedy-Drama: Act II, pp. 44–48; Mother (40ish) and Daughter (17).
Here, a mother takes her daughter to a fancy New York City restaurant to feel the young woman out as to whether she wants to have an expensive coming-out party when she graduates from high school—or go to college. The father won't pay for both. The daughter prefers college, much to her mother's utter disappointment. The playwright envisions actresses playing broad age ranges in this play so, for example, actresses in their twenties could play both of these roles. As written, a waiter moves in and out of the scene but has only one line. If you can't arrange for an actor to play that part, simply eliminate him. Start, Daughter: "Oh, Mummy! Thank you, thank you, thank you for the tennis dress, and the bathing suit, and the Bermuda shorts. They're just yummy, Mummy." End, Mother: "Now eat up, or we'll be late for *Kiss Me, Kate.*

SOCIAL SECURITY
by Andrew Bergman (Samuel French)
Comedy: Act II, Scene 1, pp. 38–46; Barbara (40s) and Sophie (70s).
Barbara is excited because an elderly artist friend is coming home with David for dinner. She thinks it will be good for her mother, Sophie, to meet someone new. Sophie, however, is less than enthused and would rather be with her old Long Island friends. Begin at the top of Act II.

Start, Barbara (on the telephone): "Hello? Oh, Hi Darling. . . ." End, Sophie: "One of the benefits of old age, darling—you're less tense about things."

SPOILS OF WAR
by Michael Weller (Samuel French)
Drama: Act II, pp. 47–53; Emma (late 30s) and Elise (mid-30s).
Elise and Emma are best friends and dedicated "leftists," politically committed since they lived together in a commune in the 1930s. In the mid-1950s, Emma and Elise are still raising their voices in a world that won't listen. Tonight, Elise is going to a party where she'll see her estranged husband. This meeting has been engineered by her 16-year-old son. Emma is upset for two reasons: Cedric, a fellow activist and friend, is being deported, and Emma is convinced that Elise is trying to take her new flame, Lew, away from her. A very good scene. Eliminate Lew's lines. Start, Emma: "My god, Elise, you look gorgeous! Why? I mean, what are you doing here." End, Emma: "Next week? Same time? Same place?"

STEEL MAGNOLIAS
by Robert Harling (Dramatists Play Service)
Drama: Act I, Scene 2, pp. 32–35; Shelby (25) and M'Lynn (50).
Shelby happily tells her mother that she is pregnant. But M'Lynn knows that the doctors have advised Shelby not to become pregnant because she has diabetes, and reacts to the news with anger rather than delight. Start, M'Lynn: "Shelby!" End, Shelby: "Please don't tell anybody yet. I want to tell daddy first."

STREETCAR NAMED DESIRE, A
by Tennessee Williams (Dramatists Play Service)
Drama: Act I, Scene 1, pp. 9–16; Blanche (early 30s) and Stella (late 20s).
Blanche unexpectedly arrives at Stella's New Orleans apartment. This is basically an expository scene, a setup for what is to come. The audience gets a hint about the sisters' differences, but the scene doesn't contain a great deal of overt conflict. Start, Stella: "Blanche! Blanche!" End, Blanche: "Oh, Stella, Stella, you're crying!"
Drama: Act I, Scene 4, pp. 43–51; Blanche (early 30s) and Stella (late 20s).
Last night, Stella and Stanley had a knock-down, drag-out fight, and then reconciled and made passionate love. Blanche anxiously watched all of this, and now she tries to convince Stella to leave her husband in this excellent scene. Stella won't hear of it. Begin at the top of Act I, Scene 4. Start, Blanche: "Stella?" End, Blanche: "Don't hang back with the brutes!"

SUMMER AND SMOKE
by Tennessee Williams (Dramatists Play Service)
Drama: Part II, Scene 4, pp. 66–69; Alma (25–29) and Nellie (18–22).
Nellie, Alma's longtime music student, gives her a Christmas gift and a card signed by Nellie and John, Alma's lifelong love. This is the first time that Alma realizes that John has become serious about someone else. It is important that Alma appears to be at least eight years older than Nellie. One of the points of the scene is that time has passed, and Nellie has grown up. Start, Nellie: "Here you are!" End, Nellie: "Goodbye, Miss Alma."

TASTE OF HONEY, A
by Shelagh Delaney (Grove Press)
Drama: Act I, Scene 2; Jo (17) and Helen (40).
Jo's bar-hopping, sluttish mother is moving out of their flat to marry a young boyfriend. As Helen packs, she discovers that Jo has been given an engagement ring. After the mother and daughter argue about Jo's readiness for marriage, and the conversation then turns to the identity

of Jo's natural father. Helen says that he was a half-wit she picked up in a bar, a man with "strange eyes." This 6-page scene is excellent. Written in the British vernacular. Start, Helen: "Jo! Jo! Come on. Be sharp now." End, Jo: "Good luck, Helen."

TOP GIRLS
by Caryl Churchill (Samuel French)
Comedy-Drama: Act II, Scene 2, pp. 88–98; Marlene (30s) and Joyce (30s).
In the final scene, which clarifies everything that has taken place so far, the audience learns that Marlene gave up her daughter 16 years ago to pursue success in the competitive business world. Marlene's sister, Joyce, has reared the rather slow-witted child. This is the sisters' first visit in six years. During this time, Marlene has acquired all of the worst traits of successful business-people and is a philosophical conservative, while Joyce is still a country person at heart. The sisters argue about class differences, business philosophy, and family loyalty. Written in the British vernacular. Start, Joyce: "So what's the secret?" End, Joyce: "No, pet. Sorry."

TOYS IN THE ATTIC
by Lillian Hellman (Dramatists Play Service)
Drama: Act II, pp. 39–45; Lily (21) and Albertine (45).
Lily, who is frail, needy, and uncertain, is worried that she is losing her husband, Julian, to another woman. Here, she asks her mother, Albertine, if the real reason Julian married her in the first place was because he was paid to. Start, Albertine: "How are you, Lily? I haven't seen you in a whole year." End, Albertine: "Then be very careful. Same thing as loving it."

TWO ROOMS
by Lee Blessing (Dramatists Play Service)
Drama: Act I, Scene 3, pp. 21–24; Lainie (30s) and Ellen (40s).
Ellen, a government official, tells Lainie that Walker Harris intends to publish an unauthorized article on the kidnapping of her husband in Beirut and her subsequent vigil. Ellen implores Lainie to publicly disavow the article so that it won't impede the efforts of the U. S. State Department to free the hostages. Start, Ellen: "I got a call today." End, Lainie: "Mine was. Now offer me hope."

VIEW FROM THE BRIDGE, A
by Arthur Miller (Dramatists Play Service)
Drama: Act I, pp. 31–33; Beatrice (40) and Catherine (17).
Beatrice has seen the depth of her husband's anguish over the romance developing between Catherine and Rodolpho and is starting to become a bit jealous of the younger woman. In this scene, Beatrice advises Catherine that if she wants Eddie to stop treating her like a child, she must stop acting like one. For example, Catherine should stop sitting on the edge of the tub to talk to Eddie while he is shaving in his underwear, and should stop letting him see her in her slip. Start, Beatrice: "Listen, Catherine. What are you going to do with yourself?" End, Catherine: "Okay."

WAITING FOR THE PARADE
by John Murrell (Talonbooks, Canada)
Drama: Scene 9; Janet (late 30s) and Marta (30s).
Janet, the self-appointed and sanctimonious monitor of local patriotism, pays Marta an unannounced visit at her father's small tailoring shop. Janet is upset because Marta plays recordings of German love songs too loud in the store. In addition, Marta's father is currently being imprisoned as a suspected Nazi sympathizer. When Janet strongly suggests that Marta herself is a Nazi, Marta almost bodily tosses her out of the shop. Marta has a slight German accent.

Start, Janet: "Good afternoon. I rang the bell on the counter, but nobody came." End, Marta: "Get out of my shop."

WATERMELON BOATS

by Wendy MacLaughlin [*Twenty-Five Ten-Minute Plays from Actors Theatre of Louisville* (Samuel French)]

Comedy-Drama: One-act play, pp. 149–155; Kitty (21) and Kate (21).

In the course of three short scenes covering 6½ pages, Kitty and Kate age from 11 to 21. Everything takes place on the bank of a lake as Kitty and Kate watch the watermelon boats they handcrafted (dug-out watermelon rinds with candles for masts) blow across to the other side. The trip becomes a metaphor for their aging. This very charming scene is challenging for the age-adjustment requirements. Start, Kitty: "How much longer?" End, Kate: "Wouldn't it be nice if now could be always?"

WHAT I DID LAST SUMMER

by A. R. Gurney, Jr. (Dramatists Play Service)

Drama: Act II, pp. 45–51; Anna (60s) and Grace (30).

Grace is worried about the growing influence that Anna "the Pig Woman" has over Charlie, her 14-year-old son. In this showdown, Grace demands that Charlie be made to return home. Anna responds with good humor and a firm commitment to let Charlie decide for himself. It turns out Grace was once one of Anna's "students." Start, Grace: "Anna!" End, Grace: "Good night, Anna."

WOMEN, THE

by Clare Boothe Luce (Dramatists Play Service)

Comedy: Act I, Scene 2, pp. 18–20; Mary (mid-30s) and Olga (any age).

Olga, the gossipy manicurist at Michael's Salon, tells Mary all about Mr. Stephen Haines and his affair with Crystal Allen. Unbeknownst to Olga, however, Mary happens to be Mrs. Stephen Haines. When Olga discovers this, she is mortified. Start, Olga: "Funny, isn't she?" Continue through Mary's exit at the end of the scene. End, Mary: "Thank you. Good day."

Comedy: Act I, Scene 3, pp. 24–26; Mrs. Morehead (55–60) and Mary (mid-30s).

Mary's wealthy husband is having an affair with a young store clerk, and she doesn't know what to do about it. In this scene, Mrs. Morehead, her colorful mother who has successfully been around the track a couple of times and understands all there is to know about men, counsels her. Start, Mary: "Mother, Dear!" Continue to the end of the scene, stopping just before Jane enters. End, Mary (on the telephone): ". . . No dear—I won't wait up—Stephen. I love—."

Comedy-Drama: Act I, Scene 4, pp. 34–36; Mary (mid-30s) and Crystal (early 20s).

Mary gets her nerve up and confronts "the other woman." This short, classic showdown takes place in the dressing room of a clothing store. Start, Crystal: "Come in!" End, Crystal: "Oh, what the hell!"

Part Six
Male/Female Scenes

AFTER THE FALL
by Arthur Miller (Dramatists Play Service)
Drama: Act I, pp. 28–30; Quentin (40s) and Louise (35).
Quentin and Louise, two complex, sophisticated people debate the true meaning of a mature relationship in this short, 3-page scene. Start, Louise: "Quentin, I'm trying to understand why you got so angry with me at the party the other night." End, Louise: "Good God! What an idiot!"
Drama: Act I, pp. 36–40; Quentin (40s) and Louise (35).
Quentin has innocently met and spent a little time in the park with Maggie, the switchboard operator in his business firm. When he arrives home, Louise, his wife, reminds him that he has missed an important business meeting. Quentin tells her about Maggie, and they fight. Start, Quentin: "Hi . . . What's the matter? . . . Well, what's the matter?" End, Louise: "It's all it's been about the last three years. You don't want me." For a longer version, end with Quentin's line, "God! Can that be true?"
Drama: Act II, pp. 47–52; Quentin (40s) and Maggie (25–30).
Quentin visits Maggie in her apartment. This is their first face-to-face meeting since they met in a park two years ago. Since then, she has become a celebrity singer, and he has followed her progress. Maggie is based on Marilyn Monroe, who playwright Arthur Miller was briefly married to. Omit Louise and Mother's lines. Start, Maggie: "I can't hardly believe you came! Can you stay five minutes?" End, Quentin: "Not yet, dear; but I intend to try. Don't be afraid to call me if you need any help."

AH, WILDERNESS!
by Eugene O'Neill (Samuel French)
Comedy: Act II, Scene 1, pp. 66–71; Belle (20) and Richard (16).
Determined to teach his steady girlfriend a lesson, Richard accepts a blind date with a young woman who has loose morals and, as he is to learn, charges for her services. Despite all of Richard's big talk, he is still a kid; as such, when Belle and Richard meet in a seedy bar, he is thoroughly intimidated. The peroxide blonde is as worldly as he is innocent. Cut the bartender's interruption of the scene. Start, Belle: "You shouldn't be so generous, Dearie. Gets him in bad habits." End, Belle: "And don't want to. Shut up about her, can't you?"
Comedy: Act III, Scene 2, pp. 108–117; Muriel (15) and Richard (16).
Shades of Romeo and Juliet in 1906. Richard and Muriel, two young lovers, sneak out of their respective homes, defying specific parental edicts, and rendezvous on a nearby moonlit beach. They quarrel and spoon and kiss, the very vision of innocent romance. Start, Muriel: "Oh, Dick." End, Muriel: "That'll be wonderful, won't it?"

ALL MY SONS
by Arthur Miller (Dramatists Play Service)
Drama: Act I, pp. 29–31; Chris (32) and Annie (26).
Chris has secretly been in love with Annie for a long time, even though she was the girlfriend of his late brother, Larry, who died in World War II. Judging that enough time has gone by, Chris decides to declare his love. When the moment arrives, however, he finds that he is still standing in his brother's shadow. Start, Annie: "It's lovely here. The air is sweet." End, Chris: "Oh Annie, Annie . . . I'm going to make a fortune for you!"

AMADEUS
by Peter Shaffer (Samuel French)
Drama: Act I, pp. 54–59; Salieri (35–45) and Constanze (20s).
Mozart is attracting attention, but little money. Salieri, his more successful competitor, is jealous of the younger man's talent and attempts to injure him by seducing his wife, Constanze. Salieri offers to intercede on Mozart's behalf with the emperor if she'll sleep with him. Though she wants to help her husband, she refuses to cooperate. Start, Salieri: "If she did, how would I behave? I had no idea of that either." End, Salieri: "I will study them overnight—and you will study my proposal. Not to be vague, that is my price. Good afternoon."

AMEN CORNER, THE
by James Baldwin (Samuel French)
Drama: Act II, pp. 66–71; Margaret (35–45) and Luke (40–50).
Luke is dying, and he is spending his last days with his ex-wife, Margaret, who, 10 years ago, took their infant son and left him. Now she is the pastor of a small Harlem church, having buried the pain of her marriage in courtship of the Lord. The prospect of death, however, presents an opportunity for reassessment. Margaret and Luke talk about the joys and challenges in their marriage, as well as how she struggled with their poverty and his love of music, which caused him to be away from home so much. Start, Margaret: "Luke, ain't you never going to learn to do right?" End, Margaret: "You's going to die, Luke."
Drama: Act III, pp. 84–89; Margaret (35–45) and David (18).
David has made his choice: he'll leave home and pursue a life as a professional musician. More important, however, he is determined to be his own man, not a puppet of his mother's religious teachings. In this scene, David has been out all night and comes home with a hangover. Margaret recognizes his sad state and slaps him in the face—hard. He lifts his head, and she slaps him again. It is a moment of truth for mother and son. Both characters have excellent monologues. You'll have to cut and paste, eliminating Odessa's lines. Start, Margaret: "Where you been until this time in the morning, son?" End, David: "No, Mama. I ain't hungry now."

AMERI/CAIN GOTHIC
by Paul Carter Harrison [*Totem Voices, Plays from the Black World Repertory,* edited by Paul Carter Harrison (Grove Press)]
Drama: Act II; Harper (mid-30s) and Cass (30s).
As Harper and Cass talk about life and fears, he keeps an eye on the motel across the street, the one Martin Luther King will soon stay in. Start, Harper: "That creep is on the prowl again!" End, Cass: "I don't believe you, Harper."

AMERICAN PLAN, THE
by Richard Greenberg (Dramatists Play Service)
Comedy-Drama: Act I, Scene 1, pp. 5–12; Lili (20) and Nick (20s).
This scene isn't what it appears to be. On the surface, it is a boy-meets-girl-in-the-Catskills scene. But what the audience doesn't know is that Nick is actually gay, and Lili has serious

emotional problems. Challenging work for resourceful actors. Start, Nick: "Oh . . . Hi!" End, Lili: "I don't think so."
Comedy-Drama: Act I, Scene 3, pp. 19–24; Lili (20) and Nick (20s).
Lili has started a rumor that Nick has a venereal disease, causing the young woman he has been dating all summer to panic and very abruptly leave the Catskills with her family. In this scene, Nick confronts Lili and demands an explanation for her actions. Then he stays for tea. Start, Lili: "Bobby Darin." End, Nick: "All these words!"
Drama: Act I, Scene 6, pp. 32–36; Eva (40s) and Nick (20s).
Eva has investigated Nick's background and discovered that almost everything he has told her daughter about himself is a lie. In this tense scene, Eva confronts him, and he explains. At least the audience thinks he explains, but he isn't telling the whole story. Although the script doesn't call for the actress playing Eva to have a slight German accent, this would work. Start, Eva: "It has warmed my heart to see the change in Lili over these last weeks." End, Eva: "That is no longer either here or there."

ANASTASIA
by Marcelle Maurette [adapted by Guy Bolton (Samuel French)]
Drama: Act II, pp. 56–59; Empress (79) and Paul (25–30).
Paul is apparently convinced that Anna is the real Anastasia, the only-surviving daughter of the Russian Tsar Nicholas II, and he has brought his aunt, the Dowager Empress, to see for herself. It is February 1926, and the Empress has met many pretenders since the royal family was assassinated in 1918, so she is inclined to be skeptical. After all, where would a real princess have hidden for so many years? Paul asks the empress her to keep an open mind. Start, Paul: "Does Anastasia know you are here?" End, Empress: "Leave them. Leave them wrapped in the dignity of death."
Drama: Act III, pp. 77–79; Empress (79) and Bounine (40s).
A woman believed to be the real Princess Anastasia, the only-surviving daughter of the last Russian Tsar Nicholas II, is about to be presented to the press. If all goes well, Bounine and his cohorts, the group that discovered the young woman, will come into their share of the heiress's huge fortune tomorrow. In this scene, the Dowager Empress, evidently convinced that Anna is the real Anastasia, surprises Bounine by announcing that she knows the whole plan is a scam. Cornered, he at first denies the charge but then caves in, blaming everything on Anna. When the empress doesn't go for that, he switches gears again, urging her to go ahead with a public endorsement of the young woman so they can all gain access to the fortune. This short scene is interesting for its many twists and turns. Start, Bounine: "I assume from Your Majesty's attitude that the—the Princess has told you certain things?" End, Empress: "The audience is over. I am through with you, Arcade Arcadievitch Bounine."
Drama: Act III, pp. 81–83; Anna (20s) and Dr. Serensky (25–35).
Anna's former lover, Dr. Serensky, has shown up on the day she is to be presented to the world as the real Princess Anastasia. He knows it isn't true. As the scene progresses, however, it is clear that Anna can pass, whether it is true or not, and she is going for the gold. All Dr. Serensky has to offer is love and a struggling medical practice. Still, Anna seems unsure. Start, Serensky: "How lovely you look. And how well." End, Anna: "If we are parting, Michael."

ANGELS IN AMERICA: A GAY FANTASIA ON NATIONAL THEMES, PART I: MILLENNIUM APPROACHES
by Tony Kushner (Theatre Communications Group)
Drama: Act I, Scene 5; Harper (early 30s) and Joe (early 30s).
Joe tells his wife, Harper, that he wants to accept a political position and move from Brooklyn to Washington, DC. Harper, an agoraphobic and a borderline valium addict, is terrified of such a move. Disregard Louis and the Rabbi's appearance in this split scene. Start, Harper:

"Washington?" End, Harper: ". . . skin burns, birds go blind, icebergs melt. The world's coming to an end."

Drama: Act I; Scene 7; Harper (early 30s) and Prior (30).
In this sequence, Harper and Prior appear in one another's dreams. She is an agoraphobic and dependent on valium; he is gay, flamboyant, and dying of AIDS. They meet here for the first time but, because it is a dream, they already seem to know much about each other. The whole scene is slightly disconnected from reality. Start, Prior: "I'm ready for my closeup, Mr. DeMille." End, Prior: "People come and go so strangely here. I don't think there's any uninfected part of me. My heart is pumping polluted blood. I feel dirty."

Drama: Act I, Scene 8; Harper (early 30s) and Joe (early 30s).
Harper and her husband, Joe, have a troubled marriage. She is addicted to various prescription drugs, and since they stopped having sex regularly, Joe has stayed out much later at night and his business trips seem longer. Sensing some kind of fundamental change in the man, she hysterically confronts him in this scene, asking if he is a homosexual. Joe doesn't provide a straightforward answer to the question; instead, he suggests that they pray more and ask God for guidance. This only serves to infuriate Harper more. Simultaneous scenes are being played on stage here, so disregard Louis and Prior. Start, Harper: "Where were you?" End, Harper: "No. Yes. No. Yes. Get away from me. Now we both have a secret."

ANNA CHRISTIE
by Eugene O'Neill (Vintage Books)
Drama: Act II; Anna (20) and Mat Burke (30).
For the past 10 days, Anna has been living happily on her father's coal barge, relishing the fresh sea air. Then a group of shipwrecked sailors comes on board, and Anna is swept off her feet by one of them, an Irishman named Mat Burke. Fifteen minutes after he meets her, he asks her to marry him. Mat has a slight Irish accent. Start, Anna: "Here you are. Here's a drink for you. You need it, I guess." End, Burke: "I'm telling you there's the will of God in it that brought me safe through the storm and fog to the wan spot in the world where you was!"

Drama: Act IV; Anna (20) and Chris (50).
After her father, Chris, and Mat reacted so terribly when Anna disclosed that she'd been a prostitute, Anna decided to return to the streets. She is packed to leave when her father returns from his drunken binge, asks her forgiveness for having been a bad parent all her life, and announces that he is shipping out to Cape Town. The role of Chris requires a heavy Swedish accent, and playwright Eugene O'Neill has written it with those inflections. The scene calls for a revolver, but it is never fired. Begin at the top of Act IV. Start, Anna: "Come in." End, Anna: "Good-night."

Drama: Act IV; Anna (20) and Burke (30).
Mat has decided that despite Anna's sordid past, he loves her and again asks her to marry him. She accepts this time. Mat has a slight Irish accent. Also, the scene calls for a revolver that doesn't get shot. Start, Anna: "What are you doing here?" End, Mat: "We'll be happy now, the two of us, in spite of the divil."

ANOTHER ANTIGONE
by A. R. Gurney, Jr. (Dramatists Play Service)
Comedy-Drama: One-act play, pp. 10–14; Judy Miller (early 20s) and Dave (early 20s).
Judy Miller has written a modern, anti-war adaptation of the Greek classic *Antigone* and, now that her Greek drama teacher has refused to give her a passing grade for the effort, she has become defiant; she is determined to mount a university production of her play. In this scene, Judy tries to enlist her boyfriend, Dave, to play Antigone's sister, a character she has changed into Antigone's lover. He isn't excited by the prospect. Begin as Dave reads aloud from the script. Start, Dave: "'No, Antigone, no. Please reconsider. Do not take on this dangerous

enterprise. The risks are too great, the payoff insignificant.'" End, Dave: "'No, Antigone, no. Please reconsider.'"
Comedy-Drama: One-act play, pp. 14–23; Diana (35–45) and Henry (40–50).
Diana, the dean of Humane Studies has been caught up in the growing conflict between Henry Harper and his defiant student, Judy Miller. Diana visits Henry's office and asks him to back off, but he won't consider it. Then she tells him that campus whispers portray him as anti-Semitic. Start, Diana: "Henry?" End, Diana: "Now where did she get an idea like that?"
Comedy-Drama: One-act play, pp. 41–47; Diana (35–45) and Henry (40–50).
In this terrific scene, Diana delivers the news that Henry is being granted a year off with full pay so he can visit Greece and do some research. He refuses the offer, however, because his wife has left him and because Diana shows no interest in accompanying him on the trip and beginning a romance. Then she levels him by reporting that there are practically no pre-enrollments for his course next year, and that the college is, in fact, laying him off for a while. Henry leaves their meeting determined to drum up some enrollments. Start, Henry: "Woman at her work. I am reminded of Penelope at her loom." End, Henry: "Then I'll have to get them, won't I?"
Drama: One-act play, pp. 49–55; Judy (early 20s) and Henry (40–50).
In this final scene between Judy and her teacher, he offers an olive branch if she'll help him get some students in his class for next year. Judy doesn't need Henry anymore, however, because another teacher—significantly, a Jewish teacher—has agreed to give her an "A" on the project that Henry dismissed. Excellent scene, a power struggle. Start, Judy: "You wanted to see me, Professor Harper?" End, Henry: "Good God. What have I done?"

ARTICHOKE
by Joanna M. Glass (Dramatists Play Service)
Comedy-Drama: Act I, pp. 22–24; Margaret (mid-30s) and Gibson (40).
Gibson was adopted at the age of eight by Margaret's father and raised in the same home. As an adult, he has broken completely away from the farm, becoming an educated man, a teacher of and expert on Alexander Pope. Gibson has returned to the farm for a summer visit, and this is the first brief scene between him and Margaret. They're already attracted to each other in "that" way, but no one knows. They talk about why Margaret has lived in a separate bedroom from her husband for the last 14 years. Start, Margaret: "Good morning." End, Margaret: "Gibson McFarland, a true friend would see there is only one side to this story. Mine."
Comedy-Drama: Act II, pp. 31–34; Margaret (mid-30s) and Gibson (40).
This is a more active scene because Margaret and Gibson's longing for one another is closer to the surface. They talk about this and that, and then he reads her palm. Of course, the Venus mound, the place just below the thumb that signifies love, is "quivering." Margaret and Gibson are so worked up that they have to head for the berry patch. Start, Margaret: "You're preoccupied, aren't you?" End, Gibson: "Oh, please, lady! Have mercy!"

AUTUMN GARDEN, THE
by Lillian Hellman (Dramatists Play Service)
Drama: Act II, Scene 1, pp. 49–52; Rose (43) and Mrs. Griggs (53).
Rose is desperately trying to save her 25-year marriage, which is in shambles. Her husband, however, is intent on divorce, wants to start a new life for himself, and is unmoved even when she tells him that another man may be standing in the wings. Start, Rose: "Nasty old thing. I'm driving over to see him." End, Rose: "I am going to try, dear. Really I am. It's evidently important to you."
Drama: Act II, Scene 2, pp. 68–70; Sophie (17) and Nick (45).
The oh-so-continental Nick has had far too much to drink and is feeling lonely and full of self-pity when he discovers Sophie preparing her bed in the living room. He makes a fumbling

attempt at seducing her, but his efforts disgust her, and he falls asleep. Sophie has a slight French accent. Start, Nick: "Constance! What is this—A boys' school with lights out at eleven!" End, Nick: "Have a little pity. I am old and sick."
Drama: Act III, pp. 78–82; Nina (40) and Nick (45).
Stung by Nick's drunken insults last night, Nina, his wife, has packed to leave. When he realizes that she is serious about separation, he begs forgiveness. She relents, sending him on ahead to Mobile, Alabama, to wait for her while she tries to clean up the human mess he has left in his wake. This is an excellent scene in which two adults redefine the terms of their relationship, essentially lowering their expectations. Start, Nick: "Nina. I just want to say before you go that they're making an awful row about nothing." End, Nina: "You love me and I love you and that's that and always will be."

BAD HABITS
by Terrence McNally [1990 revised edition (Dramatists Play Service)]
Comedy: "Dunelawn," pp. 46–48; April (late 20s) and Roy (30s).
April and Roy are professional actors who have been married only three months and can't get along because they are so competitive. Here, they lounge in the sunshine and tear each other to shreds. Start, Roy: "Honey! You're blocking my sun." End, April: "Give him skin cancer, God, give him skin cancer, please!"
Comedy: "Dunelawn," pp. 27–32; Dolly (late 20s) and Harry (30s).
Dolly arrives for a visit and discovers that after three months of treatment, her husband, Harry, is a changed man. Now he drinks, smokes, dances, sings, and sculpts. In this scene, they talk about why they've tried so often to kill each other, and he tells her how great he is doing. Eliminate Dr. Pepper in the beginning of the scene, and the interruptions of the public-address system. Start, Harry: "You look wonderful, Dolly." End, Dolly: "Doctor! . . . What have you done to him?"
Comedy: "Ravenswood," pp. 83–90; Ruth Benson (late 20s) and Hugh Gumbs (30s).
Hugh Gumbs was the love of Ruth's life until he ran off with Mildred Canby five years ago. To win him back, Ruth has remade herself, giving up smoking and drinking, and losing a great deal of weight. Now she is an attractive nurse employed at Ravenswood. Unexpectedly, Hugh checks in for treatment, a man in the gutter, an alcoholic, a loser. When she reveals her new identity to him, he still rejects her, this time because she is too good for him. Eliminate Dr. Toynbee. Also, the scene calls for Hugh to be in a wheelchair and, though that is ideal, you can work without it. Start, Hugh: "Aaaaaaaaaaaa!" End, Benson: "All right, Hugh, and remember, you asked for it."

BEAR, THE
by Anton Chekhov [*The Sneeze, Plays and Stories* by Anton Chekhov, translated and adapted by Michael Frayn (Samuel French)]
Comedy: One-act play, pp. 47–55; Smirnov (45–55) and Popova (45–55).
Smirnov has arrived at the widow Popova's home to collect a debt owed by her late husband. When she can't pay, Smirnov refuses to leave, staging a kind of sit-in. For workshop purposes, eliminate Popova's servant, Luka, completely. You'll have to do some careful editing, but it is worth the effort. Start, Smirnov: "Smirnov. Grigory Stepanovich Smirnov, landowner and lieutenant of artillery, retired." End, Popova: "I've no desire to converse with impertinent hobbledehoys! Kindly get out of here!"

BEAU JEST
by James Sherman (Samuel French)
Comedy: Act II, Scene 2, pp. 60–68; Sarah (20s) and Bob (20s).
In order to fool her parents into thinking she has a nice Jewish boyfriend, Sarah called an escort service, asked for a Jewish date for the evening, and arranged a dinner with the folks.

It turns out, however, that Bob, the escort, isn't Jewish at all. Fortunately, he is a charming actor and manages to play his role beautifully, winning over Sarah's parents. In this scene, which takes place immediately after the second visit with the parents, Bob and Sarah relax together at her place. They're clicking for real, a sexual buzz is in the air, love is happening. He massages her shoulders, they talk, he gets up to leave, they kiss. They kiss again. He stays. Start, Bob: "You got anything to drink in this place? Besides wine?" End: "You're not Jewish! Oy!"

BEDROOMS, FIVE COMEDIES
by Renée Taylor and Joseph Bologna (Samuel French)
Comedy: "Bill and Laura," pp. 15–22; Bill (35–45) and Laura (30–40).
Recently separated and now dating other people, Bill and Laura find themselves invited to the same party. Alone in the bedroom with the coats, the claws come out as they rehash their incompatibility and upcoming divorce settlement. The argument builds to a fever pitch, at which point they fall into one another's arms. Eliminate Grace's interruptions. Start, Bill: "What are you doing here?" End, Bill: "Let 'em eat quiche."
Comedy: "Mrs. Wexel and Mr. Lewis," pp. 59–70; Mrs. Wexel (75) and Mr. Lewis (75).
Love, or at least lust, comes to two senior citizens in a Florida retirement community. Mr. Lewis invites Mrs. Wexel up to his condo and tries his best moves on her. But when it is time to have sex, they're both too pooped. She wasn't all that interested anyway. A cute scene. Start, Mrs. Wexel: "Very nice. Very nice." End, Mrs. Wexel: "Sure, Leo, sure. Look, I waited this long."

BELL, BOOK AND CANDLE
by John Van Druten (Dramatists Play Service)
Comedy: Act I, Scene 2, pp. 21–26; Gillian (27) and Shep (35).
Gillian is an honest-to-goodness witch who is smitten with Shep, the handsome publisher who lives upstairs. Afraid that she was about to lose him, she cast a spell to guarantee his affections. It worked well, and he fell immediately and passionately into her arms. Three hours later, in the afterglow of lovemaking, Gillian and Shep discuss the future. He is just about ready for marriage, but she wants their romance to continue like they are for a while. Anyway, unbeknown to Shep, witches can't really fall in love. If they do, they lose their powers. Start, Shep: "Say something." End, Gillian: "Soon."
Comedy: Act II, pp. 43–47; Gillian (27) and Shep (35).
At the risk of losing Shep, Gillian confesses that she is a witch and that she used a spell to get him to fall in love with her. He, of course, doesn't believe in witches and so doesn't believe a word of what she is saying. Start, Shep: "Is anything the matter?" End, Shep: "I believe you cast an absolutely wonderful spell on me, and I'm crazy about it."
Comedy: Act III, Scene 2, pp. 65–70; Gillian (27) and Shep (35).
In the very last scene, Shep has come to say good-bye but, in the process, discovers that Gillian has truly fallen in love with him and that she has lost her magical powers. They fall into one another's arms, presumably to live happily ever after. Start, Shep: "This isn't a friendly visit." End, Gillian: "I'm only human."

BETRAYAL
by Harold Pinter (Dramatists Play Service)
Drama: Scene 1 (1977), pp. 7–12; Emma (30s) and Jerry (30s).
After learning that her husband, Robert, has been carrying on romantic affairs for years, Emma wants to talk to her former lover, Jerry. In this restaurant conversation, the first face-to-face meeting they've had since they broke up two years ago, Emma and Jerry discuss their respective families and reminisce about the glory days of their seven-year romance. She tells him that she and Robert plan to separate. Start, Jerry: "Well." End, Emma: "It's all all over."

Drama: Scene 3 (1975), pp. 17–19; Emma (30s) and Jerry (30s).
Emma and Jerry agree to end their seven-year affair. They discuss what to do with their apartment and accumulated possessions. This scene has an important subtext: Emma long ago told her husband, who is Jerry's best friend, about their affair, but Jerry doesn't know this. Start, Jerry: "What do you want to do then?" End, Emma: "Listen. I think we've made absolutely the right decision."

Drama: Scene 5 (1973), pp. 24–27; Emma (30s) and Robert (30s).
While on holiday in Venice, Emma tells Robert that she has been carrying on a longtime affair with his best friend, Jerry. Start, Emma: "It's Torcello tomorrow, isn't it?" End, Robert: "Tell me, are you looking forward to our trip to Torcello?"

Drama: Scene 8 (1971), pp. 35–38; Emma (30s) and Jerry (30s).
Their affair still young and exciting, Emma prepares lunch for Jerry in the flat they secretly maintain. At the end of the scene, she tells him that she is pregnant with her husband's child. Start, Jerry: "Hullo." End, Jerry: "Yes. Yes, of course. I'm very happy for you."

BETWEEN DAYLIGHT AND BOONVILLE
by Matt Williams (Samuel French)
Comedy-Drama: Act I, pp. 12–19; Carla (26) and Cyril (30s).
Carla wants to escape her dreary trailer-park existence. She lives with her husband, Larry, a coal miner who has allowed himself to go. In this scene, she asks Cyril, a miner who is out of work because of a hand injury, to give her and her child a lift to the bus station. Cyril is a jokester and a flirt, but he wouldn't really play around with his friend's wife. He also isn't crazy about the idea of helping Carla run away from Larry. You'll have to cut and paste a bit, eliminating Jimmy. Start, Cyril: "Waaah!" End, Cyril: "Please don't tickle. I'm goin' to pee my pants."

BEYOND THERAPY
by Christopher Durang (Samuel French)
Comedy: Act I, Scene 1, pp. 7–13; Prudence (29–32) and Bruce (30–34).
Prudence and Bruce meet through a personal ad, but the date is disastrous. It turns out that he has a male lover. Start, Prudence: "Hello". End, Prudence: "Absolutely nothing seems to get that waiter's attention, does it?"

Comedy: Act I, Scene 2, pp. 14–18; Prudence (29–32) and Dr. Stuart Framingham (35–45).
Prudence tells Dr. Framingham, her therapist, about her disastrous date with Bruce, but all the psychiatrist wants to talk about is his own masculinity and his sexual relationship with Prudence. Start, Dr. Framingham: "You can send the next patient in now, Betty." End, Prudence: "Please, don't you talk either."

Comedy: Act I, Scene 3, pp. 18–23; Charlotte Wallace (45–55) and Bruce (30–34).
Bruce tells Charlotte Wallace, his therapist, about his disastrous date with Prudence. The psychologist, however, doesn't think it sounds bad at all. Influenced by *Equus,* she thinks it is better to be outrageous and impulsive than to be boring. Start, Charlotte: "You may send in the next patient, Marcia." End, Charlotte: "Marcia, I'll buzz back when I think of it."

Comedy: Act I, Scene 4, pp. 24–33; Prudence (29–32) and Bruce (30–34).
At the insistence of his therapist, Bruce has placed another personal ad, this time completely exaggerating his physical assets and intellectual accomplishments. Of course, Prudence has responded to it and shows up at the appointed meeting place expecting to meet Mr. Tall, Dark, and Handsome. Instead, she finds Bruce. To their mutual surprise, however, this time they click. This scene isn't nearly as wild and crazy as the first encounter between Prudence and Bruce, but it is just as interesting for scene work because they must find honest values in one another. Start, Prudence: "Oh." End, Prudence: ". . . but there was something about the texture of vanilla ice cream."

Comedy: Act I, Scene 5, pp. 33–38; Prudence (29–32) and Dr. Stuart Framingham (35–45).
Prudence tells her therapist that her relationship with Bruce is progressing nicely, that she likes him after all, and that they've slept together. As a man and not as a doctor, Stuart is completely threatened by this news. Start, Stuart: "Hiya, babe, it's me." End, Prudence: "I don't think you do either."

BIRDBATH
by Leonard Melfi [*Encounters, Six One-Act Plays* by Leonard Melfi (Samuel French)]
Drama: One-act play, pp. 12–22; Velma (26) and Frankie (late 20s).
Although Velma and Frankie have been working side by side at the cafeteria, this is the first time they speak. Before the night is out, they'll go back to his place, but they won't make love. Try combining the first part of the play, which takes place in the cafeteria, and the second part, which takes place on the street outside the cafeteria. Start, Velma: "Hi." End, Velma: "You know, Frankie, maybe instead of the coffee I'd better have hot tea instead."
Drama: One-act play, pp. 30–42; Velma (26) and Frankie (late 20s).
After Frankie and Velma go to his apartment and the liquor starts to take effect, he tries to get a little closer to her. She becomes increasingly agitated, however, and finally turns on him with a knife. Start, Frankie: "Relax, Velma." Continue to the end of the play. End, Frankie: "I have a treat for you in the morning, Velma. I've just written you . . . a valentine."

BLOOD MOON
by Nicholas Kazan (Samuel French)
Drama: Act I, pp. 30–39; Manya (mid-20s, playing 19) and Alan (45).
Manya's uncle brought her to Alan's apartment and then diplomatically excused himself, leaving the two of them alone. It is immediately clear that Alan intends to have sex with Manya and that she is trapped. This scene is a tense, pre-rape seduction, a threatening game of cat and mouse with violence pushing quite near the surface. Start, Alan: "Well. Alone at last." End, Alan: "Okay, I've stopped. That's all I need to say anyway." If you want to try staging the rape sequence itself, start, Alan: "Well, I already own your uncle." Continue to the same end.
Drama: Act II, pp. 46–54; Manya (mid-20s) and Alan (45).
Manya has invited her Uncle Gregory and Alan, the man who raped her a year ago, to dinner. She does the acting job of her life, convincing Alan that she has let bygones be bygones, that the rape is water under the bridge, and that she is happy to see him. He is surprised but figures that he must have been awfully good in bed, so he is kind of flattered. What Alan doesn't know yet is that the rape resulted in a pregnancy, as well as that Manya suffered a mental breakdown and had a late-term abortion. Tonight, however, Manya will get her revenge. Unbeknownst to anyone but Manya, she froze the fetus and placenta and is serving them as the main course. Begin at the top of Act II as Manya is setting the table and talking to the audience. Start, Manya: "This part is harder for me to reveal. . . ." Stop just before Uncle Gregory arrives. End, Manya: "Well, last time I was uncomfortable, right?"

BLUE WINDOW
by Craig Lucas (Samuel French)
Comedy-Drama: Scene 2, pp. 44–46; Libby (33) and Griever (35–40).
Libby is hosting her first dinner party since her husband's death. She is embarrassed because a cap on her missing tooth fell off and, anyway, it is "too soon" for her to be trying to give a party. She fears the evening isn't going well. Griever, her friend and sometime lover, comforts and consoles her. Start, Griever: "Congratulations, it's going great, don't you think?" End, Libby: "Go!"

BORN YESTERDAY
by Garson Kanin (Dramatists Play Service)
Comedy: Act I, pp. 39–42; Billie Dawn (29) and Paul Verrall (30s).
Harry Brock, a corrupt, self-made millionaire, has hired Paul Verrall, a serious-minded journalist to tutor his dumb-but-beautiful girlfriend, Billie Dawn. Harry is worried that Billie, an ex-chorine, will be inept in social situations as he attempts to influence the movers and shakers in Washington, DC, so he wants Paul to educate her. In this first meeting between the tutor and his charge, sexual sparks fill the room. Start, Paul: "Your—friend Mr. Brock has an idea he'd like us to spend a little time together. You and me, that is." End, Billie: "Or the night!"
Comedy: Act I, pp. 43–46; Billie Dawn (29) and Harry Brock (40s).
Toward the end of Act I, Harry and Billie are alone onstage together for the first time, and the audience gets its first look at their relationship, seeing how they communicate in private. Beginning with a nonspeaking gin game that Billie readily wins and ending with Harry's attempt to draw Billie into the upstairs bedroom, this brief, 3-page scene is a fascinating power struggle. Start, Billie (singing): "'. . . Anything Goes (tata tata—tata tata—tzing!), Good authors, too, who once—.'"
Comedy: Act II, pp. 54–59; Billie Dawn (29) and Paul Verrall (30s).
Paul has been tutoring Billie for two months, and she is thriving on the newfound knowledge. To her confusion, however, he hasn't tried to sleep with her—and she's up for it. The entire scene runs about 15 pages. For a shorter version, start, Billie: "Oh, and you know that thing you gave me about Napoleon?" End, Paul: "I know. He's got a brain of gold."

BOYS' LIFE
by Howard Korder (Dramatists Play Service)
Comedy: Scene 3, pp. 14–19; Maggie (late 20s) and Jack (late 20s).
Jack and Maggie meet at a children's playground. He tries to pick her up but bombs out. Both get progressively stoned. Start, Maggie: "Oh God. Oh God." End, Jack: "One . . . Two . . . Three . . . Four . . . All right, that's it. I'm calling mommy!"

BREAKING THE CODE
by Hugh Whitemore (Samuel French)
Drama: Act I, Scene 7, pp. 48–54; Pat (early 30s) and Alan Turing (39).
Pat Green is a cryptanalyst working at the Government Code and Cipher School during World War II. Assigned to work with Alan Turing on the German code project, she falls in love with him. In this scene at his mother's home, Pat and Turing are left alone. She declares her feelings for him but, as she suspected might be the case, he tells her that he is a homosexual. Start, Pat: "She's quite right, you know." End, Turing: "It would stop me making love to you. I don't want that sort of life and I don't think you do, either."
Drama: Act II, Scene 3, pp. 72–76; Sara (60) and Alan Turing (39).
Alan Turing tells Sara, his mother, that he is homosexual and will have to stand trial for this "crime." She is shocked to learn about her son's sexual orientation, having long presumed his lack of interest in women was because he was bookish. This is a very touching scene. Start, Sara: "Alan, my dear, you are so silly!" End, Sara: "Do come and look at the guest room. I'm so pleased with it."

BUCK
by Ronald Ribman (Theatre Communications Group) [*New Plays USA, 1983* (Theatre Communications Group); *The Rug Merchants of Chaos and Other Plays by Ronald Ribman* (Theatre Communications Group)]
Drama: Act II; Shirley (mid-20s) and Frank (mid-30s).
In a cable-television station, Shirley and Frank, both actors, reenact the murder of a prostitute named Joy Bonnard by one of her tricks. This scene contains very physical and sexually explic-

it material. Shirley behaves like a whore, coming on to Frank. The scene then turns violent, ending with Shirley's stabbing death. Actors need to take special care with blocking. Start, Joy (offstage): "You make me feel like dirt! You make me feel like a whore!" End, Frank: "They want me to be God and all there is to me is a sack of testicles between my legs!"

BURN THIS
by Lanford Wilson (Hill & Wang/Noonday; HarperCollins Canada Ltd.)
Comedy-Drama: Act II; Anna (32) and Pale (36).
Anna tells Pale not to mistake their two nights of intimacy for something permanent. Start, Anna: "Pale, would you do me a favor.?" End, Anna: "There is no reason for you to come here. I have nothing for you. I don't like you and I'm frightened of you." For scene-study purposes, you can play this with Larry onstage or omit his presence altogether. To eliminate him, cut from Pale's line, "Hawaii, Brazil. See places" to Anna's line, "Pale, I don't even know how this nonsense started; it never should have." Cut Larry's lines, too. This will get around the problem of Pale having to leave and change clothes.

CANDIDA
by George Bernard Shaw (Signet)
Comedy-Drama: Act II; Prosperine (30) and Eugene Marchbanks (18).
Eugene accuses Prosperine, Morell's secretary, of not being honest about her romantic longings. He manages to elicit something of a confession that she secretly loves Morell, a fact that depresses Eugene because he is convinced that Morell is unlovable. Start, Prosperine: "Bother! You've been meddling with my typewriter." End, Prosperine: "Yes."

CAT ON A HOT TIN ROOF
by Tennessee Williams (Dramatists Play Service)
Drama: Act I, pp. 10–16; Margaret (early 20s) and Brick (27).
Margaret, who is also called Maggie, is dressing for Big Daddy's party as she and her husband, Brick, bicker and then argue more violently about their nonexistent sex life, his alcoholism, his curious relationship with Skipper, and Big Daddy's fatal disease. Start, Maggie: "Y'know—your brother Gooper still cherishes the illusion he took a giant step up on the social ladder when he married Miss Mae Flynn of the Memphis Flynns." End, Margaret: "They're impossible conditions!"

CAT'S-PAW
by William Mastrosimone (Samuel French)
Drama: Act I, pp. 18–24; Jessica (25–35) and Victor (25–40).
Jessica, a local television reporter has been brought to a terrorist hideout near Washington, DC, to interview the guerrilla leader responsible for a terrible car bombing and, she hopes, an Environmental Protection Agency employee who is being held captive. As Jessica sets up her camera, she and Victor, the leader, negotiate interview terms. Start, Jessica: "Why don't we get started? Sit down so I can focus, please. Now I'll be making some prefatory remarks." End, Victor: "The Nazarene carpenter. Luke, 14: 26."

CHAPTER TWO
by Neil Simon (Samuel French)
Comedy: Act I, Scene 6, pp. 40–49; Jennie (32) and George (42).
Actress Jennie Malone, newly divorced after a six-year marriage, meets novelist George Schneider, whose wife of 14 years recently died. The sparks fly in this scene, which is full of wit, embarrassment, and awkwardness. Start, Jennie: "Hello? . . . Faye, I can't talk to you now." End, George: "I can't believe you're from the same man who gave us Bambi and Vilma."

Comedy: Act II, Scene 5, pp. 93–104; Jennie (32) and George (42).
George and Jennie had an awful time on their honeymoon. Having just walked into George's apartment with their luggage, they think that they may have made a big mistake by marrying. Play entire scene. Start, Jennie: "That was fun! Three days of rain and two days of diarrhea." End, George: "We got, as they say in the trade, problems, kid."
Comedy: Act II, Scene 6, pp. 105–114; Faye (35) and Leo (40).
George's brother, Leo, and Jennie's friend, Faye, are launching an affair, using Jennie's old apartment for a clandestine meeting. However, Faye is guilt-ridden, and Leo wants only sex, no romance, so the liaison isn't working out. Start, Leo: "I'm sorry." End, Leo: "Hold on to your sheet, kid, kissing is my main thing."

CHASE, THE
by Horton Foote (Dramatists Play Service)
Drama: Act I, Scene 3, pp. 26–29; Mrs. Reeves (60ish) and Sheriff Hawes (38–45).
Mrs. Reeves tries to bribe Sheriff Hawes not to kill her son, who is an escaped convict. This scene gets pretty emotional as Mrs. Reeves begs for her son's life. As such, the role of the mother is best suited for an experienced actress. The play is set in Texas, so southern accents are appropriate. Start, Sheriff Hawes: "Mrs. Reeves, where have you been?" End, Mrs. Reeves: "I hope your child is hunted and killed some day. I hope it is. I hope it is."

CHEATERS
by Michael Jacobs (Samuel French)
Comedy: Act I, Scene 3, pp. 20–25; Michelle (20s) and Allen (20s).
Allen and Michelle have been living together for 18 months and are returning to their apartment tonight after attending a friend's wedding. Michelle is mortified because Allen caught the bridal bouquet—and tossed it back. She presses him to make a commitment to marry her. When he balks, she walks out on him. A delightful scene you'll need a bed or futon for. The characters often dress and undress and get into and out of bed as they fight with and seduce one another. Start, Michelle: "I want to thank you for the most embarrassing night of my life!" End, Allen: "I really showed her."

CHILDREN OF A LESSER GOD
by Mark Medoff (Dramatists Play Service)
Drama: Act I, pp. 23–25; Sarah (mid-20s) and James (30).
Because Sarah, who is deaf, refuses to speak, preferring to sign, she has been in conflict with James, who is supposed to teach her to speak. But something else is going on. The teacher/student relationship is turning romantic, although neither Sarah nor James has acknowledged this yet. In this short scene, which takes place at a duck pond, Sarah gets jealous of James's relationship with another student, and her jealousy makes him angry. Then they kiss. Start, James: "Well, at last. 'Dear Sarah, Please meet me at the duck pond after dinner. I'll bring the stale bread. James Leeds.'" End, James: "It's always worked before. See, when I get in trouble, I kiss the girl and make everything better. (She exits) Oh, come on, Sarah! . . . Sarah!"
Drama: Act I, pp. 27–28; Sarah (mid-20s) and James (30).
James meets Sarah while she is working at her regular job as a maid in a school for the deaf. After finding out that she was thought to be retarded until she was 12 years old, he confronts her with this information. James wants to know if this is why she hates hearing people, or if she hates herself. Sarah then accuses him of wanting to teach her the joys of sex with a hearing man and tells him that she was quite promiscuous in her teens. Start, James: "Hello. I left you a note. It said: 'Please see me this afternoon, I'll bring the boxing gloves.' You didn't come so I ate all the gloves myself. I'm sorry to interrupt your work." End, James: "Your secret. No hearing person has ever gotten in there to find out . . . No person, period."

Drama: Act I, pp. 32–34; Sarah (mid-20s) and James (30).
In this scene, James and Sarah talk about marriage and the prospect of having deaf children. Start, James: "Sorry I'm late. I got held up." End, James: "I know you want to, but we can't. The point is, it's all possible. And you know it. Say it. Say: 'I know it's possible.'"

Drama: Act I, pp. 36–38; Sarah (mid-20s) and James (30).
A lovely scene that takes place in Sarah's childhood bedroom. James tells her about his mother's suicide, and they cling to each other. Start, Sarah: "My room." End, Sarah: "You and me. Joined."

Drama: Act II, pp. 64–68; Sarah (mid-20s) and James (30).
Sarah is going to make a speech before the Equal Employment Opportunity Commission, asking that the school for the deaf be forced to hire more deaf people. She offends James by telling him that she wants Orin, a hearing-impaired person, not James, to translate for her. Their conversation escalates into a big argument, during which James accuses Sarah of refusing to speak just so she can control people. He holds her arms when she tries to sign and, for the first time in the play, she speaks. It isn't really clear speech, but an expression of passion and frustration. This is an extremely powerful scene. Start, James: "You're home from work." Sarah: "It's exciting to feel I have a job." End, Sarah: "Me have nothing. Me deafy. Speech inept. Intelligence—tiny blockhead. English—blow away. Left one you. Depend—no. Think myself enough. Join. Unjoined."

CHILDREN'S HOUR, THE
by Lillian Hellman (Dramatists Play Service)
Drama: Act III, pp. 61–64; Karen (28) and Dr. Joseph Cardin (35).
Karen's fiancé, Dr. Joseph Cardin, guiltily asks her if the allegations about her being a lesbian are true. Deeply hurt, she assures him that they aren't and then gives him the opportunity to back out of their relationship with grace. Excellent scene. Begin after Martha's exit. Start, Cardin: "You'll like Jake and he'll like you." End, Karen: "I don't think so."

COASTAL DISTURBANCES
by Tina Howe (Samuel French)
Comedy-Drama: Act I, Scene 2, pp. 20–24; Leo (28) and Holly (24).
Holly arrives at the beach to take some photographs. Leo, the lifeguard, helps her unfold her tripod, and a relationship begins. Start, Leo: "Well, well, long time, no see." End, Holly: "Or at least take some pictures of other people for a change—widen my focus for God's sake!"

Comedy-Drama: Act II, Scene 4, pp. 73–81; Holly (24) and Andre (49).
Andre, Holly's lover for the last three years, arrives at the resort for a weekend visit, hoping to patch up their relationship. Elegant and European born, Andre is the owner of an art gallery. The scene requires a tall life guard stand. If you can't believably and safely simulate the structure in class, just omit the references to it and work around it. Start, Holly: "Well, here we are again . . . the little beach where I spent all my summers as a child. It doesn't have anywhere near the sweep of Crane's where I took you yesterday, but . . . Are you O.K.?" End, Holly: "I just . . . can't."

COME BACK, LITTLE SHEBA
by William Inge (Samuel French)
Drama: Act I, Scene 2, pp. 33–38; Lola (39) and Doc (mid-40s).
In this short scene, Lola wants to talk about the early years of their relationship, but Doc, her husband, doesn't. Start, Lola: "I love to watch you shuffle cards, Daddy. You use your hands so gracefully. Do me one of your card tricks." End, Lola: "What are we sitting round here so serious for? . . . Let's have some music."

Drama: Act II, Scene 3, pp. 60–63; Lola (39) and Doc (mid-40s).
Doc comes home drunk and abusive. He verbally destroys Lola and then threatens her with a hatchet. Start, Lola: "Mr. Anderson? Mr. Anderson, this is Mrs. Delaney again." End, Doc: "Lola . . . my pretty Lola."

Drama: Act II, Scene 4, pp. 73–76; Lola (39) and Doc (mid-40s).
Doc arrives home after drying out, humbled and quiet. His long-suffering wife, Lola, does her best to affect an air of normality; she tells him about her dream last night and fixes him dinner. Everything is subtext. Start, Lola: "Docky!" End, Lola: "I'll fix your eggs."

CRIMES OF THE HEART
by Beth Henley (Dramatists Play Service)
Comedy-Drama: Act I, pp. 26–29; Barnett (26) and Meg (27).
Barnett meets Babe's older sister, Meg, for first time. Meg is concerned about his qualifications to defend Babe. Barnett then tells Meg that he excelled in law school; furthermore, he has a personal vendetta against Zachary, the man Babe shot. Start, Barnett: "How do you do?" End, Barnett: "Goodbye".
Comedy-Drama: Act II, pp. 34–38; Babe (24) and Barnett (26).
This is the first in-depth interview between lawyer and client. Barnett has a secret crush on Babe. Start, Barnett: "Mmm-huh! Yes! I see, I see!" End, Babe: "Goodbye, Barnett."
Comedy-Drama: Act II, pp. 49–51; Meg (27) and Doc (early 30s).
Meg meets her former flame again, and that old feeling still exists. This scene contains plenty of subtext. Start, Meg: "I feel like hell." End, Meg: "Yeah—forget the glasses. Forget the goddam glasses."

CROSSING DELANCEY
by Susan Sandler (Samuel French)
Comedy: Act II, pp. 39–43; Bubbie (80s) and Sam (early 30s).
Bubbie is a Jewish grandmother with one foot still in the old country. She has employed a matchmaker to cook up a romance for her unmarried granddaughter, Isabelle, but the young woman isn't interested. Bubbie tells the matchmaker's choice, Sam, that he is going to have to pursue Isabelle with more fervor if he wants to win her heart. Sam is more than willing. You'll need a doorbell to ring. Start, Bubbie: "In that corner." End, Bubbie: "Who invited her?"
Comedy: Act II, pp. 60–63; Isabelle (late 20s) and Tyler (early 40s).
Isabelle has become infatuated with Tyler, a romantic novelist who frequents the bookstore where she works. In some fairly unsubtle ways, she has let him know that she is interested in him. In this scene, Isabelle and Tyler are alone for the first time in a romantic setting. She quickly discovers that he primarily wants to go to bed with her, that he is a smooth-talking fast mover. She then tells him to kiss off. Start, Isabelle: "You put on a new hat, you become a new person." End, Isabelle: "There's an old Yiddish expression my Bubbie taught me—quite appropriate here—kush mir in tuchas."
Comedy: Act II, pp. 63–68; Isabelle (late 20s) and Sam (early 30s).
Sam and Isabelle's introduction was arranged by a matchmaker, but she has resisted such an old-world custom. Even though Sam has charmingly pursued her, Isabelle has had her sights fixed on a romantic novelist who frequents the bookstore where she works. Earlier this evening, Isabelle stood Sam up, opting for dinner with the novelist, a date that turned into disaster when he was too sexually aggressive. Now, hat in hand, Isabelle returns to her grandmother's apartment and discovers that Sam has been waiting for her all this time. By the end of the scene, love blooms, and they are in each other's arms. A very sweet and romantic 5-page scene. Start, Isabelle: "I didn't think you'd still be here." End, Isabelle: "It's all right."

CRUCIBLE, THE
by Arthur Miller (Dramatists Play Service)
Drama: Act I, Scene 2, pp. 27–31; Elizabeth Proctor (25–32) and John Proctor (mid-30s).
At first, this appears to be a scene of domestic tranquillity in the Puritan community, but it turns out that John committed adultery with young Abigail Williams several months ago and,

although he has confessed and asked for forgiveness, Elizabeth is still madly jealous. Abigail and a group of other young women and girls have accused some local citizens of being witches, and trials are underway in Salem. Elizabeth wants John to go to Salem and discredit Abigail, which he could easily do, but he resists because he doesn't want his adultery to become public knowledge. From Elizabeth's perspective, of course, it appears that John is still lusting after Abigail and simply doesn't want to hurt her. Start, Elizabeth: "What keeps you so late? It's almost dark." End, Proctor: "Oh, Elizabeth, your justice would freeze beer."
Drama: Act II, Scene 1, pp. 48–51; Abigail Williams (17) and John Proctor (mid-30s).
It is the night before Elizabeth Proctor's trial for the charge of practicing witchcraft. Here in the woods near Salem, John Proctor is meeting urgently with Abigail Williams, his former lover and the young woman who is responsible for Elizabeth's arrest. He warns Abigail that if she doesn't recant, he is prepared to announce publicly in court that they've been lovers and that she is motivated by jealousy. Furthermore, John claims to have documented evidence that Abigail knew all along that Elizabeth isn't a witch; he is ready to present this in court, too. Abigail, reacting with furious defiance, challenges him to carry out his threat. Start, Proctor: "I must speak with you, Abigail." End, Abigail: ". . . From yourself I will save you."
Drama: Act II, Scene 3, pp. 84–86; Elizabeth Proctor (25–32) and John Proctor (mid-30s).
John is sentenced to hang for being a witch. He can save his own life only by admitting that he is under control of the devil. In this short, emotional scene, he tells his pregnant wife, Elizabeth, that he has decided to confess and to tell the judges what they want to hear so that he can live. She responds that whatever his choice, she can't be his judge because she has sinned, too. Had she been a good and loving wife in the first place, John wouldn't have been tempted to enter into adultery with Abigail. This is a very difficult scene, played out almost literally on the gallows steps. Start, Elizabeth: "You have been chained?" End, Proctor: ". . . Good then, it is evil, and I do it!"

DANNY AND THE DEEP BLUE SEA
by John Patrick Shanley (Dramatists Play Service) [*13 by Shanley* (Applause Books)]
Drama: Scene 1, DPS pp. 12–19; Roberta (31) and Danny (29).
Danny and Roberta meet in a Bronx bar and, despite their hostile, defensive façades, are attracted to one another. They talk across the room, she moves to his table, they talk some more and, finally, they go to her place for the night. Danny tells Roberta that he thinks he killed a man, and she confesses to him that she had sex with her father when she was a child. This is a difficult scene because the characters are alternately vile and kind to one another. Start, Roberta: "You ever been in jail?" End, Roberta: "Come on. Let's get outta here. Let's go home."
Drama: Scene 2, DPS pp. 23–32; Roberta (31) and Danny (29).
After Danny and Roberta make love, their defenses begin to slowly crumble. It is hard, very hard, for Roberta and Danny to accept love or kindness. He asks her to marry him. Start, Roberta: "I went to the deli this mornin' to get a roll. Chinese guy put it in the bag." End, Danny: "Are you asleep? I love you."
Drama: Scene 3, DPS pp. 32–39; Roberta (31) and Danny (29).
In the cold light of day, the tenderness of the night before embarrasses Roberta, and she climbs back inside herself, trying to reject Danny. He refuses to be unkind, saying he meant everything he said last night and still wants to marry her. Finally, Roberta moves toward Danny. Start, Roberta: "Tag!" End, Danny: "Yeah. I do. I definitely definitely think I do."

DARK AT THE TOP OF THE STAIRS, THE
by William Inge (Dramatists Play Service)
Drama: Act I, pp. 22–28; Rubin (36) and Cora (34).
This scene features an emotionally and physically abusive fight between a husband and a wife. Rubin, struggling to makes financial ends meet, is furious when he discovers that Cora has

secretly bought an expensive party dress for their daughter, Reenie. The argument escalates when Cora accuses him of fooling around with other women during his business trips. Rubin slaps her and storms out. Omit Reenie's brief interruption of their fight. Start, Rubin: "What the hell's been goin' on behind my back?" End, Cora: "I'll never forget what you've said. Never! Don't you ever come back in this house again!"

DAYS OF WINE AND ROSES
by J. P. Miller (Dramatists Play Service)
Drama: Act III, pp. 45–48; Joe (36) and Kristen (30).
Joe has been sober for almost a year, has a steady job, and is pulling himself and Debbie, his young daughter, out of the gutter. His wife, Kristen, unexpectedly appears at the apartment one night when Debbie is asleep; Kristen asks Joe to take her back, telling him that she hasn't had a drink in two days. Although he longs for her, he realizes that, as long as she in denial about her alcoholism, the relationship will be impossible. He refuses. Start, Kristen: "Debbie asleep?" Continue to the the end of the play. End, Joe: "God—grant me the serenity to accept the things I cannot change."

DEATH AND THE MAIDEN
by Ariel Dorfman (Penguin)
Drama: Act II, Scene 1; Paulina (40) and Gerardo (45).
Paulina is convinced that Roberto is her former torturer. She tells her husband, Gerardo, that she intends to put the man, who is tied up in the living room, "on trial." Eliminate the short section when Paulina goes to Roberto, tightens his bonds, and speaks to him. Start, Gerardo: "What are you trying to do? What are you trying to do, woman, with these insane acts?" End, Gerardo: "No need to smile at him but basically yes, that is what we have to do. And start to live, yes."
Drama: Act III, Scene 1; Paulina (40) and Gerardo (45).
Paulina agrees to tell Gerardo the truth about the details of her captivity and torture 15 years ago if he'll tell her the truth about a woman she found in his bed. Start, Paulina: "I don't understand why." End, Paulina: "That's when I met Doctor Miranda."

DEATH OF BESSIE SMITH, THE
by Edward Albee (Plume)
Drama: Scene 2; Nurse (26) and Father (55).
Both father and daughter are southern racists. They argue about who is going to have use of the car. The daughter, who is a nurse, wants to use it to drive to work, and the father wants to use it to go down to the Democratic Club and hang out with the other politicos. A nasty duo. Start, Father: "Stop it! Stop it! Stop it!" End, Father: "And don't you stay out there all night in his car, when you get back. You hear me? You hear me?"
Drama: Scene 4; Nurse (26) and Orderly (28).
The white nurse is a racist, and the African-American orderly is trying to improve himself. In this rough scene, he talks about what he hopes to do in life, and she shoots him down, accusing him of bleaching his skin so that he'll be more acceptable to whites. The nurse has a very foul mouth. Start, Orderly: "The mayor of Memphis! I went into his room and there he was; the mayor of Memphis." End, Nurse: "Yes'm . . . yes'm . . . ha, ha, ha! You white niggers kill me."
Drama: Scene 6; Nurse (26) and Intern (30).
The intern has been trying unsuccessfully for some time to get the nurse into bed, but she continues to tease him. In this scene, he presses his case, and she cruelly reminds him that he can't afford her on an intern's salary. They argue about politics, she insults him again, and he remarks that he is probably the only under-60 white man in the vicinity who hasn't had sex with her. After the nurse threatens to have the intern fired, she backs off, instructing him instead to court her. This difficult scene is appropriate for experienced actors. Start,

Nurse: "Well, how is the Great White Doctor this evening?" End, Intern: "You impress me. No matter what else, I have to admit that."

DELICATE BALANCE, A
by Edward Albee (Samuel French)
Drama: Act II, Scene 1, pp. 36–39; Julia (36) and Tobias (early 60s).
Julia's fourth marriage is on the rocks, and she has returned to her parents' home. Tensions that usually run high here are exacerbated by the strange presence of family friends Harry and Edna in the upstairs bedroom. Like a couple of adversarial and wary woods animals, Julia and Tobias, her father, talk about these events. Start, Tobias: "What was that . . . all about?" End, Tobias: "Your brother would not have grown up to be a fag."
Drama: Act III, pp. 68–73; Agnes (late 50s) and Tobias (early 60s).
Because all the guest bedrooms are full of visitors, both welcome and unwelcome, Tobias had to sleep with his wife, Agnes, last night. This morning, they discuss the implications, and Agnes presses Tobias to make a decision regarding the guests. Begin at the top of Act III. Start, Agnes: "Ah, there you are." End, Agnes: "I don't know. I'm listening."
Drama: Act III, pp. 73–76; Agnes (late 50s) and Tobias (early 60s).
In this continuation of the preceding scene, Agnes and Tobias talk about the death of their infant son 34 years ago and how the event altered their sex life. Start, Agnes: "Well, isn't that nice that Julia's making coffee? No?" End, Agnes: "Whatever you like. Naturally."

DIVISION STREET
by Steve Tesich (Samuel French)
Comedy: Act I, pp. 23–27; Sal (30s) and Dianah (30s).
Sal is Dianah's nebbish Legal Aid Society lawyer. An unassertive man most people ignore, Sal is desperately in love with Dianah, but she still has eyes only for her estranged husband, Chris. Here, Sal declares his undying love while Dianah carries on about Chris and how great their life was during the 1960s radical movement. Both characters have good comic monologues in this scene. Start, Dianah: "Chris! Chris! Chris!" End, Sal: "Hurt me! I don't care!"
Comedy: Act I, pp. 39–43; Chris (37) and Nadja (19).
Nadja the slut shows up a Chris's apartment, mistaking him for a john. They share their stories and are attracted to each other. You'll need an actor to play dead on the floor the whole time. Start, Chris: "I'm coming." End, Nadja: "Well, I will not be a whore. I'm a slut."

DOES A TIGER WEAR A NECKTIE?
by Don Petersen (Dramatists Play Service)
Drama: Act I, Scene 2, pp. 34–42; Linda (18) and Conrad (20).
Linda and Conrad have just finished having sex in a midnight session on the floor of Mr. Winter's office. In this postcoital scene, they talk about the future. Conrad hopes to kick his drug habit, but Linda is more cynical, looking at a short life as a junkie hooker. As the scene progresses, they become more polarized while, at the same time, they experience a true "connection." Eliminate Tonto's interruption. Start, Conrad: "Baby, if old Pete could see us now, he'd flip." End, Linda: "You keep 'em! The trick was on the house. I don't want your cigarettes . . . or nothing else you got!"

DOLL'S HOUSE, A
by Henrik Ibsen [a new version by Christopher Hampton (Samuel French)]
Drama: Act I, pp. 28–34; Nora (25–35) and Krogstad (35–45).
Krogstad threatens to blackmail Nora with the loan document that she has forged her father's name on. Start, Krogstad: "Excuse me, Mrs. Helmer. . . ." End, Krogstad: "But I'm telling you one thing: If I'm thrown out again, you're coming with me."

Drama: Act II, pp. 49–53; Nora (25–35) and Doctor Rank (58–65).
Nora is going to ask longtime family friend, Doctor Rank, for a secret loan so that she can pay off her blackmailer. Before she can ask, however, Doctor Rank tells her that he has always loved her. With that knowledge, she can't ask for the money. Start, Nora: "Good afternoon, Dr. Rank. I knew it was you by the way you rang." End, Nora: "Oh no, Dr. Rank dear, I didn't mean it like that. But I'm sure you understand that with Torvald it's just like it was with Daddy."

Drama: Act II, pp. 56–59; Nora (25–35) and Krogstad (35–45).
Krogstad, now formally fired from the bank, is bent on revenge and determined to follow through with his blackmail threat unless Nora intercedes immediately on his behalf with her husband. Start, Nora: "Keep your voice down. My husband's in there." End, Krogstad: "I will never forgive him for that. Good-bye, Mrs. Helmer."

Drama: Act III, pp. 79–91; Nora (25–35) and Helmer (35–45).
The play's final, climactic confrontation. Krogstad had followed through on his threat to tell Helmer about Nora's illegal loan, and she has defended her action by telling him that she borrowed the money to pay for his medical care after a terrible illness. If she hadn't found a way to borrow the money on her own, he surely would have died. Still, rather than subject her husband to public shame, Nora is prepared to commit suicide.

As Helmer continues to berate her, Nora realizes that it makes no difference to him what her motives were. He is furious with her for jeopardizing his good image and standing. Nora also realizes that she has terribly misjudged this man—and herself. Calmly, she changes clothes, dressing for travel, and when Helmer notices a difference in her manner, he falls silent. Nora tells him that she is leaving him and her children. Before he can protest, Nora turns and walks out, determined to experience independence and find self-respect. Start, Helmer: "Nora!" End, Helmer: "Nora! Nora! Empty. She's gone. The most wonderful miracle. . . ."

DRAMA

by Anton Chekhov [*The Sneeze, Plays and Other Stories* by Anton Chekhov, translated and adapted by Michael Frayn (Samuel French)]
Comedy: One-act play, pp. 22–30; Pavel Vasilyevich (35–50) and Murashkina (25–50).
In this 8-page play, Pavel Vasilyevich wants to be nice to the woman who shows up on his doorstep because, after all, she is an avid admirer of his writing. But Murashkina has written a drama and wants his feedback on its merits. Refusing to leave it for him to read later, she begins to read it aloud. At first Pavel is patient, but when she continues to read the quite-awful material, he becomes increasingly distraught. Finally, when Murashkina won't stop, he takes out a knife and kills her. Start, Murashkina: "Such an admirer! Every book, every play! Such a talent!" End, Pavel: "Nice twist at the end, though."

DREAM GIRL

by Elmer Rice (Dramatists Play Service)
Comedy: Act I, pp. 25–30; Georgina Allerton (23) and Clark Redfield (28).
Clark Redfield sells a few review copies of some books to Georgina Allerton at the Mermaid Bookshop. She is both attracted to and repelled by him; eventually, however, her hate-at-first-sight turns into love. Clark says that he has finished reading the novel she wrote, and it is awful. This criticism outrages her. Omit the telephone call Georgina places to her mother. Start, Clark: "Good morning, Miss Allerton." End, Georgina: "You great big ape!"

DRESSER, THE

by Ronald Harwood (Samuel French)
Drama: Act II, pp. 60–63; Sir (about 60) and Her Ladyship (50s).
During an act break of *King Lear,* Her Ladyship talks to Sir in his dingy dressing room. She implores the increasingly frail man to retire and to make the announcement after that night's

performance, but he won't entertain the notion. They speak of their relationship, having lived together for years as husband and wife without the benefit of marriage. In fact, Sir has never obtained a divorce from his first wife, probably because he didn't want to jeopardize his chances for knighthood. Start, Sir: "Is it my cue?" End, Sir: "I shall never forgive them for what they wrote about me."

DUET FOR ONE
by Tom Kempinski (Samuel French)
Drama: Act I, Session 1, pp. 1–8; Stephanie Abrahams (33) and Dr. Feldmann (45–60).
World-famous violinist Stephanie Abrahams was diagnosed with multiple sclerosis seven months ago. Now deprived of the defining skill in her life, she has become depressed and suicidal. Here, Stephanie meets Dr. Feldmann, a psychiatrist, and tries to cover her pain with airs, humor, and other diversions, but he isn't fooled. Dr. Feldmann has a slight German accent. Stephanie is in a wheelchair almost all the time. Written in the British vernacular. Start, Feldmann: (offstage) "Mrs. Liebermann." End, Stephanie: "Well, good-bye, and thank you."

DYLAN
by Sidney Michaels (Samuel French)
Drama: Act I, pp. 11–20; Caitlin (mid-30s) and Dylan (38).
Caitlin doesn't want Dylan to go on the scheduled lecture-tour of the United States. She is afraid that he'll spend his money on liquor and his time with other women, and that he'll burn out as an artist. What is worse, she'll be left in Wales to care for their three young children—with no money. Dylan speaks with an English accent, while Caitlin has an Irish accent. Start, Caitlin: "So here you are, you scum." End, Caitlin: "Oh, Dylan, Dylan—Hurry up!"
Drama: Act II, pp. 52–59; Meg (mid-20s) and Dylan (38).
Meg is educated, responsible, attractive, and not the least charmed by Dylan's little-boy-lost persona. Or is she? In this scene, which takes place at 4:30 A.M. in Meg's Greenwich Village apartment, she tends to a quite-drunk Dylan. He is bloodied from a random fight, looks sloppy, and is soaking wet from standing in the rain. As Meg undresses Dylan, he makes haphazard romantic passes. As he sobers up a bit, they discuss his sad financial status, the unhappy state of his marriage, and his lack of artistic output. She gives him some hard-nosed advice. Then they go to bed together. The scene calls for a practical bathtub. You can get around that by eliminating reference to it and simply having Meg undress Dylan to dry his clothes. Also, you'll need an offstage telephone to ring. Start, Dylan: "The sky's divorced! The weather's go boom. What are we doing? Who am I?" End, Meg: "There are needs in this world that have nothing to do with love, and marriages that never get recorded in a court house. Happy birthday, Dylan."

EASTERN STANDARD
by Richard Greenberg (Dramatists Play Service)
Comedy: Act I, Scene 2, pp. 13–19; Phoebe (late 20s) and Peter (30s).
Phoebe meets her brother, Peter, for lunch in a Manhattan restaurant. During the meal, she tells him about her failing romance with a charming investment banker who is in trouble with the law. Peter tells her that he is dying of AIDS. The scene isn't as heavy as it sounds. Cut the few lines involving the waitress. Start, Peter: "I'm sorry, sweetheart, it's been a mess." End, Peter: "Nobody ever looked at me without thinking I'd live forever."

ECCENTRICITIES OF A NIGHTINGALE, THE
by Tennessee Williams (Dramatists Play Service)
Drama: Act I, Scene 1, pp. 11–13; Alma Winemiller (25–29) and John Buchanan (25–29).
This later version of *Summer and Smoke* takes place during a Fourth of July celebration in Glorious Hill, Mississippi, just before World War I. Alma, the high-strung daughter of the

local Episcopal minister, has just performed a song before the celebratory crowd. What is really on her mind, however, is seeing John, the next-door boy she has loved from afar all these years. In this scene, Alma and John sit near the fountain and catch up. He has finished medical school and will soon leave for Cuba on a grand adventure to fight some mysterious epidemic—and to meet some senoritas, the "caviar among females." Start, John: "Hello, Miss Alma." End, Alma: "Be careful you don't get caught. They say that the tropics are a perfect quagmire. People go there and never are heard of again!"

Drama: Act I, Scene 2, pp. 15–20; Alma Winemiller (25–29) and Rev. Winemiller (60s).
Rev. Winemiller, Alma's father, is concerned about his daughter's ever-more-apparent eccentricities, and he urges her to control them. Start, Rev. Winemiller: "Actually, we have about the same number of communicants we're had for the past ten years." End, Alma: "I can't breathe!" For a shorter version, start, Rev. Winemiller: "Alma. Sit down for a moment. There's something I want to talk to you about." Continue to the same end.

Drama: Act II, Scene 1, pp. 29–32; Mrs. Buchanan (50–60) and John Buchanan (25–29).
Mrs. Buchanan, John's doting mother, tries to steer him away from any involvement with Alma, warning him that she is an eccentric—one of those odd people you'll find in almost any southern town. Start, Mrs. Buchanan: "Son?" End, Mrs. Buchanan: "Heavens, yes, that's a story, but it's too long for bedtime. Good night, my precious! Sleep tight!"

Drama: Act II, Scene 3, pp. 38–43; Alma Winemiller (25–29) and John Buchanan (25–29).
Alma is having a panic attack and goes next door to John's house at 2 A.M. to get some medicine. He lowers the lights and gives her some brandy, and she settles down. He unbuttons her blouse to listen to her heart and diagnoses her as "lonely." This makes her angry, and she tells him off for being condescending. John then invites Alma to go to the movies the next day. This is a pretty intense scene for Alma, and it ends with an oblique hint of future sexual activity between them. Eliminate Mrs. Buchanan's lines. Start, John: "Why, it's you, Miss Alma!" End, John: "I'll take you to see Mary Pickford at the Delta Brilliant tomorrow."

Drama: Act III, Scene 1, pp. 44–49; Alma Winemiller (25–29) and John Buchanan (25–29).
Alma behaves in a fashion she never would have in *Summer and Smoke*. She is quite aggressive with John, openly inviting him to go to a hotel room "you rent by the hour." Start, Alma: "God." End, Alma: "Give me something to guarantee your return!"

Drama: Act III, Scene 2, pp. 49–53; Alma Winemiller (25–29) and John Buchanan (25–29).
A terrific scene that takes place on New Year's Eve in a cheap hotel room. At first, the fireplace won't light, and the romantic adventure seems to be a flop. Then the fire springs to life, and the scene ends with Alma and John moving toward the bed. Start, John: "Here it is, the room is cold." End, John: "No one has ever been able to answer that question."

ECHOES
by N. Richard Nash (Samuel French)
Drama; Sam (25–35) and Tilda (20–25).
Echoes is a two-act, two-character drama that takes place in a single room in a mental institution. Sam and Tilda move continually in and out of reality, playing pretend games and fighting pretend enemies. Editing this material for scene work is challenging but worthwhile. For a 6-page scene, begin at the top of Act I (pp. 5–11). Here, Sam and Tilda wake up in the morning and decorate an imaginary Christmas tree. Tilda talks to herself, a problem that they discuss, and Sam hears someone call him a name. Start, Tilda: "Sam! . . . Sammy! . . . Sa-mu-el! Sammy—please—wake up!" End, Sam: "There are only two of us! Who the hell can I blame?! I don't know his name any better than I know my own."

For another 6-page excerpt, begin shortly after the preceding dialogue ends (pp. 11–17). After Sam and Tilda talk about names, she wants to play teacher. He resists because he is a real teacher. Then Tilda tries to break the imaginary window that she sees her unwanted reflection in. Next, they play imaginary baseball. Start, Tilda: "I wish we didn't have any fixed names." End, Tilda: "There's still nobody there . . . except me."

Another option is to begin in Act I where Tilda sings "Take Me Out to the Ballgame" and climbs to place the angel on top of the imaginary tree (pp. 35–41). Once there, she becomes transfixed. Start, Tilda: "Is she on all right?" End, Sam: "Help me! Hey, you—Person!" This excerpt runs about six pages, and the following scene from Act II runs about seven pages long. Begin at the top of the act as Tilda tries to wake up Sam (pp. 43–50). She pretends to take off her clothes, and he touches her cheek in a gentle moment. Tilda then tells Sam about her bad dream, in which he was talking to "The Person" (the doctor)—but it wasn't a dream at all. Sam and Tilda then talk of death and the illusion of communication, as well as play with echoes. Sam is beginning to have real difficulty staying with Tilda in the "pretend" world. Start, Tilda: "Good morning! Good morning, Sammy!" End, Tilda: "I'm sorry, Sam."

Act II provides other opportunities. In a 5-page dialogue, Sam has heard the doctor call a name and is trying to figure out what it means (pp. 50–55). Tilda is increasingly desperate to keep Sam in their "pretend" world, but he is having trouble staying there. She pretends to watch television, but he doesn't. Start, Sam: "Jess!" End, Sam: "I don't know."

A longer, 7-page scene in Act II is another choice (pp. 61–68). Here, Sam has just finished talking to the doctor again and is reporting what he said to Tilda. The doctor told Sam about his wife and 3-year-old son and said he'll soon be allowed to visit with them. More than anything, Tilda doesn't want Sam to leave her, but that is exactly what happens as the curtain falls. Start, Sam: "You were right. He didn't answer any of the big questions. About God." End, Tilda: ". . . Mama! . . . Ma-ma! . . . Ma-ma!"

EDUCATING RITA
by Willy Russell (Samuel French)
Comedy: Act I, Scene 5, pp. 22–27; Rita (26) and Frank (50s).
This is the first major transition in the play. Last night, when Rita's husband discovered that she is secretly going to school, he burned her books. She arrives for her regular tutorial session with Frank, and they connect on a deeper level than before. She talks him into going with her to a movie. Written in the British vernacular. Start, Frank: "You know, this is getting to be a bit wearisome." End, Rita: "Don't go spoilin' it for me."
Comedy: Act II, Scene 7, pp. 50–52; Rita (26) and Frank (50s).
Almost a year has gone by since Rita began studying with Frank, and they know each other pretty well, though not romantically. Because of his drinking, he is being exiled to the university system in Australia and, as the 2-page final scene begins, is packing his stuff. Rita arrives to tell Frank that she has developed a deeper appreciation for him and his values. He invites her to go to Australia with him. Maybe she will, and maybe she won't. Before she does anything else, she gives him a symbolic (as in quick surface change) haircut. He sits down, and she begins. Written in the British vernacular. Start, Rita: "Merry Christmas, Frank. Have they sacked y'?" End, Frank: "Ouch!"

EMPRESS OF CHINA
by Ruth Wolff (Broadway Play Publishing)
Drama: Act I; Tsu-Hsi (60s) and Jung Lu (60s).
Tsu-Hsi's long-banished former lover, soldier Jung Lu, has returned to warn the empress about a spirit of rebellion in the land and urges her to stop it. Start, Jung Lu: "Empress." End, Jung Lu: "The day you cease to be in power will be the day you cease to live."
Drama: Act I; Tsu-Hsi (60s) and Kang Yu-Wel (30s).
Kuang-Hsu, the ineffectual emperor, has issued a series of edicts that are heavily influenced by his activist tutor, Kang Yu-Wel. When Tsu-Hsi reads them, she flies into a fury, not only

because this was done behind her back, but because the clear intent of the rulings is to embrace western culture. She summons the tutor and, in this scene, they battle over the wisdom of the papers. Finally, Tsu-Hsi signs an order banishing Kang Yu-Wel from the country. Start, Tsu-Hsi: "I have read—the Emperor's—new edicts. They are immensely edifying." End, Tsu-Hsi: "From the moment you leave my sight, your life is in peril! Go!"

ENTER LAUGHING
by Joseph Stein (Samuel French)
Comedy: Act I, Scene 5, pp. 24–28; David (20) and Angela (28–32).
David is definitely smelling the greasepaint and anticipating the roar of the crowd when he comes to sexy Angela's theater dressing room to rehearse their big scene. He is dazzled by her relaxed sensuality and jaded glamour; she is bemused by his youth and innocence. He is a very young 20, while she is a fully-seasoned 28. An extremely funny scene. Start, Angela: "Entrez!" End, David: "'You're a better man than I am, Gunga Din!'"

EVERYTHING IN THE GARDEN
by Edward Albee [adapted from the play by Giles Cooper (Dramatists Play Service)]
Drama: Act I, Scene 2, pp. 28–35; Jenny (late 30s) and Richard (43).
Jenny has secretly begun working as a high-priced prostitute and is making good money. She mails a bundle of cash to her husband from an "anonymous" donor. He is shocked by this blessing from heaven but, with her encouragement, agrees to keep the money and not take it to the police. Begin at the top of Act I, Scene 2. Start, Jenny: "Hello." End, Jenny: "Call it five thousand even; sounds so much nicer."
Drama: Act I, Scene 2, pp. 41–47; Jenny (late 30s) and Richard (43).
Richard discovers that Jenny, his very respectable wife, is working as a hooker. This powerful scene provides plenty of fun for actors who want to chew the scenery. Begin after Jack's exit. Start, Jenny: "Is Jack gone?" End, Richard: ". . . men kill their wives for this sort of thing!" Jenny: "Oh, darling."

EXTREMITIES
by William Mastrosimone (Samuel French)
Drama: Act I, Scene 1, pp. 8–15; Marjorie (25–30) and Raul (30–45).
This very physical scene centers on an attempted rape, which begins with a psychological cat-and-mouse-style pursuit and then turns violent. At the last minute, Marjorie gets the upper hand: she sprays poison in the face of Raul, her attacker, and then ties him up. Actors need to be careful with blocking. Start, Raul: "Joe? Hey, Joe? It's me. O. How ya doin'? Joe in?" Stop when Marjorie sprays insecticide in his face. End, Marjorie: "Just for you!"
Drama: Act I, Scene 3, pp. 18–24; Marjorie (25–30) and Raul (30–45).
Raul is tied up in the fireplace, blindfolded, and in pain from the insecticide Marjorie sprayed in his eyes when he tried to rape her. She tries to find out how he knows her name and so many details of her life. She becomes increasingly violent toward him. Here, the victim becomes the victimizer. Start, Raul: "Where am I? Marjorie? Where am I?" End, Marjorie: "Talk again and I smash you like a fuckin' bug!"

FALLEN ANGELS
by Noel Coward (Samuel French)
Comedy: Act III, pp. 46–51; Julia (late 20s) and Willy (30s).
When Willy returns early from his golf weekend, he discovers that his wife, Jane, isn't at home, so he goes to see if she is with her friend Julia. Julia and Jane had a terrible fight last night, however, and Julia is jealous and convinced that Jane is somewhere with Maurice, the handsome Frenchman. Julia tells Willy everything about the women's respective pre-marriage

romances with Maurice. Willy is stunned to learn that his wife might be having an affair at this very moment. Start, Willy: "Good morning, Julia." End, Julia: "I don't care if she's feeling heavenly, she won't be when I'm finished with her."

FAR COUNTRY, A
by Henry Denker (Samuel French)
Drama: Act II, Scene 2, pp. 61–66; Elizabeth (20s) and Freud (37).
Under Freud's insistent encouragement, his patient Elizabeth recalls painful childhood events surrounding her father's illness and death. She goes from being flirtatiously happy to sobbing and dissolving into anguished hysteria. Start, Freud: "Elizabeth." End, Elizabeth: "Dead? Oh! No! Oh! No!"
Drama: Act III, pp. 71–84; Elizabeth (20s) and Freud (37).
Freud has determined that the mysterious pain and paralysis in Elizabeth's legs are caused by guilt over her love for Frederick, her brother-in-law. In this very emotional scene, she reluctantly acknowledges that she has been in love with Frederick and that she was, in fact, happy to see her sister, Charlotte, die. The guilt resulting from these feelings led to Elizabeth's phantom leg pain and made her an invalid. As Freud points out to her, the pain assured that people would think of her as "poor Elizabeth" rather than "terrible Elizabeth."

As these thoughts surface, Elizabeth cries out in anguish and discovers that she can once again walk. Begin as Freud enters his office to greet Elizabeth. Simply ignore the argument between Martha and Frederick that takes place simultaneously outside Freud's office. Start, Freud: "Good morning, Lisl—how do you feel today? No crutches today?" Stop as Elizabeth walks toward the door. End, Elizabeth: "No, let me! I've never opened that door myself." This scene runs 13 pages. For a shorter, 8-page version, begin immediately after the Martha/Frederick argument outside the door. Start, Freud: "Elizabeth! Right now—do you have a pain?" Continue to the same end.

FATHER'S DAY
by Oliver Hailey (Dramatists Play Service)
Drama: Act II, pp. 46–50; Louise (30–35) and Tom (32–38).
Louise is distraught because her 7-year-old son has chosen to live with his father in the Midwest. She makes one last futile—and pathetic—attempt to reconstruct the ideal family that never was. When Louise asks Tom to divorce his present wife and remarry her, he refuses. Start, Louise: ". . . what are you smirking about?" End, Louise: "Admitted!"

FENCES
by August Wilson (Samuel French)
Drama: Act II, Scene 1, pp. 62–68; Troy (53) and Rose (43).
Troy tells Rose, his wife, that he is going to have a child by another woman. She isn't happy to hear this. For scene-study purposes, omit Gabriel's interruption and few lines. Start, Rose: "What they say down there? What's happening with Gabe?" End, Troy: "Don't you tell that lie on me!"

FIRST BREEZE OF SUMMER, THE
by Leslie Lee (Samuel French) [*Black Thunder, An Anthology of Contemporary African American Drama* (Mentor/Penguin)]
Drama: Act I, SF pp. 15–23; Lucretia (17) and Sam (20).
This flashback sequence takes place during the late 1920s or early 1930s in the deep south. Sam, who is African American, got into an altercation with a white customer at the train station when he defended an elderly porter who had dropped some baggage. Instead of being grateful to Sam, the old fellow apologized to the white man, humiliating Sam. Determined

now to move on to the next town, he bought his girlfriend, Lucretia, a strand of imitation pearls as a going-away present. When Sam tells her he is leaving, she flies into a rage and calls him names, and he slaps her. Then they reconcile and, as the scene ends, move to the bed to make love. What he doesn't know is that she is already pregnant. Start, Lucretia: "Oh, Sam, these are lovely!—They really are!" End, Lucretia: "Sam? . . . Sam, I—I want to talk to you about . . . something."

Drama: Act I, pp. 27–29; Lucretia (17) and Sam (20).
Sam is packed to leave and is standing at the door. When Lucretia tells him that she is pregnant, he isn't happy to hear the news. He says that he'll send her his address and that when the baby comes, she should contact him. They both know, however, that this is the last time they'll see each other. This short scene is filled with emotion. Start, Lucretia: "Are you leaving now, Sam?" End, Lucretia: "Sam, I'm scared . . . all of a sudden I'm scared!"

Drama: Act I, pp. 32–35; Lucretia (18) and Briton (early 20s).
Lucretia and her child live with the southern white family she works as a domestic for. Briton, the family's adopted son, lusts for Lucretia and aggressively pursues her. She doesn't really love him; she longs to be held, even if it is by "Mr. Briton." In this scene, he pursues, and she resists. Finally, he grabs her, kisses her, and she responds. Then she pulls away as she hears the family coming home downstairs. Start, Lucretia: "Mr. Briton, I—I haven't finished my cleaning, and—and I got cooking to do." End, Briton: "Tomorrow, Lucretia, do you hear? . . . Lucretia? . . . Tomorrow! We're outcasts—okay?"

Drama: Act I, pp. 42–47; Lucretia (18) and Briton (early 20s).
When Lucretia tells Briton that she is pregnant, suddenly he isn't so affectionate with his favorite "negra." Start, Briton: "I've decided, goddammit, Lucretia! Just now, laying here with you! I'm not going back to school!" End, Lucretia: "Briton . . . don't . . . don't say no more, please?"

Drama: Act II, pp. 62–66; Lucretia (20s) and Harper (30s).
Lucretia now has two illegitimate children, and she is trying to get a husband. She has her eye set on Harper Edwards, a very shy and sexually inexperienced miner who is studying for the ministry. In this scene of chaste courtship, it is clear that she has told him she is a widow, and he already is planning on having her in his future. Start, Lucretia: "You have to go now, Harper?" End, Lucretia: "Your hat, Harper, don't forget it!"

Drama: Act II, pp. 71–73; Lucretia (20s) and Harper (30s).
In this short scene, Lucretia's lie about being a widow is about to catch up with her. On Harper's first day of preaching, a man in the congregation told Harper that he recognized Lucretia's child. When Harper confronts her, Lucretia lies again, claiming that she has never been in Roanoke. Still trusting her, Harper plans to marry her soon. Start, Lucretia: "I keep saying to myself: That's Reverend Edwards—Reverend Edwards!" End, Lucretia: "never been to Roanoke in my life—not even near it . . . wouldn't know it if I stumbled over it!"

FOB
by David Henry Hwang (Dramatists Play Service)
Comedy: Act I, Scene 1, pp. 14–19; Grace (20) and Steve (late 20s).
Grace is alone at her parents' Chinese restaurant when Steve enters, declaring that he is Gwan Gung, the Chinese god of warriors, writers, and prostitutes. To Steve's dismay, Grace seems unimpressed and sends him outside to see if anyone recognizes him. Start, Grace: "Aaaai-ya!" End, Steve: "Very well. You will learn—learn not to test the spirit of Gwan Gung."

FOOL FOR LOVE
by Sam Shepard (Dramatists Play Service)
Comedy-Drama: One-act play, pp. 8–13; May (early 30s) and Eddie (late 30s).
Eddie has found his half-sister/lover in a motel on the edge of the Mojave Desert, and he intends to take her back to their trailer home. This is the opening scene of the play, and the

fact that May and Eddie are related hasn't been revealed yet. Start, Eddie: "May, look. May? I'm not goin' anywhere. See?" End, May: "You can take it, right? You're a stuntman."

FRANKIE AND JOHNNY IN THE CLAIR DE LUNE
by Terrence McNally (Dramatists Play Service)
Comedy-Drama: Act I; Frankie (40) and Johnny (46).
Frankie and Johnny, co-workers in a greasy-spoon restaurant, have just made love for the first time. Although this two-act, two-character play has potential male/female excerpts throughout it, the scenes in Act I are more appropriate for scene-study purposes simply because they involve fewer props. One option is to begin as Frankie enters from the bathroom, having changed into a brightly colored kimono (pp. 14–21). During this scene, she good-naturedly tries to edge Johnny out the door, but he angles to stay all night. You'll need the makings of a meatloaf sandwich. Start, Frankie: "Hello." End, Johnny: "There you go."

In the next scene, Johnny bandages Frankie's finger (pp. 21–27). They're getting to know each other a little better, and they've started exchanging private information. But Frankie still wants Johnny to leave, and he is still scheming to stay. Start, Johnny: "There you go." End, Johnny: "It was a crime of passion. They were the last of the red hot lovers. We're the next."

Another good scene to work on involves a revelation (pp. 27–33). Here, Johnny tells Frankie that he loves her, and she responds by trying to reject him. Start, Frankie: "You're not from Brooklyn." End, Frankie: "Did anyone ever tell you you talk too much?"

GENIUSES
by Jonathan Reynolds (Samuel French)
Comedy: Act II, pp. 53–55; Jocko (33) and Skye (early 20s).
Skye, a former Playmate of the Year, has decided that Jocko's hostility toward her is actually veiled lust and agrees to go to bed with him even though he hasn't asked her. Jocko appreciates the gesture but declines on the grounds that she has the runs. Start, Skye: "You win. Let's go." End, Jocko: "Good night and so forth."

GINGERBREAD LADY, THE
by Neil Simon (Samuel French)
Comedy-Drama: Act I, pp. 31–36 ; Evy (43) and Lou (33).
Evy dried out for 10 weeks in a Long Island sanitarium and has been back in her apartment for just a few moments when Lou Tanner, her former lover, shows up and asks if he can move back in. Although he still pushes her buttons, Evy can't stand the thought of returning to a relationship in which she is the caretaker of this younger, rootless, needy man who is inclined to chase other women and to beat her up occasionally. Evy's better jugdment rules the day, she refuses his appeal, and Lou beats a petulant retreat. Cut and paste around Polly's slight interruption at the top of the scene. Start, Lou: "Hello, Evy." Stop with Lou's exit. End, Lou: "Probably not."
Comedy-Drama: Act II, pp. 44–49; Evy (43) and Jimmy (40).
Jimmy, Evy's flamboyant actor/friend, is morose, having just been fired from a play. Evy consoles him and pours champagne. He is horrified to see her drinking since she only recently returned home from drying out. You'll have to cut and paste a bit. Omit Jimmy's line, "Ten thousand kids a month getting drafted and they leave this one behind to produce my show." Start, Evy: "No kiss? . . . No hello?" End, Jimmy: "Some mood I'm in for a party. Christ!"

GIRL ON THE VIA FLAMINIA, THE
by Alfred Hayes (Samuel French)
Drama: Act I, pp. 27–31; Lisa (early 20s) and Robert (early 20s).
Facing dire economic prospects in war-ravaged 1944 Rome, Lisa has agreed to be kept by Robert, an American occupation soldier. This kind of arrangement was quite common at the

time, but Lisa feels cheapened by it nonetheless. In this scene, Robert and Lisa are alone in their bedroom for the first time. She explodes at him, telling him how awful Americans are, and he responds by reminding her that her country lost the war. She slaps him, and he slaps her. After they calm down, Robert apologizes, and they settle into bed, presumably to consummate their union. Lisa is Italian, so a slight accent is appropriate. Start, Robert: "It's cold. There's a big villa at Anzio. In the pine wood." Continue to the end of Act I. End, Robert: "It came all the way from America."

Drama: Act II, Scene 1, pp. 36–42; Lisa (early 20s) and Robert (early 20s).
It is the day after the "honeymoon" night, and Lisa is disgusted with herself; she is ashamed that she sold herself so cheaply. Robert enjoyed the sex but is still lonely because he knows that Lisa didn't really want to sleep with him. In this scene, they're still trying to establish the terms of their relationship, but their conversation is colored now by their forced intimacy. Start, Robert: "I bought a clock so Adele won't have to knock on the door in the morning. See? That looks almost matrimonial, doesn't it—the clock and the bed?" End, Robert: "All right. I'll go smoke a cigarette."

Drama: Act II, Scene 2, pp. 51–56; Lisa (early 20s) and Robert (early 20s).
This classic love/hate scene takes place on New Year's Eve, a night for lovers and celebration. It is clear by this point in the play that, under different circumstances, Lisa and Robert might have made a good couple, but that is never to be. Here, they talk about how they got together in the first place and what the future holds. Start, Robert: "Would you like some cognac? Ugo thinks I was overcharged for it." End, Robert: "I ought to kiss somebody a Happy New Year's."

Drama: Act III, pp. 77–81; Lisa (early 20s) and Robert (early 20s).
Unable to produce marriage documents, Lisa has been officially designated a prostitute by the Italian government and issued a yellow identification card so that she can work the streets. Robert feels bad over his part in bringing about her dilemma, but there is nothing he can do about it now. In what is probably the most powerful scene between them, Lisa and Robert act out the fantasy of what their lives would be like if they'd met under different circumstances and they were free to be in love. He tears up Lisa's identification card in this dramatic excerpt. Start, Robert: "Lisa—If there was anything I could have done, I'd have done it." End, Robert: "Then kiss him. He just came home from a tough day in the office. Kiss him."

GLASS MENAGERIE, THE
by Tennessee Williams (Dramatists Play Service)
Drama: Act I, Scene 5, pp. 28–32; Amanda (40s) and Tom (21).
Amanda tries to enlist Tom's help in finding a gentleman caller for his sister, Laura. This scene highlights the conflict between mother and son. Tom is late for work, but Amanda wants to talk. Start, Tom: "I'm sorry, mother. I'm sorry for all those things I said. I didn't mean it. I apologize." Stop with Tom's exit. End, Tom: "Yes!"

Drama: Act II, Scene 7, pp. 54–64; Laura (23) and Jim (23).
At his mother's insistence, Tom invited his co-worker Jim home for dinner. Unbeknownst to Tom, however, Amanda has made elaborate preparations for the event, seeing this as an opportunity to fix up her shy daughter, Laura, with a gentleman caller. When Jim arrives, Laura is embarrassed to recognize him as the high-school hero she had a secret crush on.

After dinner, Laura and Jim are finally alone in the parlor and, for a while, it is a very sweet meeting as the two of them replay the good old days and wax ecstatic about what a swell and talented fellow Jim was. Soon, however, he figures out that Laura is looking for a potential mate, and he awkwardly explains that he is engaged. Laura is mortified, but she covers her discomfort in ladylike fashion. This classic scene runs about 15 to 20 minutes. Start, Jim: "How are you feeling now? Any better?" End, Laura: "A—souvenir."

GOLDEN BOY
by Clifford Odets (Dramatists Play Service)
Drama: Act I, Scene 4, pp. 27–31; Lorna Moon (20–25) and Joe Bonaparte (22).
Joe Bonaparte is an exciting young boxer with a great deal of potential, but he is pulling his punches in the ring, trying to protect hands that also play the violin. His fight manager and promoters are stymied, as well as frustrated because they can't get Joe to give 100 percent. Lorna Moon, the promoter's sexy, streetwise girlfriend, volunteers to help. She intends to use her feminine wiles to convince Joe to fight. Start, Lorna: "Success and fame! Or just a lousy living." End, Joe: "I know."
Drama: Act II, Scene 2, pp. 44–48; Lorna (20–25) and Joe (22).
Joe has fallen in love with Lorna and tries to convince her to leave Tom Moody. Although she has fallen in love with Joe, her allegiance is to Moody because he got her out of the gutter. Start, Joe: "Some nights I wake up—my heart's beating a mile a minute!" End, Joe: "Poor Lorna!"

HATFUL OF RAIN, A
by Michael Vincente Gazzo (Samuel French)
Drama: Act I, Scene 1, pp. 20–26; Celia (early 20s) and Johnny (27).
Unaware that her husband has become a drug addict and fearful that he is having an affair on the nights when he isn't at home, Celia presses Johnny for an explanation about his increasingly withdrawn and erratic behavior. The truth is that he is roaming the streets at night trying to get a fix. Start, Celia: "There's no hot water, is there?" End, Celia: "The rain's stopped. I think I'd better open the windows. Everything's so damp in here."
Drama: Act I, Scene 2, pp. 30–36; Celia (early 20s) and Polo (mid-20s).
Johnny's brother, Polo, is drunk and unable to sleep. He stumbles into the kitchen to get some water. Celia is also restless because her husband is out on the street somewhere. She hears the noise in the kitchen and joins Polo. They talk about their mutual attraction for each other, and she tells him that he had better move out of the apartment before they get into trouble. Start, Celia: "Don't do that, Polo! You'll give yourself a stomach cramp." End, Polo: "I'm not Johnny, I'm Polo."
Drama: Act II, Scene 3, pp. 57–61; Celia (early 20s) and Johnny (27).
Johnny can't bring himself to confess his drug addiction to his wife, Celia. Instead, he tries to revive their relationship by surprising her with flowers and a clean apartment when she gets home from work. Celia, however, is convinced that their relationship is damaged beyond repair and that Johnny must be having an affair. She wants to separate from him even though she is pregnant. Start, Celia: "Polo." End, Celia: "No, Johnny, I'm gonna get an apron."

HEDDA GABLER
by Henrik Ibsen [translated by Christopher Hampton (Samuel French)]
Drama: Act II, pp. 37–42; Hedda Gabler (29) and Judge Brack (45).
Judge Brack is a confirmed bachelor, part of the rather wild social scene that Hedda longs for. They engage in some cat-and-mouse verbal exchanges about the kind of relationship he wants to have with her now that she is married to the very boring George Tesman. The conversation has sexual undertones, but nothing overt. Begin at the top of the act. Start, Hedda: "Hello, Judge, back again!" End, Hedda: "And the train moves on."
Drama: Act IV, pp. 95–99; Hedda Gabler (29) and Judge Brack (45).
Judge Brack knows that Hedda gave Eilert Lovborg the pistol he killed himself with. He uses that information as leverage to pursue a relationship, possibly a romantic one, with Hedda. Realizing that Brack now has power over her life, she commits suicide moments after this scene ends. Cut George and Thea's interruption of the scene. Start, Hedda: "Oh, Judge, there's such a sense of release in what Eilert Lovborg's done." End, Hedda: "Possibly."

HEIDI CHRONICLES, THE

by Wendy Wasserstein (Dramatists Play Service)

Comedy: Act I, Scene 2, pp. 13–18 (1968); Heidi (age varies) and Scoop (age varies).

Heidi, a 19-year-old volunteer for the Eugene McCarthy presidential campaign, meets Scoop Rosenbaum at a dance in New Hampshire. The Princeton dropout and underground-newspaper publisher is about her same age. When Scoop puts some intense, highly philosophical moves on her and challenges her intellectual independence, sparks fly. Heidi and Scoop leave the dance to go have sex. Actors play a wide age range, from 16 to 40, because the play spans 24 years. Start, Scoop: "Are you guarding the chips?" End, Scoop: "No. I trust them."

Comedy: Act I, Scene 5, pp. 35–40 (1977); Heidi (27ish) and Scoop (27ish).

After being involved with Heidi sexually and otherwise off and on for 10 years, Scoop is settling down and marrying Lisa. This scene takes place at their wedding reception where Heidi and Scoop find a moment alone, and he confides that despite the fact they'll never marry, he'll always love her. Heidi suffers a great deal from the loss, but she knows that their lives are taking different paths. You'll need someone offstage to announce a song and play it on a tape recorder. Start, Heidi: "Did she just say 'shake your booties, doctor?'" Continue through the end of the act. As the lights fade, Heidi and Scoop are romantically dancing to a Sam Cooke recording of "You Send Me." End, Scoop: "Honest you do. Honest you do."

Comedy: Act II, Scene 5, pp. 63–68 (1987); Heidi (37ish) and Peter (37ish).

Peter is "the best pediatrician under forty" in New York City and is running a hospital clinic for children. Heidi, his lifelong friend, pays a midnight visit to drop off a box of Christmas gifts for the young patients before leaving for Minnesota to write and teach. Peter behaves strangely, acting cold and aloof. Finally, he admits that his former lover has AIDS. Peter and Heidi talk about the value of friendship and the point of work. She then decides to stay in New York. Start, Heidi: "He seems very nice." End, Heidi: "Merry Christmas, Peter."

Comedy: Act II, Scene 6, pp. 68–75 (1989); Heidi (40) and Scoop (40).

The final scene in the play provides a summing up. Scoop sold his magazine for millions two hours ago and has dropped by Heidi's new apartment with a gift for the baby she has adopted. They talk about where they've been in their lives, where they are going, and shifting values. You'll need a baby carriage, preferably, or a bassinet. Start, Scoop: "Hello. Hello." End, Heidi: "Honest you do, honest you do, honest you do."

HELLO AND GOODBYE

by Athol Fugard (Samuel French)

Drama; Johnny (late 20s) and Hester (late 30s).

This two-character, two-act drama between a brother and a sister contains many possible scenes that expose interesting character points and contain tension. Both characters are Afrikaner, so accents are appropriate. You'll find a good scene in Act I (pp. 18–25). Here, Johnny picks up a packet of unopened mail to look for a letter from his sister, Hester. After a moment, she reenters. It becomes clear that Johnny has given up his dreams of a career and is tending to their father, who is evidently dying in the next room. Start, Hester: "What you up to?" End, Johnny: "None of you know me and you went for good. What is it this time? Why have you come back?"

Another potential scene immediately follows (pp. 25–33). In this excerpt, Johnny learns that Hester is a prostitute and that she has come home to collect her share of their father's insurance money. Start, Hester: "Must I have a reason to visit my own home?" End, Hester: "I've got a funny feeling." An excerpt in the second act doesn't contain as much hysteria and dramatic revelation as those in the last part of the play, but it is arguably better for scene work because Hester is opening boxes that contain remnants of her childhood and her family history (pp. 34–45). The revelations are more subtle and personal. If you decide to who work on this scene, keep in mind that you'll have to accumulate all of those remnants: newspapers, photographs, old dresses, shoes, and plenty of boxes and twine. Start, Hester: "Frickie—Frickie who—Must have been a relative!—Who's she?" End, Johnny: "Dear God, please let Hester find the money! . . . Any luck?"

In a later excerpt from Act II, Johnny learns that Hester has had abortions, a fact that wounds his religious sensibility even more than learning that she is a prostitute did (pp. 45–52). And Hester learns that Johnny applied to railroad school, was accepted, and just didn't go. Start, Johnny: "All those in favor of sleep hold up their hands!" End, Hester: "I couldn't stop hating and it hurts, it hurts."

HELLO OUT THERE
by William Saroyan (Samuel French)
Drama: One-act play, pp. 5–28; Young Man (25–30) and The Girl (17).
A drifter wakes up in jail after being falsely accused of rape. He then begins a relationship with the unsophisticated teenager who cooks and cleans there. Although doing the entire scene is best, you can shorten it slightly for scene purposes by eliminating all of the young woman's offstage dialogue and beginning with her entrance. Start, Young Man: "I'm lonesome. I'm as lonesome as a coyote. Hello—out there!" End, Young Man: "Now, hurry. And don't forget, if I'm not here when you come back, I'll meet you in San Francisco."

HERE WE ARE
by Dorothy Parker [*24 Favorite One-Act Plays,* edited by Bennett Cerf and Van H. Cartmell (Doubleday/Dolphin)]
Comedy; He (early 20s) and She (18–23).
This 1931 one-act comedy is only 10 pages long. Young newlyweds are on the train en route to their New York City honeymoon. He is eager to consummate the union, while she is just a little nervous about the prospect. They banter, argue, hedge, and hug, talking about everything except what is really on their minds. A cute and fun scene. Were people ever really this innocent? Start, He: "Well!" End, She: "Yes, here we are, aren't we?"

HOOTERS
by Ted Tally (Dramatists Play Service)
Comedy-Drama: Act II, Scene 3, pp. 58–61; Ronda (22) and Ricky (19).
Ronda and Ricky's friends have returned to the motel to have sex, leaving them alone on the beach. At first, they were very hostile to one another because Ronda didn't want to party in the first place, and Ricky is jealous that his buddy is scoring with the prettier woman. But as Ricky and Ronda talk, mutual respect evolves. A nice scene. Start, Ronda: "See that buoy out there?" End, Ricky: "Whatever that is in Spanish."

HOPSCOTCH
by Israel Horovitz (Dramatists Play Service)
Drama: One-act play, pp. 19–24; Elsa (30) and Will (30).
Elsa is playing hopscotch by herself in the park when Will walks up and starts talking to her. It seems at first that they don't know each other, but gradually, their true relationship unfolds. It turns out that Elsa and Will were married for a short time when they were in high school, she became pregnant, and Will ran away. But much about this unusual couple remains unexplained as their reunion becomes increasingly violent. Will pushes Elsa to the ground, kissing her, demanding that she tell him intimate details about her life and about the baby they conceived. Did she deliver the child? Did she have an abortion? Elsa won't say. Start, Will: "I'm ready to hear about this frocked and collared husband of yours . . . Do you two enjoy each other?" End, Will: "I was sure you'd . . . well . . . you'd understand."

HOTHOUSE
by Megan Terry (Samuel French)
Drama: Act II, pp. 41–47; Jody (19) and David (25).
David, an all-American Korean War vet and college student bound for a career in education wants to marry Jody and take her away from her fighting, alcoholic, abusive, uneducated family. Jody loves him but is strongly bound to her roots. In this scene, she dodges the marriage question, and they get hot for each other. Start, Jody: "I'm sorry I wasn't ready when you came." End, Jody: "I need to feel you . . . all over me . . . deep in me . . . make me real."

HOUSE OF BLUE LEAVES, THE
by John Guare (Samuel French)
Comedy: Act I, pp. 9–15; Artie (45) and Bunny (late 30s).
Bunny excitedly bursts into Artie's apartment at 4:45 A.M., rousing him to go see the Pope pass by in a parade. Artie is depressed because his songs bombed during Amateur Night at the El Dorado Bar & Grill last night. Both actors need to have a good feel for New York regional speech patterns. Start, Bunny: "You know what your trouble is? You got no sense of history." End, Bunny: "And I'm sorry last night went sour."

HOUSE OF RAMON IGLESIA, THE
by José Rivera (Samuel French)
Drama: Act II, Scene 1, pp. 57–61; Javier (22) and Caroline (28).
Now that Javier is a college graduate and is about to pursue the American Dream, he intends to leave his Puerto Rican background behind him—and this includes his old girlfriend, Caroline. In this scene, he tells her about his decision, hurting her deeply. Start, Caroline: "Hi." End, Javier: "Here I come Dad—again!"

HURLYBURLY
by David Rabe (Samuel French)
Drama: Act II, Scene 1, pp. 104–111; Bonnie (late 30s) and Eddie (mid-30s).
Eddie fixed Bonnie up with Phil, who just signed his divorce papers today, thinking that the two of them would happily go have sex. Once out in the car, however, Phil exploded and shoved Bonnie out of the moving vehicle. Furious and bruised, Bonnie storms back to tell off Eddie for putting her in such jeopardy. Eddie, already drunk, is unfazed by her dilemma. This is a full-throttle, brakes-off scene for Bonnie. Start, Bonnie: "You know, Eddie, how come you gotta put me at the mercy of such a creep for?" End, Eddie: "For myself."
Drama: Act III, Scene 1, pp. 128–137; Darlene (30s) and Eddie (mid-30s).
Darlene tells Eddie about an abortion she had seven years ago, and how she didn't know which of two men was the father. Eddie, who is already upset, is further depressed by this news and is soon talking about how his sadistic minister father beat him as a child. At the end of the scene, Eddie receives word that his best friend, Phil, has been killed in a car crash on Mulholland Drive. If you can stand all the gloom, you'll find that this is a good, tight scene with plenty of subtext. Start, Eddie: "Let's just hang around a little in case he calls." End, Eddie: "What?"

HUSBANDRY
by Patrick Tovat (Samuel French)
Drama: Scene 2, pp. 21–29; Harry (37) and Dee (55).
Dee gets a little drunk and tells her son, Harry, how rough it has been to keep the family farm going. She hints that he should take it over. Start, Harry: "Hey, what are you doin' up at this hour?" End, Harry: "I'll go down there, Ma, and you go up . . . and sleep well . . . I love you, Ma . . . even when I don't know what the dickens to do."

Drama: Scene 2, pp. 46–52; Harry (37) and Bev (34).
Bev argues with her husband, Harry, about the wisdom of taking over his parents' farm. She wants to get back to New York City immediately because she just found out that their daughter, Sadie, has gotten sick. Start, Bev: "Why didn't you get me up?" End, Bev: "If you can't understand why I have to go . . . I'll go without you. I'm going up."

I AM A CAMERA
by John Van Druten (Dramatists Play Service)
Drama: Act II, Scene 1, pp. 40–42; Sally (20s) and Christopher (20s).
This scene is short on conflict but long on mood. Sally is recovering from the abortion she had. Christopher is bemoaning his aimless summer, and the fact that he isn't writing enough. They take stock of their poverty, sort out their lives, and declare their friendship. Start, Christopher: "This awful, obscene laziness! I ought to be flogged." End, Sally: "So do I."
Drama: Act II, Scene 2, pp. 58–63; Sally (20s) and Christopher (20s).
Sally has just received a note from her rich American friend, Clive, saying that the world cruise he promised is off. On an impulse, he has departed for America. Since Sally and Christopher are already packed to leave on the cruise, they greet the news with shock and disappointment. After they calm down, they decide to turn over a new leaf, to get jobs, and to lead responsible lives for a change. Then, just as abruptly, Sally changes her mind, deciding to throw herself back into the party scene. You'll have to cut and paste, eliminating Fraulein Schneider's lines. Start, Christopher: "Really, Sally, that was a little cruel. Fritz really is in trouble." Then, cut from Sally's line: "We could ask Fraulein Schneider to phone" to Christopher's line: "You know he's gone, don't you?" Next, cut from Sally's line: "I don't think we're much good as gold-diggers, are we, darling?" to Christopher's line: "Do you want to come out and have some lunch?" Continue to the end of Act II. End, Sally: "Can't you laugh now? Come on."
Drama: Act III, Scene 1, pp. 64–69; Sally (20s) and Christopher (20s).
This scene contains the strongest conflict. Sally is hungover and has been "away" for the past couple of days. She and Christopher exchange some low-key pleasantries and, when he asks how she likes the article he has written, she dismisses it as dull. In fact, Sally explains, she has asked someone else to write the article. His artistic pride wounded, Christopher rages at her. She rages back and then storms out, promising to move out altogether. As he mutters to himself about how awful she is, Sally bursts back in to say that her mother is unexpectedly in town and is coming up the stairs! She asks Christopher to masquerade as her fiancé because that is what her mother thinks he is to Sally. Before Christopher can protest, Sally's mother enters. This is a good scene because of all of its emotional twists and turns. Start, Christopher: "I haven't seen you for a day and a half." End, Sally: "Don't believe everything I said at first. She isn't easy. Please, darling. Please!"

I HATE HAMLET
by Paul Rudnick (Dramatists Play Service)
Comedy: Act II, Scene 1, pp. 54–57; Lillian Troy (70s) and John Barrymore (45–50).
This is a magical scene in which Lillian Troy, now in her 70s, reminisces with her old sweetheart, John Barrymore, who is actually a ghost. He would be in his 70s, too, but he stopped aging when he died 20 years ago. At any rate, Lillian is older than John, and they dance and laugh and talk about how lovely it was back then. A very sweet scene. Start, Lillian: "You. You look terrible." End, Lillian: "Surprise me."

IMMIGRANT, THE
by Mark Harelik (Broadway Play Publishing)
Drama: Act I, Scene 9; Leah (20s) and Haskell (20s).
Leah is distressed because she and Haskell have settled in Texas, far from their Russian Jewish roots, and because there are no other Jews anywhere near. She is also upset that they don't eat

kosher or pray at sundown. He thinks that this is all part of becoming American and says that he has no intentions of abandoning his Jewish faith. Then Leah tells Haskell that she is pregnant. At the top of the scene, Leah speaks Russian; at the end, Haskell sings a verse from a Yiddish song. Start, Leah: "Ach, mei' Gott, siz ah meshugenneh velt." End, Haskell (singing): "Fraylich lustik iz gevain ihr meene Ot axoy gevain is mein kusine."

IMPASSIONED EMBRACES
by John Pielmeier (Dramatists Play Service)
Comedy: "An Intellectual Discussion (or The Poor Man's Samuel Beckett)," pp. 71–73; He (20–35) and She (20–35).
In this sketch, which takes place at a kitchen table, the dialogue is in the spirit of the Abbott and Costello "Who's on First?" routine, full of double negatives and confusing context. The scene ends with a modified food fight. Start, He: "You're wrong." End, She: "Forget it."
Comedy: "Goober's Descent," pp. 87–93; He (30–45) and She (25–40).
He is a business executive looking for a new position, and she is interviewing him. In this reverse sexual-harassment scene, the woman gets the man stripped down to his underpants and then reminds him that she briefly worked as his secretary years ago. She was the one who wouldn't have sex with him and who quit when he started coming on to her. Revenge is sweet. Start, He: "Hi there." End, She: "Zilla, you can start sending in the next year."

I NEVER SANG FOR MY FATHER
by Robert Anderson (Dramatists Play Service)
Drama: Act II, pp. 51–54; Gene (40) and Alice (early 40s).
Alice traveled from Chicago to Long Island to help her brother, Gene, with family arrangements after their mother's death. The most pressing issue is what to do with their father, who is now almost 80 and increasingly frail. Gene and Alice have just had a very tense discussion with him, in which he became furious at Alice's suggestion that he hire a live-in housekeeper. Ideally, the father wants Gene to remain close at hand, but Gene wants to move to California to remarry. Overcome with guilt, Gene suddenly told his father that he'll stay, at least for a while. When the older man stalks off, Alice yells at Gene for not standing his ground, for giving in to his father, for not being a man. Start, Gene: "For God's sake, Alice." End, Alice: "Suddenly I miss Mother so."

IN THE BOOM BOOM ROOM
by David Rabe (Samuel French)
Drama: Act II, pp. 73–77; Chrissy (early 20s) and Harold (50s).
Chrissy talks to Harold, her alcoholic father, about abuse she suffered as a child. She asks him why he once put vodka in her baby bottle, causing her to be hospitalized, as well as why he is still with Helen, her mother, who has shown in many ways that she wishes her daughter were dead. Harold is remorseful about what happened years ago but makes excuses; he says he was just kidding around at the time. An excellent, low-key scene. Start, Chrissy: "Hi, Pop." End, Harold: "Here comes your mother. She's been shopping at the store."
Drama: Act II, pp. 82–87; Chrissy (early 20s) and Eric (mid-20s).
Eric loves Chrissy. She wants his help with her astrology chart while he wants to talk about how much he loves her and how wonderful their life could be together. Chrissy gets progressively frustrated with him. Start, Eric: "Come in!" End, Eric: "Don't worry. Just call. Just call."

I OUGHT TO BE IN PICTURES
by Neil Simon (Samuel French)
Comedy: Act I, Scene 1, pp. 14–24; Libby (19) and Herb (45).
Herb wakes up one morning in Hollywood to discover his daughter, who he hasn't seen since she was a small child, sitting in his living room. If you have access to a telephone that rings,

begin the scene when Libby answers the phone. If not, begin with Herb's entrance. Start, Herb: "I didn't hear you get up." End, Libby: "Hello."

Comedy: Act II, Scene 2, pp. 50–57; Steffy (39) and Herb (45).
Steffy tells Herb that, after a two-year relationship, it is time for him to make a deeper commitment to her. His response is typical of many men. Start, Steffy: "It's okay. I know how you feel." End, Herb: "You're just dumb when it comes to picking men."

IT HAD TO BE YOU
by Renée Taylor and Joseph Bologna (Samuel French)
Comedy: Act I, pp. 26–36; Theda (28–35) and Vito (40).
Theda and Vito came back to her place, spent the night, and this morning Vito is beginning to grasp just how eccentric this woman is. He has discovered that she eats health food and has been writing a perfectly awful play for herself for the past three years. Just a minute ago, Theda hid his clothes all over her small apartment, including in the freezer. Vito tries to make a graceful exit, chalking this one up to experience. However, the door seems to be locked, so he can't get out. Furthermore, it is snowing hard, and he may have to stay longer. Start, Vito: "The door seems to be stuck. Would you please open it?" End, Theda: "I know it doesn't look good for my love story but I had one thing going in my favor. He was still here!" This excerpt includes a great deal of physical comedy. For a longer version start, Vito: "Uh . . . look, I've got to be going. I'm all disoriented." Continue to the same end.
Comedy: Act II, pp. 37–43; Theda (28–35) and Vito (40).
Vito tries to help Theda write her one-woman play, wanting to add rubber-chicken jokes and such to her very Russian plot line. It doesn't work. Begin at the top of Act II as Theda reads her play-in-progress aloud. Start, Theda: "'In the name of Mother Russia, stop the torturing.'" End, Theda: "Well they should have! Now I want another idea for my play! And this time I want a good one!"

JIMMY SHINE
by Murray Schisgal (Dramatists Play Service)
Comedy: Act II, pp. 51–55; Jimmy (early 30s) and Elizabeth (early 30s).
Jimmy Shine has loved Elizabeth Evans since they were children together, but she never loved him. In this scene, which comes at the end of the play, she shows up at his apartment, informs him that she has left Michael, and asks Jimmy to run away with her to Denver. Although he wants to believe that Elizabeth has finally fallen in love with him, he slowly realizes that she is doing all of this simply to make Michael jealous. Jimmy sends Elizabeth away and, at the final curtain, he is wiser, stronger, and more content with himself. Start, Elizabeth: "It's me. Open up." End, Jimmy: "You have to be very careful with women like that. They can turn on you in a minute and whoop! Off go your badookas!"

JOINED AT THE HEAD
by Catherine Butterfield (Dramatists Play Service) [*Women Playwrights—Best Plays of 1992* (Smith & Kraus)]
Comedy-Drama: Act II, DPS pp. 53–57; Maggie (late 30s) and Jim (late 30s).
Maggie and her former high-school lover, Jim, spend an evening together at his place while his wife undergoes chemotherapy at the hospital. After dinner, he plays snippets from a couple of songs on the piano. This leads to a discussion about who-left-whom at the high-school prom 20 years ago, which, in turn, leads to talk about whether or not Maggie is being honest in her best-selling book about a father/daughter relationship. Jim's piano playing is a very important part of the scene. If you don't have access to a piano, you probably shouldn't attempt this scene. Start, Maggie (to audience): "I went to dinner at Jim's that night. I'll make this quick, then we'll move on to other things." End, Maggie: "You didn't screw it up, Jim. You did just fine."

KEY EXCHANGE

by Kevin Wade (Dramatists Play Service)

Comedy: Scene 4, pp. 19–23; Lisa (late 20s) and Philip (about 30).

Lisa wants to deepen the level of commitment in her relationship with Philip, which is signified by the exchanging of apartment keys. Philip, however, doesn't want to be fenced in. A good short scene. Start, Philip: "So great. So we get keys made for each other's apartments." End, Lisa: "Please. Go."

Comedy: Scene 6, pp. 26–31; Lisa (late 20s) and Philip (about 30).

When Lisa invites Philip to meet her father, he hedges because he doesn't want to be pushed too fast in their relationship. She gets angry, and the confrontation ends with the couple breaking up. Begin at the top of Scene 6. Cut Michael's appearance in the scene. Start, Philip: "Yes." End, Lisa: "No. You're getting what you want. I won't push you anymore. You win. I don't want to play anymore."

LANDSCAPE OF THE BODY

by John Guare (Dramatists Play Service)

Drama: Act I, pp. 9–16; Capt. Holohan (40–45) and Betty (36).

Capt. Holohan interrogates Betty at the police station. He is convinced that she murdered her 14-year-old son, but the truth is that she didn't do it. Omit Raulito and Rosalie's brief interruptions. Start, Betty: "I don't see how you can ask me these questions." End, Betty: "I can look you right in the eye. I didn't throw up. I won."

Comedy: Act I, pp. 23–27; Betty (36) and Raulito (35–45).

Betty takes over her deceased sister's old job at Dawn's Promising Star Travel Agency in New York City. Raulito, the owner/operator, is a flamboyant Cuban refugee whose modus operandi is scamming newlyweds into buying honeymoon vacations. In this scene, after he shows Betty the ropes and describes his colorful background, she gives scamming a try. The scene calls for a cassette recording of audience cheers and applause, but this isn't absolutely essential. Start, Raulito: "You take the *Daily News*. You take the Sunday *Times*." End, Betty: "I'm me. I can't do the job. I don't want the job."

LARGO DESOLATO

by Vaclav Havel [translated by Tom Stoppard (Grove Weidenfeld)]

Comedy-Drama: Scene 6; Marguerite (early 20s) and Leopold (45–50).

Marguerite, a university philosophy student, comes to Leopold's flat, declares her intellectual indebtedness to him, and, when she recognizes his despair, decides to rescue him with affection. Start, Marguerite: "Good evening." End, Marguerite: ". . . and now, I'll awaken love in you!"

LARK, THE

by Jean Anouilh [adapted by Lillian Hellman (Dramatists Play Service)]

Drama: Act I, pp. 15–18; Joan of Arc (18) and Sire de Beaudricourt (40–50).

After listening to the "voices" of God for three years, Joan of Arc accepts her calling and prepares to raise an army and march on Orleans to repel the British. As a first step, she has come to the manor of the Sire de Beaudricourt to ask for an armed escort and a horse. Initially, he toys with the idea of a sexual trade with the young woman, but because she appeals to his intelligence, he gives her what she wants. Start, Sire de Beaudricourt: "What's the matter with you, young woman? You've been carrying on like a bad girl. I've heard about you standing outside the doors ragging at the sentries until they fall asleep." End, Joan: "Good. Now that we have got that out of the way, let's pretend that you've given me the clothes of a boy and we're sitting here like two comrades talking good sense."

LAST OF THE RED HOT LOVERS
by Neil Simon (Samuel French)
Comedy: Act II, pp. 41–51; Barney (47) and Bobbi (27).
Barney entices Bobbi, a pretty singer/actress, up to his mother's apartment for a tryst. Bobbi turns out to be a dingbat, and Barney winds up smoking his first marijuana cigarette. This scene fills the entire 20 pages of Act II. For scene-study purposes, beginning halfway through the act. Start, Bobbi: "Are you married?" Continue to the end of the act. End, Bobbi: ". . . That's the only thing that there's just too little of. . . ."
Comedy: Act III, pp. 54–63; Barney (47) and Jeanette (39).
Jeanette is a longtime friend of Barney and his wife. He brings her to his mother's apartment for a tryst. She turns out to be quite depressed and pops tranquilizers. Start, Jeanette: "Why am I here, Barney?" End, Jeanette: "You actually found three people who you consider gentle, loving and decent. I congratulate you."

LES LIAISONS DANGEREUSES
by Christopher Hampton [based on Choderlos de Laclos's novel of the same name (Samuel French)]
Drama: Act I, Scene 1, pp. 16–22; Mme Merteuil (25–35) and Valmont (28–35).
Mme Merteuil's lover, Gercourt, has jilted her and is now planning to marry Cécile, the young virgin. Bent on revenge, Mme Merteuil tries to convince her sometimes-lover Valmont to seduce the young woman before her wedding night, just to teach Gercourt a lesson. Valmont refuses because he doesn't see much sport in seducing a 15-year-old. Furthermore, he is in pursuit of a much bigger prize, the very married, very religious, and very straight-laced Mme de Tourvel. Mme Merteuil is skeptical of Valmont's ability to bed Mme de Tourvel, so she challenges him to a bet with a sexual payoff if he can deliver proof of his seduction. Start, Merteuil: "Your aunt?" End, Merteuil: "Good night, Vicomte."
Drama: Act I, Scene 2, pp. 28–32; Mme de Tourvel (22) and Valmont (28–35).
Valmont is determined to seduce Mme de Tourvel because she is such an unwilling victim. Start, Tourvel: "I can't understand how someone whose instincts are so generous could lead such a dissolute life." End, Valmont: "I only want to say what I hardly thought it would be possible for me to say to you: Goodbye . . . I'll write soon."
Drama: Act I, Scene 5, pp. 51–55; Mme de Tourvel (22) and Valmont (28–35).
Although Mme de Tourvel has strongly rebuffed Valmont, her heart is beating with desire. In this short scene, he raises the stakes and increases the tempo of his pursuit. Begin as Tourvel reenters after her walk in the garden. Start, Valmont: "I trust you're feeling a little better, Madame." Continue to the end of the scene. End, Valmont: "Nothing."
Drama: Act II, Scene 2, pp. 83–86; Mme de Tourvel (22) and Valmont (28–35).
Valmont succeeds in his seduction of Mme de Tourvel. She has literally been driven to the edge of emotional collapse with sexual desire and internal conflict. The only blemish on Valmont's otherwise perfect seduction is that he has made the mortal error of actually falling in love with the woman. This short, intense scene ends with Tourvel succumbing to his passion. Start, Valmont: "I understand Father Anselme has explained to you the reasons for my visit." End, Tourvel: "Yes. You're right. I can't live either unless I make you happy. So I promise. No more refusals and no more regrets."
Drama: Act II, Scene 3, pp. 86–91; Mme Merteuil (25–35) and Valmont (28–35).
Unbeknownst to Valmont, Mme Merteuil has taken young Danceny as her lover. Her passion for this dalliance, however, has been dulled by her discovery that Valmont has fallen in love with Mme de Tourvel and impregnated 15-year-old Cécile. These games of cruel seduction aren't supposed to involve true emotion or weaknesses. In this scene, Mme Merteuil and Valmont take stock of their feelings for each other. Start, Valmont: "Success." End, Merteuil: "Goodbye."

LIE OF THE MIND, A
by Sam Shepard (Dramatists Play Service)
Comedy-Drama: Act II, Scene 3, pp. 54–60; Beth (early-to-mid 20s) and Frankie (late 20s).
In order to find out if Jake has murdered his wife, Beth, Frankie has traveled to her parents' place in Billings, Montana. Beth's father mistook Frankie for a deer and shot him in the leg. Now he is recuperating right alongside Beth, who suffered brain damage from Jake's violent beating. Here, Beth tends to Frankie's wound by taking off her shirt and wrapping it around his leg. Then, because her brain still isn't working right, she starts to fantasize about how it would be if Frankie were a gentler version of Jake. Beth comes on to Frankie, but he doesn't want to get involved with his brother's wife. Start, Frankie: "Uh—look—Beth—Don't you think you oughta put your shirt back on?" End, Beth: "Then why is this so empty? So empty now. Everything. Gone. A hole."

LIFE AND LIMB
by Keith Reddin (Dramatists Play Service)
Drama: Act I, Scene 3, pp. 13–16; Franklin (mid-to-late 20s) and Effie (mid-to-late 20s).
Franklin and his wife, Effie, have an awkward reunion. This is the first time they've seen each other since he lost his arm in the Korean War. Start, Effie: "Hi, Franklin!" End, Effie: "Sure."
Drama: Act I, Scene 5, pp. 19–21; Franklin (mid-to-late 20s) and Effie (mid-to-late 20s).
Franklin is deeply depressed about his injury and inability to land a job, and he is taking it out on Effie, who is doing the best she can to be a good wife. In this tense scene, Franklin seems to pick a fight with Effie for no reason at all. Start, Franklin: "Take your coat off." End, "No shit."
Drama: Act II, Scene 6, pp. 45–48; Franklin (mid-to-late 20s) and Effie (mid-to-late 20s).
Effie was killed in a freak accident at the movie theater and in this fantasy sequence, she returns from the dead to tell Franklin about the affair she had. He tells her how much he misses her. A lovely scene. Start, Franklin: "Effie, is that you?" End, Effie: "I miss you. I miss you and the movies."

LION IN WINTER, THE
by James Goldman (Samuel French)
Drama: Act I, Scene 2, pp. 16–20; Eleanor of Aquitaine (61) and Henry II (50).
Henry II and Eleanor of Aquitaine have become loving and comfortable adversaries. In this scene, they argue about which of their sons will be the heir to the English throne. Start, Eleanor: "Henry, I have a confession." End, Eleanor: "Good. That will make this pleasanter."
Drama: Act I, Scene 4, pp. 33–37; Eleanor of Aquitaine (61) and Henry II (50).
Henry and Eleanor strike a deal: her freedom in exchange for her endorsement of their youngest son John getting the Aquitaine. This would be a major capitulation for Eleanor because she is in favor of their oldest son, Richard Lionheart, ascending to the throne. Start, Henry: "Well, how'd you do with Richard? Did you break his heart?" End, Henry: "Where's a priest? I'll do it. I'll show you. By Christ, I will."
Drama: Act II, Scene 1, pp. 61–70; Eleanor of Aquitaine (61) and Henry II (50).
Henry tells his wife that he wants their marriage annulled. Eleanor refuses, threatening open war if he tries to have it done against her will. Their dispute takes a nasty, even more personal turn when she claims to have slept with Henry's father. Shortening this scene without disrupting the flow and tension is hard. Start, Eleanor: "I'm rather proud; I taught her all the rhetoric she knows." End, Eleanor: "It's cold. I can't feel anything. Not anything at all. We couldn't go back, could we, Henry?"
Drama: Act II, Scene 2, pp. 70–73; Alais (23) and Henry (50).
Henry tells Alais, his mistress, that they're going to Rome to have his marriage annulled; he'll then be able to marry her. Before Alais will accept Henry's proposal, she wants him to promise

to keep his sons by Eleanor locked in a dungeon forever. Alais believes that if Henry's plan succeeds and his sons were free, they would band together to wage war against him and, in time, to probably kill him. This short scene has interesting dynamics and a great deal of subtext. Start, Henry: "Get up, wake up, it's morning." End, Henry: "I shall have to, shan't I?"

LITTLE FOXES, THE
by Lillian Hellman (Dramatists Play Service)
Drama: Act II, pp. 41–44; Regina (40) and Horace (45).
Regina is more interested in her husband Horace's money than in the fact that he is dying from a heart ailment. She lured Horace home from the hospital under the pretense that she has decided to be romantic. Regina and Horace haven't had sex for 10 years. But all she really wants to do is to get $75,000 from him to seal a business arrangement with her unethical brothers. Start, Regina: "Well. Here we are. It's been a long time." End, Regina: "You will see what I've done while you've been away. How I watched your interests."
Drama: Act III, pp. 62–66; Regina (40) and Horace (45).
Horace tells his wife that her brothers and nephew have conspired to steal $80,000 from him, that he considers her to be part of the same pack of dogs, and that he intends to punish her—and them—in his will. Regina responds by telling Horace how much she has always hated him. As their tempers and tensions rise, he suddenly suffers another major heart attack. Regina watches dispassionately as he dies, not even moving to get his medicine for him. Start, Regina: "We had agreed that you were to stay in your part of this house and I in mine." End, Regina: "Horace. Horace. Addie! Cal! Come in here!"

LONG DAY'S JOURNEY INTO NIGHT
by Eugene O'Neill (Yale University Press)
Drama: Act I; Mary (54) and Edmund (23).
Edmund tells Mary, his mother, that he is afraid she is lapsing back into morphine addiction. Although this accusation is true, Mary is angry about it. Edmund then agrees not to spy on her further. The scene begins late in Act I and continues to the end of the act. Start, Mary: "Here you are. I was just going upstairs to look for you." End, Edmund: ". . . I'll go down and help Jamie bear up. I love to lie in the shade and watch him work."

LOOK HOMEWARD, ANGEL
by Ketti Frings [based on the novel of the same name by Thomas Wolfe (Samuel French)]
Drama: Act I, Scene 2, pp. 32–37; Laura (23) and Eugene (17).
Eugene talks quietly on the porch with Laura, the new boarder. Even though they both realize that he is too young for her, there is an immediate and profound attraction between them. Eugene tells Laura about his dreams in this lovely scene. What he doesn't know is that she is engaged. Omit Jack Clatt's interruption. Start, Laura: "Good evening." End, Laura: "Gene, if we keep rushing together like this, we're going to have a collision."
Drama: Act I, Scene 2, pp. 37–40; Eliza (57) and W. O. Gant (60).
After a drunken uproar, Gant, Eliza's husband, is sleeping it off when she enters his bedroom. He lurches awake, mistakenly thinking his daughter, Helen, has come to take care of him. Eliza, furious earlier, soothes him now and seems to be genuinely concerned with the old man's well-being. The truth is that she wants to pressure him to sell the valuable property where his business is located. You'll need a bed for this scene. Start, Gant: "Helen?" End, Gant: "Have mercy and pity upon me. Give me another chance in Jesus' name . . . Oh-h-h!"
Drama: Act III, pp. 76–78; Laura (23) and Eugene (17).
For reasons of her own, Laura hasn't told Eugene that she is engaged to a man in another town; instead, she lets this new romance blossom. Now deeply in love, Eugene asks Laura to

marry him in a very brief, very tender, lovely scene. It is best to have a bed for this scene, but you can get away without using one. Start, Laura: "Gene? What was that?" End, Laura: "Eugene . . . I will love you always . . . Gene!"

Drama: Act III, pp. 83–85; Eliza (57) and Eugene (17).
Now that Laura is gone, Eugene knows that his dreams of romance with her were empty. Suddenly, he realizes that he must leave this place and, in this dynamic 2-page scene, he and Eliza, his domineering mother, finally come to terms. Start, Eliza: "Gene. You know what I'd do if I were you? I'd just show her I was a good sport, that's what!" End, Eugene: "Ah, you were not looking, were you? I've already gone."

LOSS OF ROSES, A
by William Inge (Dramatists Play Service)
Drama: Act I, Scene 1, pp. 10–17; Kenny (21) and Helen (mid-40s)
Kenny discovers that he is being temporarily moved out of his bedroom to make space for house guest Lila Green. He and Helen, his mother, argue about this and about his unwillingness to move out of the house altogether. Kenny is, after all, 21 years old. Start, Kenny: "All right. How long's she gonna stay?" End, Helen: "All right, Kenny! All right."

Drama: Act II, Scene 1, pp. 44–49; Kenny (21) and Lila (32).
Lila has been living with Kenny and his mother for a month and is comfortable with the situation. This afternoon, Kenny comes home from his job at the gas station to find Lila on the front steps. A mild flirtation turns lustful, and Lila reluctantly pushes Kenny away. Start, Lila: "Good evening, Mr. Kenny Baird." End, Lila: "Yes you are. I can tell. Oh, sometimes I wish I'd never been born."

LOU GEHRIG DID NOT DIE OF CANCER
by Jason Miller [*Three One-Act Plays by Jason Miller* (Dramatists Play Service)]
Drama: One-act play, pp. 43–50; Barbara (28) and Victor (32).
Barbara and Victor are a husband and wife on the verge of separating. This scene is tense, biting, and honest. Playwright Jason Miller describes Barbara as "lean, tanned, large-breasted," and you should make an effort to cast an appropriate actress. Barbara's body is a point of reference when Victor makes comments to hurt her. Similarly, Miller describes Victor as "a sad little clown underneath a coarse and sometimes volatile temperament." Find a suitable actor. Start, Barbara: "Barbara speaking! . . . No, Mr. Toomey, my husband is not here." End, Victor: "Have a nice time."

Drama: One-act play, pp. 51–57; Helen (mid-30s) and Victor (32).
Helen Martin comes to Victor's home to talk about her shy son, a bench-sitting player on the little-league team that Victor coaches. Because he just got fired from his coaching position, their meeting turns into an introspective and, ultimately, poignant event during which Victor gives Helen a present for her son; the gift, his prized possession, is a baseball personally autographed by Lou Gehrig. Start, Victor: "Who are . . . don't tell me, I know, I have it. You are Mrs. Martin." Continue to the end of the play. End, Victor: "One cream and two sugars."

LOVER, THE
by Harold Pinter (Dramatists Play Service)
Drama: One-act play, pp. 20–26; Sarah (30–35) and Richard (30–40).
Sarah is having an affair with her "pretend" lover, who is actually her own husband, Richard. He decides to call the whole arrangement off because he is getting jealous of her relationship with this other self. But it is too late because they're both addicted to the game. This scene, the last one in the play, is appropriate for advanced actors. Written in the British vernacular. Start, Richard: "Hello." End, Richard: "You lovely whore."

LOVERS AND OTHER STRANGERS
by Renée Taylor and Joseph Bologna (Samuel French)
Comedy: "Brenda and Jerry," pp. 5–12; Brenda (20s) and Jerry (20s).
Jerry and Brenda met 30 minutes ago at Maxwell's Plum, and he managed to get her up to his apartment after they left the restaurant. He tries to seduce her, she resists, and then she gives in. The scene is funnier than it sounds. Start, Jerry: "My apartment is right over here." End, Brenda: "Oh, Jerry! Aren't you glad we waited?!"
Comedy: "Hal and Cathy," pp. 12A–12F; Hal (48–52) and Cathy (30s).
Cathy wants Hal to divorce his wife of 32 years, but he keeps dragging his feet. She threatens to marry another man if he won't come round. Nothing is resolved by the end of the scene, and they continue their affair as before. As written, this scene takes place in a small bathroom while a party is going on in another part of Hal's house. If this setting isn't practical for class work, simply change the setting to a guest room. Start, Hal: "Cathy? Are you in there, Cathy?" End, Hal: "then the responsibility rests not with me, not with you, Cathy, not with Bernice . . . but with Phil!"
Comedy: "Johnny and Wilma," pp. 13–22; Johnny (40s) and Wilma (30s).
Wilma wants to make love tonight, but Johnny wants to go to sleep, so they fight, verbally and physically. They argue about male-female relationships, submissive-dominant roles, and lovemaking frequency. Johnny finally confesses that he has had a bad day at work and lost a big account, so he needs her to be submissive. Wilma complies. Wilma and Johnny move around a great deal here: they are in and out of bed, and in and out of the bathroom. You'll need a pretty complete bedroom setting. Start, Wilma: "Are you going to make love to me, or not?" End, Wilma: "Are you going to let me surrender to you, or not?"

LUV
by Murray Schisgal (Dramatists Play Service)
Comedy: Act I, pp. 32–38; Harry (late 30s) and Ellen (mid-30s).
Harry has been swept up in Ellen's hysteria and pain as she talks about her failed marriage to Milt. She pulls out the knife she was going to use to kill Milt and, in an emotional fit, almost kills Harry. Begin the scene as Ellen and Harry regain their composure. Start, Ellen: "I've been a great deal of trouble to you." End, Ellen: "I love you! I love you!"
Comedy: Act II, pp. 42–48; Milt (late 30s) and Ellen (mid-30s).
Milt's recent marriage to Linda hasn't been working out. In fact, Linda has maintained a dirty house, let her underarm hair grow, and quit her job. Even worse, she left Milt three days ago, and now he is in despair, longing to reconcile with Ellen, his former wife. As it happens, Ellen's recent marriage to Harry Berlin has also been rocky; he has taken to lying in a corner of the living room with a paper bag over his head, moaning. As Act II evolves, Milt and Ellen finally do get back together, but this 6-page excerpt ends before that happens. Start, Milt: "El? Ellen? Is that you?" End, Ellen: "The door is closed, Milt."

MATCHMAKER, THE
by Thornton Wilder (Samuel French)
Comedy: Act I, pp. 24–29; Mrs. Dolly Levi (40–50) and Horace Vandergelder (60).
Dolly Levi intends to marry Horace Vandergelder, but he doesn't know it yet. In this fun and innocent scene, she double-talks him into believing that she is going to fix him up with a 17-year-old who has secretly fallen in love with him. Later on, he'll get even more confused and wind up marrying Dolly! Start, Mrs. Levi: "Oh, Mr. Vandergelder, how handsome you look! You take my breath away!" End, Mrs. Levi: ". . . very well; I'll meet you on one of those benches in front of Mrs. Molloy's hat store at four thirty, as usual." For a longer version, eliminate Cornelius's lines. End, Mrs. Levi: ". . . and the only way you can save yourself how is to be married to somebody by the end of next week. So think that over!"

M. BUTTERFLY
by David Henry Hwang (Dramatists Play Service)
Drama: Act II, Scene 6, pp. 41–44; Gallimard (30s) and Renee (late teens).
Gallimard, a French diplomat, begins an affair with Renee, a bored American university student he meets at a party in the Austrian embassy. The first part of the scene takes place in the embassy, the second in a bedroom. Renee, who is always perky, shares her theories on the correlation between penis size and world wars with the diplomat. Start, Gallimard: "1963. A party at the Austrian embassy." End, Gallimard: "This was simply not acceptable."

MIDDLE AGES, THE
by A. R. Gurney, Jr. (Dramatists Play Service)
Comedy-Drama: Act I, pp. 5–10; Eleanor (playing 40s) and Barney (playing 40s).
Eleanor tries to talk Barney out of making an embarrassing speech at his father's memorial service. Unbeknownst to her, he has purchased the private men's club that has figured so significantly in all of their lives and in which the service is taking place. Start, Eleanor: "I knew you'd be in here." End, Eleanor: "Nuts to you, Barney. Just—nuts to you."
Comedy: Act I, pp. 21–28; Eleanor (playing late teens) and Barney (playing late teens).
Barney is madly in love with Eleanor, but she is leaning toward his younger brother, Billy. In this very physical scene, Barney makes a hopelessly romantic, virginally awkward play for her in the trophy room of the men's club. He wants to have sex with her tonight, right here, right now. If Eleanor goes on that Bermuda trip tomorrow with Billy, it will be too late. To play this properly, you'll need dressy clothes, a man's robe, the makings of a picnic, and someone to operate offstage music to simulate the dance party going on in the next room. Begin as Eleanor and Barney dance into the room, as the action shifts from the 1940s to the 1950s. Start, Eleanor: "Hey!" End, Barney: "Not at all. I'll be right back."

MIDDLE OF THE NIGHT
by Paddy Chayefsky (Samuel French)
Drama: Act II, Scene 2, pp. 40–44; The Manufacturer (53) and The Girl (23).
After an unsatisfactory attempt at lovemaking, The Manufacturer feels awful that he wasn't able to perform sexually. The Girl is very understanding. He asks her to marry him. The actor playing The Manufacturer must have a good feel for New York regional speech patterns. This skill is less critical for the actress playing The Girl. Start, The Manufacturer: "I'm sorry, Betty." End, The Manufacturer: "Oh, my sweet girl, I love you so much you don't know. If you change your mind tomorrow, I won't be angry with you. I won't lie to you, Betty. I'm afraid."
Drama: Act III, Scene 1, pp. 65–68; The Girl (23) and The Husband (late 20s).
The Girl sent The Husband a letter asking for a divorce. He flew in from Las Vegas to try to talk her out of it. But The Girl is determined; anyway, she is in love with The Manufacturer. Start, The Girl: "George, I'd like to know why you came back. I mean it really." End, The Husband: "I swear I won't do it again."

MISS JULIE
by August Strindberg [*Six Plays of Strindberg*, translated by Elizabeth Sprigge (Doubleday/Anchor)]
Drama: One-act play; Julie (25) and Jean (30)
This 90-minute, one-act play is divided into two parts: a seduction scene between Miss Julie and her father's valet, Jean, and the consequences of their passion. In this scene, Kristin, a minor character, has conveniently fallen asleep. Julie invites Jean to go outside into the night and pick lilacs. As they prepare to leave, Jean gets something in his eye, which Julie tends to. As she does, she becomes more sexually provocative. This is fairly outrageous behavior for a woman of that era, particularly with a man from a lower class. The tempo of the dance

between Jean and Julie increases until they go into Jean's room, presumably to make love, as a group of party revelers approaches. Start, Julie: "Now come out and pick some lilac for me." End, Jean: "I swear."
Drama; Julie (25) and Jean (30).
Julie and Jean emerge from his bedroom, having just made love. She is agitated, trying to determine what to do now that she has violated a class-line taboo and made herself submissive to a lowly valet. She decides to run away and attempts to get Jean to accompany her. Perhaps they'll run a hotel somewhere. For Jean's part, their lovemaking has transformed him into someone cruelly dominant. In fact, Jean insults Julie now that she is "his." Start, Jean: "Now you see! And you heard, didn't you? Do you still think it is possible for us to stay here?" End, Jean: "Orders always sound unkind. Now you know. Now you know."

MISS LONELYHEARTS
by Howard Teichmann [adapted from Nathanael West's novel of the same name (Dramatists Play Service)]
Drama: Act I, Scene 4, pp. 24–27; Betty (early 20s) and Miss Lonelyhearts (26).
Betty's fiancé hasn't been around for three weeks, ever since he started writing a daily lovelorn column for the newspaper. He is now known as Miss Lonelyhearts. In this short, intense scene, he appears unexpectedly at Betty's apartment, and she can tell right away that he has changed in some way. No longer quite as glib and cynical, he seems more introspective and disturbed. Start, Betty: "God only knows about men, too. Women don't." End, Betty: "Why don't you let me alone? I felt swell before you came, and now I feel rotten. Go away. Please, go away!"
Drama: Act I, Scene 8, pp. 42–45; Fay (30s) and Miss Lonelyhearts (26).
Miss Lonelyhearts has agreed to a face-to-face meeting with a troubled reader who wrote to him for advice. Fay, a sad, physically strong woman, comes to his apartment. As she shares her terrible story, the sexual tension between them increases. Within minutes, they head for the bedroom. This is a difficult scene, particularly for the actress playing Fay. Best for experienced actors. Start, Miss Lonelyhearts: "Come in . . . Want to give me your coat?" End, Fay: "Oh, honey, turn off the light."
Drama: Act II, Scene 1, pp. 51–54; Betty (early 20s) and Miss Lonelyhearts (26).
Concerned about Miss Lonelyhearts's mental and physical health, Betty has brought him to the country for some rest and relaxation. After four days, however, he is more troubled than ever, and he has made no effort at all to sleep with her. In this scene, Betty lets Miss Lonelyhearts know that she is ready to go to bed with him but he refuses, explaining that he has decided to give himself to all people, not just one special woman. The scene calls for a telephone that rings, but they don't answer it. You can easily omit the references to it if you want. Start, Miss Lonelyhearts: "Hullo." End, Betty: "That's not for us either. Good night."

MODIGLIANI
by Dennis McIntyre (Samuel French)
Drama: Act I, Scene 4, pp. 26–34; Modigliani (31) and Bea (late 20s).
Modigliani's girlfriend, Bea, tries to make Modigliani work, but he is demoralized, sick, hungry, and a bit manic. At one point in this scene, she challenges him to paint by stripping off her clothes and posing. You can easily adjust this moment to stop short of nudity. Start, Modigliani: "A day-and-a-half!" End, Bea: "I know. Sleep."

MONDAY AFTER THE MIRACLE
by William Gibson (Dramatists Play Service)
Drama: Act I, pp. 15–17; Annie (35) and John (26).
This short scene begins with John trying to convince an angry Annie to help him with the book he is writing about Helen Keller. Annie is tired of living in Helen's shadow and wants to

be appreciated for herself. Then, suddenly, the action turns romantic when Annie tries to make a dramatic exit. John grabs her, and they roll on the ground and kiss. At age 35, Annie has no experience with romance. Start, John: "My, you're a contrary type. If you ever drown, I'll look for you upstream." End, Annie: "It—deserves its reputation."
Drama: Act I, pp. 20–22; Annie (35) and John (26).
Annie and John are hiding from Helen because she doesn't know they're romantically involved. They want each other, and John asks Annie to marry him. Annie is excited by the proposal but doesn't accept for two reasons. John is younger than she is, and she feels that she is already married—to Helen Keller. Start, Annie: "She's gone." End, John: "How many children are you planning on?"
Drama: Act II, pp. 51–54; Annie (35, playing 40) and John (26, playing 31).
Annie came home to find John kissing Helen by the fireplace, and this scene is the fallout. He tells Annie that he feels he is married to Siamese twins, Annie and Helen, that he has neither wife nor child, and that he feels unfulfilled. Annie damns him for taking advantage of Helen and for not appreciating all of her own hard work. Start, John: "Kissed the girls and made them cry." End, John: "She makes me feel tender. You don't."

MOON FOR THE MISBEGOTTEN, A
by Eugene O'Neill (Samuel French)
Drama: Act III; Josie (28) and Tyrone (early 40s).
Josie and Tyrone are alone in the moonlight. She longs for romance but discovers that he wants only forgiveness for the sins he committed while accompanying his mother's body across country last year. Actors who try this material should pay particular attention to the very specific casting guidelines playwright Eugene O'Neill demanded for Josie: "She should be a big woman, perhaps 5'11", weighing maybe 180 pounds, full-breasted, not mannish."
The material, which takes up all of Act III, is dense, rich, and demanding. As such, it is much too long for most workshops. You can divide it into two sections. For the first excerpt, begin with Josie's entrance at the top of Act II (pp. 66–78). Start, Josie: "You'd think I'd been gone years." End, Tyrone: "Thanks, Josie." The second scene begins where the first excerpt ends (pp. 78–93). Start, Tyrone: "Why did you say a while ago I'd be leaving for New York soon?" End, Josie: "God forgive me, it's a fine end to all my scheming, to sit here with the dead hugged to my breast, and the silly mug of the moon grinning down, enjoying the joke!"

MRS. CALIFORNIA
by Doris Baizley (Dramatists Play Service)
Comedy: Act II, pp. 33–36; Dot (25–35) and Dudley (30s).
Dot's sponsor from the Gas Company wants to send Babs home before she seriously jeopardizes Dot's chances of winning the 1955 Mrs. California contest. Babs has become a liability because of her take-no-prisoners attitude toward the competition. It seems she'll do anything, up to and including sabotaging the other contestants, to help Dot win. The subject matter makes this a very funny scene, but these individuals take themselves seriously. Start, Dot: "Poor Mrs. Modesto's wound up like a top." End, Dudley: "Night, Dot."

MRS. DALLY HAS A LOVER
by William Hanley (Dramatists Play Service)
Drama; Mrs. Dally (38) and Frankie (18).
This two-character, one-act play presents several possibilities for scene work. In one 7-page scene, it is late afternoon, and Mrs. Dally and Frankie are organizing themselves after what was apparently a very passionate lovemaking session (pp. 45–52). Start, Frankie: "What happened to my . . . ?" End, Mrs. Dally: "Wait a sec."

In the second excerpt, Mrs. Dally tells Frankie that she'd like to go out in public with him, to visit museums and such (pp. 59–68). They talk about what makes them happy, the differences in their ages, and religious guilt. Start, Mrs. Dally: "I'd like to go for a walk. Down by the river, maybe." End, Mrs. Dally: "Well . . . you'll understand soon enough."

Yet another choice for scene work overlaps the preceding excerpt (pp. 66–75). Here, Mrs. Dally tells Frankie about her show-business career and plays the trombone a tiny bit, and then they discuss John Donne's poetry. If you don't want to attempt playing the trombone, simply eliminate all mention of it. Start, Mrs. Dally: "Frankie . . . did you ever wonder if I did this before?" Continue to the end of the play. End, Mrs. Dally: "Just remember what I said: listen to the sweet music . . . and pass it on."

MURDER AT THE HOWARD JOHNSON'S
by Ron Clark and Sam Bobrick (Samuel French)
Comedy: Act I, Scene 1, pp. 8–11; Arlene (38) and Mitchell (36).
Arlene and her dentist/lover, Mitchell, wait at Howard Johnson's for her husband, Paul, to show up so she can ask him for a divorce. If he balks, they plan to murder him. The closer they get to the moment of truth, the more sexually turned on they get. Start, Mitchell: "Well, the bathtub is ready." End, Mitchell: "Think positive."
Comedy: Act I, Scene 2, pp. 27–32; Arlene (38) and Paul (40–45).
Arlene has discovered that Mitchell is having an affair with his dental assistant, and she is bent on revenge. Faking a suicide attempt, she tricks her ex-husband, Paul, into rescuing her and then enlists his assistance in killing Mitchell. Start, Arlene: "Hello, Mitchell. This is Arlene." End, Paul: "Who needs a hundred percent? Don't do it!"

NEVIS MOUNTAIN DEW
by Steve Carter (Dramatists Play Service)
Drama: Act II, pp. 31–34; Zepora Pilibert (43) and Ayton Morris (49).
Zepora Pilibert lives with her older brother, Jared, who is confined to an iron-lung machine. For years, she has carried on a romance with Ayton Morris, a childhood friend who currently lives with another woman and who has fathered two grown sons. Today is Jared's fiftieth birthday, so there is a great deal of activity in the house. In a quiet room, Zepora tells Ayton that she wants him to marry her. He says he would if she would leave this house, but he isn't going to reside here where "only one person rules . . . and he can't even hold orb and scepter."

Furthermore, Jared feels he isn't good enough for Zepora—that he is too uneducated, too old, and too black in color. She tells him that he is a good man, that it is him that she wants, that he can't be black enough. Both characters have West Indian heritages, so very slight accents are appropriate. Start, Ayton: "What you doin' sittin' in the dark? Why you don't come downstairs and join the festivities?" End, Ayton: "And when we get through . . . you either shit . . . or get off the pot!"

NIGHT OF THE IGUANA, THE
by Tennessee Williams (Dramatists Play Service)
Drama: Act II, pp. 49–52; Maxine (40s) and Shannon (35).
Shannon is struggling with inner demons, trying to choose between returning as a priest to a hypocritical church he despises or committing suicide. Here, he composes a letter to the dean of the divinity school at Sewanee as the lusty Maxine, recently a widow from a loveless marriage, presses him to forget all that and move in with her. Begin at the top of Act II. Start, Maxine: "Workin' on your sermon for next Sunday, Rev'rend?" End, Shannon: "I'll handle it myself you keep out of it, please."

NO PLACE TO BE SOMEBODY
by Charles Gordone (Samuel French)
Drama: Act II, Scene 2, pp. 56–59; Dee (20s) and Gabe (20s).
Gabe is a playwright and poet, and Dee is a prostitute. She comes into the bar to tell her man, Johnny, that she wants to stop working the streets. Before she can see him, however, Gabe strikes up a conversation with her. Dee tells Gabe how she got into the business, and he tells her about his first love. Start, Dee: "What's with the fish eyes? I gotta new wrinkle or sump'm?" End, Gabe: "I sure wanted to."

NORMAN CONQUESTS, THE—TABLE MANNERS
by Alan Ayckbourn (Samuel French)
Comedy: Act I, Scene 2, pp. 23–27; Ruth (30s) and Norman (30s).
Sarah has summoned Ruth, Norman's wife, to the country house for the weekend because it has come to light that Norman has been planning a romantic holiday with Ruth's sister, Annie, who is also in residence. In this scene, which takes place at breakfast time, Ruth has just arrived. After a few moments, Norman tells her outright that he was planning to go away with Annie. Ruth just laughs in his face. You'll need some breakfasts cereals, bowls, and utensils. Written in the British vernacular. Start, Ruth: "Oh, Reg how are you? I've been meaning to ring you, but I haven't had a minute." End, Ruth (laughing uncontrollably): "I never heard anything so funny."

NOT ENOUGH ROPE
by Elaine May (Samuel French)
Comedy: One-act play, pp. 5–8; Edith (25–35) and Claude (25–35).
Edith wants to borrow some rope from the new man moving in across the hall so she can hang herself. He has only some packing twine. Begin at the top of the play, and continue until Edith's exit back into her own apartment. Start, Edith: "Hi, there! I'm your neighbor from across the hall. . . ." End, Claude: "You're welcome . . . Oh God. . . ."

OF MICE AND MEN
by John Steinbeck (Dramatists Play Service)
Drama: Act III, Scene 1, pp. 59–63; Lennie (30–40) and Curley's wife (20s).
Curley's pretty wife has decided to leave her jealous husband and run away to Hollywood to pursue a career in the movies. As she hides her suitcase in the barn for tonight's escape, she encounters Lennie, who is sadly hiding there because he has accidentally killed his new puppy. Lennie tells her about the farm he and George are going to have someday, and she tells him about how she is really cut out to be an actress. Then she places his hand on her hair so he can see how soft it is. When Lennie innocently grasps her hair, she panics and tries to get away from him. He then he accidentally breaks her neck, killing her. For this scene to work, Lennie must clearly be a physically powerful man, a child with the strength of a giant. Start, Curley's wife: "What—what you doin' here?" End, Lennie: "I'll throw him away. It's bad enough like it is."

OH DAD, POOR DAD, MAMMA'S HUNG YOU IN THE CLOSET
AND I'M FEELIN' SO SAD
by Arthur Kopit (Samuel French)
Comedy: Act I, Scene 2, pp. 16–24; Rosalie (20–25) and Jonathan (18–25).
Rosalie babysits for the absentee couple in the penthouse across the way and comes to visit Jonathan, who has recently arrived in this Caribbean resort with his mother. In this comically wild first meeting, Rosalie learns that Jonathan's mother has completely shielded him from the outside world. As a result, he has no social skills or experience with the opposite sex, and he devotes all of his energy to his hobbies, coin and stamp collecting. Toward the end of the

scene, Rosalie turns seductive; this behavior stumps Jonathan. You'll need the sound of an off-stage cuckoo clock that gets progressively louder. Start, Rosalie: "But if you've been here two weeks, why haven't I seen you?" End, Jonathan: "I—I—I llllove you. I love you, I love you, I love you, I. . . ."

OLD TIMES
by Harold Pinter (Evergreen)
Drama: Act I; Deeley (40s) and Kate (40s).
As Kate and Deeley wait at home for her friend's arrival, they discuss Anna, who Kate hasn't seen for 20 years. Actually, Anna is standing onstage during all of this, but she hasn't entered the scene. Start, Kate: "Dark." End, Deeley: "Anyway, none of this matters."
Drama: Act II; Deeley (40s) and Anna (40s).
Kate is in the bathroom. Deeley and Anna talk. Did Deeley and Anna know each other before Deeley married Kate? Were Anna and Kate lovers? Only playwright Harold Pinter knows for sure. Start, Deeley: "Here we are. Good and hot." End, Deeley: "If I walked into The Wayfarers Tavern now, and saw you sitting in the corner, I wouldn't recognize you."

OLEANNA
by David Mamet (Dramatists Play Service)
Drama: Act II, pp. 30–36; John (35–45) and Carol (20).
John's tenure was derailed because of the sexual-harassment accusations one of his students filed. In this 15-page act, he has summoned Carol to his office to try to resolve the issue before more damage is done. There is, however, no reasoning with her. You'll need a telephone that rings. Start, John: "You see, I love to teach. And flatter myself I am skilled at it." End, Carol: "Let me go. Let me Go. Would somebody help me please . . . ?" For a shorter excerpt, start, Carol: "Whatever you have done to me—to the extent that you've done it to me, do you know, rather than to me as a student." Continue to the same end.

ONLY GAME IN TOWN, THE
by Frank D. Gilroy (Samuel French)
Drama: Act I, Scene 7, pp. 37–47; Fran Walker (28) and Thomas Lockwood (52).
Tom Lockwood, Fran Walker's longtime lover, shows up unexpectedly at her Las Vegas apartment and lets himself in while she is at work. Fran walks in at 2 A.M. with Joe Grady, who lives with her, and is stunned to discover Tom sitting in the living room. Joe leaves them alone, and Tom tells her that he has obtained a divorce at last and wants her to marry him. Initially ecstatic, Fran suddenly realizes that she can't go through with it. She tells Tom that she isn't going with him, that she has fallen in love with Joe. Start, Fran: "I've been living with him." End, Fran: "You too, Mister."
Drama: Act II, Scene 2, pp. 60–71; Fran Walker (28) and Joe Grady (30–35).
Joe Grady and Fran Walker have had a relationship-of-convenience for two years, neither having spoken the words, "I love you." After a traumatic day and night during which Joe gambles away all of his money—and then wins it back—he realizes his love for Fran is important. He returns to the apartment, declares his feelings, and asks her to marry him. Fran is still afraid of deep emotional commitment and resists at first. Then she agrees. This is the final scene of the play. Start, Joe: "Top of the morning." End, Joe: "One . . . two . . . three."

OPEN ADMISSIONS
by Shirley Lauro (Samuel French)
Drama: Act I, pp. 50–60; Ginny (30s) and Calvin (18).
Calvin realizes that his grades in the New York state university system mean nothing. He has been getting "Bs" but doesn't understand 10 percent of the subject matter covered. Here, Calvin

confronts Ginny, one of his teachers, as she is leaving for the day. This is a very powerful, sometimes physical scene. For a lengthy excerpt, you can begin with Ginny's telephone call, which establishes her personal problems. End, Calvin: "Burn it! Bullshittin Image bitch!!! Burn it, burn it, down, down, down down!!!" For a shorter version, begin as Ginny starts to leave the room and discovers Calvin. Start, Ginny: "OOOHH!! You scared me!" Continue to the same end.

Drama: Act II, pp. 70–75; Salina (20s) and Calvin (18).
When Calvin arrived home, he was still upset by the confrontation with his teacher and slapped his 7-year-old niece. Now he is overcome with guilt. Calvin's sister, Salina, tries to figure out what is going on with him and when she realizes he means to quit school, she hits the roof. Eliminate the niece's line, and roll up some blankets to serve as the child onstage. Start, Salina: "Calvin! . . . Calvin!" End, Salina: "Oh Lord God, where you goin? Come back! Don't do nothin' crazy, hear? Calvin?!?!? Oh God!"

Drama: Act II, pp. 80–87; Ginny (30s) and Calvin (18).
In the final scene, Calvin and his teacher come to terms with each other, and Ginny agrees to actually teach him something rather than give him "Bs" and walk him through the classes. This dynamic scene is very physical at times and quite emotional. Start, Ginny: "Oh! My God! Calvin! You scared me!" Continue to the end of the play. End, Calvin: "Asking . . . asking . . . asking . . . asking. . . ."

OTHER PEOPLE'S MONEY
by Jerry Sterner (Samuel French)
Comedy-Drama: Act I, pp. 46–50; Garfinkle (40–45) and Kate (35).
Kate and Garfinkle, two bright, aggressive people, talk business, but there is a sexual subtext, which is sometimes overt. Start, Garfinkle: "You know what kills me? I've done maybe seven—eight deals like this." End, Garfinkle: "I think I'm falling in love."

Comedy-Drama: Act II, pp. 75–78; Garfinkle (40–45) and Bea (early 60s).
Kate's mother, Bea, tries to give Garfinkle money from her personal stock holdings because she wants him to stop his efforts to take over the company she works for. Start, Bea: "Good afternoon, Mr. Garfinkle." End, Bea: "I hope you choke on your money and die!"

OTHERWISE ENGAGED
by Simon Gray (Samuel French)
Comedy-Drama: Act II, pp. 31–36; Simon (39) and Beth (30s).
Simon has suspected for months that his wife, Beth, is having an affair, but he has chosen to say nothing about it. Simon himself isn't altogether sexually faithful. In this comically tense scene, Beth returns from a supposed business trip, which was actually a tryst, and all the cards are laid on the table. Written in the British vernacular. Begin after Stephen exits. Start, Beth: "What did he say?" Stop just before Dave's entrance. End, Beth: "Because I hate you."

PHILADELPHIA STORY, THE
by Philip Barry (Samuel French)
Comedy: Act II, Scene 2, pp. 76–82; Tracy Lord (24) and Mike Connor (30).
Mike Connor and a female photographer are on assignment for a gossip magazine, reporting on the wedding of wealthy socialite Tracy Lord to successful, self-made businessperson George Kittredge. One thing has led to another and, in this scene, Tracy and Mike find themselves in a romantic embrace. It is almost dawn, and both of them have had a bit to drink. Nice romantic-comedy scene. Start, Tracy: "Hello, you." End, Tracy: "Not me—oh, not me! Put me in your pocket, Mike."

PIANO LESSON, THE
by August Wilson (Plume)
Comedy-Drama: Act II, Scene 2; Avery (38) and Berniece (35).
Avery tries to get Berniece to marry him, telling her she can use the piano in his new church. But she doesn't want to get married. Start, Berniece: "Who is it?" End, Avery: "God says He will soothe the troubled waters. I'll come by tomorrow and bless the house."

PICNIC
by William Inge (Dramatists Play Service)
Drama: Act II, pp. 54–56; Madge (18) and Hal (early 20s).
Everyone except Madge and Hal have departed for the picnic. Hal is trying to sort out his feelings from an earlier confrontation with Rosemary Sidney, who accused him of being a bum and a fraud. Madge and Hal talk and kiss, and at scene's end, walk off hand in hand, presumably to make love. Start, Madge: "Don't feel bad. Women like Miss Sidney make me disgusted with the whole female sex." End, Hal: "Do we? There's other places . . . with not so many people."
Drama: Act III, Scene 1, pp. 57–60; Rosemary Sidney (about 40) and Howard (42).
After making love with Rosemary Sidney, Howard brings her home. She is depressed and shaken. As he turns to leave, she suddenly and intensely demands that he marry her but he, being a confirmed bachelor, hedges. Start, Howard: "Here we are, honey." End, Howard: "Good night."

PLAY MEMORY
by Joanna M. Glass (Samuel French)
Drama: Act II, pp. 59–62; Jean MacMillan (20s, playing early teens) and Cam (late 50s).
Jean MacMillan comes home from school and, as usual, finds Cam, her father, sitting alone, immersed in self-pity. She tells him how much she longs for a "normal" family, and he launches into a speech about how despicable "normal" is. Jean is frustrated and sad that she can't seem to inspire her father to get his act together. Cam knows how his behavior appears to others, but he is evidently unable to change. His is a slow, steady descent into alcoholism and poverty. Start, Cam: "Hello . . . May I deduce that things did not go well at school today?" End, Cam: "I can see you need to—change your clothes."
Drama: Act II, pp. 68–72; Ruth (50s) and Cam (late 50s).
After Cam swapped his 12-year-old daughter's beautiful carved closet door for some liquor, she stopped talking. She hasn't made a sound for two weeks. This scene begins as Ruth, Cam's wife, comes in, having spoken to the school counselor about options. The counselor has suggested that mother and daughter move out of this home and has arranged a place for them to go. But Ruth wants more than anything to hold the family together, even in the face of its poverty and alcoholism. Cam, however, knows that the situation has gone too far, and he encourages Ruth to take the girl and leave him. He insists and, finally, Ruth agrees. A very touching, intense scene. Start, Ruth: "Any change in Jean?" End, Cam: "Should have paid more attention since he's now to be the—steward of my family."

PORCH
by Jeffrey Sweet (Samuel French)
Drama: One-act play, pp. 8–14; Amy (early 30s) and Ernest Herbert (early 60s).
Ernest Herbert is a widower facing exploratory surgery tomorrow. In this scene, he presses Amy, his daughter and only surviving child, to marry and have a family, to give him grandchildren. Start, Herbert: "So tell me." End, Herbert: "No, you're not."
Drama: One-act play, pp. 21–31; Amy (early 30s) and Sam (early 30s).
Amy is visiting with her father when her old high-school boyfriend, Sam, shows up. Amy's father told Sam that she was in town, hoping that sparks would fly again between these two

......, who haven't seen each other for 11 years. Begin after Herbert leaves them alone on the porch. Start, Amy: "Subtle, isn't he?" End, Amy: "Yup."
Drama: One-act play, pp. 30–39; Amy (early 30s) and Sam (early 30s).
Amy still believes that the decision she made years ago to abort her pregnancy by Sam was the right one. Even though she hasn't seen him or answered his letters for 11 years, some of those old sparks are still warm, however. In this excerpt, Sam and Amy talk about what might have been, but she refuses to rekindle their romance. Start, Sam: "You ever wonder what would have happened if we'd gone through with it? Gotten married, had the kid?" Stop with Sam's exit. End, Amy: "Yuh."

PRELUDE TO A KISS
by Craig Lucas (Broadway Play Publishing)
Comedy: Act I; Rita (mid-to-late 20s) and Peter (mid-to-late 20s).
Because most scenes in this play are quite short, you'll probably want to combine two. In this excerpt, the first part takes place in Rita's apartment. After Peter and Rita make love, they talk about sexual fantasies, whether or not to have children, and political preferences—the kinds of topics you would expect new lovers to talk about. In the second part, which takes place in Rita's apartment six weeks later, Peter asks Rita to marry him. As written, the scenes are intended to be played back-to-back. Start, Peter: "Christ!" End, Rita: "Uh huh."

PRISONER OF SECOND AVENUE, THE
by Neil Simon (Samuel French)
Comedy: Act I, Scene 2, pp. 18–29; Mel (46) and Edna (early 40s).
Mel is in a bad enough mood because he lost his job. Then he comes home to discover his apartment has been robbed. The thieves even took his dental floss. This rather long scene moves fast. You'll need props that suggest the apartment has been ransacked. Start, Edna: "Edison . . . Mrs. Edna Edison . . . I've just been robbed." End, Mel: "Because it's not a heart attack. It's pains in my chest."

PRIVATE LIVES
by Noël Coward (Samuel French)
Comedy: Act I, pp. 10–12; Sybil (23) and Elyot (30).
The setting: the terrace of Elyot and Sybil's honeymoon suite on a romantic, moonlit night in the south of France. Sybil went inside to dress for dinner and, as she returns, is shocked to hear an inexplicably rattled Elyot announce that he wants to leave the hotel immediately. His insistence leads to an argument when she balks. What Sybil doesn't realize, however, is that Elyot discovered only a few moments ago that his ex-wife, Amanda, is honeymooning with her new husband in the adjacent suite! Start, Sybil: "Cocktail, please." End, Sybil: "Oh, Elli, Elli, Elli."
Comedy: Act I, pp. 13–15; Amanda (late 20s) and Victor (35).
The setting: the balcony of Amanda and Victor's honeymoon suite on the same romantic, moonlit night in the south of France. Victor went inside to dress for dinner and, as he returns, is shocked to hear an inexplicably rattled Amanda announce that she wants to leave the hotel immediately. Her insistence leads to an argument when he balks. What he doesn't realize, however, is that Amanda discovered only a few moments ago that her ex-husband, Elyot, is honeymooning with his new wife in the adjacent suite! Start, Victor: "You were certainly right when you said you weren't normal." End, Amanda: "Go away, go away, go away."
Comedy: Act I, pp. 15–22; Amanda (late 20s) and Elyot (30).
Amanda and Elyot's new spouses have left their respective hotel suites in anger, and Amanda and Elyot confront each other on their respective terraces. Still madly in love, the formerly married couple soon decides to abandon their new spouses, cast caution to the wind, and run away together to Paris. The characters refer to offstage music at key points in this scene. If you

don't use music, omit the corresponding references. Start, Amanda: "Thoughtful of them to play that, wasn't it?" End, Elyot: "Solomon Issacs." For an alternative, shorter excerpt that doesn't require smoking, start, Amanda: "I'm in such a rage." Continue to the same end.
Comedy: Act II, pp. 24–29; Amanda (late 20s) and Elyot (30).
Act II is a prolonged scene between Amanda and Elyot in her Paris flat. The scene begins very romantically and ends with the couple literally rolling on the floor fighting, obviously on the road to breaking up again. Start, Amanda: "I'm glad we let Louise go." End, Elyot: "I think I love you more than ever before. Isn't it ridiculous? Put your feet up."

PROPOSAL, THE

by Anton Chekhov [*The Sneeze, Play and Stories* by Anton Chekhov, translated and adapted by Michael Frayn (Samuel French)]
Comedy: One-act play, pp. 84–89; Natalya Stepanovna (25) and Lomov (35).
Lomov has finally gotten up the nerve to ask Natalya Stepanovna to marry him. But before he can get to the important part of his proposal, the exchange degenerates into an argument about whether her family or his owns a nearby parcel of property, Ox Lea Meadows. Start, Natalya: "Oh, good Lord, it's you!" End, Lomov: "They're mine!"

P. S. YOUR CAT IS DEAD

by James Kirkwood [revised edition (Samuel French)]
Comedy: Act I, Scene 1, pp. 15–23; Jimmy (38) and Kate (32).
Kate has chosen New Year's Eve to break off her relationship with Jimmy. While he is out of the apartment, she is packing her stuff. Jimmy comes home unexpectedly, and he and Kate have a breakup scene. Start, Kate: "Oh — Jimmy." End, Kate: "Enchanting! . . . Good-bye!"

RAINMAKER, THE

by N. Richard Nash (Samuel French)
Drama: Act II, pp. 64–70; Lizzie (27) and File (late 30s).
File has traveled to the Curry place supposedly to apologize for hitting Lizzie's brother Jim earlier in the day. The truth is that File wants to see Lizzie. They're attracted to each other, but neither is comfortable with the opposite sex. This nice scene is frequently overlooked because everyone wants to do the Lizzie/Starbuck scenes. Eliminate Noah's brief interruption. Start, Lizzie: "How about a cup of coffee?" End, File: "Don't be so damn ridiculous. Be yourself."
Drama: Act II, pp. 75–79; Lizzie (27) and Starbuck (30s).
Lizzie was humiliated by her brother Noah when he called her an old maid and suggested that she get used to the idea that she is, in fact, plain, not pretty. Distraught, she ran from the room, picking up Starbuck's bed linen on the way. She came directly to the barn where he is spending the night, intent on delivering the linen to him. During the scene, Starbuck tells Lizzie that she is pretty. They kiss. Start, Starbuck: "Who's that? . . . Who's there?" Continue to the end of the act. End, Lizzie: "Oh, is it me? Is it really me?!"
Drama: Act III, pp. 88–90; Lizzie (27) and Starbuck (30s).
In the afterglow of lovemaking, Starbuck confesses to Lizzie that he is a fraud and a dreamer, and that, contrary to his claims, he has never made it rain. Start, Starbuck: "And I always walk so fast and ride so far I never have time to stop and ask myself no question." End, Lizzie: "And then one night you look down—and there it is—shining in your hand!"

RAISIN IN THE SUN, A

by Lorraine Hansberry (Samuel French)
Drama: Act III, pp. 113–119: Beneatha (20) and Asagai (mid-20s).
Beneatha's older brother, Walter Lee, has foolishly entrusted the family nest egg to a would-be business partner who promptly stole it. Now, facing a future with no funds for medical

school, Beneatha is growing more embittered about the sorry state of humanity. When Asagai, her Nigerian friend and fellow student, arrives, they have a full-force philosophical disagreement over these matters. Then Asagai asks Beneatha to marry him, to go live in Nigeria, and to rediscover her African roots. Start, Asagai: "I came over . . . I had some free time." End, Asagai: "How often I have looked at you and said, 'ah—so this is what the New World hath finally wrought.'"

RED COAT, THE
by John Patrick Shanley [*Welcome to the Moon and Other Plays* (Dramatists Play Service); *13 by Shanley* (Applause)]
Comedy: One-act play, DPS pp. 9–12; Mary (16) and John (17).
In this short play, John is at a festive party but still feels lonely, so he goes outside to sit in the light of the full moon. When Mary, who is on her way to the same party, arrives, they talk. Their conversation quickly becomes an exultant declaration of mutual love and understanding. Start, John: "Hi, Mary." End, John: "I know I can feel them shining."

REUNION
by David Mamet (Samuel French)
Drama: One-act play; Carol (24) and Bernie (53).
The subject of this one-act play is the reunion of a father and daughter after a 20-year separation. Just 23 pages long, the play is divided into 14 brief scenes that take place during a single conversation. One option is to perform scenes 1, 2, and 3 without interruption; together, they contain plenty of subtext (pp. 9–16). This excerpt includes the opening moments of Carol and her father Bernie's meeting. They're trying to figure out how to talk to one another and feeling their way in the dark. Start, Bernie: "I would have recognized you anywhere. it is you. Isn't it?" End, Bernie: "I'll be goddamned if I don't feel like I'm gonna bust out crying.' And I almost did."

A second option is to perform scenes 10, 11, 12, 13, and 14 without interruption for an excerpt that runs about 5½ pages (pp. 27–32). In the final moments of the play, Carol tells her father that she looked him up because she simply "felt lonely . . . I never had a father." He gives her a gift, a gold bracelet he had specially inscribed to mark the occasion. Start, Bernie: "But I can't work for the phone company anymore. When they finally pulled my license, that was it." End, Bernie: "Thank you."

ROAD TO NIRVANA
by Arthur Kopit (Samuel French)
Comedy: Act II, pp. 79–89; Jerry (30s to 40s) and Nirvana (late 20s).
Nirvana, rock's biggest female star, and Jerry spend their first moments alone next to her massive swimming pool. They talk about reincarnation, loyalty, and movie deals. What Jerry doesn't know is that Nirvana is sizing him up and, very soon, will ask for his testicles, or at least one of them, as proof of his loyalty to her and the price of her participation in the movie project he is producing. Start, Nirvana: "Have you any coke?" End, Nirvana: "You're my protector now."

SCENES AND REVELATIONS
by Elan Garonzik (Samuel French)
Comedy-Drama: Scene 6, pp. 20–24; Millie (23, playing teens) and Dennis (20s, playing teens).
Millie dreams of being a famous painter. In this flashback scene, she paints a portrait of Dennis, the young man from the farm next door. He is feeling his oats and wants her to be the first one he kisses, so after a while they go ahead and do it. Dennis discovers that kissing Millie "ain't like kissin' old Aunt Eleanor or huggin' my horse." Start, Millie: "Dennis

Houser, how could you speak such an awful lie! Why you make me just indignant!" End, Millie: "Oh, Dennis Houser, eat your raspberries."
Drama: Scene 10, pp. 32–37; Helena (25) and Samuel (27).
The year is 1893, and Samuel, the manager of Helena's Pennsylvania farm, is trying to save up enough money to head west. But he and Helena have known one another for a few weeks, and romance is in the air. In this 5-page scene, which takes place in a ripe raspberry patch, they dance around the issues of commitment and marriage. In a nice monologue, Helena tells Samuel about her first true love and how it evaporated. Then they kiss. Start, Samuel: "And we spent seven dollars on new planking for the barn." End, Samuel: "Wanting so much. Desiring so much."
Comedy-Drama: Scene 12, pp. 40–46; Millie (21) and Dennis (21).
It is Dennis's birthday, and Millie has bought him a pipe. They smoke the pipe together as they talk about the future. She admits that she has always loved him, that she knows he loves her, and that she expects them to marry. Dennis then tells Millie that he has been courting another woman. Millie may be crushed, but she takes the high road, wishing him all the luck in the world. Then they go skinny-dipping. Start, Millie: "Dennis! Deeennnisss! Hurry up! Or the moon'll go down and we won't see a thing." End, Millie: "Anyway, Dennis Houser, this is 1893. And that's not the Middle Ages!"

SEA GULL, THE
by Anton Chekhov [a new version by Jean-Claude Van Itallie (Dramatists Play Service)]
Drama: Act IV, pp. 49–53; Nina (21) and Treplev (27).
Two years ago Nina left her father's comfortable home outside Moscow, moved to the big city to become an actress, and began an affair with Trigorin, a famous novelist much older than she. The affair resulted in a child who died and, ultimately, Trigorin abandoned her. Nina's acting career has been mediocre but since she has been disowned by her father, she is forced to make her meager living from the stage.

In this scene, Nina appears unexpectedly one night in Treplev's studio. He is ecstatic to see her since he has loved her madly for years. He again declares his undying love; she, in turn, tells him she still loves Trigorin even though the man has treated her badly. As quickly as Nina appeared, she bids farewell to Treplev, leaving for a winter acting engagement in a distant province. After her departure, Treplev is in despair over this love that will never be fulfilled and takes his own life. Start, Treplev: "I've talked a lot about new forms." End, Treplev: "I hope no one sees her in the garden and tells Mamma. Mamma would be upset."

SEA HORSE, THE
by Edward J. Moore (Samuel French)
Drama: Act I, pp. 11–19; Gertrude (late 30s) and Harry (late 30s).
This two-character play examines the relationship between a strong, independent woman and the sailor who has come to love her, and there are a number of possibilities for scenes. In one scene, which is filled with conflict, Harry tells Gertrude about his plans to buy a fishing boat and marry her. She doesn't like the idea because she can't accept that kind of intimacy. They argue, and then make up. If you decide to use this play for scene-study work, keep in mind playwright Edward J. Moore's important casting consideration: Gertrude is described by the playwright as a "big woman," and she should be overweight. Start, Gertrude: "This run was a lot longer, wasn't it?" End, Gertrude: "Yeah, I think you better tell me about it now!"
Drama: Act II, pp. 33–41; Gertrude (late 30s) and Harry (late 30s).
Gertrude wakes up to find Harry fixing breakfast for her and trying to make amends for the fight they had last night. Still unwilling to accept this kind of intimacy, she gets angry. Start, Harry: "Oh . . . morning . . . Wow!" End, Harry: "Yeah, yeah, yeah, yeah!"

SEXUAL PERVERSITY IN CHICAGO
by David Mamet (Samuel French)
Comedy: One-act play, pp. 14–17; Bernard (30–35) and Joan (about 25).
In this short scene, Bernard tries to pick Joan up in a singles bar. He is arrogant, crude, dishonest, and insulting. It is unclear why Joan is in a singles bar in the first place. Start, Bernard: "Evening. Good evening." End, Bernard: "You got a lot of fuckin' nerve."

SHADOW BOX, THE
by Michael Cristofer (Samuel French)
Drama: Act I, pp. 13–18; Joe (48–55) and Maggie (38–45).
Joe hasn't seen his wife, Maggie, and their young son for six months. During his time here in the hospital, he has come to terms with his prognosis of terminal cancer, but she is still in denial. Maggie continues to put on a happy face, hoping everything will turn out okay. During this scene, Maggie tries to get Joe to come back home and talks about plans for the future. But Joe resists. He insists that she realize how very much he loves her even though he is dying. In the end, the reality of the situation drags Maggie into despair. Start, Maggie: "End of line." End, Maggie: "I knew it. I knew it."
Drama: Act I, pp. 22–27; Beverly (mid-30s) and Mark (25–30).
Beverly has come to the hospital to visit her ex-husband, Brian, who is dying of cancer. She drinks herself into a party mood and when she happily bursts into his room, she is surprised to find herself face-to-face with his male lover, Mark, who isn't happy at all to see her. Start, Beverly: "Surprise!" End, Beverly: "Hey!"
Drama: Act I, pp. 37–44; Brian (mid-40s) and Beverly (mid-30s).
Beverly gets reacquainted with Brian, her ex-husband, now that he is dying. They talk about their feelings and come to terms with his prognosis. Laughter through tears. No longer married, they are still good friends. Start, Beverly: "Caro! Caro! You old fart!" End, Beverly: "Yes. But why is it I always seem to end up in Naples?"
Drama: Act II, pp. 76–80; Joe (48–55) and Maggie (38–45).
Here, Joe and Maggie talk about the farm they never had and their life together, and Maggie begins to accept the fact that Joe is going to die from cancer. Start, Joe: "It would have been nice." End, Maggie: "I can't. I can't."

SIGHT UNSEEN
by Donald Margulies (Dramatists Play Service)
Drama: Act I, Scene 1, pp. 9–20; Patricia (35–45) and Jonathan (35–45).
During the years following the failure of Jonathan and Patricia's love affair, he has become a celebrated and financially successful painter. On the occasion of his first major exhibit outside North America, he looks Patricia up. She is now married to an archaeologist and living on a farm in Norfolk, England. Start, Jonathan: "You look beautiful." End, Patricia: "You aren't invited. You're cold. I think it actually is warmer inside."
Drama: Act I, Scene 4, pp. 32–36; Patricia (35–45) and Jonathan (35–45).
In this flashback scene that takes place shortly after Jonathan's mother's death, he tells Patricia, who has come to console him, that he no longer loves her. Start, Patricia: "Jonathan?" End, Jonathan: "I don't love you, Patty."

SIGN IN SIDNEY BRUSTEIN'S WINDOW, THE
by Lorraine Hansberry (Samuel French)
Drama: Act II, Scene 1, pp. 66–69; Iris (29) and Sidney (late 30s).
Iris and Sidney sit on the terrace of their Greenwich Village apartment at dawn and pretend that they're gazing at the mountains. The couple talks about the forces that are tearing their marriage apart. Sidney longs for simplicity, innocence, and quiet in his life; Iris longs to make

it in the big city. A brief, lovely, and poetic scene. Start, Iris: "Sid-? Sidney? What are you doing outside?" End, Iris: "Take me into the cabin." If you can arrange the offstage clatter of a garbage can clatter, end, Iris: "Take a shower, Mountain Man!"
Drama: Act II, Scene 2, pp. 73–78; Iris (29) and Sidney (late 30s).
Push is coming to shove in Iris and Sidney's relationship, and tonight she is going to a cocktail party—without Sidney. He isn't happy about this. Start, Sidney: "Say, Iris, what did Mavis say about Fred's new promotion, the Folk River Dam thing?" End, Iris: "Teaching little kids there was such a thing."
Drama: Act II, Scene 3, pp. 97–102; Iris (29) and Sidney (late 30s).
This is the breakup scene. Iris is moving out, and Sidney believes she is heading down the wrong road, selling her principles cheaply by appearing in television commercials. Iris, however, believes she is growing up. Start, Iris: "Thanks for covering. I couldn't have taken Mavis tonight." End, Iris: "For God's sake, Sidney, take down that sign! It's like spit in your face!"

SILENT NIGHT, LONELY NIGHT
by Robert Anderson (Samuel French)
Drama: Act I, Scene 2, pp. 33–43; Katherine (mid-30s) and John (40).
John and Katherine occupy adjoining rooms in a New England inn this Christmas Eve. The only other guests in the inn are the honeymooners upstairs. After meeting for the first time a few hours ago, Katherine and John went to a movie and had drinks in Katherine's room with the other couple afterward. Alone again now, with dawn approaching, the prospect of whether or not to go to bed together hangs in the air.
   Katherine says that it isn't going to happen and then tells John about the trouble she is having with her husband. He, in turn, tells her about other Christmases abroad. Both of them need to be close to someone tonight, so rather than return to his room, John sleeps on the sofa. Start, Katherine: "Maybe I'd better say something. It may sound ridiculous, but . . . Oh, no, it is ridiculous." End, John: "Christmas Eve is Hell, isn't it? The Fourth of July is much easier." For a 5-page version of this scene, start, Katherine: "What are you doing here alone in a God-forsaken spot on Christmas Eve?" Continue to the same end.
Drama: Act II, Scene 2, pp. 57–62; Katherine (mid-30s) and John (40).
This scene is filled to the brim with subtext. John and Katherine have bared their souls and finally slept together only a few hours ago. Now they're going their separate ways with no regrets, certain that the experience was significant, important, and perhaps even lifesaving. John enters Katherine's room as she is packing. You'll need a telephone to ring. Start, John: "Good morning." End, Katherine: "I have nothing either . . . (reaches in her pocket) A handkerchief."

SNOWANGEL
by Lewis John Carlino [*Cages* (Dramatists Play Service)]
Drama: One-act play; John (40s) and Connie (35–45).
This 19-page, one-act play centers on a meeting between a prostitute and a john at 4 A.M. Several excerpts capture the essence of Connie and John's involvement. One option is to begin at the top of the play and continue through John's suggestion that Connie reenact the first meeting he had with his first love (pp. 7–15). Connie responds with outrage and telephones her pimp, who tells her that she has to do it. Start, John: "Connie? . . . Connie? End, Connie: "You got your way! Now what'a ya want me to do?"
   The second scene choice begins where the first excerpt ends and continues to the end of the play (pp. 15–26). This excerpt is far more physically and emotionally demanding than the first one. Connie gets progressively drunker while she attempts to act out John's fantasy, and he is frustrated with her inability to do it as he remembers it. Finally, he slaps her. When Connie recovers, they begin to act out her first-love fantasy. Start, John: "Your dresses in here?" End, Connie: "A dark angel . . . it's me. Me!"

SOCIAL EVENT, A
by William Inge [*Eleven Short Plays by William Inge* (Dramatists Play Service)]
Comedy: One-act play, pp. 30–35; Randy (25–30) and Carole (25–30).
A rare comedy from William Inge. Randy and Carole are two Hollywood actors on the make. They're trying to get an invitation to the funeral of a prominent actor they cared little about. All that matters to them is being seen at this social event. Start, Randy: "Muriel? We're getting up now. Bring up the usual breakfast." End, Randy: "Just a slight case so you could tell them with a straight face."

SORROWS OF STEPHEN
by Peter Parnell (Samuel French)
Comedy: Act I, Scene 2, pp. 11–17; Stephen (mid-20s) and Liz (mid-20s).
When Stephen arrives at the apartment he shares with Liz, he is stunned to discover her packing to leave him. He tries to talk her out of her decision while she packs. They discuss the situation in a civil and enlightened way, they kiss and hug, and then she leaves. Start, Stephen: "I don't believe it." Stop with Liz's exit, or continue to the end of the scene and end, Stephen: ". . . Sorry. I'm sorry to disturb you . . . I must have copied the wrong . . . number. . . ."
Comedy: Act II, Scene 2, pp. 53–61; Stephen (mid-20s) and Christine (mid-20s).
Christine loves William, but she has begun an affair with his best friend, Stephen. Both Stephen and Christine feel conflicted about this romantic triangle, but they kiss and hug a great deal. Start, Christine (reading): "As you know me, you will understand only too clearly what attracts me." End, Stephen: "Let me embrace you. Let me make you feel safe."
Comedy: Act II, Scene 5, pp. 69–75; William (mid-20s) and Christine (mid-20s).
William has booked a lovely suite at the Plaza Hotel for Christine and himself. He is still apologizing for last night's mix-up at the opera when he punched the man he erroneously suspected was having an affair with her. William has been drinking champagne and is now tipsy. When he asks Christine to marry him, she agrees even though she also secretly loves Stephen. You'll need a bed for the scene. Start, Christine (reading): "Lotte had slept little that night." End, Christine: "The Yanamam. Yes."
Comedy: Act II, Scene 7, pp. 77–83; Stephen (mid-20s) and Christine (mid-20s).
On a romantic, rainy afternoon in the sculpture garden at New York's Museum of Modern Art, Stephen asks Christine to marry him. She refuses, explaining that she is going to marry Stephen's best friend, William. She then says that she and Stephen have to end their affair. This is a good scene because Christine legitimately loves both men. Start, Christine: "It's nice out here, isn't it?" End, Stephen: "Christine, please! Go!"

SPEED OF DARKNESS, THE
by Steve Tesich (Samuel French)
Drama: Act II, Scene 1, pp. 47–50; Joe (mid-40s) and Anne (mid-30s).
Joe and his wife, Anne, talk about the fact that he isn't their daughter's natural father. How are they going to break this to her? Although the scene is only about three pages long, it contains a great deal of texture. Start, Joe: "I thought you were asleep. Where're you going?" End, Joe: "As soon as Lou leaves, we'll tell her."

SPEED-THE-PLOW
by David Mamet (Samuel French)
Comedy: Act I, pp. 37–44; Karen (20s) and Gould (35–45).
This is a good scene in which studio executive Gould has most of the lines. He is "teaching" Karen, his sexy temp secretary, about the movie system before assigning her a boring book on radiation to read. Gould is actually after a roll in the hay with Karen. She comes off as more naive than she is. Start, Karen: "Mr. Gould." End, Gould: "And tell him that he owes me five hundred bucks."

Comedy: Act II, pp. 45–55; Karen (20s) and Gould (35–45).
Karen, the sexy office temp, has read the boring radiation book and is pushing it for movie development. Gould wants to get her in bed. Start, Karen: "He puts his hand on the child's chest." End, Karen: "You asked me to come. Here I am." For a shorter version, start, Gould: "You've done a fantastic job." Continue to the same end.

SPLIT SECOND
by Dennis McIntyre (Samuel French)
Drama: Act I, Scene 4, pp. 33–41; Alea (28–35) and Val (28–35).
Val is an African-American New York City cop who, a few hours ago, lost his temper and killed a racist white car thief he'd taken into custody. After shooting the thief, Val restaged the crime scene to make it look like a case of self-defense. It is now 4:30 A.M., and he is arriving home where his wife, Alea, has fallen asleep on the sofa. At first Val lies about what happened earlier, but then he tells Alea the truth. Her reaction is to tell him he made the right choice by officially altering the facts. Start, Alea: "What time is it?" End, Val: "No."
Drama: Act II, Scene 4, pp. 65–69; Alea (28–35) and Rusty (55–60).
Alea and Rusty, Val's father, both know what actually happened when Val shot and killed a white car thief who was already handcuffed and in custody. Rusty, a retired cop, is ashamed of his son's actions and the subsequent lie he told to cover up the crime. Alea thinks that expediency was the best choice, that it was better for Val to distort the truth than to risk going to jail. In this tense, 4-page scene, Alea tries to get Rusty to change his position to one of support for his son. Start, Rusty: "We could have talked about it over the phone." End, Alea: "As long as he's here, that's all that counts."

SPOILS OF WAR
by Michael Weller (Samuel French)
Drama: Act I, pp. 7–16; Elise (mid-30s) and Martin (16).
Martin comes home from boarding school to find the electricity turned off in his mother's small Greenwich Village apartment. Elise doesn't realize that he has been seeing her estranged husband on the sly, planning to engineer a reconciliation between them. An interesting scene because of the age differences between the characters and their complex relationship. Elise is quite the bohemian. Start, Martin: "Mom!" End, Elise: "Angel!"
Drama: Act I, pp. 39–41; Penny (20s) and Martin (16).
In this short scene, Martin talks to Penny, his father's girlfriend, and tries to convince her to not show up at the party next Sunday. Penny doesn't know that Martin is scheming to get his mother and father together at that function. Start, Martin: "I got lost after the Sheep Meadow, sorry." End, Penny: "I know my overalls stink, but I can still smell bullshit when a truckload of it falls on my head. The answer is no, en-oh."
Drama: Act I, pp. 42–46; Elise (mid-30s) and Martin (16).
Martin finally tells his mother that he has been secretly seeing his father for some time. He then tells Elise that next Sunday he wants her to come to a party that his father will be at. Elise resists at first but then agrees to attend. Start, Elise: "Martin, hurry up in there, what are you doing, plotting the Revolution?!" End, Elise: "After all the pains taken, how could I disappoint? We should call and warn him, it's only fair. But on the other hand, in love and war. Well? What a pair we are, you and I."

STRANGE SNOW
by Steve Metcalfe (Samuel French)
Drama: Act I, Scene 2, pp. 30–41; Megs (late 30s) and Martha (mid-30s).
Megs and Martha share a common high-school-prom fantasy that leads to a moment of true affection, but Martha resists it. The scene requires props because Martha fixes Megs some soup,

which he eats. Stop just before Megs puts his fist angrily through a pane-glass window. Start, Megs: "Martha! Hey, Martha!?" End, Megs: "That bad a dancer, huh!" If you can figure out a way to safely break a window on stage, end, Megs: "Joseph. You're too much, Martha. M-A-R-T-H-A!" **Drama: Act II, Scene 1, pp. 42–48; Dave (late 30s) and Martha (mid-30s).**
Dave, who is unwilling to confront his personal demons, definitely doesn't want Megs, his old Vietnam War buddy, to come for dinner. But Martha, Dave's sister, is attracted to Megs and definitely wants him to come. Start, Dave: "What a ya mean you invited him over for dinner?" End, Dave: "Get'm for me, huh?"

STRANGEST KIND OF ROMANCE, THE

by Tennessee Williams [*The Theater of Tennessee Williams,* Volume 6 (New Directions)]
Drama: Scene 2; Landlady (40) and Little Man (35–40).
Little Man has moved into this seedy rooming house and keeps to himself, becoming friends with the cat that was left behind by a former boarder. In this scene, Landlady, who is lonely, walks in on Little Man and tries to seduce him. This event only makes him more nervous and uncertain. Later in the play, Little Man has a complete nervous breakdown. This scene is appropriate for sophisticated actors. Start, Landlady: "Oh—you were playing possum." End, Landlady: "Nature says—'Don't—be lonesome!'"

STREETCAR NAMED DESIRE, A

by Tennessee Williams (Dramatists Play Service)
Drama: Act I, Scene 2, pp. 20–24; Stanley (about 30) and Stella (late 20s).
Stanley returns to the apartment and discovers Blanche's fine clothing and jewelry lying around. He figures she bought these relatively expensive items with the money she swindled from Stella. This scene requires some specific props, including clothes and jewelry. Start, Stanley: "Hiya, sweetheart." End, Stanley: "You're damn' tootin' I'm goin' to stay here."
Drama: Act I, Scene 2, pp. 27–29; Stanley (about 30) and Blanche (early 30s).
Stanley demands that Blanche show him the documents of sale for Belle Reve, Stella's family home. This short but powerful scene contains their first confrontation. Start, Blanche: "The poor little thing was out there listening to us." End, Blanche: " I didn't know she was going to have a baby."
Drama: Act II, Scene 2, pp. 61–68; Blanche (early 30s) and Mitch (about 30).
In this 7-page scene, Blanche has been coming on to Mitch. Alone in the apartment after a date, they move cautiously toward a deeper relationship. He still doesn't know the truth about her sordid past. If you decide to work on this scene, keep in mind playwright Tennessee Williams's reference to the specifics of Mitch's build. He is 6 feet tall and weighs 207 pounds. Begin at the top of the scene. Start, Blanche: "Well. . . ." End, Blanche: "Sometimes—there's God—so quickly." For a shorter version, start, Mitch: "Blanche—Blanche—guess how much I weigh?" Continue to the same end.

SUBJECT WAS ROSES, THE

by Frank D. Gilroy (Samuel French)
Drama: Act I, Scene 1, pp. 6–10; Nettie (45) and John (50).
It is 1946. Timmy has been discharged from the Army and has returned to the Bronx apartment he has always shared with his parents, Nettie and John. Last night the family celebrated, and Timmy is sleeping it off as John and Nettie talk in the kitchen. They are both grateful that he wasn't killed or injured in World War II, as so many other young men were, and they have plans to really enjoy him now. Their conversation, however, seems to be more like sparring than discussing, and it becomes clear that they are in competition for Timmy's affections. This is the first glimpse of a tense relationship that has been sexless for many years. Start, Nettie: "It's a lovely day . . . Timmy still asleep?" End, John: "Did I say it wasn't? There."

Drama: Act II, Scene 1, pp. 48–51; Nettie (45) and Timmy (21).
Last night, the family ate out in a fancy restaurant and then went to a dance club. After Timmy went to bed, John tried—for the first time in a long time—to make love to Nettie and was rebuffed. This morning, he is in a foul mood and takes his frustration out on Timmy. A few moments ago, John stormed out, apparently on his way to church. In this scene, Timmy blames his mother for the problems at home, says she has never really understood or been supportive of John, and has been too involved with her own mother and cousin. Nettie is stunned by the assault. Start, Nettie: "Now what was that all about?" End, Nettie: "Thank you for the roses."

SUBSTANCE OF FIRE, THE
by Jon Robin Baitz (Samuel French)
Drama: Act II, pp. 48–55; Issac Geldhart (60s) and Marge Hackett (50s).
Marge Hackett, a psychiatric social worker, is sent by Issac Geldhart's children to determine if he is competent to manage his own affairs. It turns out Marge and Issac have much in common. Start, Marge: "We usually do this at the office. It took a bending of the rules." End, Marge: "I'm not from Sotheby and I shouldn't be here. Goodbye, Mr. Geldhart."

SUMMER AND SMOKE
by Tennessee Williams (Dramatists Play Service)
Drama: Part I, Scene 1, pp. 14–19; Alma (25–29) and John (25–29).
John teases Alma for "putting on airs," and she gets angry. Then they make up. Start, Alma: "What book is she talking about?" End, John: "Get one!"
Drama: Part I, Scene 7, pp. 45–51; Alma (25–29) and John (25–29).
John and Alma are on a date, and he wants to go to the cockfights at the Moonlight Casino. When Alma won't hear of it, they argue and she leaves. For scene-study purposes, eliminate Dusty, the waiter. Start, John: "I don't understand why we can't go in the casino." End, Alma: "You're not a gentleman."
Drama: Part II, Scene 5, pp. 69–75; Alma (25–29) and John (25–29).
Alma comes to John's office to let him know that she loves him and is now willing to sleep with him. She discovers that he has changed his mind, however, and that it is too late. Time has passed them by. Start, Alma: "No greetings? No greetings at all?" End, John: "I'll write a prescription for you."

SWEET BIRD OF YOUTH
by Tennessee Williams (Dramatists Play Service)
Drama: Act II, Scene 2; Chance (29) and Aunt Nonnie (35–45).
Aunt Nonnie tries to get Chance to leave town before Boss Finley's henchmen hurt him. But Chance is sinking more deeply into a drug-induced haze and only wants to talk about his love for Heavenly. Start, Aunt Nonnie: "I've got just one thing to tell you, Chance, get out of St. Cloud." End, Aunt Nonnie: "I'll write to you. Send me an address. I'll write to you." (This scene doesn't appear in the DPS acting edition, but you can find it in earlier library compilations.)

TASTE OF HONEY, A
by Shelagh Delaney (Grove Press)
Drama: Act I, Scene 1; Jo (17) and Boy (22).
Jo finds romance with a sailor. In her mind, Boy is a black prince of mysterious origins. And in Boy's mind, Jo is a delightful convenience while he is in port. They haven't been intimate yet, but they will be. A sexual charge is in the air. Written in the British vernacular. Start, Jo: "I'd better go now. Thanks for carrying my books." End, Jo: "Because you're daft."

Drama: Act II, Scene 1; Jo (17) and Geoffrey (20s).
Geoffrey, a homosexual student, has moved in with Jo to care for her during her pregnancy. As this scene begins, they've been living together for about two months, and she isn't looking forward to motherhood. Although there is no sexual attraction between Geoff and Jo, he would love to be a father. He kisses her, trying to get something started, but it is hopeless. An excellent 6-page scene for two people trying to define the parameters of their relationship. Written in the British vernacular. Start, Jo: "God, it's hot." End, Jo: "I don't suppose so."
Drama: Act II, Scene 2; Jo (17) and Geoffrey (20s).
Jo, who is in her ninth month of pregnancy, is still unhappy about having a baby. Geoffrey wants to marry her, even though he is gay. Written in the British vernacular. Start, Jo: "'Ninth month, everything should now be in readiness for the little stranger.'" End, Jo: "I think I'll give it to you, Geoff. You like babies, don't you? I might call it Number One. It'll always be number one to itself."

TENTH MAN, THE
by Paddy Chayefsky (Samuel French)
Comedy-Drama: Act III, pp. 78–82; Evelyn (18) and Arthur (30s).
As Arthur and Evelyn await final preparations for her exorcism, she tells him that she has fallen in love with him. Arthur says that this is impossible for several reasons. They've known each other for only five hours, he doesn't believe in love, and, at any rate, she is schizophrenic and doesn't know her own mind. When Evelyn insists, Arthur resists. Still, there is a very strong attraction between them. Eliminate the group of elderly Jewish men eavesdropping on this scene from an adjacent room. Start, Evelyn: "I am very frightened, Arthur." End, Evelyn: "We could be very happy if you would have faith in me."

TIME OF YOUR LIFE, THE
by William Saroyan (Samuel French)
Comedy-Drama: Act II, pp. 55–60; Joe (25–35) and Mary (25–35).
Mary is "an unhappy woman of quality and great beauty." Joe is a man trying to lead a life in which he doesn't hurt anybody. They meet in Nick's waterfront bar in 1939. Joe and Mary are attracted to one another but after this conversation in which they speak of life and philosophy, she leaves, never to return. A wonderfully poetic scene, classic Saroyan. Start, Joe: "Is it Madge—Laubowitz?" End, Joe: "Good-bye."

TO GILLIAN ON HER 37TH BIRTHDAY
by Michael Brady (Broadway Play Publishing)
Drama: Act I, Scene 3; Esther (39) and David (37).
Esther, David's sister-in-law, admonishes him for not being a good father. It is one thing for him to still be in mourning two years after his wife died, but it is another when his self-imposed extended isolation begins to affect Rachel. After all, she is only 16 years old and needs her father. Start, David: "Whose idea is Kevin? Yours?" End, Esther: "Good. We'll go to the cemetery tomorrow, put down some flowers, irises would be nice. Then we'll discuss this as a family."
Drama: Act I, Scene 4; Gillian (35) and David (37).
David plays out another moonlit scene with his wife, Gillian, who appears regularly in his imagination. He keeps this loving relationship with her "alive" even though she was killed in a boating accident two years ago. Here, Gillian gently chides David for not getting involved with other women and for remaining secluded. Start, David: "What's life? What's it cost? No . . . Who took the cookie from the cookie jar?" End, David: "That's cheap."
Drama: Act II, Scene 3; Kevin (28) and David (37).
A subtle but tangible courtship is developing between David and Kevin, his delightful former university student who has an unusual name. In this scene, they're just returning from a jog

on the beach. As they settle down, Kevin tells David about her ex-husband and her 4-year-old daughter. Start, David: "God, you've been practicing." End, Kevin: "I know a little about jumping, that's all."

TOUCH OF THE POET, A
by Eugene O'Neill (Random House/Modern Library)
Drama: Act I; Nora (40) and Melody (45).
Cornelius Melody, one of Eugene O'Neill's most colorful characters, has an ambivalent relationship with Nora, his wife. He loves her deeply, but he is ashamed of her working-class roots. During this scene, Melody remembers that today is the anniversary of his war victories and decides to celebrate. Nora has a slight Irish brogue. Start, Melody: "Good morning, Nora." End, Melody: "Yes! In a while. Fifteen minutes, say. But leave me alone now."
Drama: Act I; Sara (20) and Melody (45).
Sara's contempt for her father is barely disguised when she discovers him preening in front of a mirror. She is on her way to beg Neilan the storekeeper for more credit in her father's name, resenting every moment of the humiliating task. Father and daughter discuss the possibilities of her romance with wealthy young Harford, who is recovering from an illness in an upstairs room. Melody wants them to marry so that he can get some of Harford's family money. Start, Melody: "Thank God, I still bear the unmistakable stamp of an officer and a gentleman." End, Sara: "Father! Will you never let yourself wake up—not even now when you're sober, or nearly?"
Drama: Act III; Sara (20) and Melody (45).
Still devising ways to get his hands on young Harford's family money, Melody tells Sara that he has talked to the fellow, prodding him to make a marriage commitment and a financial "settlement." Sara is, of course, outraged by this development. In this scene, Melody is supposed to be wearing his old military uniform, a garment that somewhat transforms him into the strong, daring soldier he used to be. Such a costume is rarely practical for workshops, but the actor playing this role should make some kind of appropriate substitution. Start, Sara: "You're drunk. If you think I'm going to stay here and listen to." End, Melody: "I believe I have said all I wished to say to you. If you will excuse me, I shall join Corporal Cregan."

TOYER
by Gardner McKay (Samuel French)
Drama: Act I, Scene 1, pp. 14–24; Maude (30s) and Peter (20s).
This two-character, two-act drama turns on whether or not Peter is a serial mutilator/rapist, an actor doing a weird acting exercise, a voyeur, or all of the above. He terrorizes Maude, a psychiatrist, in her Hollywood Hills home. Peter sends her through extreme emotional peaks and valleys. First, he makes her think that she is about to die, and then he tells her that he was only joking. Then Peter seduces Maude. Then he tells her that, yes, he is the criminal after all. The later scenes are more difficult for the actress because of all the accumulating transitions. Maude is alternately terrorized and relieved, to the point that she becomes disoriented.
Drama: Act I, Scene 1, pp. 26–37; Maude (30s) and Peter (20s).
Peter makes his first entrance into Maude's house. He is going to make a telephone call, and she thinks he is a strange but helpful biker who did her a favor earlier in the day. This expository scene is worth doing for the subtext involved. Maude is wary of strangers because of the highly publicized stalker on the loose, and Peter, alias Toyer, is looking for victim number 12. Start, Peter: "This is fun." End, Maude: "I am an expert."

Peter has made a fake call to the police to report a voyeur. He acts as though he is going to leave and then suddenly admits that he is, in fact, the voyeur. Danger hangs in the air. Peter then tells Maude that he loves her. As a psychiatrist, Maude has first-hand knowledge of scopophilia (voyeurism), so she strikes a deal with Peter. She'll let him watch her undress if he'll leave. He agrees, and she takes off her blouse and bra, letting him watch in a mirror.

But as Peter puts his hand on the doorknob to leave, he turns and admits that he is actually Toyer. Start, Peter: "Maybe I'd better go." End, Peter: "Yeah. Really. You sure are. Sort of."
Drama: Act II, Scene 1, pp. 37–45; Maude (30s) and Peter (20s).
This excerpt, which runs for eight pages, begins with Maude believing that Peter is Toyer. She is in fear for her life. As she emotionally collapses into tears, he jumps up gaily and says it was all a joke, that he is really an actor doing an elaborate acting exercise. Doubtful at first, Maude slowly comes to believe him. Then just as Peter is about to leave, he changes course again, saying that he is, after all, Toyer. Start, Peter: "I'm always touched by someone I can completely control." End, Peter: "I love you."
Drama: Act II, Scene 1, pp. 52–60; Maude (30s) and Peter (20s).
Maude has turned the lights off, grabbed a knife, and cut Peter on his arm. Suddenly, he is docile again, claiming the stunt was a joke and that he is afraid of blood. She feels sorry for him, treats his wound, and apologizes for having cut him. They drink some liquor, start dancing, undress each other, and head for the bedroom. You can eliminate the nudity from this 8-page scene. Start, Peter: "You still hate me." End, Maude (offstage): "Where are you?"
Drama: Act II, Scene 2, pp. 63–70; Maude (30s) and Peter (20s).
The next morning, Maude discovers that Peter actually is, after all, Toyer. He tries to give her an animal tranquilizer, and she pretends to drink it while she slips him some powerful tranquilizers of her own. Then she fakes the effects of the poison she supposedly ingested while he gets excited that she is becoming incapacitated.

As Peter starts marking Maude's neck with a magic marker, preparing to sever her spinal cord, the stuff she gave him kicks in, and he collapses. She jumps up and ties him to a chair. Because her emotional state is a complete mess, she decides to sever his spinal cord—just as he did to all those other women. As the curtain falls on this 7-page scene, Maude is reaching for the knife. Start, Maude: "How do you like it?" End, Maude: "I'm sorry for you, Peter, dreadfully sorry for what I'm about to do."

TRIBUTE
by Bernard Slade (Samuel French)
Comedy: Act I, pp. 43–48; Maggie (mid-40s) and Scottie (51).
Scottie reluctantly shares his true feelings about being terminally ill with Maggie, his ex-wife. She comforts him in a scene filled with laughter and tears, and they fall into a romantic embrace. Start, Scottie: "Hello, Operator—Hi there, how are you?" End, Scottie: "Times have changed. I used to laugh you into bed."

TRIP BACK DOWN, THE
by John Bishop (Samuel French)
Drama: Act II, pp. 82–87; Bobby (37) and Barbara (39).
Depressed by the state of his life, Bobby has been driving around Mansfield. He winds up at his brother's home, where he is staying. He finds himself alone with his brother's wife, Barbara. After they commiserate, they recall how hot they used to be for each other back in their dating days. Bobby and Barbara then fall into one another's arms. At the end of the scene, it looks as if they are about to go upstairs and make love. But they don't. Start, Barbara: "What are you doing here?" End, Barbara: "Oh, Christ, I've wanted you for so long. Upstairs. All right?"

TWENTY-SEVEN WAGONS FULL OF COTTON
by Tennessee Williams [*The Theater of Tennessee Williams*, Volume 6 (New Directions)]
Drama: Scene 2; Silva Vicarro (35–50) and Flora Meighan (35–45).
Silva Vicarro, the manager of the Syndicate Plantation, is alone on the porch with Flora Meighan, Jake's uneducated, childlike wife. She quickly lets it slip that her husband is the one

who set the big fire last night, burning down Silva's cotton gin. Silva responds by cruelly seducing the woman, who behaves much like a trapped animal. The erotic build in this 15-page scene is slow and deadly, difficult to shorten, and appropriate for sophisticated actors. These characters are rural, earthy, sweaty, dusty, and raw. Start, Silva: "The good-neighbor policy!" End, Flora: "Don't follow. Please don't follow!"

TWICE AROUND THE PARK
by Murray Schisgal (Samuel French)
Comedy: "A Need for Brussels Sprouts," pp. 13–20; Margaret (40s) and Leon (50s).
Leon is a New York actor who has been practicing for an upcoming commercial audition in which he must mime an opera singer. His upstairs neighbor has complained about the volume of his opera tapes to no avail. Margaret, a police officer, knocks on the door and gives Leon a summons for disturbing the peace. It turns out that she is actually the upstairs neighbor. After the initial shock, Leon and Margaret begin to establish a relationship that, very soon, will result in true love. You'll need a tape recording of a Tosca opera and, ideally, a recording of a dog barking. If you can't get the latter, simply omit the reference to it. Start, Margaret: "Are you the tenant of this apartment?" End, Margaret: "Margaret. Margaret Heinz."
Comedy: "A Need for Brussels Sprouts," pp. 28–33; Margaret (40s) and Leon (50s).
Margaret is role-playing with Leon. She is a judge, and he is going to testify about his three failed marriages. Start, Leon: "Margie, all men aren't the same." End, Margaret: "If you can't stand the heat, mister, stay out of the kitchen!"
Comedy: "A Need for Less Expertise," pp. 54–60; Edie (50s) and Gus (50s).
Edie and Gus have been married for 26 years, live on the East Side of New York, and are experiencing sexual difficulties. The main problem is that he isn't interested. Edie has been spending a great deal of money on therapy, self-help groups, and sexual-advice gurus. Today, she has convinced Gus to grudgingly follow the recorded instructions of one Dr. Oliovsky. After a while, Gus quits in disgust, and Edie begins to sulk. In this excerpt, he confronts her, and they rehash their problems. Start, Gus: "I don't know what the hell is going on. Every week, you find a reason to start a fight." End, Gus: "Be fair now, Edie. You have to be fair, too. Didn't I tell you to get a job?"

TWO ROOMS
by Lee Blessing (Dramatists Play Service)
Drama: Act I, Scene 2, pp. 16–20; Lainie Wells (30s) and Walker Harris (30s).
Walker Harris is a newspaper man who wants Lainie Wells to go public with the story of her husband's kidnapping in Beirut and her subsequent painful vigil. Although she is supposed to be showing him slides, you can substitute a photo album. Start, Lainie: "This is a hotel in Beirut near where he lives." End, Lainie: "Get out! If I want to see a scavenger, I'll go to the marsh."

TWO SMALL BODIES
by Neal Bell (Dramatists Play Service)
Drama: Act I, Scene 5, pp. 14–17; Eileen Mahoney (late 20s) and Lt. Brann (40s).
Lt. Brann has been investigating the disappearance of Eileen Mahoney's children for some time when he drops by her place for a talk. By now, she is close to the edge and fed up with his continual probing. Tension, including vague sexual tension, bristles between them. Start, Lt. Brann: "Nice night." End, Eileen: "Do you know what I mean?"
Drama: Act I, Scene 6, pp. 17–20; Eileen Mahoney (late 20s) and Lt. Brann (40s).
Lt. Brann changes clothes in front of Eileen Mahoney as they discuss the kidnapping of her children. This scene has more overt hostility and sexuality than the preceding one. You'll need a table, a tablecloth, and unbreakable dishes. As written, Lt. Brann has to rip the tablecloth off

the table, sending the dishes flying. A gun and shoulder holster would also be useful. Start, Eileen: "What's that?" End, Lt. Brann: "That was a joke, huh? See, I'm catching on."
Drama: Act I, Scene 8, pp. 23–25; Eileen Mahoney (late 20s) and Lt. Brann (40s).
The investigation of her children's kidnapping is stretching Eileen Mahoney to the breaking point emotionally. Lt. Brann is apparently enjoying the tension. Start, Lt. Brann: "Let me show you something." End, Lt. Brann: "There are walls and walls."
Drama: Act II, Scene 1, pp. 26–39; Eileen Mahoney (late 20s) and Lt. Brann (40s).
Although Eileen Mahoney's lawyer advises her not to talk to Lt. Brann, they can't resist each other, and their relationship is becoming sexual. At one point in this scene, Eileen strips to her underwear and, at another, she places Lt. Brann in handcuffs and then massages his shoulders. At the end, he tells her the police have caught her children's killer, that a man has confessed and they have positive proof. The question is: why doesn't Lt. Brann tell Eileen this at the beginning of the scene? Precisely what is the nature of their relationship? This challenging 13-page scene is hard to shorten because it contains transitions on several levels and is best played by experienced actors. Start, Eileen: "Can't you knock?" End, Lt. Brann: "I don't know."

VALUE OF NAMES, THE
by Jeffrey Sweet (Dramatists Play Service)
Drama: One-act play, pp. 23–27; Norma Teitel (early 20s) and Leo Greshen (late 60s).
After the original director of a new play suffers a stroke, Leo Greshen replaces him. As a result, the female lead, Norma Silverman, threatens to withdraw. Leo learns that Norma is the daughter of his old crony Benny Silverman, who he named as a communist sympathizer when testifying before the House Un-American Activities Committee during the 1950s. Leo goes to Benny's Hollywood Hills home, where Norma is staying, to convince her to remain with the production and to make up with Benny. Start, Leo: "Miss Teitel?" End, Leo: "You're a lot like him, Miss Teitel. By the way, that's a compliment."
Drama: One-act play, pp. 48–52; Norma Teitel (early 20s) and Benny Silverman (late 60s).
Norma tries to convince her father that his unwillingness to forgive Leo Greshen is self-destructive. Begin after Leo's exit. Start, Norma: "OK, I think I've got it now." Continue to the end of the play. End, Benny: "'Norma Teitel is the daughter of actor Benny Silverman.'"

VIEUX CARRÉ
by Tennessee Williams (New Directions)
Drama: Part II; Scene 9; Jane (20s) and Tye (25–30).
No one in the rooming house knows that Jane has leukemia, not even her low-life lover, Tye. So when she received word from a medical clinic that her blood count "had changed for the worse," she kept the news to herself. In this 8-page scene, Jane orders Tye out of her life, citing two reasons. He has begun to shoot heroin again, and she has given up fashion illustration in favor of prostitution. The first reason is true, but the second one probably isn't. Jane may have toyed with the idea of prostitution, but her primary problem is the blood disease. This terrific scene, which is full of rough material and a great deal of physicality, is best suited for experienced actors. Start, Jane: "Tye, Tye, oh-Christ." End, Tye: "Yes, yes, yes, yes, yes!"

VIEW FROM THE BRIDGE, A
by Arthur Miller (Dramatists Play Service)
Drama: Act I, pp. 24–26; Eddie (40) and Beatrice (40).
Eddie is becoming increasingly jealous of the love affair that is developing between Catherine, his wife's beautiful 17-year-old niece, and Rodolpho, the Sicilian immigrant who is staying with the family. Since Eddie reared Catherine from childhood, however, his relationship with her is parental, and he would never even speak of his secret lust for her. This is the first scene to expose the depth of his conflict. Eddie is so distressed by recent developments that he has

stopped making love with Beatrice, his wife. She sees the situation for exactly what it is. Start, Eddie: "It's after eight." End, Eddie: "I'll be in right away. Go ahead."

Drama: Act I, pp. 29–30; Eddie (40) and Catherine (17).
Eddie finally confronts Catherine about her feelings for Rodolpho, and she says she is in love. Eddie warns her that Rodolpho is only interested in her because, through marriage, he can become an American citizen. The truth is, however, that Eddie is jealous. Catherine begins to sob and runs into the house. Start, Catherine: "Why don't you talk to him, Eddie? He blesses you, and you don't talk to him hardly." End, Catherine: "I don't believe it and I wish to hell you'd stop it!"

Drama: Act II, pp. 45–48; Catherine (17) and Rodolpho (early 20s).
Catherine and Rodolpho are very much in love, but Eddie, her guardian and surrogate father, is deeply jealous and has been trying to break them up. He warned Catherine that Rodolpho is only interested in her because, if she marries him, he'll get his United States citizenship. In this excellent scene, she first entertains the idea of getting married and living in Italy instead of America. When Rodolpho realizes that she is questioning his love and motives, he becomes angry. Catherine knows right away that he loves her and that she was wrong to be doubtful. They fall into one another's arms and then head for the bedroom to make love for the first time. Rodolpho is an Italian immigrant, so an accent would be appropriate. Start, Catherine: "You hungry?" End, Rodolpho: "There's nobody here now. Come inside. Come . . . And don't cry any more."

Drama: Act II, pp. 52–54; Eddie (40) and Beatrice (40).
Eddie has made an anonymous call to the Immigration Bureau to report Rodolpho and Marco, knowing that the men will be deported. It is his last resort in trying to break up the romance between Rodolpho and Catherine. Arriving home, he discovers that the lovers have moved upstairs with Mrs. Dondero. This is a disastrous development because Mrs. Dondero has two other illegal immigrants living with her, and they'll soon be included in the Immigration Bureau sweep. As Eddie suffers for what he has done, Beatrice tells him that Catherine and Rodolpho are getting married right away. This news crushes Eddie even more. Start, Eddie: "Where is everybody? I says where is everybody?" End, Eddie: "I'm goin', I'm goin' for a walk."

VISIT, THE
by Friedrich Dürrenmatt [translated by Patrick Bowles (Grove Press)]
Comedy-Drama: Act III; Claire (63) and Schoolmaster (40–55).
The schoolmaster tries to convince Claire to withdraw her offer of a million pounds to the citizens of the town if they'll murder Alfred III, the man who done her wrong many years ago. She refuses, explaining that she can make her own rules in the game of life with the money she already has. You'll have to do a little editing to make this a two-character scene. Eliminate the doctor, perhaps give his lines to the schoolmaster, and eliminate Roby and Toby. Start, Schoolmaster: "Madam." End, Claire: "Guellen for a murder, a boom for a body."

WAITING FOR LEFTY
by Clifford Odets (Grove Press)
Drama: Scene 1, "Joe and Edna"; Edna (30) and Joe (30s).
In 1935, the Depression is making life tough. Joe arrives home to discover that creditors came today and repossessed all the furniture, and his wife is threatening to leave him for another man if he can't become a better provider for the family. The children aren't eating regularly, their shoes are worn out, and the family is about to fall two months behind in the rent. Joe argues that he is doing his best and tries to give Edna the $1.04 he earned today, but they both know it isn't enough. At the end of the scene, Joe vows to support a strike action in the hope of winning higher wages for cab drivers. Although the language is very dated now, this

play is still powerful, and it unquestionably is one of the most important dramas in American theater history. Start, Joe: "Where's all the furniture, honey?" End, Joe: "I'll be back!"
Drama: Scene III, "The Young Hack and His Girl"; Flor (20s) and Sid (20s).
Flor can't afford to marry Sid because he doesn't make enough as a cab driver to support them both. Furthermore, Flor's immediate family needs the $9 she brings home each week. Sid and Flor try to smile through their misery, but it is no use. Sid ends the scene by falling to his knees, sobbing into Flor's skirt. Start, Sid: "Hello, Florrie." End, Flor: "Hello, honey. You're looking tired."

WAIT UNTIL DARK
by Frederick Knott (Dramatists Play Service)
Drama: Act II, Scene 2, pp. 64–68; Susy (late 20s) and Mike (30s).
Susy has figured out that Mike and the others are impostors. He tells her the truth about the elaborate deception they invented in their attempts to locate the missing doll that is stuffed with valuable heroin. Then, as Mike exits to the hallways, Roat stabs him. Susy's blindness presents interesting acting challenges. Start, Mike: "Susy. Susy . . . there's something I must tell you." End, Susy: "Good luck."

WARM PENINSULA, THE
by Joe Masteroff (Samuel French)
Comedy: Act I, pp. 38–42; Joanne (30) and Steve (20–25).
After a romantic movie date, Joanne proposes marriage. Jack stuns her by announcing that he is already married and has been for four years. Then he mysteriously clams up; he won't say anything else except that he can't get a divorce and that if Joanne wants to continue seeing him on their current terms, that is fine. If not, he is ready to end their relationship. Joanne thinks about Jack's ultimatum for a few minutes and decides to continue the affair. Start, Joanne: "Wait—wait a minute." End, Steve: "Just beautiful."
Comedy: Act I, pp. 45–50; Ruth (25–30) and Jack (28–35).
Ruth thought she had a good relationship with Jack, but then he mysteriously disappeared and didn't call her for a month. She is packing for the 10 P.M. plane to Milwaukee when he walks in suddenly, declaring his love. Ruth is doubtful at first, but then gives in. They kiss, and Ruth doesn't get on the plane. Start, Jack: "Are you really leaving tonight?" End, Jack: "I love you."
Comedy: Act II, pp. 53–58; Ruth (25–30) and Jack (28–35).
Ruth's neighbor and elderly friend, Iris, just told her that she saw Jack at a party the other night and, no question about it, this man is a gigolo! No sooner has Iris reported this than Jack walks in, and she exits. Ruth hints about what Iris has said, and Jack breaks down and confesses. He has been a kept man for years and feels just awful about it. Ruth wants to continue her relationship with Jack anyway, but they agree to not see each other any more. Start, Ruth: "Was it a nice party?" End, Jack: "Okay, if you want to. I'll never call you again. Don't you know that? . . . Take it easy."

WASH, THE
by Philip Kan Gotanda (Dramatists Play Service) [*Between Worlds, Contemporary Asian-American Plays* (Theatre Communications Group)]
Drama: Act II, Scene 8, DPS pp. 45–47; Masi (67) and Nobu (68).
Masi and Nobu are Nisei, second-generation Japanese Americans, and have been married for 42 years. But Masi left Nobu 13 months ago, has taken up with a new man, and wants to marry him. In this excellent and tense scene, she tells Nobu that she has seen a lawyer and is filing for divorce. It is important to remember that divorce is very unusual among older-generation Nisei. Start, Masi: "I want to talk, Nobu." End, Masi: "Because I want to be happy, Nobu. I have the right to be happy."

WHEN YOU COMIN' BACK, RED RYDER?
by Mark Medoff (Dramatists Play Service)
Drama: Act I, pp. 7–11; Stephen (19) and Angel (mid-20s).
For the most part, this is an expository scene, but it captures the oddly affectionate relationship between Stephen and Angel. It also establishes the circumstances of their lives and the day-in, day-out routine of an isolated diner in the New Mexico desert. Playwright Mark Medoff describes Angel as "obese," but this isn't essential to the logic of the scene. Start, Angel: "Good mornin', Stephen." End, Stephen: "I'll get the hell outta here and go to the goddamn cemetery or someplace."

WHO'S AFRAID OF VIRGINIA WOOLF?
by Edward Albee (Dramatists Play Service)
Drama: Act I, pp. 5–12; George (46) and Martha (52).
George and his wife, Martha, arrive home after a faculty reception and prepare to entertain Nick, the new young biology professor, and Honey, his wife, who are dropping by for late-night drinks. As the curtain goes up, George and Martha have already been drinking most of the evening and are engaged in their customary verbal sparring. This is definitely the easiest George/Martha scene for workshop use. You'll need an offstage doorbell. Begin at the top of Act I, and continue until Nick and Honey's entrance. Start, Martha: "Jesus. . . ." End, Martha: "Screw you!"
Drama: Act II, pp. 71–75; George (46) and Martha (52).
George has completely humiliated Honey, who has once again headed for the bathroom to throw up. Nick furiously goes to comfort her, leaving George and Martha alone. The verbal warfare between them escalates. Begin after Nick's exit. Start, Martha: "Very good, George." George: "Thank you, Martha." Stop just before Nick reenters. End, George: "Total war?" Martha: "Total."
Drama: Act II, pp. 82–85; George (46) and Honey (26).
During the last moments of Act II, Martha humiliates George by making out with Nick in the kitchen. Honey comes out of the bathroom, weak, still drunk, and vulnerable, and George berates her. Then he gets the idea to tell Honey that he and Martha's "son" has died. Begin as Honey enters, and continue to the end of the act. Start, Honey: "Bells. Ringing. I've been hearing bells." End, George: ". . . It's about our . . . son. He's dead. Can you hear me, Martha? Our boy is dead."
Drama: Act III, pp. 86–91; Martha (52) and Nick (30).
Martha took Nick to her bedroom, but he was unable to have sex with her because he was too drunk. Now back in the living room and deep in her own alcoholic haze, Martha belittles him for his impotence and says that George is the only man who has ever made her happy. You'll need an offstage doorbell. Begin at the top of the act, and stop when George arrives with flowers. Start, Martha: "Hey, hey . . . Where is everybody . . . ?" End, Nick: "Christ."

WHOSE LIFE IS IT ANYWAY?
by Brian Clark (Dramatic Publishing Company)
Drama: Act I; Ken Harrison (35–45) and Mrs. Boyle (35).
Mrs. Boyle, a medical social worker, is sent to see Ken because the hospital staff thinks he is depressed. In this first encounter between them, he tells Mrs. Boyle that he chooses not to go on living with his physical limitations. Start, Mrs. Boyle: "Good morning." End, Ken: "Go . . . For God's sake get out . . . Go on . . . Get out . . . Get out."
Drama: Act I; Ken Harrison (35–45) and Dr. Scott (25–30).
Ken became angry during his confrontation with the medical social worker, and the nurses had to give him oxygen to breathe. As he calms down, Dr. Scott enters to find out what is going on. During this scene, Ken tells her what it is like to still have sexual desires and not be

able to act on them. Start, Dr. Scott: "And what was all the fuss about?" End, Ken: "You still have lovely breasts."

WILD HONEY
by Michael Frayn [adapted from an early, untitled play by Anton Chekhov (Samuel French)]
Comedy: Act I, Scene 2, pp. 49–51; Anna Petrovna (late 20s) and Platonov (28–32).
Alone with Platonov in the garden, Anna Petrovna suddenly declares her love for him. He resists, admitting his attraction to her but worried about the threat to his marriage. Start, Anna Petrovna: "And here he is. Our philosopher. Shunning us all." Stop with Platonov's exit. End, Anna Petrovna: "Intolerable man! Come back here! Misha! Misha!"
Comedy: Act II, Scene 1, pp. 61–64; Anna Petrovna (late 20s) and Platonov (28–32).
Anna Petrovna continues her attempted seduction of Platonov, and he continues to resist, although less enthusiastically now. This scene is a little stronger than their Act I encounter. Start, Anna Petrovna: "Platonov! I knew you wouldn't be asleep. How can anyone sleep on a night like this?" End, Anna Petrovna: "To the old summerhouse!" For a longer version, eliminate Sasha's offstage lines and end, Anna Petrovna: ". . . I'll come in and fetch you."
Comedy: Act II, Scene 2, pp. 77–81; Sofya (early 20s) and Platonov (28–32).
Sofya and Platonov were lovers back in their university days but are now married to other partners. During a night of mad love and confusion three weeks ago, they started an affair. Platonov's wife, who mistakenly believes that he has become involved with Anna Petrovna, left him and took the baby. Since then, he has hung around the house in something of a drunken stupor. In this scene, Sofya convinces Platonov to run away with her, an option he accepts unenthusiastically. She surprises him by saying that she has told her newlywed husband of their affair. Start, Sofya: "Platonov! Wake up!" End, Sofya: "I've got some money—we'll eat on the way. And smarten yourself up a bit for the journey!"
Comedy: Act II, Scene 2, pp. 89–95; Anna Petrovna (late 20s) and Platonov (28–32).
Anna Petrovna doesn't realize that Platonov has begun an affair with her daughter-in-law, Sofya. Anna Petrovna seeks him out, wanting to know why he hasn't been responding to her letters. Then she suggests a plan that has them running away together. Platonov, for his part, is miserable with all of this romance and primarily wants to reunite with his wife. Start, Anna Petrovna: "Come here, Platonov. Why are you running away from me?" End, Anna Petrovna: "He can easily give me some of it. That's all we need, my love."

WOOLGATHERER, THE
by William Mastrosimone (Samuel French)
Comedy-Drama: Act I, pp. 5–12; Rosie (mid-20s) and Cliff (25–35).
Cliff picks up Rosie and goes back to her place, hoping for a one-night stand. The evening doesn't go as he planned, however, and she turns out to be just a little bit strange. Start, Rosie: "And there was this girl . . . She was a poet." End, Cliff: "How would you know if the boards were up when you moved in?"
Comedy-Drama: Act I, pp. 38–45; Rosie (mid-20s) and Cliff (25–35).
Cliff gets frustrated with Rosie's avoidance of intimacy, decides that she is something of a fruit, and leaves. As he does, she asks if she can keep his sweater. Start, Cliff: "Someday I'm gonna take you cross country in my truck." End, Cliff: "Me? Cold? Hey, Rosie, you're lookin' at the only survivor of the Great Ice Age."

Part Seven
Three-Person Scenes

ABSURD PERSON SINGULAR
by Alan Ayckbourn (Samuel French)
Comedy: Act I, pp. 29–35; Sidney (30s), Geoffrey (30s), and Ronald (40s).
On the surface, this scene is about three men in a kitchen, discussing the women in the other room. It offers a kind of leering, low-ball comedy. What the scene is actually about, however, is the male pecking order. If you are careful not to underestimate playwright Alan Ayckbourn, you'll get a lot out of this material. Written in the British vernacular. Eliminate Jane's appearance at the outside window. Start, Ronald: "Ah, there you are, old chap." End, Geoffrey: "I mean face it, there's just too much good stuff wandering around simply crying out for it for you not . . . (Eva enters) . . . Anyway, I think that would be a good idea. Don't you?"

ABUNDANCE
by Beth Henley (Dramatists Play Service)
Comedy-Drama: Act I, Scene 1, pp. 7–11; Bess (20s), Macon (20s), and Jack (30s).
Bess and Macon are mail-order brides who meet in a stagecoach depot in Wyoming Territory during the 1870s. In this scene, they meet for the first time and get to know one another. Then Jack arrives to tell Bess that her would-be husband, his brother, has been killed. She breaks down in hysterics, he hits her, Macon comes to her defense, and he carries Bess off to marry her himself. Jack's time onstage is considerably shorter than that of the women, but his entrance is demanding. Start, Bess (singing): "Roses love sunshine." End, Jack: "Let's go."

AND MISS REARDON DRINKS A LITTLE
by Paul Zindel (Dramatists Play Service)
Comedy-Drama: Act I, pp. 13–20; Anna (30s), Ceil (40s), and Catherine (40s).
Catherine and Ceil try to figure out what to do about their sister, Anna, who has had a nervous breakdown after becoming involved sexually with one of her high-school students. Anna, although distressed, frequently makes more sense than both of them. Start, Catherine: "Remember when Mama took us to St. Mary's Bazaar and we put her on that little ferris wheel. There was only enough money for one, and Mama said she could go alone." End, Catherine: "That noise might have been just what we needed. Nowadays you need nice noises every so often—like Lebonnons Indian-wrestling under your window."

BABY DANCE, THE
by Jane Anderson (Samuel French)
Comedy: Act I, Scene 2, pp. 28–39; Rachel (30s), Wanda (late 20s), and Al (30s).
Good old boy Al returns to his trailer home to meet the Hollywood visitor he and his wife Wanda are waiting for. Rachel and her husband, Richard, have agreed to purchase the as-yet-unborn

child Wanda is carrying. The scene functions on several levels: Hollywood meets Louisiana, liberalism meets bigotry, and money meets poverty. The play is billed as a drama, and the ultimate message is quite serious. The individual scenes, however, are funny. Start, Rachel: "Hello. Are you Al?" End, Rachel: "Well, Al, that's another way of looking at it."
Comedy: Act II, Scene 1, pp. 58–67; Richard (30s), Ron (30–50), and Al (30s).
Richard and his lawyer, Ron, are waiting in a Louisiana hospital for Wanda to have her baby. Richard and his wife, Rachel, have agreed to purchase the child from poverty-stricken Wanda and her husband, Al. In this scene, Al arrives and tries to up the ante, asking for a new car as part of the deal. Richard balks, and a fistfight erupts. Finally, Al settles for a new set of tires. Start, Ron: "Al? Ron Davis. We talked on the phone." End, Richard: "Well, good. Thank you . . . Jesus, I'm exhausted."
Comedy-Drama: Act II, Scene 1, pp. 67–74; Richard (30s), Rachel (30s), and Ron (30–50).
Rachel rushes into the waiting room to announce to Richard and Ron that Wanda's baby has been born. The euphoric celebration is short-lived, however, when learn that the baby was oxygen-deprived and may have brain damage. Rachel and Richard then decide to back out of the deal to buy the baby. Start, Richard: "Jesus, I'm exhausted." End, Richard: "Do you want to look at this?"

BABY WITH THE BATHWATER
by Christopher Durang (Dramatists Play Service)
Comedy: Act I, Scene 1, pp. 3–11; John (late 20s), Helen (late 20s), and Nanny (30–50).
John and Helen have a new baby and don't know what to do with it. In fact, they aren't even sure what gender it is. Nanny arrives from who knows where and helps out. This is outrageously surreal comedy, full of transitions that don't make much sense and wildly fluctuating emotions. Begin at the top of the scene. Start, Helen: "Hello, baby. Hello." End, Nanny: "Very well! Let's just do it in the kitchen. Come on."

BEYOND THERAPY
by Christopher Durang (Samuel French)
Comedy: Act I, Scene 6, pp. 38–53; Bruce (30–34), Bob (30–34), and Prudence (29–32).
Prudence comes to Bruce's apartment for dinner, thinking that his male lover, Bob, is out for the evening. Bob has changed his mind, however, and the romantic evening turns into a competition between Bob and Prudence for Bruce's affections, a struggle that Prudence would rather not participate in. Start, Bruce: "Hi, Come on in." End, Bruce: "Mrs. Wallace, this is Bruce, we have a bit of an emergency, I wonder if you can help . . . We're in desperate need of some therapy here."

BOYS' LIFE
by Howard Korder (Dramatists Play Service)
Comedy: Scene 2, pp. 8–14; Karen (late 20s), Phil (late 20s), and a Man (late 20s).
Karen and Phil unexpectedly meet at Jack's party. Phil tries to rekindle their love affair, but Karen reminds him that it was, in fact, just a one-night stand, and he hasn't called her for two months. He persist even more, inviting her to go away with him for a weekend. Karen resists at first but gradually softens. Through it all, a Man tries repeatedly to enter the bedroom where Karen and Phil are talking, and Phil keeps shooing him out.
Finally, as Karen and Phil sink onto the coats on the bed and begin some serious necking, the Man enters once again, insisting that he be allowed to retrieve his coat. Karen is suddenly very embarrassed and flees from the room. Once she is gone, the Man tells Phil that he actually is Karen's date for the night. In terms of dialogue, Karen and Phil have the most, but the Man's role can be a hoot. Start, Phil: "Well, there you are." End, Man: "You want to reimburse me for cab fare or what?"

COVER

by Jeffrey Sweet with Stephen Johnson and Sandra Hastie [*Twenty-Five Ten-Minute Plays from Actors Theatre of Louisville* (Samuel French)]

Comedy: One-act play, pp. 205–212; Marty (20s), Frank (20s), and Diane (20s).

Marty wants Frank to lie and tell his ladyfriend Diane that the two of them were together last night, but the truth is that Marty had a date. Frank doesn't want to lie, but when Diane brings the issue up, he finds the false words coming out of his mouth. Diane sees right through him but doesn't challenge the men's story. The play, which is only 7 1/2 pages long, is interesting for the undercurrent of all the negotiations going on. Start, Marty: "Work, work, work." End, Marty: "I guess we'd better get going, hunh?"

HEDDA GABLER

by Henrik Ibsen [translated by Christopher Hampton (Samuel French)]

Drama: Act II, pp. 53–57; Hedda Gabler (29), Eilert Lovborg (33), and George Tesman (33).

In this very famous scene, by far the most sexually intense in the play, Lovborg and Hedda are supposedly looking at a photograph album but are, in fact, talking about the romance that might have been between them. Hedda's new husband, George Tesman, doesn't have an inkling about this as he moves in and out of the scene, serving food and drinks and explaining a photograph here and there. This is actually a two-person scene with occasional interruptions by Tesman. Start, Hedda: "I'll show you some photographs, shall I, would you like that?" End, Hedda: "Be careful. Don't jump to conclusions."

HOUSE OF RAMON IGLESIA, THE

by José Rivera (Samuel French)

Drama: Act II, Scene 1, pp. 49–57; Dolores (45), Ramon (49), and Javier (22).

The American Dream is a big bust for Dolores and Ramon, and they're trying to move back to Puerto Rico after a 19-year struggle in the United States. However, selling their dilapidated Long Island house involves expensive trips back and forth to Puerto Rico to untangle the title, and they're broke. In this very dynamic scene, Ramon swallows his pride and asks his eldest son, Javier, for a loan. Javier, however, is ashamed of Ramon and his peasant ways, as well as the fact that he has worked as a janitor, and refuses to help him. Start, Dolores: "I heard what he said." End, Javier: "Mom . . . (a knock at the door) Come in! It's open!"

LAUNDRY AND BOURBON

by James McLure (Dramatists Play Service)

Comedy: One-act play, pp. 25–35; Hattie (30s), Elizabeth (30s), and Amy Lee (30s).

Amy Lee has come to Elizabeth's house to sell tickets to the First Baptist Church pancake supper. She also wants to spread the juicy gossip that Elizabeth's husband, Roy, is messing around with Margaret Crowell. Amy Lee winds up in a humdinger of a fight with Hattie. Start, Elizabeth: "Hattie's had a few." Continue to the end of the play. End, Elizabeth: "Yeah. Call me."

MISTER ROBERTS

by Thomas Heggen and Joshua Logan (Dramatists Play Service)

Drama: Act I, Scene 2, pp. 17–25; Mister Roberts (25–32), Doc (35–40), and Ensign Pulver (20–25).

Ensign Pulver has been reading Mister Roberts's most recent request for a transfer when he walks in with Doc, explaining that he just gave away their treasured bottle of scotch in an effort to have the boat ordered to a liberty port. Pulver is dismayed because he had plans for the scotch that involved a certain nurse with a red birthmark on her bottom. Doc and Roberts make a new bottle of scotch out of alcohol, Coca-Cola, and Kreml Hair Tonic. Then the conversations turns again to how much Roberts wants a transfer into battle, and Doc lights into him, explaining that he is probably already doing his best for the war effort by staying where he is. Start, Roberts: "Hey, Frank, has Dolan been in here yet with my letter?" End, Pulver: "I just threw that firecracker under your goddamn bunk."

MURDER AT THE HOWARD JOHNSON'S
by Ron Clark and Sam Bobrick (Samuel French)
Comedy: Act I, Scene 1, pp. 11–20; Arlene Miller (38), Paul Miller (40–45), and Dr. Mitchell Lovell (36).
Arlene Miller has fallen madly in love with her family dentist, Dr. Mitchell Lovell, and they've decided that she'll ask her husband, Paul, for a divorce. Anticipating that he might not give her one, however, the lovers have cooked up elaborate plans to kill him. Paul arrives at the Howard Johnson's motel room where Arlene and Mitchell are secretly waiting for him. Arlene tells him about the divorce, he refuses, and an inept attempt at murder takes place. Lots of dentist jokes and cheap laughs make this a very funny scene. Start, Paul: "Arlene!?!!" End, Arlene: "Great idea. Ever since we thought of killing you at Howard Johnson's, I've had a taste for fried clams."

ODD COUPLE, THE (MALE VERSION)
by Neil Simon (Samuel French)
Comedy: Act II, Scene 2, pp. 63–68; Cecily Pigeon (30s), Gwendolen Pigeon (30s), and Felix Unger (44).
Gwendolen and Cecily Pigeon, the British sisters who live upstairs, have come down for dinner and, maybe, some fun and games. Oscar Madison happily leaves the room to fetch some drinks, leaving his friend, Felix Unger, to entertain Cecily and Gwendolen. Felix manages to transform a festive mood into utter gloom by showing them pictures of his wife and children, causing them to bemoan their own lost loves. As Oscar reenters, they're all sitting on the sofa crying into their handkerchiefs. Start, Felix: "Er . . . Oscar tells me you're sisters." End, Gwendolyn: "Oh dear Oh dear Oh dear."

OUR LADY OF THE TORTILLA
by Luis Santeiro (Dramatists Play Service)
Comedy: Act I, pp. 5–14; Aunt Dolores (50), Dahlia (49), and Nelson (early 20s).
In this scene, Nelson wants his colorful family to behave while his college girlfriend is visiting, but this is a lost cause. Aunt Dolores, who speaks with a thick Spanish accent, prays to miscellaneous saints at the drop of a tortilla and maintains a working altar in the living room. Nelson's mother, Dahlia, is a flashy dresser who is currently bent on winning back her estranged husband from that "cow . . . with an ass that goes from here to the Lincoln Tunnel." Eliminate the radio announcer. Begin at the top of the act. Start, Dolores (singing): "Ave, Ave, Ave Maria. . . ." End, Dahlia: ". . . get the pastilitos ready. I'm going to change."
Comedy: Act II, Scene 1, pp. 39–43; Dolores (50), Dahlia (49), and Eddy (mid-20s).
Aunt Dolores has discovered the face of the Virgin Mary on a tortilla shell, and now the sick, needy, and religious are crowding into the front yard wanting to share the experience. Eddy, a religious skeptic, sees a way to make a quick buck. In this scene, he tries to convince Dahlia, his mother, and his aunt, Dolores, to speak to the media. Start, Dahlia: ". . . get the pastilitos ready." Continue to the end of the scene. End, Eddy: ". . . The tortilla lady . . . right!"

PICK UP AX
by Anthony Clarvoe (Broadway Play Publishing)
Comedy-Drama: Act I, Scene 3; Keith (late 20s), Brian (late 20s), and Mick (mid-30s).
Mick, a wheeler-dealer, walks in unannounced to save Keith and Brian from financial ruin. He outlines for them the various ways they can use illegal means to get the microchips they

need delivered. Keith, the computer nerd, and his partner, Brian, are fascinated and agree to go along with Mick's scheme. Start, Mick: "Mr. Weiss? Mr. Rienzi?" End, Keith: "My appointment? I thought he was your appointment."

PIZZA MAN
by Darlene Craviotto (Samuel French)
Comedy: Act II, Scene 1, pp. 46–54; Julie (late 20s), Alice (mid-20s), and Eddie (late 20s).
Eddie, the pizza-delivery man, has no idea that Julie and Alice intend to rape him. As he relaxes on the sofa, engaging in small talk, the women begin an awkward seduction—awkward because they've never done anything like this before. Later, when this doesn't work, the play takes a more violent turn. Start, Eddie: "So when I was in the service, I started thinking about what I wanted to do with my life." End, Eddie: "We always got extra guys to cover at night, so it's cool. I'll just drop these two pizzas and I'll be right back."

PRELUDE TO A KISS
by Craig Lucas (Broadway Play Publishing)
Comedy: Act I; Peter (mid-20s), Rita (mid-20s), and a Waiter (any age).
Unbeknownst to Peter, his bride's body is now occupied by the soul and personality of a mysterious old man who kissed Rita at their wedding. Now on their honeymoon in Jamaica, Peter slowly realizes that something is very wrong with her. She suddenly can't remember the most intimate details of their lives, isn't putting salt on her food, is sleeping long hours, seems to have changed her political views, and, most significantly, has decided that she wants to have children. The role of the waiter is perfunctory but necessary to the scene. Start, Peter: "Don't you want to try one?" End, Rita: "This is me. And maybe what you saw wasn't there at all."
Comedy: Act II; Peter (mid-20s), Rita (mid-20s), and an Old Man (70s).
In the final scene, Peter orchestrates another meeting between Rita and the old man in the hope that their body transformation can be reversed. He succeeds, and the play ends on a very romantic and bittersweet note. During the first part of the scene, the old man speaks and acts like Rita, and she like him. Midway, he begins to act like himself, and she begins to act like herself. Begin after Mrs. Boyle's exit. Start, Peter: "How've you been?" Continue to the end of the play. End, Peter: "You."

PROPOSAL, THE
by Anton Chekhov [*The Sneeze, Plays and Stories* by Anton Chekhov, translated and adapted by Michael Frayn (Samuel French)]
Comedy: One-act play, pp. 93–100; Natalya Stepanovna (25), Lomov (35), and Chubukov (50s).
Lomov's marriage proposal to Natalya Stepanovna turned into disaster when they started arguing about whose family owns Ox Lea Meadows. He stormed out when Natalya's father, Chubukov, joined the argument, taking her side. Now everyone has calmed down, and Lomov returns to try again. Before long, however, they argue about who has the better dog. Then, overcome with anxiety, Lomov faints. In the end, though, the lovers get together. The challenge in this excerpt is to focus on the emotional roller coaster everyone has been on just before Lomov comes back. Start, Lomov: "Terrible palpitations! . . . My leg's gone numb . . . Pain in my side. . . ." End, Chubukov: "Champagne! Champagne! Champagne!"

RAISIN IN THE SUN, A
by Lorraine Hansberry (Samuel French)
Drama: Act I, Scene 1, pp. 20–27; Ruth (about 30), Walter (35), and Beneatha (20).
Early-morning life in this tenement apartment on Chicago's Southside is a crowded affair, especially since two families share a bathroom that is down the hall. Against the background of

constant jockeying for bathroom time, Walter tells Ruth about his dream of owning a liquor store. Then Beneatha comes into the room, and they talk about her dream of being a doctor. Start, Walter: "You know what I was thinking 'bout in the bathroom this morning?" End, Ruth: "Fifty cents? Here, take a taxi."

SIGHT UNSEEN
by Donald Margulies (Dramatists Play Service)
Drama: Act II, Scene 5, pp. 37–47; Jonathan (35–45), Patricia (35–45), and Nick (40s).
Jonathan is the house guest of his former lover and her archaeologist husband at their place in Norfolk, England. After dinner, sparks begin to fly when Nick announces that he detests Jonathan's paintings. Even worse, he considers them pornographic. Jonathan, a famous and wealthy artist, defends himself and counterattacks. Patricia, Nick's wife, is caught in the crossfire. Jonathan and Patricia are American. Nick is English and, though an educated man, comes from a rural, working-class background; his accent should reflect those origins. Start, Jonathan: "Drive down with me tomorrow." End, Nick: "Um . . . shall I? Would you like me to make your bed?"

SPOILS OF WAR
by Michael Weller (Samuel French)
Drama: Act II, pp. 68–79; Elise (mid-30s), Martin (16), and Andrew (40s).
Martin has successfully engineered a meeting between Andrew and Elise, his estranged parents. However, Martin's plan turns into a disaster as they compete for his loyalty. Elise is trying to expose Andrew to be the jerk she has always said he is, and Andrew is trying to expose Elise as the true culprit. You'll have to cut and paste a bit, eliminating Andrew's young girlfriend, Penny, who comes in and out. Start, Andrew: "You haven't changed." End, Martin: "Everything's kind of screwy tonight. She makes you all tangled up. I know why you had to get away." For a longer version, end, Andrew: "Martin . . . Martin, god damn it, you're a man now, stop asking for help."

TRUE WEST
by Sam Shepard (Samuel French)
Comedy-Drama: Act I, Scene 3, pp. 19–24; Austin (early 30s), Lee (early 40s), and Saul Kimmer (late 40s).
Austin is putting the finishing touches on his deal with movie producer Saul Kimmer when his brother, Lee, comes in with a stolen television, plops it on the kitchen counter, and proceeds to hustle Saul, wanting to pitch his own movie idea. This is a funny scene, with Lee playing out his idea of the Hollywood hustle while Austin is embarrassed and Saul is thrown off guard by the shabbily dressed, colorful man. Start, Saul: "Well, to tell you the truth Austin, I have never felt so confident about a project in quite a long time." End, Austin: "Give me the keys."

Indexes

Playwrights

Albee, Edward: *The Death of Bessie Smith*, 27, 204–5; *A Delicate Balance*, 27, 127, 176, 205; *Everything in the Garden*, 32, 177, 210; *Who's Afraid of Virginia Woolf?*, 90, 150, 170, 253; *The Zoo Story*, 92, 171
Anderson, Jane, *The Baby Dance*, 14, 152, 174, 255–56
Anderson, Robert: *I Never Sang for My Father*, 43, 103–4, 159, 220; *Silent Night, Lonely Night*, 75, 241
Anouilh, Jean, *The Lark*, 47–48, 135, 222
Athayde, Roberto, *Miss Margarida's Way*, 57, 139
Ayckbourn, Alan: *Absent Friends*, 8, 93, 121, 172; *Absurd Person Singular*, 8, 93, 255; *The Norman Conquests-Table Manners*, 61–62, 110–11, 184, 232

Babe, Thomas, *Taken in Marriage*, 81, 147
Baitz, Jon Robin, *The Substance of Fire*, 80, 116–17, 245
Baizley, Doris, *Mrs. California*, 59, 139, 183, 230
Baldwin, James, *The Amen Corner*, 10, 94–95, 122, 151, 190
Barry, Philip, *The Philadelphia Story*, 66, 234
Bell, Neal, *Two Small Bodies*, 86, 249–50
Bergman, Andrew, *Social Security*, 76–77, 185–86
Bishop, John, *The Trip Back Down*, 85, 118, 248
Blessing, Lee: *Independence*, 43, 179; *Two Rooms*, 86, 187, 249
Bobrick, Sam, *Murder at the Howard Johnson's*, 59–60, 162, 231, 258
Bologna, Joseph: *Bedrooms: Five Comedies*, 15, 96, 195; *It Had To Be You*, 44, 134, 221; *Lovers and Other Strangers*, 54, 107, 137–38, 227
Bolt, Robert, *A Man for All Seasons*, 54–55, 161–62
Brady, Michael, *To Gillian on Her 37th Birthday*, 83, 246–47
Butterfield, Catherine, *Joined at the Head*, 45–46, 105, 134, 180–81, 221

Carlino, Lewis John, *Snowangel*, 76, 145, 241
Carter, Steve, *Nevis Mountain Dew*, 60, 140, 231
Chambers, Jane, *Last Summer at Bluefish Cove*, 48, 181–82
Chayefsky, Paddy: *The Middle of the Night*, 56–57, 183, 228; *The Tenth Man*, 82, 117, 148, 246
Chekhov, Anton: *The Bear*, 15, 96, 194; *The Cherry Orchard*, 21, 97; *Drama*, 28, 206; *The Evils of Tobacco*, 32, 101; *The Proposal*, 69–70, 237, 259; *The Sea Gull*, 73, 114–15, 143, 239; *Swan Song*, 81, 117
Churchill, Caryl, *Top Girls*, 83, 148, 187
Clark, Brian, *Whose Life Is It Anyway?*, 90–91, 170, 253–54
Clark, Ron, *Murder at the Howard Johnson's*, 59–60, 162, 231, 258
Clarvoe, Anthony, *Pick Up Ax*, 67, 113, 165, 258–59
Cole, Tom, *Medal of Honor Rag*, 56, 109, 162

Coward, Noël: *Fallen Angels*, 32–33, 177, 210–11; *Private Lives*, 69, 236–37
Craviotto, Darlene, *Pizza Man*, 67, 141–42, 185, 259
Cristofer, Michael: *The Lady and the Clarinet*, 47, 105; *The Shadow Box*, 74, 115, 144, 240

Delaney, Shelagh, *A Taste of Honey*, 82, 186–87, 245–46
Denker, Henry, *A Far Country*, 33, 157, 211
Dorfman, Ariel, *Death and the Maiden*, 26, 127, 155, 204
Durang, Christopher: *Baby with the Bathwater*, 14, 174, 256; *Beyond Therapy*, 16–17, 196–97, 256; *Laughing Wild*, 48–49, 106, 136; *The Nature and Purpose of the Universe*, 60, 139–40; *Sister Mary Ignatius Explains It All For You*, 75, 145
Dürrenmatt, Friedrich, *The Visit*, 87–88, 170, 251

Foote, Horton, *The Chase*, 20–21, 155, 200
Frayn, Michael, *Wild Honey*, 91, 119, 254
Frings, Ketti, *Look Homeward, Angel*, 52, 137, 225–26
Fugard, Athol: *Hello and Goodbye*, 39, 102, 132, 216–17; *"Master Harold"... the boys*, 55, 108–9
Fuller, Charles, *Zooman and the Sign*, 92, 120, 150

Gaffney, Mo, *The Kathy and Mo Show: Parallel Lives*, 46, 134, 181
Garonzik, Elan, *Scenes and Revelations*, 72–73, 143, 238–39
Gazzo, Michael Vincente, *A Hatful of Rain*, 37–38, 215
Gibson, William, *Monday After the Miracle*, 58, 229–230
Gilroy, Frank D.: *The Only Game in Town*, 64, 111, 233; *The Subject Was Roses*, 80, 146, 168, 244–45
Glass, Joanna M.: *Artichoke*, 13, 193; *Play Memory*, 67–68, 113, 142, 235
Goldman, James, *A Lion in Winter*, 50–51, 224–25
Gordone, Charles, *No Place To Be Somebody*, 61, 232
Gotanda, Philip Kan: *The Wash*, 89, 119, 150, 252; *Yankee Dawg You Die*, 92, 120, 170–71
Graczyk, Ed, *Come Back to the 5 & Dime, Jimmy Dean, Jimmy Dean*, 23, 126, 175
Gray, Simon: *Butley*, 19, 154; *Otherwise Engaged*, 65–66, 141, 164–65, 234
Greenberg, Richard: *The American Plan*, 11, 95, 151–52, 190–91; *Eastern Standard*, 29, 207
Guare, John: *The House of Blue Leaves*, 40, 102, 132, 218; *Landscape of the Body*, 47, 106, 222; *Marco Polo Sings a Solo*, 55, 108, 138; *Six Degrees of Separation*, 76, 116, 145
Gurney, A. R., Jr.: *Another Antigone*, 13, 95, 122–23, 192–93; *The Middle Ages*, 56, 109, 228; *Scenes from American Life*, 73, 143, 185; *What I Did Last Summer*, 89–90, 188

Male Monologues

Female Monologues

Male/Male Scenes

COMEDY

Teenage range
Hooters, 158

20s age range
I Hate Hamlet, 159; Immigrant, The, 159; Lisbon Traviata, The, 160; Lonely Impulse of Delight, A, 161; P. S. Your Cat Is Dead, 165; Rosencrantz and Guildenstern Are Dead, 166; Sexual Perversity in Chicago, 166; Sorrows of Stephen, 167; Yankee Dawg You Die, 170–71

30s age range
Division Street, 156; Geniuses, 157; I Hate Hamlet, 159; Immigrant, The, 159; Lisbon Traviata, The, 160; Lonely Impulse of Delight, A, 161; Luv, 161; Murder at the Howard Johnson's, 162; Nerd, The, 163; Otherwise Engaged, 164–65; P. S. Your Cat Is Dead, 165; Rosencrantz and Guildenstern Are Dead, 166; Sexual Perversity in Chicago, 166

40s age range
Born Yesterday, 153; I Hate Hamlet, 159; Lisbon Traviata, The, 160; Murder at the Howard Johnson's, 162; Odd Couple, The, 163; Otherwise Engaged, 164–65

50s age range
Born Yesterday, 153; Geniuses, 157; I Hate Hamlet, 159

60-plus age range
Yankee Dawg You Die, 170–71

COMEDY-DRAMA

Teenage range
Candida, 154; Dance and the Railroad, The, 155

20s age range
Butley, 154; Dance and the Railroad, The, 155; Lie of the Mind, A, 160; On the Open Road, 164; Pick Up Ax, 165; Tribute, 169; Visit, The, 170

30s age range
Baby Dance, The, 152; Butley, 154; End of the World with Symposium to Follow, The, 156; Fool for Love, 157; Hurlyburly, 158–59; Largo Desolato, 160; Lie of the Mind, A, 160; On the Open Road, 164; Pick Up Ax, 165; Road to Nirvana, 165–66; True West, 169; Visit, The, 170

40s age range
Baby Dance, The, 152; Butley, 154; Candida, 154; Chapter Two, 154–55; Cold Storage, 155; End of the World with Symposium to Follow, The, 156; Largo Desolato, 160; Road to Nirvana, 165–66; Speed-the-Plow, 167; True West, 169; Visit, The, 170

50s age range
Baby Dance, The, 152; Largo Desolato, 160; Tribute, 169; Visit, The, 170

60-plus age range
Cold Storage, 155; End of the World with Symposium to Follow, The, 156; Visit, The, 170

DRAMA

Teenage range
Amen Corner, The, 151; Fences, 157; Splendor in the Grass, 167

20s age range
American Plan, The, 151–52; Breaking the Code, 153; Cat on a Hot Tin Roof, 154; Cat's-Paw, 154; Does a Tiger Wear a Necktie?, 156; Happiness Cage, The, 158; Life and Limb, 160; Little Foxes, The, 160–61; Long Day's Journey Into Night, 161; Man for All Seasons, A, 161; Medal of Honor Rag, 162; Mister Roberts, 162; Orphans, 164; San Antonio Sunset, 166; Split Second, 167–68; Subject Was Roses, The, 168; Summer Brave, 168; Sweet Bird of Youth, 168; Vieux Carré, 169

30s age range
American Buffalo, 151; American Plan, The, 151–52; Andersonville Trial, The, 152; Angels in America: A Gay Fantasia on National Themes, Part I: Millennium Approaches, 152; Bent, 152–53; Betrayal, 153; Breaking the Code, 153–54; Cat's-Paw, 154; Chase, The, 155; Death of a Salesman, 155; Does a Tiger Wear a Necktie?, 156; Enemy of the People, An, 156; Far Country, A, 157; Goose and Tomtom, 158; K-2, 159–60; Long Day's Journey Into Night, 161; Man for All Seasons, A, 161–62; Mister Roberts, 162; Modigliani, 162; Of Mice and Men, 163; San Antonio Sunset, 166; Sight Unseen, 166; Split Second, 167–68; Strange Snow, 168; Sweet Bird of Youth, 168; Who's Afraid of Virginia Woolf?, 170; Whose Life Is It Anyway?, 170; Zoo Story, The, 171

40s age range
Amen Corner, The, 151; American Buffalo, 151; Andersonville Trial, The, 152; Bent, 153; Breaking the Code, 153–54; Cat's-Paw, 154; Chase, The, 155; Death and the Maiden, 155; Does a Tiger Wear a Necktie?, 156; Far Country, A, 157; Glengarry Glen Ross, 157; Goose and Tomtom, 158; Happiness Cage, The, 158; I Never Sang for My Father, 159; Last Yankee, The, 160; Little Foxes, The, 160–61; Man for All Seasons, A, 161; Medal of Honor Rag, 162; Mister Roberts, 162; Of Mice and Men, 163; On Golden Pond, 163–64; Orphans, 164; San Antonio Sunset, 166; Sight Unseen, 166; Speed of Darkness, The, 167; Split Second, 168; View From the Bridge, A, 169–70; Who's Afraid of Virginia Woolf?, 170; Whose Life Is It Anyway?, 170; Zoo Story, The, 171

50s age range
Breaking the Code, 153–54; Cat's-Paw, 154; Death and the Maiden, 155; Fences, 157; Glengarry Glen Ross, 157–58; Happiness Cage, The, 158; Mister Roberts, 162; Orphans, 164; Splendor in the Grass, 167; Subject Was Roses, The, 168; Vieux Carré, 169; View From the Bridge, A, 169–70; Whose Life Is It Anyway?, 170

60-plus age range
Cat on a Hot Tin Roof, 154; I Never Sang for My Father, 159; Last Yankee, The, 160; Long Day's Journey Into Night, 161; On Golden Pond, 163–64

Female/Female Scenes

COMEDY

Teenage range
Importance of Being Earnest, The, 179; Women, The, 188

20s age range
Agnes of God, 172; Baby Dance, The, 174; Baby with the Bathwater, 174; Bad Habits, 174; Bell, Book and Candle, 174; Commanche Cafe, 175; Fallen Angels, 177; Hooters, 178; Importance of Being Earnest, The, 179; Isn't It Romantic?, 180; Kathy and Mo Show, The: Parallel Lives, 181; Mrs. California, 183; Pizza Man, 185; Women, The, 188

30s age range
Absent Friends, 172; Agnes of God, 172; Baby Dance, The, 174; Baby with the Bathwater, 174; Coupla White Chicks Sitting Around Talking, A, 175; Kathy and Mo Show, The: Parallel Lives, 181; Mrs. California, 183; Norman Conquests, The-Table Manners, 184; Odd Couple, The, 184–85; Women, The, 188

40s age range
Baby with the Bathwater, 174; Bell, Book and Candle, 174; Commanche Cafe, 175; Odd Couple, The, 184–85; Social Security, 185–86; Women, The, 188

50s age range
Agnes of God, 172; Baby with the Bathwater, 174; Bell, Book and Candle, 174; Isn't It Romantic?, 180; Women, The, 188

60-plus age range
Social Security, 185–86; Women, The, 188

COMEDY-DRAMA

Teenage range
Album, 172–73; Gingerbread Lady, The, 178; Scenes from American Life, 185

20s age range
Crimes of the Heart, 176; Immigrant, The, 179; Jar the Floor, 180; Lie of the Mind, A, 182; Ludlow Fair, 183; Watermelon Boats, 188; Women, The, 188

30s age range
Come Back to the 5 & Dime, Jimmy Dean, Jimmy Dean, 175; Father's Day, 177; Immigrant, The, 179; Independence, 179; Joined at the Head, 180–81; Last Summer at Bluefish Cove, 181–82; Laundry and Bourbon, 182; Lost in Yonkers, 183; Top Girls, 187; Women, The, 188

40s age range
And Miss Reardon Drinks a Little, 173; Gingerbread Lady, The, 178; Scenes from American Life, 185

50s age range
Independence, 179; Lie of the Mind, A, 182

60-plus age range
Jar the Floor, 180; Lost in Yonkers, 183

DRAMA

Teenage range
Autumn Garden, The, 173; Effect of Gamma Rays on Man-in-the- Moon Marigolds, 176; Hothouse, 178–79; Summer and Smoke, 186; Taste of Honey, A, 186–87; View From the Bridge, A, 187

20s age range
All My Sons, 173; Anastasia, 173; Between Daylight and Boonville, 174; Children's Hour, The, 175; Doll's House, A, 176; Fox, The, 177; Getting Out, 177; Girl on the Via Flaminia, The, 178; Hedda Gabler, 178; Independence, 179; In the Boom Boom Room, 179; Jar the Floor, 180; Life and Limb, 182; Middle of the Night, The, 183; Mrs. Warren's Profession, 183–84; Steel Magnolias, 186; Streetcar Named Desire, A, 186; Summer and Smoke, 186; Toys in the Attic, 187

30s age range
Between Daylight and Boonville, 174; Dark at the Top of the Stairs, The, 176; Delicate Balance, A, 176; Doll's House, A, 176; Effect of Gamma Rays on Man-in-the-Moon Marigolds, 176; Everything in the Garden, 177; Hothouse, 178–79; In the Boom Boom Room, 179; Joined at the Head, 181; Keely and Du, 181; Later, 182; 'Night, Mother, 184; Night of the Iguana, The, 184; Other People's Money, 185; Spoils of War, 186; Streetcar Named Desire, A, 186; Two Rooms, 187; What I Did Last Summer, 188; Waiting for the Parade, 187–88

40s age range
All My Sons, 173; Autumn Garden, The, 173; Children's Hour, The, 175; Getting Out, 177; In the Boom Boom Room, 179; Jar the Floor, 180; Later, 182; Mrs. Warren's Profession, 183–84; Night of the Iguana, The, 184; On Golden Pond, 185; Taste of Honey, A, 186–87; Toys in the Attic, 187; Two Rooms, 187; View From the Bridge, A, 187

50s age range
Delicate Balance, A, 176; Everything in the Garden, 177; Independence, 179; Later, 182; Mrs. Warren's Profession, 183–84; 'Night, Mother, 184; Steel Magnolias, 186

60-plus age range
Anastasia, 173; Keely and Du, 181; Later, 182; 'Night, Mother, 184; On Golden Pond, 185; Other People's Money, 185; What I Did Last Summer, 188

Male/Female Scenes

Three-Person Scenes

COMEDY

Males: Ethnic Group, Nationality, and Race

Females: Ethnic Group, Nationality, and Race

Publishers

Anchor Books
Published by Doubleday
Division of Bantam Doubleday Dell Publishing Group
1540 Broadway
New York, NY 10036

Applause Theatre Book Publishers
211 West 71st Street
New York, NY 10023

Dramatists Play Service
440 Park Avenue South
New York, NY 10016

Samuel French, Inc.
45 West 25th Street
New York, NY 10010

Grove Weidenfeld
Division of Grove/Atlantic, Inc.
841 Broadway
New York, NY 10003

Methuen Drama
Michelin House
81 Fulham Road
London SW3 6RB

Plume Books
Coward-McCann & Geoghegan, Inc.
200 Madison Avenue
New York, NY 10016

Plume Drama
Published by The Penguin Group
Penguin Books USA
375 Hudson Street
New York, NY 10014

Signet Classics
Published by The Penguin Group
Penguin Books USA
375 Hudson Street
New York, NY 10014

Theatre Communications Group
355 Lexington Avenue
New York, NY 10017